THE STASI

Also by David Childs

BRITAIN SINCE 1945: A Political History

BRITAIN SINCE 1939: Progress and Decline

THE CHANGING FACE OF WESTERN COMMUNISM (*editor*)

CHILDREN IN THE WAR (*editor with Janet Wharton*)

EAST GERMANY

EAST GERMANY IN COMPARATIVE PERSPECTIVE (*editor*)

EAST GERMANY TO THE 1990S

FROM SCHUMACHER TO BRANDT

THE GDR, MOSCOW'S GERMAN ALLY

GERMANY IN THE TWENTIETH CENTURY

GERMANY ON THE ROAD TO UNITY

GERMANY SINCE 1918

HONECKER'S GERMANY (*editor*)

MARX AND THE MARXISTS

WEST GERMANY, POLITICS AND SOCIETY (*with Jeffrey Johnson*)

Also by Richard Popplewell

INTELLIGENCE AND IMPERIAL DEFENCE: British Intelligence and the Defence of the Indian Empire, 1904–1924

The Stasi

The East German Intelligence and Security Service

David Childs
Professor of Politics
University of Nottingham

and

Richard Popplewell
Lecturer in Politics and Contemporary History
University of Salford

First edition 1996
Reprinted (with new introduction) 1999

Published by
MACMILLAN PRESS LTD
Houndmills, Basingstoke, Hampshire RG21 6XS
and London
Companies and representatives
throughout the world

ISBN 0–333–63094–7 hardcover
ISBN 0–333–77207–5 paperback

A catalogue record for this book is available from the British Library.

This book is printed on paper suitable for recycling and made from fully managed and sustained forest sources.

10 9 8 7 6 5 4 3 2 1
08 07 06 05 04 03 02 01 00 99

Printed and bound in Great Britain by
Antony Rowe Ltd, Chippenham, Wiltshire

Contents

Acknowledgements

David Childs is very grateful to the German Academic Exchange Service (DAAD) for awarding him a scholarship which enabled him to spend some time in the former DDR in 1994.

A great many people have been very generous with their time to discuss various aspects of the DDR and/or the MfS. In Germany they include: various members of the Citizens' Committees of Berlin, Dresden and Leipzig, particularly David Gill, Heinz Meier, and Ulrich Wiegend; Andre Andrich, Neues Forum, Dresden; Dr Sabine Bergmann-Pohl, MdB, formerly President of the Volkskammer of the DDR; Dr Sc med Kay Blumenthal-Barby, Berlin/Göttinghen; Dr Heinrich Bortfeldt, formerly Akademie für Gesellschaftswissenschaften beim ZK der SED; Dr Manfred Braune, CDU, Leipzig; Dr Eberhard Brecht, MdB; Elfriede Brüning, writer, Berlin; Wolfgang Dehnel, MdB; Colonel Prof. Dr Helmut Eck, formerly of the Hochschule des MfS Potsdam-Eiche; Dr Helmut Ettinger, formerly diplomatic service of the DDR, PDS Berlin; Colonel Klaus Eichner, formerly head of *Bereich 'C'* of Department X of the HVA; Joachim Fiegel, PDS, Bonn/Chemnitz; Bernt Förster, Leipzig University; Monika Friedrich, Gauck-Behörde, Berlin; Dipl.-Psych. Svetla Friedrich, Leipzig; Prof. Dr Walter Friedrich, formerly Director of the Institut für Jugendforschung, Leipzig; Horst Gibtner, MdB, formerly Minister of Transport of the DDR; Dr Wolfgang Gudenschwager, CDU, Berlin; Dr Karlheinz Guttmacher, MdB; Hildegard Hannan Stadtmuseum, Oranienburg; Adolf Haidegger, CDU, Bürgermeister, Colditz; Dieter Herberg, FDP, Leipzig; Prof. Dr Uwe-Jens Heuer, MdB; Matthias Hinkel, Leipzig; Prof. Dr Hartmut Jäckel, Free University, Berlin; Dr Dittmar Keller, MdB, formerly Minister of Culture of DDR; Egon Krenz, formerly General Secretary of the SED and Chairman of the Council of State of the DDR; Vera (Wollenberger) Lengsfeld MdB; Dr Ekkehard Lieberran, PDS, Bonn; Roger Loewig, painter, Berlin; Dr Michael Luther, MdB; Heide-Marie Lüth, MdB; Friedrich Magirius, Stadtpräsident Leipzig, Superintendent der Nikolaikirche, Leipzig; Roland May, SPD, Leipzig; Lothar de Maiziere, formerly Minister-President of the DDR; Captain Wilfried Mannewitz, formerly of the MfS; Rudolf Meinl, MdB; Barbara Miller, research student Edinburgh University; Dr Hans Modrow, MdB, formerly Minister-President of the DDR; Uwe Müller, formerly SPD Leipzig; Dr Hermann Pohler, MdB, Gert Poppe, MdB; George Pumfrey, PDS, Bonn; Klaus Reichenbach, MdB, formerly Minister in the Office of the Minister-President of the DDR; Hans

Jürgen Richter, MdL, SPD, Chemnitz; Colonel Dr Klaus Rösler, formerly head of Department XII of HVA; Christina Schenk, MdB; Dr Gerald Schmidt, CDU, Berlin; Richard Schröder, MdB, formerly Chairman of the SPD group in the Volkskammer; Dr Sigrid Semper, MdB; Werner H. Skowron, MdB; Arni Snaevarr, Foreign News Editor, Icelandic National Broadcasting Service; Dr Gerald Thalheim, MdB; Rolf Thieme, CDU, Dresden; Cenzi Troike-Loewig, Berlin; Dr Wolfgang Ullmann, MdB; Joachim Walter, writer, Gauck- Behörde, Berlin; Konrad Weiss, MdB; Wolfgang Wiemer, SPD, Bonn, and several individuals who did not wish to be identified.

For their kind hospitality David Childs would also like to thank: Patricia Clough; Prof. Dr Hartmut Jäckel and Frau Margarete Jäckel; Svetla and Martin Friedrich; Prof. Dr Siegfried Prokop; Ceszentia Troike-Loewig; Dr Axel and Frau Hai-Oh Noack and Lenny.

Among those resident in the United Kingdom, the authors would particularly like to thank Professor Christopher Andrew of Corpus Christi College, Cambridge; Peter Johnson, former Reuter and BBC correspondent in Berlin and Moscow, O.J. Bachmann and Dr Tilman Remme.

Abbreviations and German Terms

AfNs – *Amt für Nationale Sicherheit.* Office for National Security, November 1989 to December 1989.

Apparat – literally, 'apparatus, equipment'. Usually, closest translation is 'organization'.

BEK – *Bund der Evangelischen Kirchen.* Federation of Protestant Churches in the GDR.

Bezirk – largest administrative district of the GDR.

BfV – *Bundesamt für Verfassungsschutz*, 'Federal Office for the Protection of the Constitution'. West German security service.

BND – *Bundesnachrichtendienst*, the Federal Intelligence Service, West Germany's foreign intelligence organization.

Bundestag – the directly-elected chamber of the (West) German parliament.

CDU – *Christlich-Demokratische Union*, the Christian Democratic Union. Main right-wing party in West Germany, roughly equivalent to 'Conservatives'. Also, the SED-dominated party in East Germany.

CSCE – Conference on Security and Cooperation in Europe.

CSPU – the Communist Party of the Soviet Union

CSU – *Christlich-Soziale Union*, 'Christian Social Union'. Bavarian sister-party of the CDU.

DBD – *Demokratische Bauernpartei Deutschlands*, Democratic Peasants Party of Germany, one of four SED-'allied' parties.

DDR – *Deutsche Demokratische Republik*, 'German Democratic Republic', East Germany.

DKP – *Deutsche Kommunistische Partei*, the German Communist Party, the successor to the KPD from 1968.

DVdI – *Deutsche Verwaltung des Innern, (DVdI)*, German Administration of the Interior in the Soviet-occupied zone of Germany, 1945–9.

ECCI – the Executive Committee of the Communist International.

FDJ – *Freie Deutsche Jugend*, 'Free German Youth'. East German communist youth movement.

Freikorps – Volunteer units outside the regular army (*Reichswehr*) of the Weimar Republic.

FRG – the Federal Republic of Germany, West Germany.

GDR – the German Democratic Republic, East Germany. In German, the DDR, short for 'Deutsche Demokratische Republik'.

Gestapo – Secret State Police of the Third Reich.
GI – *Geheime Informatoren.* Pre-1968 designation of Stasi informers.
GRU – *Glavnoe razvedivatelnoe upravlenie*, 'Main Intelligence Directorate'. Soviet Military Intelligence.
GST – *Gesellschaft für Sport und Technik*, 'Society for Sport and Technology'.
HVA – *Hauptverwaltung Aufklärung*, 'Main Administration Reconnaissance'. The Stasi's foreign intelligence organization.
IM – *Inoffizielle Mitarbeiter*, 'Unofficial Colleagues' or collaborator. Stasi informers.
INO – *Inostranny Otdel* – the Foreign Department. The first foreign espionage agency of Soviet Intelligence.
ISH – Seamen's International in the interwar period.
IWF – *Institut für Wirtschaftswissenschaftliche Forschung*, 'Institute for Economic Research'. Cover for first East German foreign intelligence service.
Junkertum – 'Junkerdom', the squirearchy of Prussia.
KGB – *Komitet gosudarstvennoi bezopasnosti*, 'Committee of State Security'. Soviet security and foreign intelligence agency. See below.
K5 – *Kommissariat 5*, political secret police forerunner of MfS, 1945–50.
KPD – *Kommunistische Partei Deutschlands*, Communist Party of Germany.
KoKo – *Kommerzielle Koordinierung*. Clandestine MfS department within Foreign Ministry of GDR.
Kripo – *Kriminalpolizei*, criminal police,
Kreis – 'district'. Sub-division of the *Bezirk.*
KVP – *Kasernierte Volkspolizei*, People's Police in barracks.
Land – province of West Germany. Largest administrative district of the Eastern Zone of occupied Germany, 1945–52.
LDPD – *Liberal-Demokratische Partei Deutschlands*, Liberal Democratic Party of Germany, one of the four SED-'allied' parties in the GDR.
MAD – *Militärischer Abschirmdienst*, West German Military Counter-Intelligence.
MfS – *Ministerium für Staatssicherheit*, Ministry of State Security. East German intelligence agency, 1950–89.
M-Gruppen – Military groups (i.e.: sub-units) of the *Militärapparat.*
Militärapparat – Military Organization of the KPD.
Mitarbeiter – literally, 'co-worker'. Closest English equivalent is 'collaborator' without its usual, pejorative sense.
Nachrichtenapparat – Intelligence Organization of the KPD.
Narkomindel – *Narodny Komissariat Innostranych Del* – the People's Commissariat of Foreign Affairs, the Soviet foreign ministry in the 1920s and 1930s.

NDPD – *National-Demokratische Partei Deutschlands*, the National Democratic Party of Germany, one of the four SED-'allied' parties in the GDR.

N-Gruppen – Intelligence groups (i.e.: sub-units) of the *Nachrichtenapparat.*

NKVD – *Narodny komissariat vnutrennych del*, 'People's Commissariat of Internal Affairs'. Soviet ministry of the interior, including secret police and foreign intelligence agencies, in the the 1930s and 1940s.

NSDAP – *Nationalsozialistische Deutsche Arbeiterpartei*, the Nazi Party.

NVA – *Nationale Volksarmee*, 'National People's Army', the East German armed forces.

OGPU – *Ob'yedinyonnoe glavnoe politicheskoe upravlenie*, 'United Main Political Department'. Designation of Soviet intelligence and security service.

OiBE – *Offiziere im besonderen Einsatz*, 'Officers on special duties'. Stasi regulars operating under cover.

OMS – *Otdel Mezhdunarodnych Svyazyey* – the Department of International Communications. The Comintern's foreign intelligence section.

Ostpolitik – 'Eastern policy'. The West German government's policy towards the Soviet Bloc in general and East Germany in particular.

Paß-Apparat – Passport Organization of the Comintern.

RAF – 'Red Army Faction'. West German terrorist group, best-known abroad as the 'Baader-Meinhof Gang'.

Reichswehr – German regular armed forces from 1919 to 1935.

RHSA – *Reichssichorheitshauptamt*, 'Reich Main Security Office', 1939–45.

RIAS – Radio in the American Sector (of West Berlin).

SED – *Sozialistische Einheitspartei Deutschlands*, the 'Socialist Unity Party of Germany'. In effect, the East German Communist Party.

SMAD – Soviet Military Administration (in the Eastern Zone of Occupied Germany, 1945–9).

Smersh – short for *Smert' Shpionam*, 'Death to Spies'. Designation of Soviet military counter-intelligence in, and immediately after, the Second World War.

SOUD – KGB-administered computerized storage system to which MfS and other 'socialist' security services contributed.

Spartacists – Members of the *Spartakusbund*, the 'Spartakus Federation', a left-wing radical-revolutionary organization founded in 1916 out of ex-members of the SPD.

SPD – *Sozialdemokratische Partei Deutschlands*, 'Social Democratic Party' of Germany.

Stasi – short for *Staatssicherheit*, 'State Security'. Colloquial term for the MfS. Now Anglicized so that it does not require italics.

TASS – *Telegrafichnoye Agenstvo Sovietskovo Soyuza* – the Telegraphic Agency of the Soviet Union, the Soviet Press Agency.

Treff – Clandestine meeting between officer and agent.

UB – *Urząd bezpieczeństwa*, the Polish security service.

VBK – *Verband Bildender Künstler der DDR*, 'Association of Creative Artists of the GDR'.

Volkskammer – the East German parliament.

Volksschule – 'People's School', roughly equivalent to 'elementary school', providing basic primary and secondary education. Inferior to *Gymnasium* or 'grammar school'.

Volkspolizei, the regular police of the GDR.

V-Mann – *Vertrauensmann*, term often used in German for informer or surveillance agent.

Wehrmacht – German armed forces, excluding SS divisions, 1935–45.

die Wende, literally the 'turning-point'. Popular term for the East German revolution of 1989.

WES – the Western European Secretariat of the Comintern.

ZAIG – *Zentrale Auswertungs und Informationsgruppe*, Central analytical department of MfS.

Zentrale – Directing Committee of the KPD.

The Changing Names of the Soviet Domestic and Foreign Intelligence Agency

Cheka – 1917–22.
GPU – 1922–3.
OGPU – 1923–34.
GUGB – 1934–41. But intelligence organization generally referred to as NKVD, the ministry of internal affairs within which it was contained.
NKGB – 1941–3. As above, NKGB was part of the NKVD.
NKVD – 1943–6.
MGB – 1946–53.
MVD – 1953–4.
KGB – 1954–91.

Introduction to the 1999 Reprint

WOLF AND MIELKE AT LOGGERHEADS

Since the hardback of our book was published in 1996 a number of other volumes have appeared, especially East German intelligence chief Markus Wolf's memoirs.[1] It is gratifying to be able to write that this and other volumes have in no way lessened the relevance of *The Stasi*. Interesting though Wolf's *Spionagechef im geheimen Krieg* is, like all memoirs, it is an attempt by its author to present himself in the best possible light. Wolf does this convincingly. Understandably, he distances his work in intelligence gathering from the *security* side of the Ministry for State Security. He also distances himself from his boss, Minister for State Security, Erich Mielke, whom he claims openly called himself a Stalinist.[2] According to Wolf, he and the Minister for State Security, Erich Mielke, were at loggerheads throughout their nearly 40 years in intelligence and security. Regarding the security side of the MfS's activities, Wolf uses the excuse, used so often by others in relation to Nazi crimes, that he did not know what was going on:[3] he confesses that he did not know the mood of the East German population on the eve of the 1953 June revolt;[4] he first heard of the building of the Berlin Wall in 1961 from the radio;[5] he did not have a clear picture about the situation in Prague in 1968.[6] He quotes approvingly the Soviet expert on Germany, diplomat Valentin Falin, as saying the number of DDR citizens supporting the regime was never more than 30 per cent and was usually lower.[7] He admits he was shocked by Khrushchev's exposure of Stalin at the Twentieth Soviet party congress in 1956,[8] but then claims that although he and others knew about repression in the Soviet Union, they thought it was due to Stalin's lieutenants acting without the leader's knowledge.[9]

Many of the unsolved mysteries described in the original book, still carry question marks. Dr Manfred Stolpe, Minister-President of Brandenburg, remains under suspicion in some circles of having worked for the Stasi. He vigorously contests such accusations. The brief passage of time between the hardback and the paperback has seen some of the mysterious figures mentioned, notably Otto John and Jürgen Kuczynski, go into that faraway land from which no traveller returns, and take their remaining secrets with them. Interestingly, Wolf supports John's claims that he was abducted by the KGB.[10] My friend, Stasi victim Roger Loewig has also died, but at least in his case we have his art, a lasting testimony to the strength of the human spirit against dictatorship.

WEHNER NOT 'AGENT IN CLASSICAL SENSE'

Wolf devotes a whole chapter to Herbert Wehner, the leading Social Democrat and one-time minister in Bonn. Wehner, a Communist in the Weimar Republic who turned to Social Democracy after the war, was denounced by the East Germans as a renegade and traitor. Then, in 1973, it all changed after an open visit by Wehner to East German leader Honecker. Wolf tells us that Wehner had kept up secret contacts with East Berlin for many years but was 'never an agent in the classical sense'.[11] He reveals how Wehner persuaded Communist official, Kurt Vieweg to return to the DDR after he had defected in March 1957. Vieweg did so on the understanding that he would not be prosecuted, but he ended up in jail. The negotiations were carried on in Wehner's Hamburg flat with Social Democrat parliamentarian and future ambassador to Yugoslavia, Peter Blachstein, in attendance. To me this is intriguing because I knew Blachstein. He arranged for me to meet Wehner at that time in Wehner's flat. We conversed alone for something like two hours. I knew nothing of any negotiations. Of course, my visit could have been a cover to prove that nothing was going on at the time; the controversy surrounding Wehner continues.[12] I did not know anything about my friend Blachstein's contacts with the East Germans. He would only have conducted them with the authority of Wehner and possibly his friend Willy Brandt. Blachstein introduced me to one or two of his Social Democratic contacts in East Berlin, at that time the SPD could still run an office openly there. He worked closely with Stefan Thomas of the dreaded (for the Stasi) *Ostbüro* of the SPD. I also met Thomas. Blachstein, like Wehner, from what had become 'East' Germany, was a severe critic of Soviet-type 'Socialism'. Mielke had imprisoned him in the Spanish Civil War when he joined George Orwell and others in the anti-Stalinist POUM. Blachstein introduced me to Rosa Luxemburg's critique of Leninism, *Die Russische Revolution*.

'GENERALS FOR PEACE' INFILTRATED

Wolf gives us details of contacts with his organization and politicians of the other main West German parties – Christian Democrats and Free Democrats.

These actors in the East–West drama from the 1950s to the end of the 1980s, were not always clear with whom they were dealing, and pursued their contacts for a variety of motives. In some cases, especially in the early years, they hoped to make a contribution to restoring German unity, later they sought to improve the conditions of the East German people. They worked to avoid a nuclear war or they wanted to pursue business deals. In some cases they wanted to feel they were pursuing their own foreign policy agenda. Some hoped to gain information that would put their rivals out of business. Most loved the idea of possessing secret knowledge. Most of them were not 'classic' agents. The Bavarian leader, Franz Josef Strauss, is reported as having spoken freely about political and military matters with Colonel Alexander Schalck-Golodkowski of the MfS.[13] Schalck presented himself as a commercial trader with contacts at the highest level in the DDR.

As opposition to the renewed arms race grew in Europe in the late 1970s and early 1980s, so did the Stasi's interest in the various peace movements. The East German propaganda machine applauded the peace movements when they held demonstrations in Munich or Manchester, Bremen or Birmingham, but vilified any independent peace movements in the Soviet bloc. The anti-nuclear West German Greens were the most successful of these movements gaining entry into the Bundestag, the German parliament, in 1983. They became a target for Wolf's HVA. Convincing opposition to NATO's nuclear plans came from the Generals For Peace. These were six generals and two admirals from Britain, France, Germany, Italy, the Netherlands, Portugal and the US. All were veterans of the Second World War who went on to become professional soldiers. The leading advocates from West Germany were General Graf von Baudissin and ex-tank commander, General Gert Bastian. To me, when I interviewed him in 1983, with his noble Nordic features, slim figure and bow tie, von Baudissin looked more like a Swedish aristocrat than a German general. He was of course a *German* aristocrat who was famous for having evolved the concept of the 'Citizen in Uniform', the democratic military code of the West German armed forces, the Bundeswehr. This code gave West German soldiers rights their East German counterparts could only dream of. Von Baudissin trod on the toes of traditionalists both young and old and felt towards the end of his career that his work was being undermined.[14] Wolf managed to establish contact with the German naval officer, Professor Gerhard Kade who was 'head and motor' of the movement. Through him payments were made to enable the generals to pay their travel and other expenses. Wolf admits[15] he does not know whether the soldiers were informed about the true source of the money. He also makes it clear that he does not believe the Generals were the kind of people who could be manipulated.[16]

OPERATION ROSEWOOD

In the US the FBI arrested a senior Defense Department employee, her husband and a private detective. Taken into custody in October 1997, they were accused of working for the Stasi. The woman involved is alleged to have said she had worked for the East German intelligence service (HVA) for '17 or 18 years'.[17] The US were not the main field of Stasi operations, however, Wolf claims he had two long-term agents there who were never discovered. He admits it was not easy to place agents in the US.[18] He reminds us of two agents, Warrant Officer James Hall of the National Security Agency and Sergeant Jeffrey Carney of the US Air Force, who offered their services. For years they gave valuable information to the Stasi until they were exposed at the end of the 1980s. Both were then sentenced to long prison terms.

Despite such arrests, the names of many of the Stasi's foreign agents have still not been revealed. In Operation Rosewood, in 1990, the CIA was able to purchase film material containing the entire list of names from rogue Stasi officers. The Americans have repeatedly resisted German requests for the return of the material to the *Gauck-Behörde*, the custodian of the MfS files, in Berlin. In 1993 the CIA did allow their German colleagues the chance to see nearly 2,000 cards giving details of relevant individuals. Arrests followed in Germany. It is thought that these 2,000 cards are only a small part of the CIA collection.[19]

The man who led the Stasi, as Minister for State Security, General Erich Mielke, is still alive and well at the time of writing. He celebrated his ninetieth birthday in December 1997. Apparently he neither smokes nor drinks and takes daily exercise. He lives with his 89-year-old wife, Gertrud, in their two room flat in the Hohenschönhausen district of east Berlin. In 1991, when he faced imprisonment, he claimed to be on his death bed. For this reason, he was released by the Berlin legal authorities. At this level he is having the last laugh. His comrades in the ruling Politburo,[20] Egon Krenz, Günther Schabowski and Günther Kleiber, were not so lucky. In 1997, they were called to account for the shooting of would-be escapers on the Berlin Wall. Krenz had served longer than Schabowski and Kleiber and was officially responsible for security matters in the DDR. Krenz employed the argument that in reality the Soviets controlled the frontier regime, he was, therefore, powerless to change things. There is some truth in this argument, but did he ever raise his voice in an attempt to moderate the policing of the frontier? He was unable to claim that he had done. All three accused were sentenced to terms of imprisonment for manslaughter. Krenz received six years and six months, Schabowski and Kleiber three years each.

PUBLISHERS AS INFORMERS

A book, by Joachim Walther,[21] is an important contribution to our understanding of how the Stasi infiltrated the DDR's literary world and used writers, editors and publishers for its purposes within East Germany and beyond. He is able to take the story beyond our survey in Chapter 4, revealing that the Stasi recruited, not just writers as informers, but also literary editors, publishers and so on. Would-be writers were subject then to control by the ruling party, SED, by their 'union', by laws which could be used to make criticism illegal, and by the Stasi through its informers. One example, Walther gives us, is Armin Zeissler, deputy chief editor of the prestigious literary journal *Sinn und Form*, 1963 to 1988. He worked for department HAII of the MfS from 1984 to 1988. One of his jobs was to report on the literary/publishing scene in West Berlin and West Germany.[22] Likewise, *neue deutsche literatur*, the monthly journal of the writers' association was heavily infiltrated by the Stasi. Key positions in publishing houses like Aufbau-Verlag were held by informers. One important case of a Stasi commissar was Klaus Gysi who served as informer 'Kurt' from 1957, having been recruited by a 22-year-old Stasi NCO, Peter Heinz Gütling. Gysi worked as head of the Aufbau-Verlag, 1956–66. Gütling wrote of Gysi in 1957 that he had conscientiously fulfilled all the tasks set him and shown himself open, sincere and reliable.[23] Gysi had collected material which helped to convict Harich. Although he was an atheist of Jewish background, at Christmas 1956, the Stasi gave him as presents a leather brief case for himself and an electric train for his children,[24] Gysi gave up his informer activities in 1964. As the Stasi pointed out, they would meet him officially through his position as Minister of Culture, 1966–73.[25] He went on to serve as Ambassador to Italy and Malta, 1973–78 and State Secretary for Church Affairs, 1979–88, Gütling crept up the ladder in the Stasi reaching the rank of major in 1980. He continued in his attempts to keep DDR literature clean and pure until the Stasi was abolished in 1989. Walther was himself a victim of the Stasi. After negative comments about his DDR loyalty by a British academic when Walther visited Britain in the 1980s, he was banned from travelling abroad.

STASI IN BRADFORD AND LEEDS

I am still hoping to recover more of my own file. I wish I knew for instance how the Stasi came to believe I was in contact with Hermann von Berg, for many years deputy head of the DDR press office, who left East Germany to settle in the West. Von Berg had worked for Wolf's HVA. In the meantime

I have had to be content with references to me in other official DDR archives. I forgive those who informed on me who were brought up in Communist homes and lived in Marxist–Leninist environments. They were only 'doing their duty' in the 'struggle for peace'.[26] I am less sympathetic to those in Britain who informed on me and caused me the occasional setback. The identities of at least two Stasi informers in the British academic world located in Bradford and Leeds are now known.

INFORMERS ON BAHRO COMMITTEE

Controversy has continued about access to the Stasi files and about the use to which they are put. The exposure of informers (IM) by reference to the files had inevitably led to some individuals claiming that they have been wrongly named, mixed up with other people or wrongly quoted. American Jerry Hodges was one of them. According to the Stasi files, he was an IM who gave regular reports on the meetings of the committee in West Berlin set up to free imprisoned East German dissident, Rudolf Bahro. Hodges denies the charges. Of the 26-member committee no less than four were Stasi informers; another two were on the periphery.[27] Whatever the exact truth about Hodges, clearly the files, though vitally important for our understanding of the East German system, must be treated with some caution. There have been calls to close the Stasi archives. The majority of Germans do not support this view: a poll in 1997 revealed that, overall, 37 per cent favoured closing the files, but 57 per cent wanted them to remain open. In West Germany 56 per cent wanted the files kept open, 60 per cent of East Germans took the same view.[28]

Again and again Markus Wolf admits his disappointment and dismay as he was forced to face the realities of the Soviet Union and the DDR, and as he realized he was not a equal partner with the Soviets.[29] He was forced to admit the ugliness of the system he served. This book describes and analyzes that system in a way Wolf does not. Despite his disappointments, Wolf claims he has remained convinced of the ideals of his youth. He and so many others had a wasted journey. Would he not have done better to have left the DDR early on and use his great talents to campaign for Democratic Socialism in the West?

David Childs
Nottingham
July 1998

NOTES

1. Markus Wolf, *Spionagechef im geheimen Krieg* (Munich, 1997); Markus Wolf with Anne McElvoy, *Man Without a Face* (New York, 1997). These two books vary in their contents.
2. Wolf, *Spionagechef*, *op. cit.*, p. 107.
3. *Ibid.*, p. 49.
4. *Ibid.*, p. 76.
5. *Ibid.*, p. 129.
6. *Ibid.*, p. 222.
7. *Ibid.*, p. 132.
8. *Ibid.*, p. 105.
9. *Ibid.*, p. 106.
10. *Ibid.*, p. 103.
11. *Ibid.*, p. 218.
12. *Der Spiegel*, 23 June 1997, p. 85. See also Wolf as above, Egon Bahr *Zu meiner Zeit* (Munich, 1996) and Heinrich Potthoff, *Bonn und Ost-Berlin 1969–1982* (Bonn, 1997) for opposing views on Wehner.
13. Wolf, *op. cit.* p. 191.
14. Baudissin's views are elaborated in Wolf Graf von Baudissin, *Nie Wieder Sieg! Programmatische Schriften 1951–1981* (Munich, 1982).
15. *Ibid.*, p. 343.
16. *Ibid.*, p. 344.
17. *Der Spiegel*, 13 October 1997, p. 61.
18. Wolf, *Spionagechef*, *op. cit.* p. 407.
19. *Der Spiegel*, 22 June 1998, p. 60.
20. The relationship between the Ministry for State Security and the SED is fully researched in Siegfried Suckut and Walter Süss (eds) *Staatspartei und Staatssicherheit: Zum Verhältnis von SED und MfS* (Berlin, 1997).
21. Joachim Walther, *Sicherheitsbereich Literatur Schriftsteller und Staatssicherheit in der Detschen Demokratischen Republik* (Berlin, 1996).
22. Walther, *op. cit.* p. 529.
23. *Ibid.*, p. 565.
24. *Ibid.*, p. 567.
25. *Ibid.*, p. 567.
26. Timothy Garton Ash, *Die Akte Romeo* (Munich, 1997); Timothy Garton Ash, *The File: A Personal History* (New York, 1997). Seems to also take this view in his interesting account of the Stasi's interest in him.
27. *Der Spiegel*, 30 June 1997, p. 54.
28. *Der Spiegel*, 1 September 1997, p. 38.
29. See Wolf p. 324 and p. 339, for instance.

Introduction

This is the first book in English to appear on the security and intelligence service of the former East German state, or the 'Stasi' as it commonly known. The study of this subject has been greatly facilitated by the continuous appearance of documentary material since the revolution of 1989. Indeed, it would be fair to say that the Stasi, or at least its domestic branches, is a more accessible field for study than any other secret service in the second half of the twentieth century. It will hopefully become clear from this work that the study of East German intelligence is significant in its own right, since the organization involved employed, directly or indirectly, a sizeable part of the population and consumed an increasingly burdensome portion of the state budget. But the Stasi had a far wider importance than that reflected in histories of East Germany or of intelligence services. Through its espionage East Berlin played a significant role in the foreign policy of the Soviet Bloc as a whole. Furthermore, the Stasi's spying had an impact on West German politics the effects of which can still be felt.

By now the Stasi have acquired a legendary status on two counts. First, because of the almost unbelievably extensive spying on the citizens of the DDR which, it has been claimed, debased and corrupted two generations of postwar Germans. Second, because of the foreign wing of the Stasi's huge success at spying on the West. The reality of the Stasi's success and the nature of the beast itself are, of course, central to this book. It will be seen that nothing can dispel the gargantuan reality of this organism at the heart of the Party-State. The Stasi, it can be argued, came very near to its leaders' desire to know everything worth knowing about their own population and about the outside world. It can be argued strongly that the Stasi played a major role in maintaining a state as vulnerable as East Germany for four decades. Yet despite all their efforts, they could do nothing to prevent revolution in 1989 and the subsequent collapse of the DDR.

David Childs
Richard Popplewell
Nottingham
August 1995

1 German Communism, the Comintern and Secret Intelligence 1918–43

> Freedom only for the supporters of the government, only for members of one party – however numerous they may be – is no freedom at all. Freedom is always and exclusively freedom for the one who thinks differently.

Rosa Luxemburg, pamphlet entitled *The Russian Revolution*, Breslau (Wrocław) prison, summer 1918.

> From the very beginning we called upon the tradition of eminent people – such as Richard Sorge – or on the intelligence officers, who belonged to the 'Red Orchestra'.

Markus Wolf, former head of East German foreign intelligence, 1990.[1]

THE KPD, THE COMINTERN AND SOVIET INTELLIGENCE, 1918–33

Close links between secret intelligence and German communism predated the creation of the East German state by over a quarter of a century. From the outset of the Russian Revolution, Lenin and the Bolsheviks intended that such links should exist. The first leaders of the German Communist Party, the KPD (*Kommunistische Partei Deutschlands*) realized that involvement in clandestine work for the Bolsheviks might well be a snare binding them to Moscow from which they could never break free. Their fears proved well-founded, for throughout the Twenties, the secret organization of the KPD developed in tandem with Moscow's increasing control over the German Party.

In the period 1917 to 1923, Germany was of central importance in Lenin and the Bolsheviks' global plans. Though Lenin seized power in Russia at the end of 1917, he firmly believed at this time that the Revolution could only be successful if it rapidly spread to the belligerent states of Western Europe, and above all to imperial Germany. Lenin's initial hopes were not realized, for despite the destruction of the First World War, the European state structures proved far more resilient than he had forseen. When no revolution came, the Bolshevik leaders felt isolated and surrounded. Breaking this encirclement became the priority of their foreign policy. At the end of 1918 one possibility still gave them heart. It seemed to the Bolsheviks that although Red October had not sparked off any spontaneous proletarian revolution outside Russia, still the capitalist states of the West would come tumbling if further preparations for revolution were made. In October 1918 Lenin wrote to the Spartacists, as the German communists were known before February the next year:

> The decisive hour is at hand: the rapidly maturing German revolution calls on the Spartacist group to play the most important role, and we all firmly hope that before long the German socialist proletarian republic will inflict a decisive blow on world imperialism.[2]

In practical terms, preparation for the European revolutions meant two things: first, the rapid development of communist parties in all the industrial states; and second, the establishment of close control over these parties by the Bolshevik leadership in Moscow.

At the end of 1918 the Bolsheviks put forwards plans for the creation of the Third International, or as it was to become known, the Comintern. This organization was to be based in Moscow with the task of coordinating and disciplining the work of communists throughout the world. The founding Congress was held in Moscow in March 1919.

The leaders of the KPD did not receive the plans of their Bolshevik comrades with unmixed enthusiasm. To varying degrees they were suspicious of an organization based in Moscow, purporting to speak for communists throughout the world, but which the Russian Bolshevik leadership would most likely be in a position to dominate. Rosa Luxemburg, the commanding personality within the KPD, held this opinion more strongly than anyone else. From the confines of prison she had already in the summer of 1918 written a study of the Russian Revolution in which she sharply criticized Bolshevik methods. In particular, she condemned the Red Terror which Lenin had inflicted on all classes of Russian society potentially hostile to the Revolution through the agency of his secret police, the *Cheka*.[3]

Luxemburg chose a KPD delegate named Hugo Eberlein to go to the founding Congress of the Third International, but instructed him to vote against the Comintern's creation on the grounds that it was premature. Indeed, the personal qualities of Eberlein which appealed to Luxemburg for the furtherance of this end were not his diplomatic skills, but his narrow-mindedness and stubbornness.[4] Eberlein was the only true representative of a communist party outside Russia at the Comintern's foundation. As Aino Kuusinen, a Finnish communist who was present at the time recalled in her memoirs, most of the other 'so-called delegates had never even seen the country they were supposed to be representing'.[5] Besides Eberlein there were only four delegates who had come specially from abroad, while the other participants were foreign supporters of the Bolsheviks who happened to be in Russia at the time. Some of them spoke for parties which did not yet exist in their home countries.

Only the KPD had an independent voice, since Eberlein did as Luxemburg instructed. As a result, the Third Communist International came into being without the support of the KPD, which was by far the most important communist party outside Soviet Russia at this time. This was the first and last time that a foreign communist party was to play an official role equal to that of the Russian Party.[6]

Lenin's set-back was only momentary, for the KPD soon voluntarily joined the Comintern which it had not created. Even before Eberlein left for Moscow, Rosa Luxemburg was dead, as was Karl Liebknecht, the KPD's second most prominent leader. The two had been taken prisoner in the Berlin Rising of 1919, a localized insurrection which neither the KPD nor the Russian Bolsheviks had planned, and had been wantonly murdered by government soldiers on their way to jail. The murders of Luxemburg and Liebknecht and the KPD's subsequent joining of the Comintern were events of great moment in the history of German communism. The early loss of its most able and independent leaders made it much more difficult for their inexperienced successors to resist Moscow's demands. The murders marked the beginning of a process by which German communism became subject to increasing interference from Moscow, until by 1923, the KPD could justifiably be seen as no more than an auxiliary of the Communist Party of the Soviet Union. In this process the Comintern played a major role. In particular, the secret service operations associated with it were of key importance in the process whereby, in the course of just four years, the KPD became inextricably enmeshed with the revolutionary apparatus of the Soviet Union centred on Moscow.

Luxemburg's fears about the nature of the Third International were well-founded. In theory, the Comintern was to serve the needs of world revolution; in practice, the needs of the Russian state came first. From the beginning, Russian control over the Comintern was total. The first Executive Committee of the Communist International, or ECCI, scarcely disguised the Russians' overwhelming influence. It included the towering personalities of Lenin, Bukharin, and Trotsky, with Zinoviev as its president.[7] Trotsky recalled that: 'on all basic questions involving the International, Lenin called the tune'.[8] German influence was represented by Karl Radek, a communist from the former Austria-Hungary, who was in prison in Berlin when the Comintern was founded. After his arrival in Moscow in 1920, Radek soon established himself as Lenin's main adviser on German affairs. But he did so as a loyal subject of the Bolshevik regime, going so far as to assume Russian citizenship.

The ECCI saw itself, as it stated on festive occasions, as 'the general staff of world revolution'. In practical terms, this meant that it had four basic aims, which were: the formation of communist parties throughout Europe, but above all in the industrialized states; the subsequent organization of the new parties and, in particular, training them in Bolshevik-style clandestine habits; financing of the parties, largely in secret through Comintern couriers sent from Moscow; and, in the German case, organizing revolution.

The Comintern launched its western European campaign in October 1919, with the establishment of two secret agencies; these were the Western European Secretariat (WES) at Berlin and the Western Bureau at Amsterdam. The Amsterdam organization had only a short life. It was soon infiltrated by the Dutch police and had folded up by spring 1920. The Berlin agency, on the other hand, existed in Germany until Hitler's seizure of power in 1933. Thereafter it moved to Copenhagen, where it only finally wound up after the German invasion of Denmark in 1940.

The first head of the WES was Yakov Reich, whom Lenin had personally chosen for the job. Reich went by the pseudonym of 'Comrade Thomas'. He was a German-speaking Jew born in the Austro-Hungarian province of Galicia but who had taken up residence in Russia before the October Revolution.[9] His first assignment for the Bolsheviks was as an official in the Bolshevik embassy in Bern, where he also carried out propaganda duties, putting out the official communist bulletin, *Russische Nachrichten* ('Russian News').[10] Reich's mission was funded out of the treasures of the Bolsheviks' enemies. Before setting out he was allowed to choose from a huge horde of jewels and valuables which the Cheka had seized and deposited in the Palace of Justice.[11] According to one account, Reich arrived in Berlin with at least 25 million marks in cash and valuables worth 37 million marks.[12] Reich remained head of the WES until 1925.

Reich joined two Comintern emissaries who were already in Berlin. They were a Pole named Mieczysław Broński and a Russian-born German, Felix Wolf.[13] Another important member who joined the WES shortly after Reich's arrival was a German lawyer called Dr Eduard Fuchs. Fuchs had a reputation as an art connoisseur and intellectual writing books on the subject of mores in society. Though not appearing in public as a communist at all, Fuchs played a major role in the secret section of the KPD and in the WES. He was the treasurer of the WES from when it was founded, and served as liaison between important foreign communists and the KPD leaders, in which capacity, he sat on the Directing Committee (*Zentrale*) of the KPD.[14]

The official emissaries from Moscow formed the most important section of the WES. With the exception of Reich, Wolf, Broński, and a further member, Abraham Heifetz, who was more commonly known by his pseudonym 'Guralsky', these men served only for fairly short periods of time in Berlin. The rest of the WES personnel was drawn from the top ranks of the KPD. German communists serving in this organization included Paul Levi, who was head of the KPD in the period 1919–22, August Thalheimer, the German Party's chief theoretician, and Willi Münzenberg, who brilliantly conducted the Comintern's secret propaganda work in Europe in the interwar period.

It is almost superfluous to note that secrecy was the essence of the WES's work. Its practices stood in a tradition going back to the origins of the Russian revolutionary movement in the nineteenth century and which the Bolshevik Party had developed after its foundation in 1903. This aspect of the WES's work has been summed up with clarity by Branko Lazitch and Milorad Drachkovitch, who have written the authoritative account of the Comintern's early years. They note that to

> play its role effectively, the WES had to follow from the outset the Bolshevik rules about working legally and illegally at the same time. False papers, false identities, the use of diplomatic and nonpolitical covers, conspiratorial domiciles where hunted militants could take shelter, liaison plans ensuring contact and conversations between underground agents, the use of a middle-class false front as regards residence, dress, and style of life so as not to attract the police attention – all this came into being for the first time in Western Europe thanks to that Comintern branch installed in Berlin.[15]

The principal task of the WES was to serve as the chief clandestine centre of communications between, on the one hand, the Comintern in Moscow and the European communist parties and, on the other, between the Comintern and its secret agents. These channels were quite separate from those of the KPD, which had its own secret communications with Moscow. The clandestine operations of the WES were under the general supervision of Felix Wolf, while communications in particular were the charge of a man named Slivkin.[16] Like Wolf, the Comintern had sent Slivkin from Moscow. He arrived in Berlin in 1920. In the years 1919–20, the Comintern's foreign communications were very shaky. At this time the WES was the only contact which the Bolsheviks had with the KPD, and even this link was maintained through no more than an intermittent courier service.[17] But by all accounts, the WES quickly made good this situation. The veteran communist Victor Serge praised Slivkin's contribution to the Comintern's communications in his memoirs. He met Slivkin on a trip to Russia which he made in 1921, remembering him as 'a big merry fellow in charge of every imaginable kind of smuggling and who had bribed all the police, customs agents, and border guards along our route'.[18]

Within its communications brief the WES played the crucial role of paymaster to European communism. Over the course of the Twenties, it came to distribute funds both to the KPD and to the other European communist parties.[19] In the years 1919 to 1925 Moscow paid the KPD more than 200 million Reichsmark.[20] This gave it great leverage. With the exception of the Swedish Party, none of the European communist parties was able to make ends meet without subsidies from Moscow in the interwar period.[21]

The importance of the WES within the Bolsheviks' plans for world revolution was reflected in its relations with the leadership of the KPD. Members of the WES attended the meetings of the KPD Central Committee.[22] Thus they knew in detail about the KPD's work. Yet knowledge of the existence of the WES was restricted to the inner circle of the KPD.[23] Despite the secrecy surrounding the WES, the KPD was closely involved with the Comintern's operations acting in the passive yet vital capacity as an agency carrying out the Russian Bolsheviks' instructions.[24] From the beginning, the relationship seems to have been that of masters and men. The Moscow emissaries had two enormous advantages over the local German communists. First, they were supported by Lenin's writ. Second, when they took decisions they did not have to answer to the KPD rank and file, unlike the German communists, who had to think about re-election to their offices.[25]

Collaboration between the WES and the KPD enabled the Comintern to fulfil certain important intelligence requirements. One such requirement was the provision of false papers for communist agents. The production of secret documents was carried out by the Comintern's *Paß-Apparat* (Passport Organization), which was founded in Berlin in the years 1919–20. The covert German communist artisans who staffed this agency acquired a high level of expertise. They are said to have been able to forge all European passports, though they regarded British ones as particularly difficult. On the eve of the Nazi take-over in 1933, the *Paß-Apparat* had acquired considerable dimensions. According to one source, its Berlin headquarters always held 2,000 passports at the ready, backed up by a collection of 30,000 rubber stamps, while in 1931–2 its total personnel both in Germany and abroad numbered 170.[26] By this time the *Paß-Apparat* had ramified throughout northern and central Europe, with branches in Denmark, Sweden, Norway, Holland, Belgium, Switzerland, Austria, Czechoslovakia and the Polish-German port of Danzig (Gdańsk).[27] The WES's printing operations were not restricted to agent support. At the time when Reich was its head, the WES set up a publishing house which was the Comintern's main producer of propaganda for Western Europe.[28]

The international ramifications of the *Paß-Apparat* reflected the importance of WES and of Berlin within the Communist International's schemes for revolution. It was natural that an organization so important to Moscow should always be in the hands of one of the Comintern's most prominent disciples. In 1929 the WES received a new head. This was the charismatic Bulgarian communist, Georgi Dimitrov. Dimitrov had started his political career within the Bulgarian trade union movement, where he had been active in organizing strikes. In 1917 he became a secret communist, directing the Party's clandestine operations inside Bulgaria. In September 1923 he led an armed communist rising which the government rapidly suppressed. Unlike many of the Bulgarian Communist Party (BCP) leaders, Dimitrov escaped arrest and fled to Moscow. It was only then that his importance within the BCP was recognized, when he was officially proclaimed as it co-leader.[29] In appearance Dimitrov did not seem the formidable politician that he was. Richard Krebs, a German communist, recalled his first meeting with him:

> My first impression of Dimitrov was disappointing. I had expected to meet a steely man, a hardened veteran of many campaigns. Instead there came out of an inner office a large, soft, flabby-faced individual, stout and dark, dressed like a dandy and smelling of heavy perfume. He wore a thick ring on his left hand. His well-manicured fingers held a black cigar. His eyes were large and bold. I soon found that he was a driving, domineering personality. He spoke German with remarkable fluency. His words came loud and hard.[30]

Dimitrov's powers were revealed in 1933, when he achieved international prominence after his arrest by the Nazis, who put him on trial on a charge of complicity in starting the *Reichstag* fire. Dimitrov conducted his own defence and brilliantly outmanoeuvred his accusers, including Hermann Göring, whom he held up to ridicule. This won his acquittal and gave a fillip to the communist cause throughout the world. Dimitrov returned to the Soviet Union where he survived the Purges, possibly helped by his friendship with Stalin. From 1935 he served as the secretary-general of the Comintern, until Stalin disbanded the organization as a sign of goodwill to the Western Allies in 1943. The climax of Dimitrov's career came after the Second World War, when he was prime minister of the Bulgarian People's Republic in the years 1946–9.

Shortly after establishing operations in Berlin, the Comintern took measures to coordinate its intelligence operations from the centre in Moscow. At the end of 1920 or at the beginning of 1921, it set up a formal intelligence agency, the OMS, short for *Otdel Mezhdunarodnych Svyazyey* (Department of International Communications). This was to serve as a secret liaison department, running the Comintern's agent networks abroad.

The formation of the OMS was part of a general reorganization and systematization of Bolshevik intelligence – something which had been very much lacking during Lenin's first years in power. The circumstances of the creation of the communist state ensured that the Party would always be dependent upon the large-scale use of intelligence. Most obviously, the Bolsheviks realized the need for a massive and ruthless counter-intelligence service at home, because of the hostility of the majority of their own population. They had this from December 1917 onwards in the form of the Cheka.[31] A well-founded realization of the need for protection was a powerful motive which impelled the Bolsheviks to establish regular foreign intelligence services alongside the operations of the Comintern. The Bolsheviks were acutely concerned to discover the intentions both of the capitalist powers whom they perceived were encircling them, as well as of the numerous émigrés who had fled Russia during the Civil War and some of whom were now plotting against the Bolshevik regime. A further key factor leading to the establishment of Bolshevik intelligence abroad was the desire to assist the Comintern in spreading the world revolution.[32]

The first head of Soviet intelligence was the legendary Feliks Dzerzhinsky, who held this post until his death in 1926. Dzerzhinsky had built up his reputation as a revolutionary at the beginning of the century through his daring activities among the workers of Russian Poland, which had led to his frequent imprisonment. In this capacity he has been described as 'the pupil of Rosa Luxemburg', who was then the leader of Poland's embryonic Marxist party the SKDPiL (the Social Democratic Party of the Kingdom of Poland and Lithuania).[33] This is ironic in that it was above all the cruelty of Dzerzhinsky's Cheka which Rosa Luxemburg castigated in her treatise, *The Russian Revolution*.

In December 1920, Dzerzhinsky formed a regular political intelligence agency within the Cheka. This was known simply as the Foreign Department or *Inostranny Otdel*, but usually just as the INO.[34] Its targets were the establishments of capitalist states, and Russian émigrés. At about the same time a third Bolshevik foreign intelligence agency came into being, namely the Fourth Department of the General Staff of the Red Army. Little, however, is known about this military organization. In German communist slang the two regular Soviet intelligence organizations were feminized, perhaps surprisingly given the ruthless reputation which they acquired, as 'Greta' for the INO and 'Klara' for the Fourth Department.[35]

The operations of the INO and the Fourth Department were largely kept separate from one another. Very few agents worked simultaneously for both departments. The same is not true, however, of the regular intelligence agencies and the OMS. As one authority has concluded, the 'OMS performed a valuable service for INO by drawing into secret-service work foreign communists and fellow travellers (communist sympathizers) who were more likely to respond to an appeal for help from the Communist International than to a direct approach from Soviet intelligence. Many of the best OGPU and NKVD foreign agents in the 1930s believed initially that they were working for the Comintern.'[36]

Thus as head of the Cheka, Dzerzhinsky was closely involved in the affairs of the Comintern. He briefed Yakov Reich before he set out to establish the WES in Berlin.[37] Indeed, Dzerzhinsky symbolized in his person the intimate links between Soviet intelligence and the world revolutionary movement. At the first three Congresses of the Comintern it was he who represented the Russian Communist Party, while at the fourth he represented the barely existent Polish Communist Party.[38]

The operations of Bolshevik intelligence were greatly assisted by the improving diplomatic relations between Moscow and most of the capitals of Western Europe. Moscow and Berlin resumed semi-official relations in 1920. The concrete result was the Russians' establishment of a huge trade delegation, the *Handelsvertretung*, in Berlin's Lindenstraße. This was to remain until 1933 the main centre for the INO's operations.[39]

One of the most important espionage activities which the Comintern carried out in its own right was the maintenance of a check on local communists. That the ECCI regularly sent out agents on counter-intelligence missions was well-known to their targets, who gave these unwelcome guests the nickname, the 'eyes of Moscow'. The Comintern exercised these functions as just one of the many ways in which it tried both to build up European communist parties and at the same time to ensure that they remained firmly tied to Moscow from the outset. Reich recalled this aspect of his work:

> In my capacity as the 'eye of Moscow,' that is as emissary of the Executive Committee of the Communist International and of the Central Committee of the Russian Communist Party, I regularly attended the meetings of the German Communist Party's Central Committee … I sent regular reports to the Central Committee [of the Russian Communist Party], in which I frankly described the situation within the German Communist Party and included information about some of its militants …[40]

This aspect of the Comintern's work particularly galled Paul Levi, the KPD's leader from 1919 to 1921. Reich recalled the origins of a row which had blown up between them in 1920 after Levi had been visiting the Second Comintern Congress in Moscow:

> [Levi] was at Comintern headquarters in an office of Radek's, the latter having become one of the secretaries of the Third International. I never found out what they were talking about. I know only that Radek opened a drawer and said that he had there my secret reports on the German

> Communist Party. I even believe that Radek read him a passage from one of them. Then, without closing the drawer again, he went out. Left to himself, Levi picked up the reports and started to read them. Among them were those that described the members of the Central Committee of the German Communist Party and in particular Levi himself, reports which had especially interested Lenin and which he had requested me to continue sending ... At the first meeting of the German Communist Party's Central Committee, Levi gave a detailed report on his trip to Moscow, adding that he must end his report on a personal note. He then brought up my reports ... He concluded by demanding that I be censured and that a request be sent to the Communist International and of the Central Committee of the Russian Communist Party that I be recalled to Moscow.[41]

THE KPD'S SECRET ORGANIZATION

From its creation, the German Communist Party had its own secret apparatus at its disposal. After the fall of the Kaiser's regime in November 1918 secret communist underground organizations sprang up throughout Germany. But for the next two years they remained generally outside the control of the KPD's Directing Committee, or *Zentrale*, in Berlin. Because of this lack of coordination the communist underground was weak and played no significant role whatsoever in the period 1918–20.[42] Most conspicuously, the military power of German communism was greatly inferior to that of the German Right. The KPD had nothing to compare with the nationalist and violently anti-Bolshevik *Freikorps*, the irregular, but well-armed units which had emerged out of the collapse of the imperial German army at the end of 1918.

The Second Comintern Congress, held at Petrograd in 1921, ordered all foreign communist parties to set up illegal organizations, which 'at the decisive moment will help the party to do its duty to the revolution'.[43] The KPD dutifully echoed these instructions at its Seventh Party Congress in August that year.[44] Thus one of the first tasks of the Comintern in its organization of German communism was to provide the KPD, or more exactly Bolshevism, with the power not just to defend itself but to take on the *Freikorps* and the German establishment, and to bring revolution to Germany. This was a difficult task, which indeed was never remotely accomplished, because the KPD never attracted more than a minority of German workers. Nonetheless, from the point of view of the Comintern and the KPD, the situation seemed to improve in 1921, after the KPD gained an accession of strength from its absorption of the left wing of German Social Democracy, the USPD. Thus in 1921, the KPD and the Comintern began work in earnest to set up an illegal organization. This meant strengthening the two illegal KPD organizations which had already come into existence. These were the N-group (*Nachrichtenapparat*) which was for intelligence work, and the M-group (*Militärapparat*) which was for the training cadres of the communist military forces. Both groups had the additional mission of maintaining liaison with Russian agents passing illegally through Germany.[45]

Two further branches seem to have been added to the illegal *Apparat* at this time: the Z-groups, or *Zersetzungsgruppen* (Subversion Groups), which were intended to infiltrate the German political establishment and the *Reichswehr* (the 100,000-strong regular army); and the T-groups, or *Terrorgruppen*, which were to be used for sabotage and for the liquidation of traitors to the KPD.[46] There is, however, some debate about the precise date when the Z- and T-groups were created; possibly they only emerged in 1923.[47]

As the abortive revolution of March 1921 was to prove, none of these illegal groups was at all effective. The Comintern's efforts to create them, however, are of importance in its relations with the leadership of the KPD, over which it was trying to increase its control at this time. The KPD was not yet the utterly pliant tool in Moscow's hands which it was very soon to become. The leader of the KPD, Paul Levi continued the tradition of Rosa Luxemburg in trying to stake out the German Party's claims to a degree of independence from the Bolsheviks. Levi was particularly concerned about the covert operations into which the Comintern was increasingly drawing the KPD, and clearly saw the leverage which these developments gave the Russians in the KPD's internal affairs. Under Levi, control of the illegal apparatus became an issue, and a split started to develop between the KPD *Zentrale* and the communist grass-roots in the secret organizations. Levi and the KPD leadership tried to channel the activities of the illegal groups into what seemed to them to be safer channels. They wanted the illegal *Apparat* to do no more than train communists in military theory and to provide guards at party meetings. The illegals, on the other hand, wanted to build up a communist arsenal. Levi and his associates had little success in restraining the secret organizations and, whether they liked it or not, preparations for the Comintern's revolution in Germany continued.[48] Such impotence proved intolerable to Levi and his independently-minded supporters in the KPD leadership. They resigned from their posts in February 1921, resentful at the dictatorial way in which the Bolsheviks had treated them and worried at the danger into which premature preparations for revolution had placed the German communist movement.[49] Levi wrote bitterly after his resignation about the atmosphere which the Comintern had created. He drew particular attention to the Comintern's spies, the 'eyes of Moscow' stating that they

> never work with the leadership of individual Communist parties, but always behind their backs and against them. They enjoy the confidence of Moscow but the local leaders do not ... The Executive Committee [of the Comintern] acts like a Cheka projected outside the Russian borders.[50]

Levi's fears for the future of German communism were soon to become a reality. Already by the time he resigned, the Comintern was planning a German revolution. At the beginning of March 1921, a secret Comintern delegation led by the Hungarian communist, Béla Kun came to Berlin to plan the campaign. This was to be the Comintern's first attempt at world revolution. Lenin had been sceptical about its chances, but Kun had won him over. With hindsight, this seems surprising. Kun had the distinction of having been the leader of the only communist regime outside Russia. In March 1919 he had come to power in Hungary as the head of communist-dominated government. It had not lasted long, thanks largely to Kun's policies, which had included the wholesale communization of property and invasion of neighbouring Slovakia. In August 1919, Kun had been expelled when the Romanian army marched into Hungary, an invasion welcome to all but himself and his small band of supporters.

By now the KPD was weakened by the loss of the Levi faction. But it still greeted the preparations for the forthcoming revolution with enthusiasm, despite the recklessness of the Comintern's plans, and Kun's past record as a failed revolutionary. Perhaps surprisingly the main opposition to the plan within Germany came from the WES, where Reich and Wolf were firmly opposed to it, to the extent that the KPD *Zentrale* excluded Wolf from its meetings.[51] But 'plan' might be considered a misleading term by which to refer to Kun's ideas for Germany. Before March 1921 the Comintern had no specific blueprint for the insurrection.[52] The result was a fiasco. On 21 March strikes and uprisings took place, but they were completely disorganized. Only a tiny minority of German workers were involved. The secret *Apparat* of the KPD was conspicuous by its absence, which was probably fortunate for its survival.[53] The German government had the situation in hand from the outset, though the rising only finally petered out on 1 April.

The KPD's secret military organization proved a complete failure in 1921, as did its intelligence set-up, the *N-Gruppen*. Clearly they had been unable to gauge accurately the temperament of the German working class. Worse, they had not been able to protect the KPD from infiltration by the police. On 10 January 1921, the Prussian police raided communist headquarters in a number of cities and as a result became aware of the existence of a 'red army'. On 3 February Dr Robert Weismann, Prussian State Commissioner for Safeguarding Public Security obtained documents from the Soviet Mission in Berlin which 'contained strong indications that the Soviet Mission was involved in smuggling arms and explosives, furthering Communist propaganda, and financing Communist underground activities in Germany and other parts of Europe'.[54] Later in the month, police raids uncovered dynamite and other military equipment. Weismann now had the party's activities under constant surveillance. Though aware of the Comintern's determination on revolution, he stopped short of imposing further restrictions on the KPD. Nonetheless, these actions meant that the government was ready when the insurrection took place.

The Bolshevik leadership saw the failure of the 'March Action' as a major blow. It marked the end of Lenin's last real hope that his revolution would spread abroad and break Russia's encirclement. For the KPD the results were grim, and led to a sharp decline in the membership of what was already a minority party. But, from the Comintern's point of view, there was one gain from the fiasco. After March 1921, the KPD towed the party line as never before. Heinrich Brandler, co-chairman of the KPD since Levi's resignation in February 1921, denied that the Comintern had had anything to do with the 'March Action', as did the Comintern's president, Zinoviev. Thus the KPD leadership accepted full responsibility for the humiliation.

After the 'March Action', Bolshevik foreign policy entered a period of confusion. This reflected principally the declining power of Lenin who by now was clearly a dying man, and the succession struggle which had become a clear feature of Kremlin politics by 1923. Lenin now held no real hope for any German revolution in the immediate future. The Comintern in general, and Trotsky in particular, however, had not abandoned hope and finally, in the summer of 1923, persuaded Lenin on his death-bed to allow yet one more attempt to create a revolution in Germany.

It was not only Trotsky who kept up his hopes of revolution, two thousand miles away from the reality of German conditions. Far more surprisingly so did the new KPD leadership, who had decided to recover from the crisis after the March Action by improving their fighting strength. By the beginning of 1923, the KPD was already organizing for another attempt at revolution. At this time it set up a general staff, called the Revolutionary Committee or REVKO, which was headed by August Guralsky. Military operations were to be carried out under the direction of the KPD's *M-Gruppen* (M-Groups) or the Military-Political Apparat as they were now also known. These were under the German leadership of a military council led by Ernst Scheller, and which included the future East German leader, Walter Ulbricht. On the eve of the insurrection of 1923, however, the Soviet general, Skoblevski took overall command of the KPD's military operations with the rank of *Reichsleiter*. At the provincial level, military preparations for the rising were in the hands of six regional military-political commanders or *MP-Oberleiter*. These were trusted party leaders, each of whom was assisted by a Russian military adviser.[55]

The *Terror-and Zersetzungapparate* had by now taken definite shape and were expected to assist the military operations of the coming revolution. Here too the KPD took measures to improve its operational efficiency, at least on paper. The *T-& Z-Apparate* were supplemented by a newly-created Office for the Procurement of Weapons and Ammunition (*Waffen-und Munitionsbeschaffungsamt*), or WUMBA as it was euphoniously known for short. All three were coordinated by Leo Flieg, the chairman of the party's organizational bureau (*Orgbüro*).[56]

One new feature, however, which gave a boost, albeit an unwarranted one, to the KPD in 1923 was the presence of Soviet advisers in Germany.[57] It seems that numbers of Soviet agents were already operational in the Ruhr area during the disturbances which followed the French occupation of this district in January that year. Certainly the German Government sent a diplomatic protest to the Soviet Government on this account, though predictably the Soviet foreign ministry, *Narkomindel*, denied all knowledge of the affair.[58] But there is no doubt that the Soviet government sent military advisers into German to prepare for the rising of 1923. Richard Krebs (better known by his pseudonym Jan Valtin), who took part in the insurrection of 1923 wrote of the period around the end of June 1923 that 'Already it was an open secret in our midst that Soviet officers had been sent from Moscow to act as technical advisers, and that military preparations for the expected armed rising were well under way.'[59] According to the then senior member of the KPD, Ruth Fischer, they numbered 'several hundred'.[60] This figure has been taken without criticism by many authors.[61] It is, however, difficult not to agree with Werner Angress, the chief authority on the events of 1923, who considers Fischer's figures to be a 'gross exaggeration'.[62] This conclusion is supported by incidental information in Jan Valtin's *Out of the Night*, according to which there were only 'five or six' Russian instructors in the crucial Hamburg district.[63]

Overall operations were in the hands of General Pyotr Alexsandrovich Skoblevski, whose real name is not known. It is thought that he was a civil war general, named Rose, *alias* Gorev, and was a Latvian by birth.[64] Skoblevski came at the request of Brandler and of other KPD leaders, probably arriving in Germany only in September 1923.[65]

In 1923, the KPD made efforts to build up its shock troops, known as 'proletarian' or 'red hundreds'. This was a striking name for a workers' militia, since it begged obvious comparison with the notorious 'black hundreds' of Tsarist Russia in the 1890s, who had played a major role in the slaughter of scores of Russian and Polish Jews and the emigration of countless others.[66] When the revolution came the Red Hundreds were also to perform the functions of a security police, in a manner analogous to that of the Red Guards in the October Revolution. It was to be their job to round up all the principal anti-communist elements. The full strength of the Red Hundreds remains unclear. According to Gast, an East German writer, they numbered about 100,000 in October 1923 and were organized into 800 different groups. Certainly this was no more than a paper figure.[67] According to Krebs there were 'several hundred' companies of one hundred men each throughout Germany, eleven of which were in Hamburg.[68]

The Soviet advisers had the role of preparing the 'Red Hundreds'. Overall direction of this task from Moscow was apparently entrusted to no less a person than Unshlikht, Dzerzhinsky's deputy in the OGPU, as the Soviet security and intelligence service was now called.[69] Richard Krebs was at this time serving in the KPD's secret courier corps, which served communications between the German leaders and their Russian military advisers.[70] He claimed to have been trained by Soviet instructors:

> Each Sunday the hundreds marched out for military training in lonely stretches of forest or heath. Young Soviet Russian officers, most of whom spoke German, directed the training. Five or six such officers operated in the Hamburg area. They had come to Germany in the guise of sailors abroad Soviet vessels, and [KPD] 'activists' ... had smuggled them ashore at night. Under assumed names, using false German passports, they had their quarters in the homes of Party members. Their chief in Hamburg was a short, gruff, square-headed Russian who called himself Otto Marquandt, nominally an official of the Soviet Trade Mission in Hamburg.[71]

Along with Soviet manpower, came Soviet money, paid in US dollars. It was channelled to the KPD's *Orgbüro* through Jacob Mirov-Abramov, an OMS official at the Soviet Embassy in Berlin. According to Aino Kuusinen, who was then working on Scandinavian affairs in the Comintern's Information Department, Moscow also tried to provide weapons for the revolution. In her memoirs, which are generally reliable, she wrote:

> Arms were transported in a cargo steamer which plied regularly between Petrograd and Hamburg; there they were unloaded by Communist dockers and stored on wharves under Communist control. A small, slim, unimportant-looking man named Kleine (actually Guralsky) paid several flying visits to Moscow to arrange for the shipments, which included thousands of rifles.[72]

That Soviet weapons reached the KPD in 1923 is supported by Krebs, who likewise speaks of Soviet steamers making clandestine deliveries off the German coast.[73] He provides further information that the KPD and the INO made efforts to fund the revolution from within Germany.[74] Apparently they did so by providing an illegal immigration service for Central and East Europeans who wished to emigrate to the United States and Argentina. Another source of funds came from the Comintern's alcohol smuggling operations.[75] The proceeds of these operations were used to buy arms from Belgium.

Despite all the KPD's paperwork, it was by no means ready for revolution in 1923. Whatever their nominal strength, there was no more guarantee that the 'Red Hundreds' would take the field than the communist cohorts of 1921. It seems that the KPD's preparations suffered also from the overlapping of and confusion between too great a number of secret agencies, none of which were individually at all effective.[76] Furthermore, there is no doubt that the preparation for an uprising remained at the paper stage until the autumn of 1923.

The main plans for the revolution were in the Russians' hands. The basic scheme was straightforward. During the anniversary celebrations of the Bolshevik Revolution, the Red Hundreds were to attack the police who would react with excessive violence. This official repression would stimulate a workers' rising, which would be enough to overwhelm the government's forces of law and order. Meanwhile, other Red Hundreds would seal off Bavaria, which was the marshalling ground for about 50,000 *Freikorps*.

Details of the Comintern's plans for the 'revolution of 1923' are probably of more interest to students of the psychology of intelligence than to the history of intelligence. Even with the benefit of hindsight, it is difficult to see how any rational commander, such as Trotsky certainly had proved himself in the Russian Civil War, could take such a scheme seriously. The revolution faced three insurmountable obstacles. First, according to all the elections to the Reichstag since the First World War, the majority of the German working class did not support the KPD's legal activities, let alone its plans to pull down the state. Second, the Red Hundreds were expected to take on the *Reichswehr*, whose 100,000 rank-and-file were excellently armed, and had shown no signs of siding with the communists in the past. Third, the idea that the Red Hundreds could keep the powerful *Freikorps* quiet within Bavaria's borders, was ludicrous.

At the last minute, the reality of the situation in Germany became clear even to the KPD leadership, who with Radek's support called off the insurrection. News of the Comintern's change of plan did not reach the KPD's organization in Hamburg until after an insurrection had begun. The government suppressed it with little difficulty.

The failure of the 1923 insurrection had a decisive effect on Soviet foreign policy. The faction in the Politburo, supported by the Comintern, which had continued to seek revolution in Europe had to abandon its plans. The priority of Soviet foreign policy was now that which Stalin demanded, namely the consolidation of the Soviet regime at home.[77] The Comintern now saw Asia, in particular India and China, as the only fertile ground for revolution in the near future.[78] This did not mean, however, that Comintern activities in Europe were reduced. It continued to play a key roles in two fields: the maintenance of communications with, and financial support for, the European communist parties; and carrying out espionage.

The failure of revolution in Germany and the reorientation of the Comintern's plans had an immediate impact on the illegal apparatus of the KPD. It was reduced in scale and reorganized. Possibly this amounted to no more than a consolidation. The Comintern entrusted direction of this task to Hans Kippenberger, who had served as an officer in the German Army during the First World War and had fought in the Hamburg insurrection. Erich Wollenberg, a former member of the *Apparat,* later wrote about the organizations' definitive absorption into the network of Soviet intelligence at this time.[79] According to his account, the *M-Apparat* was still intended primarily to serve the aims of the German revolution, despite the dominance within it of Russian instructors and its dependence on Soviet money.[80] In 1928, it changed its name to *AM-Apparat*, or the Anti-Military Apparat (*Antimilitarischer Apparat*). This symbolized its renunciation of the initiative for armed combat. By this time the KPD's military *Apparat* had become little more that the auxiliary of Soviet intelligence, serving the ends not of German revolution, but of the Soviet State. Despite the failures of 1921 and 1923, the KPD's illegal apparatus afforded great advantages to Soviet intelligence which, before Hitler came to power, operated in Germany on a greater scale than anywhere else in Europe. The existence of the KPD, as the largest communist party outside the Soviet Union, allowed it to do so.

What the German communists lacked in military muscle, they made up for as Soviet spies. By the beginning of the 1930s, the KPD had at its disposal a network of several thousand 'worker correspondents'. These agents were usually referred to either by their Russian acronym of *rabcors*, short for *rabochiye korrespondenty* (worker correspondents) or in German as *Betriebs-Berichterstatter* or BBs. A special department of the KPD was established to organize their work. Their ostensible purpose was to report to the communist press on working conditions. But their main task was secretly to gather technical information for the construction of Soviet industry.[81]

Sometimes their work scarcely fell within the field of espionage at all. For example, Richard Krebs served as a BB while employed as a seaman in the Atlantic. His task was to find out about a new harpoon gun in use on whaling ships.[82]

The huge scale of Soviet intelligence operations in Germany at the end of the 1920s and beginning of 1930s is illustrated by the proliferation of spy scandals which occurred at this time. For example, in the period June 1931–December 1932, over 300 cases of espionage were tried in Germany, almost all of which involved Soviet intelligence.[83] The number of the trials reflected the conditions for espionage which existed in the Weimar Republic, which were more favourable than in Britain and France. Not only did Soviet intelligence have the support of a strong local communist party, but also it benefited from the attitude of the Weimar government towards the Soviet Union, with which, as a fellow victim of the Treaty of Versailles, it was anxious to remain on good terms.

THE NAZIS' DESTRUCTION OF THE KPD

This situation came to an abrupt end in February 1933 when Hitler seized absolute power in Germany. He immediately set the Gestapo to work on both the legal and illegal branches of the KPD, rapidly destroying their organization. Despite its long use of covert activities, the KPD proved incapable of providing organized resistance when the moment came.[84] In the words of the writer Arthur Koestler, then working for the Comintern, the KPD behaved like 'a castrated giant' in 1933. Why, then did the greatest communist party in Europe outside the Soviet Union collapse so quickly? Resistance to the Nazis would certainly have been very difficult, given the level of repression after 1933, as well as the efficiency of the Gestapo. In their swoop on the communists, the Gestapo were able to draw profitably on all the material which the regular police had been building up on the KPD over a period of years. For example, the Berlin police had agents inside the KPD as far as the level of the leadership, and were quite well informed about all the Party's internal affairs.[85] But even the ruthlessness and methodicalness of the Nazis does not explain the sheer speed of the KPD's collapse. Partly this was due to the KPD's own inefficiency. The degree of police infiltration of the Party reveals much about the ineffectiveness of the *Z- and N-Apparate* and the special *Parteiselbstschutz*, or Party Self-Protection unit which was created to protect the KPD leadership at the end of the 1920s. In a sense, the existence of the KPD's various illegal organizations even helped the Nazis. Hitler's propagandists were not lying when they painted the KPD as a subversive puppet of Moscow. Very few Germans, outside the KPD lamented the destruction of the Party in 1933. Furthermore, a considerable number of German communists saw little reason to fight for their old cause, and simply switched from one extreme to another, joining the Nazi Party in 1933.

Further reasons for the catastrophe of 1933 may be found in the policies of the Soviet Union to which the KPD had been bound now for a decade. This extended to the field of Party organization. The Soviet government, through the Comintern, had insisted that the KPD establish a highly centralized command structure. In the 1920s, this meant that Moscow could control German communism more easily. But it left the KPD all the more vulnerable to the Nazis. Once the KPD leadership had either fled or been imprisoned, the Party as whole, in both its legal and illegal branches, was like a body without a brain.[86] A further area in which Soviet control of the KPD proved fatal was that of domestic policy. Until 1932, the KPD had paid relatively little attention to the mounting threat from the Right. Instead, the brunt of the Party's propaganda had been directed at its enemies on the Left, namely the SPD. This had rendered the German working-class movement weak and divided before the Nazi onslaught. Finally, and perhaps most importantly, the Soviet Union contributed to the KPD's rapid demise through its foreign policy, upon which, needless to say, the KPD was utterly dependent. Stalin saw the German crisis of 1933 as a manifestation of the death throes of German capitalism, and thought it best to let events in Germany take their own course.[87] Above all, the Soviet leadership realized that little would be gained by putting the KPD's illegal apparatus into action. This was no more likely to bring success in 1933 than in 1921 or 1923. The worst that could happen was that it would poison German–Soviet relations at a time when Stalin still hoped for friendly relations with Hitler.

After the Nazis came to power, the Soviet Union made no serious move to rebuild the KPD. Far from it, Stalin was just as keen to liquidate a large number of the German communist exiles who fell into his hands as was Hitler. Many of the Germans working in the regular organizations of Soviet intelligence died during the Great Purges in the Soviet Union at the end of the 1930s. The victims included the élite of the KPD who had worked in the Comintern's clandestine organizations. Foremost among them was Hans Kippenberger, a former member of the *Zentrale* and director of the KPD's military intelligence *Apparat* with the responsibility of maintaining liaison between the Party underground and the Soviet intelligence.[88] Kippenberger was one of the few members of the KPD to come out of the fiasco of 1923 with credit. It was largely thanks to his military expertise that the Hamburg insurrectionists were able to organize an orderly retreat.[89] Thereafter he was sought by the police, but continued to work illegally for the Comintern in

Germany with the task of reorganizing the KPD's Military Apparat. In 1928 he stood for the *Reichstag*, which brought him both public notice and arrest. However, his election was successful and so long as the Weimar Republic lasted, he enjoyed parliamentary immunity. This saved him again in 1931 when he was publicly unmasked as a Soviet agent.[90] After Hitler's seizure of power Kippenberger was one of the few KPD leaders who vainly tried to rebuild the Party's secret apparatus, but not for long. Later in 1933 he escaped to the Soviet Union. For a while he continued to work for the Comintern in Western Europe, but in 1935 he was recalled to Moscow. A secret trial followed. He was forced to confess to the trumped-up charge of spying 'for the German Reichswehr'. He was shot on 3 October 1937.[91]

The worst period of the Purges, the so-called *Yezhovshchina*, abated at the beginning of 1938, when Lavrenti Beria became head of the NKVD, the Soviet Ministry for Internal Affairs, which included the secret police. But even then, there were further terrors in store for German communists. In August 1939 Germany and the Soviet Union signed the Nazi–Soviet Pact which seemed to usher in a new period of rapprochement between the dictatorships, bringing with it, from Stalin's point of view, a new impulse to conciliate Hitler. One means of conciliation was to drag German communists out of the labour camps and hand them over to the SS in exchange for Russian émigrés and Ukrainians who had tried to find refuge in Germany and Poland.[92]

Even after the Second World War, the collapse of German communism in 1933 was still a source of humiliation to German communists on both sides of the East–West divide. The speed and scale of the disaster was something which for good reason disturbed the future East German leaders. From early on, communist propaganda tried to make the best of a bad job. It was difficult for the Comintern and the writers in its pay to say much that was positive about the KPD's performance in 1933, but they were able, and with some success, to build up a myth of communist resistance to the Nazis thereafter. According to this version of events, the KPD quickly reorganized itself at the grass-roots level inside Germany. German workers heroically rallied to the cause and organized themselves in resistance cells. These were the famous *Fünfergruppen*, or 'groups of five', though not all the groups had strictly five members. The *Fünfergruppen* operated according to tried and tested methods of revolutionary conspiracy; only the leaders of each group knew the names of the other members; only group leaders were able to contact higher echelons in the resistance network.[93] This myth proved very attractive not only to German communists, but to many other Germans distressed at the absence of any armed resistance to Hitler before the end of 1944. It has even found its way into some works expressly written to reveal the dangers of Soviet and East German espionage, which is surely a singular achievement of the KGB and the Stasi who assiduously spread the story of the *Fünfergruppen*.[94] Yet the resilience of the myth remains surprising for it does not explain one obvious fact: why did the communist resistance not carry out a single act of military significance throughout the Second World War?

Stalin saw the destruction of German communism as a diplomatic necessity after 1933. This does not mean, of course, that the Soviet Union was not weakened by the collapse of the KPD. As Christopher Andrew, an authority on Soviet intelligence notes, after Hitler came to power, 'Stalin had less reliable intelligence from within Nazi Germany than from any other major power … The damage done by the near liquidation of the extensive German agent network was all the more serious because Germany was probably the one major power whose high-grade ciphers Soviet SIGINT could not read.'[95] By 1935, Abram Slutsky, the head of the INO reported that all large-scale Soviet intelligence operations in Germany had been wound up.[96] From then on, Soviet intelligence tried to work against the *Reich* from bases on Germany's borders, notably the Low Countries, France, and Switzerland. However, the main sources of intelligence on Germany came from two particular agents inside German embassies, Rudolf von Scheliha at Warsaw, and above all, Richard Sorge, in Tokyo.

Richard Sorge was one of the most famous and, perhaps, the most important spies in history. After the war he was not surprisingly placed in the fighting tradition of East German state security. In the Stasi's Berlin headquarters, small busts of his head proliferated, and were outnumbered only by those of Feliks Dzerzhinsky, the founding father of all communist intelligence operations.[97]

Sorge was born in 1895, the son of a German father and a Russian mother. He was educated in Germany and fought for the Kaiser in the First World War. He was immediately inspired by the Bolshevik Revolution. In 1924 he became a Soviet citizen. Five years later he started to work for the Fourth Department, as Soviet military intelligence was then known. His first mission was to Shanghai where, under the cover of a journalist, he was able to work his way into right-wing circles within the German community. He returned to Germany in 1933 and joined the Nazi party. His break came in autumn that year, when he was sent on a journalistic assignment to Tokyo. There, to use his own words, he won the 'absolute trust' of the German Embassy. In particular, he established a very close relationship with Colonel Eugen Ott, the Military Attaché. As a result, Sorge obtained access both to high-level German documents and to the information on Japanese military planning which the Tokyo Embassy received. Sorge acted as an important spy-master in his own right. He was singularly successful in penetrating the Japanese establishment by building up an agent network. The most important of

Sorge's sub-agents was Hotsumi Ozaki, who worked for the high-ranking statesman, Prince Konoye.[98]

Sorge had immense success in procuring political and military intelligence about the intentions of Germany and Japan. He warned Moscow of the Japanese invasion of China in 1937 and then provided reassurance that the Japanese military were not intending to start a war with the Soviet Union, despite fierce border clashes with the Red Army in 1938–9. How much weight the Soviet military attached to Sorge's intelligence about the Japanese remains uncertain. It is certain, on the other hand, that the concrete information which he provided about Operation 'Barbarossa', Hitler's plan for the invasion of the Soviet Union, was of no practical use. Stalin disregarded this information along with over a hundred other warnings that the Germans were preparing to attack. The Soviet intelligence failure of 1941 highlights an important truism: intelligence is only of use if it is accurately assessed by the leadership for which it is intended. In so highly centralized a governmental system as the Soviet Union, the assessment of high-grade information rested with Stalin himself. There is a clear analogy to be drawn here with the experience of the East German Politburo almost half a century later, on the eve of the revolution of 1989. Stalin believed that a German invasion of the Soviet Union was impossible, therefore any information which indicated that an attack was on the way could only be disinformation. Right up until the middle of 1989, the East German leadership believed that they had nothing to fear from popular unrest and had no interest in the occasionally alarming reports which filtered through to them.[99]

It might be argued that the link between East German state security and Sorge is very tenuous, despite the Stasi's adopting him as one of their ancestors. Sorge was, after all, never a member of the KPD and, indeed, not even a German national after 1924. In short, he belongs with far greater justification to the traditions and ancestry of the KGB. Yet, at least until the 1970s, it is misleading to draw an fine dividing line between Soviet and German intelligence. As argued above, links between German communism and Soviet intelligence were intimate from almost the moment of the Russian Revolution. Likewise, as will be shown in the next chapter, East German intelligence was born of the KGB in 1945 and developed in its parent's image.

The case of Sorge raises an issue. While the KPD could no longer provide the soil which fertilized Soviet intelligence operations inside and outside Germany, nonetheless, after 1933, individual German communists continued to play a significant, though not decisive role as auxiliaries in the world-wide operations of the Comintern and of the regular agencies of Soviet intelligence. In this sense, the process continued whereby German communism was grafted onto the Soviet plant. From the 1930s to the Soviet take-over in eastern Germany in 1945, many of the future leaders of the East German State were working for the agencies of Soviet intelligence. They included Walter Ulbricht, Wilhelm Zaisser, Rudolf Herrnstadt, Ernst Wollweber, Richard Stahlmann, and Erich Mielke.

RUDOLF HERRNSTADT

Rudolf Herrnstadt was the only future East German leader whose contribution to Soviet espionage approached that of Richard Sorge. Herrnstadt became an important political figure in the early years of the DDR as editor-in-chief of the East German Party daily newspaper, *Neues Deutschland* and candidate member of the SED's first Politburo.

Herrnstadt was born in 1903 at Gleiwitz in Upper Silesia into a well-to-do Jewish family. His father Ludwig was a lawyer and Social Democrat town councillor.[100] In 1921 he went to study law at Berlin University.[101] But he broke off his studies the next year to become a writer and journalist. Possibly his decision was motivated by the anti-Semitic climate prevalent in the university, which undoubtedly had a profound impact upon him.[102] Herrnstadt's career did not prosper until 1928, when he obtained the post of temporary editor with the respected liberal newspaper, the *Berliner Tageblatt*. The editor-in-chief was the famous Theodor Wolff. Herrnstadt proved good at his job and continued to work for the paper as Eastern Europe correspondent, working successively in Prague, Warsaw and Moscow, then Warsaw again.[103] After the Nazis passed the anti-Semitic Nuremburg Laws in 1935, Herrnstadt was not, as a Jew, allowed to write officially for a German newspaper. So he transferred his services to the London-based *Prague Press*, for which he worked until August 1938 when he returned to Prague as correspondent for the French newspaper, *L'Europe nouvelle*. After the German invasion of Czechoslovakia, Herrnstadt fled first to Poland, then to the Soviet Union.[104]

Herrnstadt joined the KPD in 1929. As a journalist in the Thirties he cut the figure of a 'salon Communist' of the type then common in European intellectual circles.[105] Yet Herrnstadt was in reality far from being a dilettante in the Red cause. He became an agent of Soviet intelligence, working for the Fourth Department of the Red Army's General Staff.[106]

Herrnstadt's postings to Warsaw and his frequent visits to that city were of key importance in his career as a spy. In 1937 he recruited Rudolf von Scheliha, a 40-year-old counsellor at the German embassy there. Von Scheliha and Herrnstadt had been acquainted in their student days. Von Scheliha had been chairman of the general student committee of Heidelberg University and had made a vain attempt to stop anti-Semitism.[107] He retained a dislike of the Nazis, though he was equally unattracted to the communists. He agreed to work for Soviet intelligence for one reason: he needed money to finance his gambling and whoring. He provided Moscow with value for money. In the years leading up to Barbarossa he proved to be the Soviet Union's second most important source of human intelligence on Nazi Germany. He was able to provide detailed information on two key issues of German foreign policy, namely the timing of the invasions of Poland and of the Soviet Union itself.[108]

Herrnstadt built a spy-ring around himself, which is usually referred to as 'Gruppe Alta', the name which the Gestapo gave to it. A key role in the group was played by Herrnstadt's fiancée, Ilse Stöbe.[109] She was able to receive von Scheliha's information after Herrnstadt's flight to the Soviet Union and von Scheliha's own transfer to the information section of the German foreign ministry. She was able to do because she had obtained a job in the foreign ministry's press department, which gave her regular pretexts to meet the TASS representative in Berlin.[110] Both von Scheliha and Stöbe managed to evade detection by the Gestapo until autumn 1942.[111]

WILHELM ZAISSER

Wilhelm Zaisser, the GDR's first chief of state security had, like Herrnstadt, a previous career as a Soviet intelligence officer. Also like Herrnstadt, he had some claim to belong to the communist intelligentsia. Zaisser was born on 20 June 1893 in the Ruhr, Germany's western industrial centre, where his father Karl served as a constable in the gendarmerie. Despite a relatively humble background, Zaisser received a university education, and when the First World War broke out had just started work as a teacher. His education allowed him the moderate advancement in the army which had been denied to Hitler, for by the end of the war he had attained the rank of lieutenant. In 1917 he was serving in Russia when the October Revolution started. This had a marked effect on him.[112] Upon his return home in 1919 he joined the KPD. Zaisser could justifiably claim to have defended the Red cause in this period. In March 1920, when right-wing elements of the German army attempted unsuccessfully to replace the government in Berlin, in the event known as the Kapp Putsch, Zaisser was one of the leaders of resistance in his home district of Essen in the Rhineland. This did not lead to fighting. Nonetheless, at the beginning of the next year, Zaisser was arrested and sentenced to four months' imprisonment for being a member of the Red Army of the Ruhr and was dismissed from the teaching profession. Thereafter he took up work as a local journalist, while continuing his political activities.

In 1922 he went to Moscow to attend the Second Congress of the Red Trade Unions' International. Two years later, in March–June 1924 he completed a course there at a Comintern school. Zaisser next attained an important position within the KPD, working in the *Apparat* of the Party's central committee. However, his career in the KPD was a short one. In July 1927 he left for the Soviet Union again, this time to become a regular intelligence agent of the Comintern. Zaisser was not, however, tasked by the Comintern itself. It was General Berzin, the head of the Red Army's Fourth Department who offered him the opportunity of a mission in China, then one of the key areas of Soviet intelligence work.

In China, Zaisser collected political, military and economic information for Moscow.[113] He posed as an independent arms dealer, and founded a Shanghai branch of the right-wing ex-servicemen's association, the *Stahlhelm*. He and his elegant wife established themselves as leading figures of the local German community. In this capacity, Zaisser was able to win the confidence of diplomats and army officers, which provided him with sources of intelligence. When General von Seeckt, former chief of the German army, visited Shanghai, he stayed at Zaisser's home.[114] Zaisser's cover was blown not as a result of any mistake he made in China, but as a result of a mishap in Germany. In 1930, he returned home on holiday and became involved in a case of unsuccessful industrial espionage.[115]

Now that he had been unmasked as a Soviet agent Zaisser had to return to Moscow, where he spent the next six years, in that time completing a course at the Military Academy. It was probably at this time that he took Soviet citizenship. Certainly in 1932 he became a member of the Communist Party of the Soviet Union.

The Spanish Civil War broke out in July 1936. For the KPD, insofar as it still had independent opinions, and for the Comintern, this was a major opportunity. Moscow was keen to send all emigrants with military experience to assist the beleaguered Republican government. Among these exiles were several thousand German communists. Together with volunteers from all the European countries and the United States, they formed the famous International Brigades. The troops in these units were by no means all communists. However, from their formation to the end of the War, they remained firmly under the control of the Comintern. The Comintern was able to maintain strict supervision over the International Brigades, which with justification have been referred to as the 'Comintern Army', by placing communists in all key positions and by imposing a strict police discipline on the troops, to the extent that by 1937, commanders effectively had the power of life and death over their men.[116] In leading and above all, controlling the Comintern army, certain German communists in the employ of the Soviet State played key roles. They included Wilhelm Zaisser and Erich Mielke, two future leaders of the East German State Security, as well as the GDR's first leader, Walter Ulbricht. It was with good reason that the Stasi was to include the International Brigades in its revolutionary tradition.

Zaisser served in Spain from September 1936 to the summer of 1938, when Franco's victory was certain and Stalin withdrew Soviet aid from the Republic. Acclimatizing himself, Zaisser assumed a Spanish name, General Gómez, though he did not conceal his true identity.[117] His first task was to organize and the lead the Thirteenth International Brigade, which was composed predominantly of Slavs and Frenchmen.[118] The Brigade seems first to have performed a political rather than military role. It was sent into Valencia, probably as a show of force to the local Anarchists, whom though on the Republican side, the Comintern regarded with almost as much hostility as the Fascists.[119] As a result, the Thirteenth Brigade missed participation with the bulk of the International Brigades in their heroic defence of Madrid in the autumn of 1936. Thereafter the Brigade did not play any spectacular role in the fighting, and was dissolved after being badly mauled in the Brunete campaign of July 1937.[120] Zaisser then took on a more obviously security-orientated role as commander of the international units' base at Albacete. His immediate job was to impose order after the corrupt regime of his predecessor, the French communist, Vital Gaymann.[121]

Heinz Hoffman, the future DDR Minister of Defence, recalled meeting Zaisser during the Spanish Civil War. He had arrived in Alabacete and had to report to the camp commandant.

> On the way to 'Gómez' I met an acquaintance from Moscow: Erich Mielke who was at that time working with Comrade Zaisser. I had gone straight from the training grounds at Madrigueras to Albacete without getting particularly dressed up for my report to the general ... When Erich Mielke saw me like that, with dusty shoes, creased uniform, and unshaven, he advised me that the first thing I should do was to tidy myself up and have a wash and shave. He told me that 'Gómez' was quite capable of throwing me out on the spot if I appeared before him got-up like that.

Hoffman thought this advice was exaggerated, but not for long.

> General 'Gómez', a giant in size, listened to my report, looked at me carefully from top to bottom and ordered: 'Get out!'.

Hoffman then returned, having tidied himself up. When he thought the meeting was over, Zaisser retained him, asking:

> whether it had become clear to me in the meantime why he had first had to throw me out. My answer, that I could imagine why, did not appear very convincing to him. But he just said, 'You have received a training like few other comrades in our Party. Think this over carefully, and you will understand why we demand a high degree of discipline from superiors!'

Another witness from the Spanish Civil War put more stress on Zaisser's harshness:

> The general is a gigantic man. His eyes lie deep in his massive face. His nature is jovial, but I should think that this joviality is able to fall like a mask. He who has seen the hard, strained eyes of 'General Gomez', and his hard, scar-cut face, feels that the pleasantness is only put-on and the brutality is genuine.[122]

Within the International Brigades, maintaining discipline was a task of increasing difficulty, as casualties mounted and disillusionment with the government cause grew. Nonetheless, the 'Comintern consistently and effectively used the agencies of the various national Communist parties and the Albacete commissariat to maintain its control over the internal structure and affairs of the Brigades'.[123] In achieving this end the Comintern disposed of its own secret police apparatus, known as the 'Cheka', after the organization which Lenin had established immediately after seizing power in Russia. It made systematic use of torture. Like its namesake, the Albacete Cheka had the power to imprison and execute without appeal to higher authority.[124] At Albacete, Zaisser was inevitably involved in the Comintern's police regime within its own army. The German communist, Erich Wollenberg recalled, however, that his men regarded Zaisser with respect because of 'his knowledge of his subject and his correct behaviour even towards those of different political persuasions'.[125] Apparently the same could not be said for one of the key Chekists at the camp, Walter Ulbricht. According to Ruth Fischer, who admittedly was his political enemy, Ulbricht organized the Cheka unit dealing with the German-speakers in the Brigades, 'personally directed the search for Trotskyists among his fellow Germans, and ordered the death of many of them'.[126]

Another leader of the Stasi received his grounding in secret service work at the Albacete camp. This was Richard Stahlmann, who in the 1960s and 1970s was Mielke's right-hand man in East German State Security. In Spain, Stahlmann was in charge of the training of members of the International Brigades in sabotage. He commanded the '1er Batallón Motorizado de Guerilleros'. This was composed of 70–80 specialists, most of whom were Scandinavians. These men were involved in operations not only against

Franco, but also were involved in maritime sabotage as members of the so-called Wollweber League, which is discussed below. Stahlmann's organization operated so effectively that Dimitrov, the leader of the Comintern, paid it high praise in December 1937.[127]

Participation in the Spanish Civil War might well have saved some of the future leaders of East Germany from Stalin's purges, which claimed the lives of so many other KPD exiles in the Soviet Union. Zaisser, though, did suffer briefly from the excesses of Stalinism. On his return to Moscow he was imprisoned, only to be released in 1939 on the orders of Lavrenti Beria, the new head of the Soviet secret police.[128]

ERNST WOLLWEBER

Thus the Spanish Civil War provided important military and political experience for many Germany communists and in particular for some of the future leaders of the DDR. For Ernst Wollweber, who was to succeed Zaisser in 1953 as head of East German State Security, opposition to the Nazis took a more direct form. He was employed in a sabotage operation against the shipping of the powers of the Anti-Comintern Pact.

Wollweber came from a distinctly working-class background. He was born on 28 October 1898, the son of a drunken Silesian miner. In 1913 he escaped his unhappy family life by obtaining a job as a sailor on Germany's inland waterways. Wollweber was too young for active service during the first two years of the First World War, though even this early period of his life is the subject of myth. According to one account, he was active in smuggling defeatist propaganda from Berlin to the western front and on one occasion helped to sink a number of cement barges in a canal in Belgium to block the transports of war materials to the front. Recent research has found these well-known claims to have no substance in fact.[129] In 1916 Wollweber was called up to the navy where he saw active service with the U-boats.[130] By the end of the War he had started a career as a political activist, serving as the Left Socialists' contact with the U-boat crews. Wollweber's revolutionary career started in earnest in November 1918 when the *Kriegsmarine* revolted in the Kiel naval mutiny, at which time he was serving as a stoker on board a small cruiser called the *Helgoland*.[131]

In 1919 Wollweber joined the KPD, and by 1921 had risen to a position of responsibility within the Party, as member of its Central Committee.[132] Shortly thereafter, he was talent-spotted by the Comintern. He owed his good fortune to Walter Ulbricht, who was provincial secretary for the KPD in Thuringia. He recommended Wollweber for the Fourth Comintern Congress in Moscow.[133] At this time Wollweber received education at the first of several military and political courses he was to attend in Moscow. Wollweber played no significant role in either of the KPD's attempts at revolution. In 1923 he was to have commanded the communists' military forces in Hessen-Waldeck in his capacity as M-Leader. However, on the eve of the projected uprising the authorities put Wollweber in preventive detention.[134]

Wollweber returned to the Soviet Union in 1923 and where he entered the service of Soviet intelligence, a connection which was to last up until his enforced retirement as head of East German State Security in 1957.[135] Like Zaisser, Wollweber worked for the Fourth Department of the General Staff of the Red Army, in other words, for Soviet military intelligence. Unlike Zaisser, he was not posted abroad, but continued to function as a KPD official in Germany. Also unlike Zaisser, his early work was unsuccessful. In the middle of 1924 he was denounced by a police agent within the KPD and was arrested. He spent a year and a half in custody awaiting trial until on 23 December 1925 he was sentenced to three years in prison. He served only three months after a remarkable stroke of luck, for the local state prosecutor who had had him arrested and who had sentenced him was himself arrested for fraud.

Wollweber's arrest and exposure by no means lowered his status within KPD circles or in the eyes of Soviet intelligence. Rather he was put forward as KPD candidate for parliament, which brought with it the gift of immunity from arrest. In 1928, he was elected to the Prussian Diet.[136] In November 1932, he became a member of the Reichstag.[137] Membership of Weimar parliaments offered other benefits to secret agents. The government granted substantial travelling allowances to all MPs. Thus the Weimar Republic paid for the movements of Wollweber and other agitators intent upon its destruction.[138]

Wollweber's success within the KPD in the Weimar period stemmed from the favour which Moscow accorded him as well as from the vigour of his personality. Wollweber's nature was reflected in his appearance. One of his agents described Wollweber in the 1930s:

> The man was short and burly. His thin hair was combed to cover a bald spot on his head. He had chunky hands, a hard round forehead, and a thick, straight mouth. His chunky face was of an unhealthy colour, and the expression on it was the most saturnine I had ever seen. It denoted power, patience, ruthlessness, distrust. But the really outstanding feature in this man were his eyes – unblinking, glistening slits without a trace of white.[139]

Ragnhild Wiik, a Norwegian communist whom Wollweber married for purely political reasons in 1935 was even less complementary about

Wollweber, describing him as 'repulsive'. He had greater appeal, however, to her sister Gudrun, with whom he had an affair for several years up to the start of the Second World War.[140] Wollweber's rotundity earned him an unusual nickname after he became East Germany's second head of State Security. He was known to his colleagues as 'the pancake on legs'.

Wollweber achieved a heroic status within communist circles after Hitler's seizure of power in March 1933 when he stayed behind to reorganize the KPD's secret organization. He did so by command of the Party, which soon realized that it had no alterative but to give up the fight within Germany.[141] In May 1933 Moscow ordered Wollweber to move to Copenhagen, which was now the seat of the Comintern's Western European Secretariat.

From 1933 to 1937, Copenhagen was the most important revolutionary centre outside Moscow. The offices of the WES had the cover of an engineering firm situated in Vesterpoort, the largest and most modern office building in the heart of Copenhagen.[142] Moscow maintained about 500 people there. In default of Berlin, the Danish capital was an obvious choice as centre of conspiracy, for reasons listed succinctly by Richard Krebs, who was working as a Comintern courier at this time:

> The journey Moscow–Leningrad–Helsinki–Copenhagen led through relatively harmless countries. By train and boat, it could be made in forty-eight hours. The communist positions in the Scandinavian merchant fleets were strong, particularly in Denmark, and this made Copenhagen a suitable centre for a world-wide network of conspirative marine communication. Moreover, the Danes were one of the most hospitable and liberal peoples on earth, and the amiable *laissez-faire* spirit of the Danish police had long been proverbial among Comintern men.[143]

Wollweber had a commanding role in the conduct of the WES's maritime operations which predated the move to Copenhagen. He had started making contacts with Hamburg seamen in 1930.[144] The next year he was appointed head (*Reichsleiter*) of the 'Einheitsverband der Seeleute, Hafenarbeiter und Binnenschiffer' which was a German organization subordinate to the Seamen and Dockers' International (usually known by its German acronym ISH), which in turn was a section of the Red Trade Unions' International.[145] In 1933 Wollweber was appointed to the secretariat of the ISH where he 'wielded the strongest power', though the organization was nominally controlled by Albert Walter, another member of the KPD.[146]

The ISH was founded in Hamburg in October 1930 by 38 delegates from 16 countries. The choice of location was an attempt to disguise the organization's close links with Moscow. From the start the trade union was really a wing of the Comintern, receiving subsidies from Moscow, even if this was not known to its rank-and-file members.[147] The ISH flourished. By 1932 it had branches in 22 countries and 19 colonies. The German section alone had 16,000 members.[148]

The ISH network was only part of the KPD's secret apparatus which the Nazis did not annihilate. At the end of December 1932 it moved to Copenhagen.[149] From Copenhagen it continued its old clandestine activities, which included the smuggling of persons, propaganda and weapons as well as maritime espionage and the organization of strikes.[150] As the international climate continued to deteriorate and European war seemed a strong possibility, Moscow decided to exploit the ISH to more bellicose ends. At the end of 1935, the Soviet leadership decided to build up a maritime sabotage agency for use in time of war.

In the winter of 1935, Wollweber was ordered to Moscow, where he was given the task of building up an organization for maritime sabotage. This organization was to have no official contact with either Moscow or the local communist parties in the countries where it operated. The saboteurs had to leave the Party. It received logistical support from the Fourth Department.[151]

It took a year to set up the sabotage network, which was fully operational in eight countries. At the end of 1936 there were about 300 people in the organization.[152] They were recruited from sailors and dockers. The League had units in the Baltic States, Holland, Belgium, Sweden, Norway, Denmark, France, Germany, and China.[153]

The Wollweber League was first called into action after the outbreak of the Spanish Civil War in July 1936. At this time there was a series of sensational shipping disasters, which affected German, Italian and Japanese ships – the powers of the Anti-Comintern Pact. According to a recent study of Wollweber's career, the Wollweber League sank about 250,000 tons of shipping and killed 10 seamen – as far as calculations are possible.[154] Wollweber's activities received publicity at the highest diplomatic level in June 1941, after Germany had invaded the Soviet Union. When von Ribbentrop, the German foreign minister, announced the official reasons for 'Barbarossa', the existence of the Wollweber League figured among them. According to him, Soviet-backed sabotage had resulted in the sinking of 16 German ships at the end of the 1930s.[155] This figure was more restrained than some of the Nazis' calculations for their own use. Reinhard Heydrich, the head of the security police and the SD, drew up a report in June 1941 according to which the Wollweber League had succeeded in sabotaging 21 ships.[156] Shortly after the Germans drew up their charges against him, Wollweber found himself in Swedish custody, where he was to stay until 1944. He admitted to the Swedish authorities that he had made bombs which were intended for use against German, but not Swedish ships. He did not give any indication how many he had destroyed.[157]

It is difficult to say when the Wollweber League finally came to an end. There is some evidence that it briefly survived its founder's incarceration, for there was a series of sabotage attacks on Norwegian railway lines after the Nazi invasion of Russia in 1941 in which the remnants of the League might have been involved.[158]

2 The Origins and Development of East German State Security: The Ulbricht Years, 1945–71

The East German Ministry of State Security (*Ministerium für Staatssicherheit*), or MfS, was created on 8 February 1950, four months after the foundation of the German Democratic Republic. It claimed a revolutionary tradition dating back to the abortive Spartacist uprising in Berlin of January 1919. This was not unjustified. From nearly the moment of its creation the German Communist Party had developed clandestine agencies and had always realized the necessity, when the revolution came, for thorough security measures in order to maintain itself in power and to implement its policies. In this way the KPD drew from the experience of the Soviet communists. However, at least since 1923, the KPD had not been an active partner in its relationship with the CPSU. This was reflected with particular clarity in its illegal organizations, which by the early Twenties were little more than auxiliaries of Soviet intelligence. Inevitably this tradition continued after 1945, when the predecessor of the KGB set up and trained an East German satellite service in its own image and partly staffed by its own personnel. Continuity with the interwar period also existed on a personal level. The leaders of East German State Security, Wilhelm Zaisser, Ernst Wollweber, and Erich Mielke, as well as others, had themselves been agents of Soviet intelligence and remained closely tied to it. Yet the theme of continuity can be pushed too far. Such men were but a minority of German communists who had survived Nazi repression and the Purges. Between them the Gestapo and the NKVD had all but destroyed the KPD's cadres and the major task of the Soviet administration after 1943 was to rebuild the German Communist Party so that it could support the Red Army after the occupation of Germany.

INTELLIGENCE IN THE EASTERN ZONE OF GERMANY, 1945–9

After 1945 the Soviet Government quickly built up a Soviet Military Administration in Germany, or SMAD as it was known by abbreviation. Under the leadership of Marshal Zhukov, the Commander-in-Chief of the Red Army, SMAD had control of all aspects of life in the Eastern Zone and, with one exception, was answerable only to Stalin himself. This exception was the local representation of the NKVD (after 1946, MVD), the Ministry of

Internal Affairs and the MGB, the Ministry for State Security which was closely associated with it.[1] These organizations answered directly to Moscow, not to SMAD.[2] Both Ministries were involved in setting up a security system in the Eastern Zone. Initially, a third Soviet security agency operated alongside them in Germany, this was *Smersh* or military counter-intelligence.[3] In May 1946 the Third Directorate of the MGB took over most of *Smersh*'s counter-intelligence operations in the Eastern Zone.[4]

Soviet intelligence established its headquarters in the former St Antonius hospital in the Berlin suburb of Karlshorst, where SMAD had its seat. Unlike SMAD, which was wound up in 1949, the KGB was to stay there for 46 years, only leaving in 1991. It occupied a huge complex, surrounded by barbed wire and policed by men and dogs, which was a no-go area to all but security personnel. The KGB's senior officers lived there in considerable luxury, occupying comfortable middle-class houses within the compound.[5] The military intelligence operations of the GRU in Eastern Germany were based in a separate headquarters alongside the Red Army's General Staff at the towns of Wünsdorf and Zossen, which lay some fifteen miles south of Berlin.

It is impossible to say how many Soviet intelligence officers worked within the Karlshorst headquarters in the mid-1940s. In 1960, a West German report stated that there were 1,500 KGB officers there, which made Karlshorst by far the largest KGB base outside the Soviet Union. At the same time there were 250 GRU officers at Wünsdorf and Zossen.[6] The total Soviet intelligence operation in the Eastern Zone as a whole was massive. There was an office of the MVD/MGB in every province (*Land*) and district (*Kreis*). The whole network was headed initially by Major-General Melnikov, who in 1944–5 had assisted in setting up the Polish security service, the UB.[7]

The scale of the Soviet security network in the Eastern Zone reflected the wide variety of tasks which it was to carry out. These included de-Nazification; the general oversight of political parties, trade unions and politicians; the Sovietization of the Zone; and the procuring of intelligence about the West. The Soviet security organs also had the duty of watching over SMAD itself as well as the surveillance of Soviet troops stationed in Germany.[8] However, in the aftermath of the conquest of Germany, SMAD's two priorities were: first, to set up an effective German communist party; and second, to develop a German security service. The two objectives went hand in hand. Both were very difficult indeed to achieve.

The most obvious problem facing SMAD was how to create a communist party capable of governing in the Eastern Zone. The prewar KPD had been decimated both under the Nazi regime and in Stalin's Purges. In the Eastern Zone it did not command anything like a majority of German votes. The party cadres which existed in the early years of the Soviet occupation were of doubtful reliability. The new KPD obviously included a large intake of opportunists, who had joined solely as a way of currying favour with the Soviet authorities.

Stalin's answer to the weakness of the KPD was to force the other left-wing party, the Social Democrats (SPD), to merge with it. This he did in April 1946. The result was the so-called Socialist Unity Party of Germany (SED). The SED was completely dominated by the communists, who in turn received their orders from the SMAD. Nonetheless, to begin with the SED leadership had to rely to a considerable degree on the cooperation of the non-communist rank and file of the Party, who supplemented the KPD's already dubious communist cadres. Their cooperation, or rather quiescence, could only be guaranteed by one means – coercion. In short, the SED, as an artificial party, was largely dependent upon its security forces from the outset.

To begin with, the local police looked very much the same as they had been in the Weimar Republic. In particular, they were decentralized, under the control of the provincial (*Land*) governments. Undoubtedly this contributed to the inefficiency of the German police. So, to an even greater extent, did the character of its personnel, of whom a high proportion were disorganized and corrupt.[9] The poor quality of the police reflected serious recruiting problems. From the SMAD's point of view, the situation was so pressing that inevitably former Nazis and German soldiers were enrolled. They included even former members of the SS.[10]

To Western observers at the time, the decentralization of the police in the Eastern Zone implied that Moscow was willing to leave some power in the hands of the local civilians. In fact, the SMAD was very dissatisfied with the performance of the German police, which placed strain on the already overstretched Soviet security apparatus.[11] SMAD had great difficulty in maintaining law and order at the same time as carrying out its more important political and military tasks. Lawlessness assumed crisis proportions in the Eastern Zone which was beset by marauding gangs of former German soldiers, but was afflicted above all by the licentiousness and rapine of the Red Army.

The first step on the path which ultimately led to the creation of an independent East German security organization came in July 1946 with SMAD's reorganization of the regular police in the Eastern Zone. SMAD saw the centralization of the police as the key to improving their efficiency. Thus the Soviet authorities had to create a central German authority capable of coordinating and controlling the police. The new organization in question was the German Administration of the Interior (*Deutsche Verwaltung des Innern, (DVdI)*).[12] Though described specifically as a 'German' institution, in fact the Soviet authorities retained very close control over it. The president of the DVdI reported directly to SMAD.[13] The creation of a centralised police in the Eastern Zone coincided with a worsening of tension between the Soviet Union and the Western Allies and with a general move towards political repression on the part of the SMAD and the SED.

The DVdI did not initially dispose of a clearly-defined political police force, but carried out important political functions. This is clear from an East German history, according to which

> In its work the DVdI concentrated on the general securing of the revolutionary achievements. This included the further building up and political strengthening of the Police organs as well as securing the borders, the energetic fight against subversive activities, against economic sabotage, profiteers and black marketeers; and not least the systematic education of all members of the German Administration of the Interior and all members of the State Administration.[14]

The creation of the DVdI was really the origin of the eastern German party-police for two reasons. First, because the DVdI succeeded according to plan in centralizing police activity throughout the Eastern Zone.[15] Second, because communist control of the police was guaranteed. This process found parallels in every state of the future Soviet Bloc in these years, where all the local communist parties ensured that from the outset they controlled the forces of law and order and began to set up, at varying tempos, security forces on the Soviet model. In the Eastern Zone the SED and SMAD began a drive to indoctrinate the police in Marxism-Leninism which was sustained right until the end of the DDR.[16] The first step in this process was the establishment of party-police schools and party cells within the DVdI.

Communist control at the level of the leadership of the DVdI was provided by four former revolutionaries from the interwar KPD. Erich Reschke was the first President of the DVdI, holding this office until July 1948. Reschke had not previously worked for Soviet intelligence, unlike some of his colleagues in the DVdI, though he had excellent anti-Nazi credentials, having been imprisoned in Buchenwald concentration camp.[17] Perhaps what most qualified him for the post was his 'blind loyalty' to the Soviet Union.[18] In 1948, Kurt Fischer replaced him as head of the DVdI. Fischer had received military training in the Soviet Union and had fought in the Spanish Civil War.[19] More recently, he had built up his reputation as Minister of the Interior in the state of Saxony, where he had developed an effective and centralized provincial police force.

The Deputy Presidents of the DVdI were Kurt Wagner, who dealt with the security, criminal, water, and fire brigade police; Willi Seifert, who was responsible for administration and organization; and, most importantly, Erich Mielke, who had control of personnel.[20] In summer 1948, at the same time that Fischer took charge of the DVdI, Wilhelm Zaisser was made one of its deputy ministers.

Erich Mielke was head of eastern German intelligence for most of its existence. He served basically in this capacity in the DVdI of the Eastern Zone; thereafter he was head of the GDR's secret police from 1956 to 1989. After the Second World War, Mielke passed onto the other side of the barricades, having first come to prominence as one of the KPD's armed revolutionaries in the interwar period.

Like the vast majority of the SED's postwar leaders, Erich Mielke came from a working-class background. He was born the eldest son of a Berlin cartwright on 28 December 1907. He displayed intelligence from early on and was one of 60 out of a group of 360 working-class Berlin children who were given scholarships to go on to secondary education at grammar school. He did not go on to university, leaving school at the age of 16 to become a dispatch clerk for a Berlin removal firm. Two years later, he followed in his father's footsteps by joining the KPD. Mielke's education allowed him to be of some service to the party. In 1925 he started work as a reporter for the *Rote Fahne* ('Red Flag'), the Party's main newspaper. But it was not as a journalist that Mielke was to make his mark in the KPD's interwar history. He soon found his way into more vigorous revolutionary employment when he joined the KPD's *Parteiselbstschutz* (Party Self-Defence), which was a para-military force used for the protection of meetings and demonstrations.

In the summer of 1931 Mielke and another KPD activist named Ziemer were designated for an important mission. This took place on Berlin's Bülowplatz on 9 August 1931, where the two young revolutionaries gunned down from behind two senior police officers and a senior sergeant (*Oberwachtmeister*); only the latter recovered. Mielke then fled to Moscow, having been provided with money and a false passport. According to police reports presented at the trial, the idea for the assassination came from Hans Kippenberger, the head of the KPD's Military-Political Apparatus and *Reichsleiter* of the *Parteiselbstschutz*. Kippenberger was saved from trial because he enjoyed parliamentary immunity as a member of the *Reichstag*. Mielke did not face trial in person for murder until 1994, after the reunification of Germany. But he was tried *in absentia* under the Third Reich. The court decided that it was certain that Mielke and Ziemer had fired the shots. As a result of this trial three members of the KPD were sentenced to death, one of whom received a reprieve, whilst 15 others were imprisoned for complicity in the murders. Mielke, had he been caught, would almost certainly have been executed.

The second stage of Mielke's career started in Moscow, where he attended the Comintern's International Lenin School. In 1936 he went to fight in the Spanish Civil War alongside other German communists. He served as an officer of SIM (Servicio Información Militar), the secret security service. Later he helped to organize the evacuation of units of the International Brigades to France. Mielke stayed in Spain until the Republican cause collapsed in 1939. He then fled first to Belgium and then to France, where he was interned. The third and final stage of Mielke's career started in 1945, when he returned to Berlin. Thereafter he was continuously involved with the police.

K-5

In August 1947, the Soviet authorities strengthened the powers of the police in the Eastern Zone, or the *Volkspolizei* (People's Police) as they were now known. This was the result of SMAD's order no. 201, which announced the Soviet authorities' intention to accelerate de-Nazification in the Zone and soon to bring it to an end. With the declared aim of implementing this object, order no. 201 provided for the establishment of a special department of the *Volkspolizei*, *Kommisariat-5* to carry out its provisions.

Official statements about K-5 were misleading. Though officially part of the *Volkspolizei* it was distinct from it. K-5 was far more the agency of the Party than of the State. As one contemporary observer noted, the creation of K-5 altered the system of government in the Eastern Zone by increasing 'the importance of the purely political functionaries at the expense of the administration, as the former were now the main channel for Soviet orders'.[21]

K-5 had a jurisdiction just as powerful as that of the MVD/MGB in the Soviet Union. It was given all the powers it needed to arrest suspects and seize their property as well as the powers of the public prosecutor. The only real restriction on its activities was the strict oversight of the Soviet occupation authorities themselves.

The Soviet authorities soon expanded K-5's duties, giving it work which had nothing to do with de-Nazification. Its priorities became increasingly the surveillance and crushing of all the opponents of the regime, against whom it was very convenient to level the accusation of National Socialism. As a contemporary Western observer noted: 'Actions which in other Eastern countries needed the full support of Russian Marxist theory could conveniently be carried out in Germany as part and parcel of a policy aimed at the very worthy object of eliminating National Socialism and the German *Junkertum*.'[22] Mielke stressed K-5's role in fighting the 'Schumacherites' as the communists called those members of the SPD who rejected union with the KPD after the name of the leader of the Social Democrats in the Western Zones, Kurt Schumacher.[23] Undoubtedly, the German Communists and the Soviet authorities saw them as a far greater threat than the remnants of the Nazi Party.

Before the beginning of 1947, repression of the SPD was by and large directed at those of its members who opposed the merger with the KPD into the SED. But it intensified in the summer of 1947, afflicting not just the Schumacherites, but all real and perceived opponents of the regime. Victims included not only functionaries serving within the SED, but also many who had retired from politics.[24] By the time the campaign against the SPD abated around 1950, thousands of its members and former members had been imprisoned. Thousands of members of the other parties also fell victim to K-5 and the MGB. For example, between 1948 and 1950 there were 597 documented cases of CDU members being arrested. Probably the majority of those taken found their way into Soviet, not East German labour camps.[25]

Primary responsibility for tasking K-5 lay with the Soviet authorities, but it goes without saying that the German communists played an active role in organising the purges of their opponents. A Central Control Commission of the SED was set up with smaller branches in the provinces, which had the task of vetting SED members throughout the Eastern Zone.[26] The intimate links between the SED and K-5 were clearly revealed in the Party's torture chambers, where East German Party members sometimes took part in the interrogations of political opponents.[27]

Though K-5 was assisted by the SED, it was scarcely more than an auxiliary of Soviet intelligence. In the province of Saxony K-5 handled 51,236 cases in 1948. Of these 14,137 were assigned to it by the Soviet authorities and 1,318 by the SED.[28] Soviet officers assisted at every level of the K-5 organization and played a key role in training their German counterparts. They were present at all the most important interrogations.[29] According to one account, Soviet officers reported that in order to win the confidence of the Russians, their K-5 trainees tried to surpass their teachers in cruelty.[30] Not surprisingly, K-5 acquired a reputation just as bad as that of Stalin's secret police in the Soviet Union and worse than that of the Gestapo which they succeeded. At least the Nazis had discriminated in their choice of victims.

Russian control of the German police was so great that prosecutions were routinely carried out by Soviet Military Tribunals. Prisoners could be held in special camps by order of the MVD or the MGB alone, without any judicial procedure taking place.[31] Furthermore, convicted prisoners had a good chance of deportation to Soviet labour camps – thousands of Germans were released from imprisonment in the Soviet Union after the Federal Chancellor, Konrad Adenauer visited Moscow in 1955.[32] This was a fate only somewhat worse than incarceration in the Eastern Zone, since the SED was also following the Soviet example by gaoling political prisoners in its own labour camps. Here the new German regime was assisted by the Nazis, who bequeathed to it their concentration camps. But these did not fulfil the requirements of the SED and the Soviet authorities. New camps sprang up at Frankfurt-on-the-Oder, Lieberose, Forst, Bitterfeld, Mühlberg, Bantzau, Altenhain, Stern-Buchholz, Beeskow, and just north of Berlin. At the same time the old prisoner-of-war camp at Torgau was converted into a political prison. It is very difficult to estimate the number of Germans imprisoned at any one time, particularly since so many Germans were detained in the Soviet Union, including tens of thousands of soldiers who had still not been released at the end of the 1940s. An official US survey put the number of political prisoners in the Eastern Zone at 25,000 for 1947.

The German labour camps passed into the control of the SED's police at the time of the creation of K-5 in summer 1947. In 1949, on the eve of the creation of the East German state all but one of the camps were closed. But this was little comfort to the inmates, who passed into the GDR's regular prisons instead.[33]

The large number of German political prisoners at the end of the 1940s is indicative of the burden which fell on K-5. K-5 was always subject to a manpower crisis. Not only did it have too few officers, but those it did have were not satisfactorily trained, despite Soviet assistance. On the eve of the creation of the East German state, the SED leadership concluded that its own political police were inadequate for social control.[34]

THE DEVELOPMENT OF THE 'COLD WAR'

The mounting tempo of political violence in the Eastern Zone was at least in part occasioned by a deterioration in the Cold War. In March 1947 the United States Administration had accepted the Truman Doctrine, pledging itself to contain further Soviet expansion. Many have regarded this as the definitive start of the Cold War. From the Soviet point of view there was now no serious hope of cooperation with the Western Allies on either the political or the economic levels. Correspondingly, the Soviet leadership and its associates in Eastern and Central Europe had nothing to gain by taking Western susceptibilities into account. Throughout what was rapidly becoming the Soviet Bloc, the regimes shed the mask of constitutional government over the course of 1947 and 1948.

In the eyes of some statesmen on either side of the East–West divide, including Stalin, armed conflict in Europe seemed a strong possibility in the near future. From the point of view of the Soviet authorities in Germany and of the SED, this was a conflict which had already started on the ideological front. Both saw the eastern German population as something inherently unreliable and subject to the seduction of the West. Most obviously, this reflected the unabated flight of citizens to the Western Zones. Just as seriously, it meant that what Moscow and East Berlin saw as Western subversion escalated into a counter-offensive against the Soviet take-overs in Eastern Europe. This offensive included not only a barrage of propaganda from US-funded radio stations, but also the activities of Western secret agents.

These fears seemed to reflect the hysteria which Stalin had generated in the Soviet Union in the 1930s and which had served as a perhaps essential background for the Purges which he inflicted on his political opponents. The creation of an atmosphere of 'spy-mania' which followed the establishment of communist regimes in Eastern and Central Europe facilitated the establishment of strong security states. The existence of an ubiquitous secret police was justified as a response to the threat from the West, not as a means of controlling unwilling populations. In fact, the close relationship between local communist parties and their secret police systems was essential to the maintenance of the Soviet Bloc regimes which were now coming into shape. Nonetheless, the communist rhetoric of the time, which depicted almost all enemies of the 'socialist order' as the agents of Western intelligence is also explicable by the sense of vulnerability which these regimes felt both before their own populations and before the West. Such fears were obvious in the case of eastern Germany, where the embryonic SED state was already being weakened in the mid-1940s by the exodus of its population to the West. Even the Soviet Union had to cope with internal unrest at this time. The return of the Red Army to the Ukraine and the Baltic States had not been welcomed by the peoples it had 'liberated' from the Germans. From 1944 onwards, both these regions were the scene of guerrilla war, which only petered out at the end of the 1940s and which in each case tied down substantial numbers of Soviet troops.[35]

It is arguable, therefore, that the Soviet Union and its satellites had genuine reasons to fear Western subversion. Furthermore, they had every reason to believe that the Western Powers had the capability to conduct covert action with great effect. The Second World War had seen a growth of such activities, which had hitherto played a minor role in warfare. The British in particular had conducted large-scale propaganda operations against Nazi Germany and occupied Europe, and, through the Special Operations Executive, or SOE, had successfully organized partisan resistance to the *Wehrmacht* in France and in the Balkans.[36] That the British and Americans would exploit Soviet difficulties in Eastern Europe seemed likely in 1947 if only because the Soviet Union was doing the same thing in Western Europe.

Western espionage and plans for subversion against the Soviet Bloc are an important background to the development of security regimes in the Eastern Bloc, though they are far from being the primary reason for their creation. If anything, the 'threat from the West' explains the severity of Soviet Bloc counter-intelligence measures in the occupied states after 1945. What, however, did these plans amount to in practice? It is difficult to quantify the impact of Western radio propaganda against the East. Undoubtedly its impact fell far below the expectations of Western governments. There is no doubt, however, about the failure of covert action in the Eastern Bloc. The chief operations which the British and Americans mounted in the Baltic States and Albania were ignominious failures. They would have failed even without the thorough counter-intelligence operations mounted by the MGB, simply because of the activities of the Soviet agents Philby, Burgess and Maclean within the British establishment. Nonetheless, the Western 'counter-offensive' provided a spur to the development of the secret police in Eastern Europe, and, arguably, allowed the Soviet Union an unnecessary justification of this process.

One act of the Americans was of particular concern to the SED regime. This was the formation of the Gehlen Organization in 1946. General Reinhard Gehlen was German general who had been in charge of the intelligence operations of the Wehrmacht's foreign auxiliaries, *Fremde Heere Ost* (Foreign Armies East) on the Eastern Front. The frankness and accuracy of his reports had not pleased Hitler.[37] Gehlen found himself in the hands of the Americans in 1945 and from the start, raised his voice firmly on the side of vigorous Western action against the Soviet take-overs in Eastern Europe. He accurately predicted that Stalin was determined to retain control in Poland, contrary to his agreements with the Western Allies, and to establish satellite states in Czechoslovakia, Hungary, Romania and Bulgaria.[38] As early as 1946, the American occupation authorities in Germany had given Gehlen the task of setting up an intelligence agency which they were to fund and control. Its primary aim was to penetrate the Soviet regime in the Eastern Zone. At the end of 1947, the Gehlen Organization took on a more permanent form. The Americans controlled the organization until April 1956, when it was transferred to the oversight of the West German Federal Chancellor's Office, changing its name to the *Bundesnachrichtendienst* (Federal Intelligence Service) or BND.[39]

The Gehlen Organization operated on a large scale in the Eastern Zone and DDR in the late 1940s and 1950s. It achieved some notable agent penetrations. Gehlen's most important agents who came to light were Professor

Hermann Kastner, deputy Prime Minister of the DDR and his wife. They managed to flee to the West. Much less fortunate was Ella Bartschatis, secretary to the GDR's first Prime Minister, Otto Grotewohl. She was guillotined.[40] (See Chapter 6.) It is impossible to assess accurately how useful the Gehlen Organization was to the Western Allies in the early Cold War. It is equally difficult to say how seriously the East German and Soviet authorities regarded it. The only thing certain is that the existence of the Gehlen Organization gave credibility to the SED's public statements about the threat from Western subversion.

For six years after the creation of K-5, East Germany was in the grip of spy fever. The purges of the communists' political opponents were supplemented in August 1950 when the SED's Central Committee decided to clean up the Party itself. The new wave of repression was directed at German communists who had sought refuge outside the Soviet Union in the years 1933–45. Former soldiers whom the Western Allies or the Yugoslav partisans had taken prisoner during the War were also prominent targets in the new purge. The last purge in the DDR gathered pace at the beginning of 1953 and was directed at the 'Zionists'. This was occasioned by events in the Soviet Union, where Stalin was now obsessed with the idea of a Zionist conspiracy, and claimed that a group of predominantly Jewish doctors were planning 'to wipe out the leading cadres of the USSR'.[41] The impending purge against Jews both in the Soviet Union and throughout the Eastern Bloc was cut short by Stalin's death in March 1953, though not before many East German Jews had fled to the West.[42]

The authority of the East German communists was founded through terror and always rested upon the threat of terror. The incarceration of opponents and their physical liquidation was the prerequisite for the establishment of the one-party state on the foundations of a cowed populace. In this respect the communist seizure of power in East Germany did not differ from the Soviet take-overs elsewhere in Central and Eastern Europe. But the repression in Germany was bloodless compared to the rest of the Soviet Bloc. Even de-Nazification was not nearly as fierce as the Germans themselves had expected. While Stalin lived, the SED itself was not purged. There were no show trials of disgraced party members analogous to the Slánský Trial in Czechoslovakia or the Rajk Trial in Hungary, which led to merciless secret police campaigns both against the rank and file of the party and society as a whole.[43] It is difficult to say why East Germany was not so afflicted. Certainly communist rule was if anything even more shaky there than it was in Czechoslovakia and Hungary because of the existence of West Germany next door. It is possible that the SED and the Soviet authorities were frightened of encouraging an even greater lesion of the East German population into the Western Zones and, after 1949, into West Germany. A further question which arises is that of the responsibility for restraining the repression. Should this moderation be attributed to Walter Ulbricht, then struggling for dominance within the SED? Certainly he had not hesitated to denounce his compatriots to the Soviet secret police when forced to do so in Soviet exile. There is evidence that he had even courted the favours of the NKVD as a means of destroying his political opponents.[44] In all the other purges in the Eastern Bloc, the prime mover had been Moscow, though local faction-fighting had added to virulence of the repression.

THE MAIN DIRECTORATE FOR THE DEFENCE OF THE ECONOMY

The charges levelled against the SED's political opponents mirrored those of the show trials in the Soviet Union, where political prisoners were generally accused of working for at least one foreign intelligence service and often for wrecking the economy as well. The language of the show trials was reflected in the official redesignation of K-5 in December 1948, when it became the 'Main Directorate for the Defence of the Economy and the Democratic Order' in the DVdI. The change appears to have been nominal only since K-5 continued to be the SED's political police and counter-intelligence agency, while Erich Mielke continued to be its chief.[45]

THE AGENCY FOR THE PROTECTION OF NATIONAL PROPERTY

K-5 was not the only police force engaged in defending the economy of the Eastern Zone. At the same time that it was created in August 1947, the SED and SMAD used the Western threat as the justification for the creation of a second counter-intelligence against which was to work alongside it. This was the Committee for the Protection of National Property. The stated aim of the agency was the protection of national property against misuse and sabotage. Its chairman was also Erich Mielke.[46]

PROPAGANDA AND COUNTER-PROPAGANDA

According to the SED, the Western threat amounted to more than just intelligence-gathering and sabotage. Its most obvious form was the propaganda war which the British and Americans unleashed on the air waves over the course of 1947. In November 1947 the Soviet authorities decided to back up their counter-intelligence operations in Germany with special measures to counter the Western ideological offensive. SMAD authorized the formation of a Department for Intelligence and Information of the DVdI. This was the first zone-wide propaganda service of the SED. The new organization was intended to counter Western propaganda and to spread the SED's party line.[47] It had very close relations with the press in the Eastern Zone.[48]

The Department for Intelligence and Information was far more than just a propaganda agency and press liaison bureau. It also conducted intelligence-gathering and counter-intelligence. It had the task of collecting information 'about any intentional or unintentional activities that [were] designed to hurt the SED'. This even included functions normally associated with foreign intelligence, since the Department was expected to procure information about reactionary intentions from the Western zones.[49] The methods to be used did not differ from those of the SED's other secret police agencies. The Department was to use agents 'in all branches of the economy, society, mass organisations, and political parties'.[50] Given the apparently high degree of overlap between the SED's three counter-intelligence agencies, it is not surprising that the Department for Intelligence and Information was also placed under Mielke's control within the DVdI, alongside K-5/the Main Directorate for the Defence of the Economy and Democratic Order and the Agency for the Protection of National Property. Thus Mielke had the distinction of being both the SED's first head of intelligence as well as its last.

THE CREATION OF THE MINISTRY FOR STATE SECURITY

On 7 October 1949 the East German State came into being, five months after the creation of the Federal Republic. Four months later, the SED received its own autonomous state security service or Stasi as it was popularly known, the word being an abbreviation of the word *Staatssicherheit* (state security). The question has been raised as to why the Soviet occupation authorities took so long to make this move, particularly since the secret police were an essential part of the Soviet-style party state. This question, however is misleading since the Party already had its own political police in all but name in the form of K-5 and the Committee for the Protection of National Property, not to mention the extensive services of the MGB. The Soviet Government had been loath to give the SED the formal trappings of state power while accommodation with the Allies on the German question was still on the agenda.

The extent to which the gradual build-up of German police institutions reveals anything about Soviet policy towards Germany remains unclear as do the Kremlin's real objectives in this vital area. It seems obvious that institutional changes in the secret police of the Eastern Zone closely followed events of the Cold War. To begin with, the DVdI was created in 1946 when relations with the West were worsening and when the KPD had lost the local elections at the beginning of the year. Then, in the summer of 1947, K-5 was set up just four months after the Truman Doctrine. Finally, the MfS came into being in 1950 following the definitive break between the Soviet Union and the Western Allies on the German issue because of the creation of the Federal Republic the year before. Thus it might be concluded that Soviet policy in the Eastern Zone was undecided and that the Soviet leadership was just reacting to events. Perversely, it might be argued that increasing repression in the Eastern Zone was occasioned to a significant degree by the mounting threat from the West.[51] But it is misleading to assume that the institutional history of the Soviet Bloc is a clear reflection of Soviet policy. It is clear that SMAD worked to build up the communist party and the secret police from almost the moment that the Red Army occupied eastern Germany. As far as the development of the German secret police reflected Soviet policy, it was as an indication of Stalin's intention to mask the communist take-over from the Western Allies. It was important to the Soviet authorities that K-5 and its sister secret police agencies should be hidden within the Administration of the Interior.

The creation of the Ministry of State Security (MfS) was presented to the East German people as a defensive measure in the mounting Cold War with the West. On 26 January 1950, the East German Government made a public statement in the Party daily, *Neues Deutschland*, about the growth of Western subversion in East Germany, calling on the people to be vigilant.[52] Two days later, Erich Mielke wrote in the same vein, warning of the increasing danger of British and American covert action. He explained that the Allies were now using systematic terror against the leading officials of the DDR, without of course citing any cases, since there were none. Furthermore, according to Mielke, the British and Americans had started on a full-scale campaign of sabotage against East German industry, going so far as to use explosives; again he put forward no evidence. Finally, the Allies were spying in the DDR; here the following years were to prove Mielke right, though again he did not mention any cases, since few had yet come to light.[53] These two newspaper articles, both as vague as one another, were the only official justifications for the creation of the East German secret police.

The law creating the MfS passed through the *Volkskammer*, the East German parliament, by unanimous vote, though this is hardly surprising. The law itself offered no more elucidation about exactly what State Security was supposed to do. It was only two paragraphs long, mentioning simply that the Committee for the Defence of National Property (to be exact, the Chief

Department for the Protection of the National Economy as it had briefly become in 1949) was now being established as an independent Ministry for State Security. Dr Karl Steinhoff, the GDR's first Minister of the Interior explained the new Ministry's duties to the *Volkskammer* in exceptionally vague and brief terms:

> The most important tasks of this Ministry will be to protect the national enterprises and works, transport and national property from plots of criminal elements as well as against all attacks, to conduct a decisive fight against the activities of hostile agents networks, subversives, saboteurs and spies, to conduct an energetic fight against bandits, to protect our democratic development and to ensure an uninterrupted fulfilment of the economic plans of our democratic free economy.

Thus the Ministry State for State Security was created with no legal restriction whatsoever on its activities.

The headquarters of the MfS were established in a former finance office in the Normannenstraße of East Berlin's working-class suburb of Lichtenberg. Regional headquarters were established in the five provinces *(Länder*), and a special centre was set up in Prenzlauer Allee for the general control of Berlin. A special unit, named *Verwaltung Wismut* operated in the Erfurt region in the south of the DDR for the protection of the local uranium mines.[54]

Wilhelm Zaisser was East Germany's first Minister for State Security, appointed on 8 February 1950, the day the MfS came into existence. By his own account he was appointed through the express wish of Moscow, but was also the choice of Walter Ulbricht, who in July 1950 was to become General Secretary of the SED.[55] On the same day the SED's Central Committee elected Zaisser to the Politburo. Erich Mielke was State Secretary for Security, thus once again becoming Zaisser's right-hand man, as he had been in Spain.

After his return to Moscow from the Spanish Civil War, Zaisser fell foul of the NKVD and spent a brief period in gaol during the Great Purges. Thereafter he spent five years as an editor, before resuming his career in the field of intelligence and counter-intelligence. By 1943, he was clearly recognized as a senior member of the German communist cadres which Moscow was trying to create for service after the War. In February that year he joined a working group which the KPD Politburo formed to work out proposals for the fight against the Nazi regime. Thereafter, from November 1943 to December 1946 he was employed on political propaganda work among German prisoners-of-war in the camps at Krasnogorsk and Talitsa.

Zaisser only returned to the Eastern Zone in February 1947. He retained his dual German–Soviet citizenship and became a member of the SED. His first official post was as head of the *Volkspolizei* in Saxony-Anhalt. In

September 1948, the provincial head of government (*Ministerpräsident*), Max Seydewitz, made him the province's Minister of the Interior. The relationship between the two was evidently a close one, for Seydewitz alone of the SED leaders was to write favourably about Zaisser after his death. In September 1949, Zaisser changed jobs, being appointed to train the special units of the People's Police (*Volkspolizeibereitschaften*), which were to form the basis of the GDR's army. Zaisser's career in intelligence and in the army clearly suited him for his new position. The same can also be said of his deputy, Erich Mielke. A further qualification was indispensable to their promotion: they had the Soviet Government's complete trust. In particular, Zaisser had some connection with Lavrenti Beria, the head of Soviet intelligence, who had personally ordered his release from gaol in 1939. Beria was then at the height of his powers in the Soviet Union. Exactly how close his relationship was with Zaisser before 1950 remains unclear. After 1950 Beria was automatically Zaisser's superior by virtue of their official relationship.[56] From 1950 until their common fall in 1953 the fate of the two men was closely linked.

At the senior level, then, the creation of the MfS did not lead to major changes. K-5 officers simply transferred to the new organization. It is unclear how much East German intelligence expanded with the creation of the DDR because the strength of K-5 is not known. In 1952, the MfS was composed of 4,000 regular officers, excluding its special troops, the Felix Dzierżyński Guards.[57] At the beginning of the 1950s the Stasi was purely an internal security service. Nonetheless its strength was very low indeed given the tasks which it was expected to perform. Controlling the border zone with West Germany involved a huge effort, as did the blanket surveillance of society. These were tasks which could only be performed at this time with the assistance of the KGB. Yet from the Soviet point of view this was not an adequate long-term solution. In the aftermath of the communist take-overs in the 1950s, Moscow expected the Eastern European satellite states to pay for themselves. It did not want to continue contributing to the expense of East Germany's administration.

The MfS's problems of size were compounded by problems of quality. Despite the Soviet training of K-5 there were still few intelligence professionals in the Stasi's ranks. A factor which particularly concerned the SED leadership was the low level of ideological training and commitment of the secret police who were guarding them. In May 1953, on the eve of the Berlin Uprising, Walter Ulbricht stressed that 'The first duty is significantly to improve the ideological education of the members of the MfS and to increase their knowledge of their jobs.'[58] When the MfS was created, the security department of the SED under Gustav Roebelen took overall responsibility for the ideological training of the Stasi. It received much criticism for its poor performance in the first half of the 1950s.[59]

The SED's ideological supervision of the Stasi did not prevent former Gestapo and SD officers continuing to serve or finding employment in it. They included, for example, Louis Hagemeister, a former *SS-Hauptsturmführer*, now head of the interrogation department (*Vernehmungsabteilung*) in the Schwerin provincial administration of the MfS.[60] At least he was qualified for the job. In 1955, nine former Wehrmacht and SS officers worked in the Stasi's Leipzig provincial administration, together with five former Nazi civil servants. The extent to which former Nazis were employed in the MfS only became clear after the opening of the East German archives after the revolution of 1989.[61]

As far as it had any official definition at all, the Ministry for State Security was an institution of the new East German State. In fact, it was still closely controlled by the Soviet Union. The bonds between the Stasi and the KGB existed on many levels. They claimed a shared heritage dating back to the Russian revolution, with Lenin and Felix Dzerzhinsky as their common spiritual fathers. The leaders of the MfS had been trained in the Soviet intelligence schools, while its rank and file had been instructed by officers of the MGB while in K-5. Even a superficial look at the structure of East German state security showed its Soviet parentage. Most obviously, both incorporated both the functions of a domestic secret police and a foreign intelligence agency in one organization. Furthermore, the practices of the two bodies were very similar indeed. Even minor details betrayed this. Techniques of interrogation were similar. After October 1952, Stasi officers started to hold military rank as KGB officers had done for very many years.[62] This was intended to encourage *esprit de corps*, distinguishing them from the ordinary police. Finally, large numbers of Soviet officers continued to serve in the MfS.

Soviet instructors continued to work in the MfS right down to the district (*Kreis*) level. They had two basic functions: firstly, to watch and control their German subordinates; secondly, and most importantly, to train them. The MfS was not only required to supply Soviet departments at the corresponding level with information, but also they could only carry out certain actions in agreement with the MGB.[63] Soviet representation at the district level was somewhat reduced at the beginning of the 1950s. But the same was not true at the provincial and central level. At Stasi headquarters in Berlin, there was at least one Soviet instructor in each MfS department. While at the provincial *(Bezirk)* level, the head of each department (*Verwaltung*) was controlled by a chief instructor. The work of operational departments was watched and instructed by Soviet officers even down to the details of daily work.[64]

By the time that the DDR was created the KGB and K-5 had between them crushed all potential political opposition to the SED within East Germany. But the SED continued to need a high level of repression for the construction of the 'socialist' state. The class struggle intensified. Targets of the MfS were the middle classes, against whom the state passed punitive legislation. Those particularly affected were shopkeepers and manufacturers, as the private sector of the economy was worn down. Other groups which suffered were active Christians and the peasants. The latter suffered as the SED intensified the collectivization of agriculture after the creation of the East German state. For these people repression did not necessarily signify imprisonment, as it had done for refractory Social Democrats, Usually the rank and file of the 'class enemies' were subjected to confiscation of land and property or discrimination such as withdrawal of ration books and refusal of entry into university. Repression was never restricted to specific social groups. As the SED enforced austere policies aimed at rapid industrialization, the workers too needed to be cowed. The hands of the Stasi and the KGB extended into the factories and the number of trials for economic crimes increased. Many of the accused were charged with complicity in Western sabotage. The extent to which charges of wrecking were just a convenient method of imposing strict work discipline will always be unclear.[65]

THE 1953 UPRISING

The Stasi was an essential component of the Party-State. Coercion was vital to the implementation of both the SED's social and economic policies. Yet at the beginning of the 1950s, the East German state was still not strong enough to handle serious popular unrest on its own. On 17 June 1953 the workers of East Berlin rose in protest at the regime and were soon joined by their comrades in 200 other towns and cities. This was the first revolt within the Soviet Bloc. The crisis was short-lived and after ten days the DDR was quiet again. But there was no doubt whatsoever that the SED had been saved only by the intervention in force of the Red Army. The regular East German Police, the *Volkspolizei* were neither numerous enough nor suitably well-armed to meet the rioters who, it is worth noting, did not bear firearms themselves, unlike the Hungarian insurrectionists three years later.[66] The GDR's secret police seemed to have failed even more miserably, since both the SED leadership and the Soviet authorities charged them with having failed to foresee the unrest. The justification of this accusation will be discussed shortly. At any rate, even days before the Berlin Uprising the SED leadership had not the slightest suspicion that serious trouble was about to break out. Even when rioting did start they failed to appreciate its seriousness and the depth of workers' discontent with the regime. On the morning of 17 June Walter Ulbricht is said to have reacted to the first news that the Berlin workers were on strike with the words: 'It's raining and people will go home.'[67] By that evening the workers were calling for the resignation of the government.

Ulbricht found it far easier to explain the Uprising than to foresee it. Far from being a workers' uprising, the riots had been part of a fascist-imperialist plot organized by the Americans and West Germans with the aim of subjecting the proletariat to capitalist exploitation once more.[68] By implication, therefore, the workers were lucky that the Red Army had killed over a score of them and arrested 25,000 more. The SED's official explanation found basis in only one fact: news reports about protests in Berlin on the Western radio might have encouraged the spread of the riots throughout the rest of the DDR. In all other respects, Ulbricht's explanation bore no relation to reality, though this does not necessarily mean that he and the rest of his Politburo did not genuinely believe that they were faced with a Western plot. It is true that the SED Politburo did not seriously think that the rising was the result entirely or almost entirely of fascist provocation. This is a clear indication of how they assessed the ideological threat from the West. But even members of the Politburo hostile to Ulbricht felt that Western subversion was one of three basic causes of the unrest, though not the most important one. The others were: the deep bitterness of the workers; and the disorientation of the Party *Apparat*.[69]

Ulbricht was singularly unable to explain away the West's complete inactivity whilst East Germany was in turmoil. The real causes of the Berlin Uprising have long been clear. The fundamental factor which brought the workers onto the streets was their resentment at prolonged and increasing hardship. In 1952 the SED had announced its decision to accelerate the 'building of socialism'. This meant a drive to build up heavy industry, the rapid expansion of the armed forces, and the forcible collectivization of agriculture. The workers' resentment was only aggravated when the Party admitted mistakes in an editorial of 11 June 1953, promising henceforth to raise living standards.[70] The East Germans were further confused by Stalin's death on 9 March 1953. This encouraged the belief that the communist systems throughout the Soviet Bloc would be less brutal and decisive than they had been under the great dictator. Yet there is no evidence that Western subversion in any form played a significant role in instigating the Uprising. The same was to be true 46 years later when East Germany was convulsed by popular unrest for the second and last time in its history.

The Berlin Uprising and the widespread popular discontent of which it was a manifestation was only one of the crises facing the GDR's leadership in June 1953. The second crisis was the bitter faction struggle within the SED Politburo which was fought out over the course of June and July 1953. The MfS was closely involved in both issues.

At first sight it would seem that the MfS had failed in its first task: to monitor public opinion. With hindsight it should have appeared obvious that there was widespread discontent with the SED regime. In May–June 1953, the monthly figure of those fleeing the DDR rose to 30,000.[71] There is evidence that at the local level, the MfS were aware of widespread discontent. But the information was neither collected together to present an overall picture, nor did it reach the leadership.[72] Here there is a parallel with the Stasi's intelligence failure in 1989, which is discussed in Chapter 7. Otto Grotewohl, the East German premier (*Ministerpräsident*), complained about the Stasi's incompetence to a group of SED functionaries:

> The state cannot accept a situation in which all of us were able to form a general picture of all the events from the press and archive material, [while] only our State Security was not able to ascertain what was happening and how this had happened and developed.[73]

Ulbricht blamed Zaisser for a failure of intelligence. So did the Soviet authorities. On 17 June the Soviet High Commission summoned the SED Politburo to Karlshorst. S.V. Sokolovski, the Red Army's Chief of Staff and Deputy Minister of the USSR's Armed Forces, blamed Zaisser that state security did not have the necessary intelligence and had been surprised as a result. Sokolovski assumed that the strikes in the DDR had been organized and that a 'complete enemy network' existed. This formula had several advantages for the Soviet leadership, since it allowed the GDR's side and specific persons within it to bear all responsibility for the mismanagement of East Germany. The question did not even arise as to whether the Stalinist economic model, which Ulbricht had been blindly following, was responsible for the unrest. From the outset, the Soviet authorities ascribed its causes to 'enemy influence', which could be blamed on Zaisser as he had not known about it.[74]

Zaisser accepted some of the criticisms levelled against him and the Stasi. He implied that the MfS had been too preoccupied with fighting against Western subversion and had not paid enough attention to the complaints of ordinary East Germans which had nothing to do with the Cold War. As he put it, 'We misunderstood Day X.' The Stasi had seen it 'too narrowly as the threat of war'. Zaisser defended himself against the charge that he had been lax in fighting the West. He denied that the MfS had not known about the 'nests of agents' which the West had placed in East Germany and listed some examples of its achievements in counter-intelligence. Zaisser's most powerful defence of all was that the MfS could not be blamed for its actions before June 1953 because it had not been able to make a single decision without the approval of the Soviet instructors who controlled it.[75] It is hard to disagree with this justification which Zaisser gave to the SED leadership and the Soviet authorities. If there had been an intelligence failure, it should be attributed to the KGB, not to the Stasi.

Did the KGB fail to foresee the deterioration of the public mood in East Germany? The short answer is that it did not. Over the course of 1952 and the first half of 1953 the KGB reported to the Soviet Politburo on the worsening public mood in East Germany which they believed was caused by the severity of the SED's economic policies.[76] The Politburo summarized this intelligence in a resolution drawn up at the end of May 1953, entitled 'On measures for the recovery of the political situation in the German Democratic Republic'. The Politburo had no doubt that the crisis was worsening, since from 1951 to 1953, 447,000 people had fled to West Germany, while just in January–April 1953, 120,000 had fled. The main cause of the problem was that 'the course for the accelerated building of socialism in East Germany had been mistakenly taken without the presence of the necessary real domestic and foreign policy conditions'. The Soviet leadership concluded that 'All this is creating a serious danger for the political stability of the German Democratic Republic.'[77]

There can be no doubt that the information which the Soviet leadership drew on was the product not only of the KGB but also of the MfS's inquiries. This was inevitable because of the intimate links between East German and Soviet intelligence. It was reflected also in the behaviour of Wilhelm Zaisser, who stood firmly for the moderation of the SED's economic policies in the months leading up to the Berlin Uprising.

Clearly there was no failure of intelligence collection or analysis. Was there a failure of implementation? The Soviet leadership took the bad news very seriously. The action which they took was far more decisive than their dilatory and contradictory approach to the crises in Hungary and Poland three years later. The first warning came on the occasion of Stalin's funeral in March 1953 when Ulbricht was in Moscow. Beria and Malenkov warned him that they disliked his radical course. The Soviet leadership's opposition to Ulbricht's policies became clearer in April when they issued him an official note of warning.[78] When Ulbricht continued to stall on reform, he and other members of the East Germany Politburo were called to Moscow in May. There they were called to task for their handling of the East German economy, and were ordered to take a more relaxed approach. But they did not take serious action on their return to East Berlin. As a result, the Soviet leadership recalled Ulbricht and his associates to Moscow on 2 June 1953 and told them even more forcefully to introduce reform at home. Beria in particular behaved aggressively towards the East German delegation.[79] This had an effect since on 11 June the SED Politburo agreed to publicize a change of course in the Party's daily newspaper, *Neues Deutschland*. Rudolf Herrnstadt, the paper's editor did want to announce it too precipitately, preferring to wait a fortnight. The Soviet High Commissioner, Vladimir Semyonov was closely informed of the public mood in East Germany and replied to Herrnstadt: 'Maybe in 14 days you won't have a state any more.'[80]

The Soviet authorities were aware of the unrest building up in the DDR and had tried to act upon the information which they had received. The problem in 1953 was not one of intelligence, but perhaps of the Soviet and East German leadership's failure to move quickly enough. But above all the problem stemmed from the refusal of Walter Ulbricht either to acknowledge the crisis which was developing in East German society or to follow Soviet instructions to change course.

THE FALL OF ZAISSER AND HERRNSTADT

After the Berlin Uprising, Walter Ulbricht found himself in an almost untenable position. He more than any other was responsible for the crisis because he had obstructed the Soviet leadership's demands for reforms. Furthermore he had alienated a sizeable section of his own Politburo because of his autocratic style of leadership. Yet Ulbricht survived the crisis and destroyed the political careers of his main adversaries.

Already at the beginning of 1953 there were two clear factions within the East German Politburo: the supporters of Walter Ulbricht, who included Erich Honecker; and a more numerous but disunited group who were generally dissatisfied with Ulbricht. The most prominent among Ulbricht's opponents were Wilhelm Zaisser and Rudolf Herrnstadt.

Herrnstadt was now a candidate member of the SED Politburo and editor of the SED's daily newspaper, *Neues Deutschland*. In this capacity he was closely associated with the propaganda, or 'active measures', which the Stasi and the KGB conducted, thus continuing his association with Soviet intelligence which had started in the 1930s when he was an anti-Nazi journalist in Warsaw.

The attack on Ulbricht had started at the beginning of the year when the SED Politburo gave Zaisser the task of preparing a draft resolution for changing the methods and work of the Politburo, on account of Ulbricht's 'bad style of work'.[81] What exactly were the issues dividing the two factions? Ulbricht's opponents accused him of creating a governing clique centred upon himself and the Secretariat of the Central Committee. It was he who took key political decisions without proper reference to the Politburo as a whole. This reflected Ulbricht's campaign to achieve supremacy within the German Party, which he had been conducting since his appointment as the SED's General Secretary in July 1950 and, arguably, since his time in Soviet exile. In the period 1950–3, Ulbricht succeeded in weakening the influence of the Politburo in favour of the Central Committee Secretariat, building up his own dictatorial position. In short, Ulbricht was trying to set himself up as a little Stalin.[82] This, more than his austere economic policies had alienated Herrnstadt and Zaisser. In fact, neither was in principle opposed to rapid industrialization and the collectivization of agriculture, so long as their implementation did not lead to social unrest. Herrnstadt did not want the new reform course in 1953 to involve any curtailment of the collectivization of agriculture, objecting to the ease with which Ulbricht gave in to Soviet demands.[83]

In the days after 17 June 1953, Ulbricht conducted a skilful defence against his opponents within the SED leadership. He was able to counter-attack Zaisser from three directions. First, he branded his opponent with the disgrace of the Uprising. Second, he accused both Zaisser and Herrnstadt of attempting to form a faction within the Party. Third, he seems to have encouraged feelings which had existed among SED veterans since their exile in Moscow that men like Zaisser and Herrnstadt were not pure German communists. Ulbricht's victory in the faction struggle was the result not only of his skill but also of Zaisser and Herrnstadt's incompetence. Their strength within the SED was never as great as has often been claimed.[84] They never succeeded in forming a faction and, according to their own account, did not even act concertedly together. Perhaps most important of all, they did not secure the support of any of the Soviet leaders before they began their attack on Ulbricht.

Ulbricht's most powerful weapon against Zaisser was the charge of failure to prevent the June Uprising. Despite his self-defence, Zaisser could not regain the prestige he lost in June 1953. What was worse, his role as head of East German intelligence made him a very convenient scapegoat for the Soviet authorities who, like Ulbricht, were anxious to avoid blame for the Uprising sticking to themselves.

Ulbricht's second charge against Zaisser did not fit easily with the first. If Zaisser was a powerful figure who had tried to use the secret police as a basis of support, why had he proved so incompetent in conducting counter-intelligence? Ulbricht claimed that Zaisser had devoted his attention to faction-fighting to the exclusion of all his other duties.[85]

There was a kernel of truth in what Ulbricht said. The old K-5, for example, had often acted outside the law and out of party control. Zaisser agreed with

Ulbricht that 'there had been tendencies in the MfS to set themselves above the Party', but only 'here and there'. Hermann Matern, a member of the Politburo who was not a client of Ulbricht, said that 'the whole way of working' in the Stasi was wrong. He claimed that within the MfS the habit of standing above the Party was widespread. He cited the example of Erfurt where the MfS controlled the entire provincial *(Bezirk)* Secretariat.[86]

Zaisser denied ever having used the Stasi against the Party and provided evidence that this was true. As he noted, he was not in absolute control of the MfS, which was dominated by the Russians. Unfortunately this was not an argument which Zaisser could make forcefully inside the SED Politburo, let alone in a more public forum such as the Plenum of the Central Committee. To have done so would have been an open insult to the Soviet Union and the KGB.

As intelligence chief, Zaisser was not independent of Ulbricht either. Zaisser told the SED Politburo that in the period before the Berlin Uprising 'There were no substantial decisions in principle in the Ministry for State Security down to the arrest of influential or prominent people, which were not discussed beforehand with Comrade Walter Ulbricht.'[87] Ulbricht's relations with the Stasi reflected his overall drive to centralize the leadership of the Party and the State in his own hands. He undoubtedly was vying for leadership of the organization with Zaisser. The effects of Ulbricht's interference were clear. It removed any possibility of Zaisser building up a power base upon the MfS. This was clearly demonstrated when Zaisser's lieutenants in the MfS, Mielke and Stahlmann, deserted him without a whimper when his star was falling.[88]

Ulbricht played on the suspicions of the Politburo members. There was a general feeling that Zaisser and Herrnstadt were the 'Russia faction' within the Politburo, since they were men who owed their position to their career in Soviet intelligence and to the goodwill of the Soviet authorities thereafter.[89] The ambiguity of their position was also characterized by their dual Soviet–German citizenship. Some of the SED leadership complained that they were not sufficiently concerned with specifically German issues. This bad blood went back to the period of Soviet exile. For example, in 1943 the future SED Politburo member, Anton Ackermann had organized a Christmas party for the staff of the radio station *Freies Deutschland*. Herrnstadt was furious about their lack of ideological discernment when he heard that they had sung carols and lodged a complaint with the KPD's Politburo.

Zaisser resented his comrades' refusal fully to accept him as a fellow German communist. He referred contemptuously to Ulbricht and others as the 'Pieckwick-Club' which was a pun on Charles Dickens' *Pickwick Papers* and the name of the GDR's first president, Wilhelm Pieck. Zaisser claimed explicitly that Ulbricht and his associates did not regard him as a German because he had always worked for the Soviet Union.[90] He told the German communist Hanna Wolf: 'I do not belong to that Pieckwick-Club, those comrades do not regard me as a German, because I have always worked for the Soviet Union.' He prophesied correctly that the Club would get themselves into trouble and that he would get them out of it, though he did not, of course, foresee that this would be by becoming their scapegoat.[91]

In chronological terms, Zaisser's fall corresponded roughly with the arrest and execution of Beria in the Soviet Union. In causal terms, the connection is unclear. It has been argued that Beria was Zaisser's patron and that it was primarily Beria who had encouraged Zaisser to resist Ulbricht, with the immediate aim of reversing the SED's disastrous economic policies and with the long-term aim of reuniting Germany.[92] No evidence has come to light which supports these conclusions. Herrnstadt did not mention any close bonds between Beria, himself and Zaisser in his secret testimony. On the contrary, he made it clear that he and Zaisser were ignorant of what was going on inside the Soviet Politburo.[93] Ulbricht did not make complicity in Beria's plotting one of the cardinal charges against Zaisser, even though he was aware of the extent of Beria's crimes. He had been called to Moscow and briefed by the Soviet Politburo at the time of Beria's arrest. One charge which is probably false is that Zaisser and Herrnstadt were plotting with Beria to create a reunified, neutral Germany. In 1953 none of the SED leadership knew anything about Beria's alleged plans for Germany's future.[94] Probably he had no such schemes. It was only in 1963 that Khrushchev first made the accusation that Beria wanted to liquidate the socialist state in the DDR.[95] Had Beria, Zaisser and Herrnstadt been guilty of such a major crime, they would undoubtedly have been accused of it more explicitly ten years earlier. When Ulbricht asked Zaisser whether he had had relations with Beria, Zaisser said only: 'without the help of these Soviet comrades from top to bottom, from the Ministry down to the *Kreise*, the mistakes which the Ministry for State Security made would have been much greater. All the advice which the Soviet comrades gave me, I carried out.' According to the available evidence, the matter rested there.[96] It is true that Ulbricht publicly accused Zaisser and Herrnstadt of taking 'a defeatist line towards the West' at the time of their fall in July 1953. He did not make it clear what he meant by defeatism. At any rate, he did not link this with Beria. Possibly this was to avoid embarrassment to the Soviet Union. It was not until Khrushchev's 'Secret Speech' three years later that disgraced Soviet leaders could be condemned by name. Even if this is so, it does not explain why Herrnstadt did not mention the Beria plot in his testament which was not intended for immediate public consumption and who cannot, therefore, have had qualms about embarrassing Moscow.

Beria was not the only Soviet leader who had pressed for reform in East Germany. So did many of his rivals in the Soviet Politburo. Their interests were represented in East Berlin by Vladimir Semyonov, the Soviet High Commissioner to the DDR. He was constantly present at the meetings of the SED Politburo.[97] Semyonov had arrived in East Germany on 28 May 1953, having been appointed with the main task of overseeing the 'new course' of reforms which the SED was forced to take.

Semyonov was not a supporter of Zaisser and Herrnstadt. He had known Herrnstadt for almost ten years and had worked with him on the most intimate political questions. But he had a poor opinion of Zaisser, whom he described to Otto Grotewohl, the SED's premier and party chief, as a 'prima donna and a dancer' and a person with whom one could not work. According to Herrnstadt, the antipathy was mutual.[98] On 20 July 1953 Semyonov informed Herrnstadt implicitly that the Kremlin had decided in favour of Ulbricht, telling him explicitly that his political career was finished.[99] Thus it proved that the Berlin Uprising strengthened Ulbricht by increasing his value to Moscow, even though his economic policies had been so much responsible for the unrest. Moscow did not now feel able to show any weakness before the German population. They felt that jettisoning Ulbricht would have been a sign of weakness. Thus they had to find other scapegoats. Only two were available.

By this time Zaisser and Herrnstadt were isolated within the SED Politburo. Their erstwhile supporters had either fallen silent or, like Oelßner, Matern and Jendretzky, had joined the Ulbricht camp.[100] Zaisser's end was ignominious. On 23 July, only three days after Semyonov's announcement, he voted for his own exclusion from the Politburo, accusing himself of being a defeatist and representative of Social Democracy. He burst into tears and left the room.[101] Two days later he and Herrnstadt were subjected to a more public humiliation at the Fifteenth Plenum of the SED's Central Committee. Ulbricht launched a tirade against the pair, accusing them of taking a defeatist line towards the West and having expressed Social Democratic viewpoints. Before replying, Zaisser agreed with Herrnstadt that he could not say what had really happened, because 'that could harm the Soviet Union'.[102] In an emotional speech he denied all the charges against him. Inevitably the Central Committee condemned him and Herrnstadt.[103] The two men were removed from office and excluded from the Party. They were not, however, imprisoned.

The humiliation of Zaisser and Herrnstadt in July 1953 was the nearest that East Germany ever came to the kind of great show trials of disgraced leaders which had occurred in all the other states of the Soviet Bloc. East

Germany also differed from the rest of the Soviet Empire in the selection of the men put on trial. In the countries it was the 'national communists' who suffered. These were men such as Slánský in Czechoslovakia, Rajk in Hungary, and Gomułka in Poland who were thought to be insufficiently dependent on Moscow and to have local roots which were too strong. Zaisser and Herrnstadt were Moscow's men in that most of their Party career had been spent in Soviet intelligence and they owed their appointment within the SED to Moscow.

The impact of the crisis on the Stasi was not that great. Most obviously, it lost prestige. This was reflected in an institutional change, since the MfS temporarily ceased to be an independent Ministry and was incorporated into the Ministry of the Interior. This might have been no more than an attempt to follow Soviet practice, since after Stalin's death the MGB was briefly incorporated into the Ministry of the Interior (MVD) once more, only to become independent again in March 1954, this time assuming the title it was to bear right up to the 1990s – the KGB.[104]

East German State Security was purged following the unrest, which had not left it untouched. For example, in the *Juristische Hochschule* near Berlin, about a hundred officers who were attending courses had demonstrated against Ulbricht's regime.[105] They were punished. In all about 30 state security officers were arrested in July 1953.[106]

One thing was certain after 1953: the Stasi could never be a lever in East German faction fighting. There never developed a situation similar to that in the Soviet Union in 1953 when Beria tried to build up a power base for himself based on the KGB, nor could such a situation ever have arisen. There were two reasons for this: first, as Zaisser had rightly stressed, the MfS was always under Soviet control; second, Ulbricht was very careful to ensure his own control of the Stasi. Not much changed after 1953. In political terms, the disgrace of the MfS meant very little, though it did affect its operations. The situation was inconceivable whereby either the SED leadership or the Soviet authorities could afford to restrict the Stasi's operations or disregard its intelligence. The Party was dependent upon its secret police. The chief result of 1953 was to increase the importance of the Stasi within the state, though this was not obvious for several years. But an early sign was its rapid increase in numbers from 4,000 in 1952 to 10,000 in 1955.[107]

WOLLWEBER AND THE MfS

The choice of Zaisser's successor was not an easy one. Erich Mielke was in every way suited to the job, but he was one of those whom the Party held responsible for the Stasi's failure.[108] Furthermore, because of the complete failure of the MfS in June 1953, it was not possible to appoint anyone else to head the Stasi from within its own ranks.[109] The selection of East Germany's head of intelligence fell once more to Moscow. Semyonov suggested Ernst Wollweber, as the most obvious outsider who had experience of intelligence work. Ulbricht did not like this choice, since Wollweber was too coarse and outspoken for his tastes. But he was obliged to agree with the Soviet authorities.[110]

Wollweber had spent most of the Second World War in Swedish gaols, having been captured there in May 1940 while travelling to the Soviet Union after the German invasion of Denmark and Norway where his organization was based. In 1941 a Swedish court sentenced him to three years' imprisonment for the theft of explosives. His fate hung in the balance until the War definitely turned in the Red Army's favour after the Battle of Stalingrad in early 1943. Before this the Swedish authorities had considered granting German demands for his extradition on the charge of maritime sabotage.[111]

Wollweber's connection with the sea continued after his return to Germany. Before his appointment as Minister for State Security he had been the GDR's Director of Shipping.[112] There is evidence that he once more became involved with maritime espionage in this period. This will be discussed in Chapter 5.

Though untainted by the fiasco of the Berlin Uprising, Wollweber's first task was to cope with its aftermath. Zaisser's fall did not satisfy the Party leadership who needed more scapegoats. The SED continued to present the uprising of 17 June as a fascist coup. To be able to do so credibly, the Party had to find plotters whom it could put on trial. Thus Wollweber and the Stasi were given the task of finding non-existent conspirators. When they were still empty-handed at the end of three months they came in for a barrage of criticism. At the end of September 1953, the SED Politburo criticized the Stasi for its failure to unearth the organization behind the uprising. The official complaint read: 'Although 3 months have passed since the events of 17 June, the state security organs have not even by now unmasked the organizers of the provocations.'[113] The Stasi soon fulfilled the Party's expectations. The first blow was against the Gehlen Organization. On 1 November 1953, they had arrested a few dozen people. One of the prisoners, Hans-Joachim Geyer, *alias* Grell emerged at a press conference a few days later and accused the Gehlen Organization of organizing sabotage and armed groups in the DDR, and of trying to buy its technical and scientific secrets. Geyer was a genuine West German agent based in West Berlin. He was also working for the Stasi and it was thanks to him that Gehlen's agents had just been captured. Geyer's switch to East Berlin was occasioned by fear of impending arrest. This prompted Wollweber to launch a lightning raid on the suspects. Wollweber unfairly claimed all the justification for his success. In fact, Geyer had already been recruited in Zaisser's time.[114]

The Geyer affair did not satisfy the SED's desire for culprits. At the beginning of January 1954, Wollweber, Mielke and other Stasi chiefs met in their Normannenstraße headquarters to discuss a plan for increasing their haul of *provocateurs*. This was 'Operation Vermin'. The target was a exile group known as the '17 June Committee'. This was not a counter-revolutionary group plotting the overthrow of the SED regime, but a pressure group campaigning on behalf of victims of repression in the DDR. The Committee had extensive contacts in East Germany which it was using to gather information about conditions there and to assist the flight of fugitives implicated in the Berlin Uprising. 'Operation Vermin' was a success. The Stasi succeeded in arresting 12 of the Committee's agents, four of whom were put on a show trial, where they were presented as human proof of the West's complicity in the unrest of the previous June. This was the publicity which the Party leadership wanted. Consequently the Stasi's prestige increased.[115]

By early 1954 the Stasi were receiving official recognition for their successful counter-intelligence. In April, Wollweber was rewarded by promotion to the SED's Central Committee, though he was never to reach the Politburo.[116] Exactly a year later the East German government paid public tribute to his success by announcing that 'There have been arrested 521 agents of the American and English secret services, of the Gehlen espionage organization as well as of the so-called "Task Force against Inhumanity", the so-called "Investigative Committee of Liberal Jurists", the RIAS, the Eastern offices of West Berlin parties and others.'[117] In his hauls of Western agents Wollweber managed ultimately to satisfy the Party, without filling their vengeance quota with wholly innocent victims. Such evidence that there is suggests that Wollweber was not very interested in spying on the East German population and tended to ignore Party demands that he should do so.[118]

The arrests of 1955 clearly satisfied the Party leadership. Apparently in recognition of the State Security's rehabilitation, it was elevated once more to the level of an independent Ministry. Wollweber thus became Minister of State Security with Mielke once again as State Secretary with the rank of Lieutenant-General.[119]

THE CRISIS OF 1956

The real test for Wollweber and the Stasi lay not in the capture of Western agents, but in their ability to gauge public opinion and to prevent any recurrence of popular unrest. In 1956 they faced their second crisis. In fact they faced two challenges that year: first, they had to adjust to the new wave of de-Stalinization flowing from the Soviet Union after Khrushchev's 'Secret Speech' in February; and second, they had to prevent unrest spreading from Poland where revolution threatened in June and July and from Hungary which rose against Soviet rule in November.

The way in which the Stasi faced the troubles of 1956 was conditioned, whether the SED liked it or not by events in the Soviet Union. Khrushchev's denunciation of Stalin's excesses in his 'Secret Speech' of 1956 inaugurated the rule of 'socialist legality' both in the Soviet Union and in the DDR. From the point of view of the Communist Party of the Soviet Union, one of the main achievements of the Khrushchev era was to put the security services firmly under the control of the Party, preventing the violent repressions of Stalin's time which had afflicted those in and without the Communist Party indiscriminately. The new order necessitated new modes of social control. In short, there could be no recourse to the violent repression of the years 1945–53.

The observation of 'socialist legality' involved particularly acute problems for the East German leadership, because of the existence of another German state on their borders, and the haven of West Berlin in their midst. The SED tried to achieve security before what they saw as a hostile West and unreliable population by the maintenance of blanket surveillance of society. The SED and the Stasi had already been moving in this direction before 1956, which was indicated by the relative mildness of the Purges in the DDR even in Stalin's time.

The basic principles of social control used by the Party and the Stasi remained constant between 1953 and 1989. The level of physical repression differed fundamentally from that used under pure Stalinism. This is worth mentioning since reporting on the Stasi after the East German Revolution put much stress on the technical capabilities of surveillance used by the MfS while misleading comparisons were drawn between it and the Romanian *Securitate*.[120] After Stalin's death in 1953 physical torture lessened and the death penalty was imposed less frequently.[121]

A system of 'normalization' came into being in the DDR in the 1950s, like that which the Czechoslovak Communist Party refined after 1968. This meant that the Stasi had the primary duty of ensuring that only those loyal to the Party got good or important jobs, and that those disloyal got the worst ones. This is one reason why by 1989 there were 6 million files on citizens of the DDR. The so-called 'Stasi-state' was as much a massive system of vetting as it was an apparatus of simple persecution.[122]

Despite the easing of physical repression, freedom of expression was strictly curtailed in Ulbricht's DDR. Even the relative tolerance during the

'New Course' of 1953 did not last long. On occasion in the post-1953 period, the Stasi operated as an agent of overt repression. For example, in 1956–7 they destroyed student opposition in East Berlin; in 1960 they were closely involved with the ruthless collectivization of agriculture; and in 1972 they assisted in the nationalization of the DDR's last privately owned enterprises.[123] But apart from their services as a vetting agency, their most important function in controlling society came from their very ubiquity, rather than from positive actions on their part. The pervasiveness of the security organs served to prevent public expression of any thought hostile to the SED line. The very knowledge that they were there and watching served to atomize society, preventing independent discussion in all but the smallest groups. In this sense they were far from being a 'secret' service, and would perhaps best be described as the Party's 'scarecrow'.[124] It seemed until the end of 1989, that potential terror was as effective as real terror.[125]

Wollweber's most obvious reaction to de-Stalinization was the public relations campaign which he launched in an attempt to improve the Stasi's image. Here East German practice was in advance of that of the Soviet Union, where the KGB only mounted a sustained publicity drive in the 1960s.[126] Zaisser had attempted to maintain the dignity of office, keeping himself aloof from the public. Wollweber, on the other hand, relished public appearances and addressed the workers in their factories and the rank and file of the SED at Party conferences.[127] Press conferences became regular events as the Stasi provided information about the Western espionage rings which they had uncovered. Links between state security and the press had always been close. Now the media of the DDR revelled in a real sensationalism.

East Germany was largely untouched by the popular unrest elsewhere in Eastern Europe in 1956. There were no more than a few student demonstrations. To what extent the Stasi's measures contributed to the calm is uncertain. Arguably the East German population had learned their lesson in 1953 when they had faced the Red Army and were unwilling to try their hand against the Soviet tanks. It was certain in 1956 that the Stasi did not overreact. Wollweber was far less concerned about the possibility of unrest spreading from Poland than Ulbricht. According to a recent study, the MfS might indeed have acted as a restraining influence on the Party leadership in that troubled year.[128]

THE FALL OF WOLLWEBER

Despite his apparent success and the Party's public approval of his work, Wollweber was very vulnerable. He suffered from the same two basic weaknesses as Zaisser: Ulbricht disliked and distrusted him; and he did not have the support of the Soviet authorities.

The Germany Department of the KGB, under the leadership of Major-General Alexander Korotkov, deeply distrusted Wollweber. The reason was personal. The KGB disliked Wollweber's choice of mistress, a woman named Clara Vater. She was a German communist who had fled to the Soviet Union to escape Hitler, but like many of her comrades had ended up in Stalin's labour camps. Though now a member of the SED, she remained an unreliable element in the KGB's eyes. The KGB's suspicions went so far that they kept Clara Vater and her daughter, whom Wollweber had adopted, under constant surveillance.[129] A further reason for the KGB's distrust of Wollweber was what they saw as his unduly elevated national consciousness.[130] Perhaps most importantly of all, the KGB disliked Wollweber's relatively independent attitude towards them. He did not passively accept orders from Moscow.[131] Wollweber resented the superior behaviour of the KGB, which did not keep him informed of all their operations in West Germany.[132]

The Stasi's success in averting disorder in East Germany in 1956 did not redound to Wollweber's credit in Soviet eyes; but it did much to restore Ulbricht's image.[133] Ulbricht realized his strength and moved against his opponents within the SED once more at the end of the year. He was concerned that Khrushchev might look to more moderate figures within the SED leadership once the situation in the Eastern Bloc settled down.

Unlike in 1953, the head of East German intelligence was not of key importance in the faction struggle of 1956, but was swept away by Ulbricht's broom all the same. Ulbricht's main opponents were the Politburo members Fred Oelßner and Karl Schirdewan, who objected to his autocratic style of leadership and to his economic policies, standing for the introduction of some market mechanisms. Their great weakness was that after 1956 they did not have much Soviet support. After events in Poland and Hungary, Khrushchev was more interested in encouraging stability in Eastern Europe than in tinkering with the established systems. Wollweber was linked to this group.[134]

A further group who incurred Ulbricht's displeasure in the mid-1950s was a small group of intellectuals who also wanted economic reform. Wollweber's actions in investigating one such member of the intelligentsia was the cause of the conflict between Ulbricht and Wollweber which broke out in earnest in November 1956. The MfS had just arrested a dissident group led by Wolfgang Harich, a professor of philosophy and social theorist who generally favoured a political and economic system similar to that of Tito's Yugoslavia. Wollweber agreed with Ulbricht that Harich was a counter-revolutionary, but saw him as insignificant. Ulbricht wanted to exploit the occasion to publicize the existence of a counter-revolutionary plot. Ulbricht had his way. In 1957 Harich was sentenced to ten years' imprisonment for conspiring to alter the social order of the DDR by threat of force.[135] (See Chapter 4.)

The Harich case involved the control and functioning of the MfS. Ulbricht came into possession of some of Harich's papers which he obtained without Wollweber's knowledge.[136] In retaliation, at the end of 1956 Wollweber gave orders that he was to be informed whenever MfS members had contact with members of the SED Central Committee. Ulbricht interpreted this order as Wollweber's attempting to put himself above the Party.[137]

As the attack on Wollweber developed, Ulbricht accused Wollweber of incompetence in office, just as he had Zaisser. He claimed that Wollweber was publishing unduly negative reports on public opinion.[138] In 1957, the SED leadership increasingly criticized the MfS for paying insufficient attention to the activities of 'counter-revolutionary elements' in the DDR.[139] There is evidence that Ulbricht was receiving information from Erich Mielke about Wollweber's character. According to a retired MfS Colonel, who spoke out in 1991, Mielke had reported on Wollweber to Ulbricht, presenting him as an alcoholic.[140]

There was no real question who would win the faction fight between Ulbricht and his rivals. Wollweber fell along with Oelßner and Schirdewan at the Thirty-Fifth Plenum of the SED's Central Committee in February 1958. They were charged with 'repeated infractions of Politburo discipline and refusal to become part of the collective of the Politburo'.[141] They were disgraced but suffered no greater punishment than the removal of all their offices and expulsion from the Party.

Wollweber's fall was not followed by a purge of the MfS. It led to a period of stability in the cadres of the Stasi which was to last until the end of the DDR. Erich Mielke now became head of East German State Security once more, which he was to personify for the next 41 years, making him one of the longest-serving intelligence chiefs in history. Mielke owed his success not just to his ability but also to his personality and political skill, which distinguished him fundamentally from his two predecessors. He never attempted to cut the gentlemanly, intelligent figure of Zaisser. On the other hand, he never indulged in the crude outbursts of the ruffianly Wollweber. Crucially, he avoided any scheming within the SED Politburo and he always made himself utterly acceptable to the Soviet Union, even in the Gorbachev era. In short, Mielke was a quintessential *apparatchik*; the English translation might be 'Vicar of Bray'. His success paralleled that of Walter Ulbricht who now dominated the bureaucracy and had reduced the SED to a client-system centred on his person. Thus the security service remained no different from any other part of the governmental apparatus of a Stalinist Party.

3 The MfS, the SED and the East German State

'We all remained silent, we should have spoken out more'.
Egon Krenz

MfS AND SED

According to Article 1 of its 1968 constitution, the German Democratic Republic (DDR), was 'a socialist state of the German nation'. It was 'the political organization of the working people in town and country, who together under the leadership of their Marxist-Leninist party, were realizing Socialism'.[1] In this case the party was the SED. It left open the possibility that the SED could change its name while remaining a Marxist-Leninist party, It also left open the possibility that if the SED was overrun by revisionists a new Marxist-Leninist party could be set up. However, in the official commentary[2] on the new constitution the SED was specifically named. As it was, Article 1 established the 'legal' dominance of the SED in all areas of society. Yet according to Article 2, 'All political power is exercised by the working people.' The Volkskammer (People's Chamber) 'is the highest organ of state of the German Democratic Republic. It decides in its plenary sessions the basic questions of state policy.' (Article 48) However, Article 47 laid down that, 'The Sovereignty of the working people realized on the basis of Democratic Centralism is the governing principle of the structure of the state.' This Leninist principle meant that the lower organs were subject to direction from above and from the centre. In theory, and formally, the lower organs elected the higher organs. The National Front (Article 3) united all the parties and mass organizations ultimately deciding the Volkskammer candidates who were then formally elected at regular intervals, no other candidates were permitted to stand. In the Volkskammer from 1949 until the only democratic elections in the DDR in March 1990, the SED had a de facto majority. This was gained via the mass organizations – trade unions, FDJ, women's organization (DFD) and so on – which were also represented in the People's Chamber together with the political parties: SED, CDU, LDPD, NDPD and DBD. In the same way the SED was subject to Democratic Centralism which meant ultimately domination by the Politburo. Of course the Politburo did not rely on its majority in the Volkskammer to keep power. It was by the use of force and the threat of force that it was able to do this. It was the acquiescence, resignation, acceptance of the great majority born of fear and propaganda which enabled the Politburo to achieve this. Behind everything was the knowledge that the Soviet armed forces could be called upon as in 1953 (DDR), 1956 (Hungary) and 1968 (Czechoslovakia) to crush any attempts to alter the system.

It was in this situation that Erich Mielke was 'elected' to the Volkskammer in 1958 and then at each subsequent 'election'. In the same way he was 'elected' to the central committee of the SED by the party congress in 1950 and by the central committee in 1976 to the Politburo. The Volkskammer repeatedly formally re-elected him as Minister for State Security from 1957 onwards. In theory, Mielke was subject to the judgement by the Volkskammer. In practice there was no control by that 'highest organ'. But he was also part of the Ministerrat (Council of Ministers), the government of the DDR. Under Article 79, paragraph 2, this body led, coordinated and checked the activities of the ministries, other state organs and district councils. Above all, of course, Mielke was subject to control by his colleagues in the Politburo. What was the control like in practice? There appears to be no evidence that Mielke was subjected to any scrutiny during his long years of service. Gerhard Schürer, from 1967 a deputy Chairman of the Ministerrat and from 1973 a candidate member of the Politburo, claimed that there was no control at all. He did, however, freely admit he should have been part of the control mechanism and should take the responsibility for doing nothing.[3] Horst Sindermann, who had served as Chairman of the Ministerrat (1973–6), President of the Volkskammer (1976–89), deputy Chairman of the Staatsrat and a member of the Politburo (1967–89), likewise admitted the lack of control. According to Sindermann, the Politburo did deal with MfS appointments in the higher ranks. It did not consider other questions. Sometimes there would be critical comments made about the size of the MfS but never were any resolutions passed. As for Mielke, he sat silently most of the time. In his last years most of what he said had little sense in it. When questioned about the logic of leaving the Stasi to such a senile old man, Sindermann pointed out that from 1983 onwards, Egon Krenz was the Secretary of the Central Committee responsible for security matters. 'Although in the literal sense he had no right to issue directives to Mielke, but it was completely clear that in the area of state security nothing important happened which Krenz was unaware of.' Throughout these years it was supposed that, 'If Krenz takes his responsibilities seriously, Mielke can't do any damage.'[4] Speaking in 1994 Krenz himself emphasized that the MfS was just one of his responsibilities in the general field of security and that he was not the top security chief of the DDR. He was not Mielke's boss. Mielke was responsible to the Chairman of the Staatsrat, the Chairman of the Defence Council, the General Secretary of the SED (Honecker in all three cases), and to the Chairman of the Ministerrat

(Stoph). He denied that he had any more responsibility than the other members of the Politburo, most of whom had been members much longer than he had. 'We all remained silent. We should have spoken out more.' Honecker regarded himself as infallible and members were reluctant to speak out because they had been educated to the view that there was always a danger of splitting the Party. Mielke was obsessed with power, but that was not the deciding factor, he was a 'man of the Soviets who had been awarded the Order of Lenin (by the Soviets) six times, the last time being in 1988 from the hands of Mikhail Gorbachev, that means, Mielke was a representative of the KGB in the ranks of the State Security'. This determined his position in the Politburo. According to Krenz, Mielke would have retired before 1989, but the Soviets did not wish him to so so.[5] In the view of General Markus Wolf, head of the HVA for many years and deputy Minister for State Security, Mielke would have discussed important decisions with Erich Honecker as General Secretary of the SED.[6] But Honecker in turn denied that he had detailed knowledge of what the MfS was doing.[7] He denied, for instance, knowledge of the employment by the MfS of former Nazis and of the fact that the Stasi was protecting such people by withholding files on them. In 1992 he even claimed that he had been threatened by Mielke with material about him which could have damaged the General Secretary. Allegedly Mielke had built up files of compromising material on his colleagues which he kept in a red suitcase.[8] Günter Schabowski, candidate member of the Politburo from 1981, full member, 1984–9, has described how most members spoke only about their own areas of responsibility in Politburo meetings. Within the Politburo, said Schabowski, there was a kind of inner circle comprising Honecker, Mielke, Günter Mittag, who had responsibility for the economy, and Joachim Herrmann, who supervised the media. Members rarely met outside these meetings even though they lived next to each other. Schabowski did not think Mielke was senile.[9] He was a man who could not stand criticism.[10] The MfS was out of reach of control by the Politburo which was not a collective decision-making body. It only discussed matters that the General Secretary wanted it to discuss. Had attempts been made to bring up other matters, those doing so would have been regarded as splitters. 'The key to the structure and activities of the security apparatus … was in Honecker's hands and was given to Mielke to administer.' Everything resulted from discussions between Honecker and Mielke.[11] All these witnesses, except Honecker, admit their general responsibility for what happened, but claim the Minister for State Security had a free hand. One other aspect of Mielke's MfS was the extent to which he considered himself to be the agent of the Soviet Union, and the extent to which this strengthened his independence within the SED. There is no doubt that many leading SED figures regarded their first loyalty to the Soviet Union as the leading, in their eyes, socialist state. They also knew how vulnerable the DDR was without the backing of the Soviet Union. Mielke belonged to this group. His successful career would have been impossible without Soviet KGB backing. According to Wolf, Mielke firmly believed that he was not only the best friend of the Soviet Union, but its representative in the SED. He had difficulties with Gorbachev's new ideas after 1985, but his basic loyalty remained.[12] Indeed, one of his objections to Honecker towards the end was that he was disturbing the necessarily close relationship of the SED to the CPSU. His colleagues in the SED leadership must have feared him to a degree because of his close Moscow connections.

SED ORGANIZATION WITHIN THE MfS

As in every other ministry in the DDR the SED was organized at every level of the Ministry for State Security. The MfS understood itself, like the KGB in the Soviet Union, as the 'shield and sword of the Party'. This defined its special relationship with the SED. At the head of the SED organization in the MfS from 1982 was Major General Horst Felber. He was also a member of the 14-strong *Kollegium* which was supposed to coordinate policy and advise Minister Mielke who was its chairman. Under Felber were four full-time SED secretaries and about 150 other full-time officials. There were many other 'honorary' functionaries. Within the HVA there was also a SED organization headed by a Major-General, Otto Ledermann. The significance of Felber and Ledermann can be gauged when one considers that many departmental heads only held the rank of colonel. For instance, the head of the NATO/EC department was Colonel Klaus Rösler, the head of liaison with the KGB was Lieutenant-Colonel A.K. Prinzipalow. On the other hand, there were 48 other officers who held the rank of *Generalmajor* and 14 others, including Mielke, with a higher rank.

Horst Felber officially worked under the direction of the Security Secretariat of the Central Committee of the SED. His main responsibilities were to ensure that the MfS faithfully, enthusiastically and creatively implemented the policies of the SED. He ensured that in every department of the Ministry the SED organization functioned smoothly. He was responsible for maintaining the morale of the members of the MfS. He did this by clarifying ideological matters, helping in the selection of the best cadre for promotion and dealing with problems of SED members in the MfS. Those hoping to get promotion would often take up honorary positions in the SED organization. Because of the secret nature of so much of the work of the MfS and the large scale and complexity of the Ministry, it could be expected that Felber was not totally in the picture. However, the lower SED organs were supposed to report to him on their activities. Many of the HVA agents outside the DDR were SED members even when they were not always citizens of the DDR. This fact would have given Felber some idea of the scale of the operations beyond the frontiers of the homeland.[13]

Within the SED the MfS had its informers. Their job was to ensure that any tendency towards ideological deviation – Trotskyism, Social Democratic tendencies, left-wing radicalism, Maoism, Reform Communism – or anti-Party groupings were nipped in the bud.

To a degree the SED control of the Stasi was very effective. All its officers looked to the Party for direction and explanations for what was happening at home and abroad. As one ex-officer put it, 'We were always totally faithful to the SED.'[14] There is no doubt that Stasi officers tended to follow their leaders blindly.[15] Only the arrival of Gorbachev in the Kremlin raised doubts and, in the end, the ideology of the SED had failed to prepare the Stasi for a peaceful revolution. As Horst Sindermann put it in 1990, 'The peaceful revolution did not fit in with our theory. We did not expect it, and it made us defenceless.'[16]

THE MfS AND THE NATIONAL DEFENCE COUNCIL

The National Defence Council of the DDR *(der Nationale Verteidigungsrat der DDR)* was established under the Defence Law of 20 September 1961. This Law was amended by a second law of 13 October 1978. A defence emergency could be declared by the Volkskammer or, in case this body was unable to meet, by the Staatsrat. In such a defence emergency the National Defence Council was responsible for the defence of the DDR. According to the Defence Law (Article 2), the Council was made up of its Chairman and at least 12 members.[17] Honecker was, of course, its Chairman. There were 16 other members in the 1980s including Willi Stoph (head of government), Horst Sindermann (President of the Volkskammer), the Central Committee secretaries and Politburo members Egon Krenz, Hermann Axen, Günter Mittag, Kurt Hager, Joachim Hermann, Werner Krolikowski (deputy head of government), Army General *(Armeegeneral)* Heinz Keßler (Minister of Defence), Army General Fritz Dickel (Minister of Interior), Army General Erich Mielke (Minister for State Security), the SED First Secretaries for Magdeburg, Cottbus and Suhl, Werner Eberlein, Werner Walde and Hans Albrecht, and Wolfgang Herger (head of the Security Department of the Central Committee). According to Sindermann[18] members had military ranks, thus he was a Major-General of the NVA, perhaps significantly, a rank below that of Mielke, Keßler and Dickel. Sindermann tells us that mock alerts involving all members of the Council were carried out once or twice a year with members wearing battle dress. The National Defence Council was responsible for policy relating to the armed forces even in normal times although formally its proposals had to be agreed by the Volkskammer.

In each of the 15 administrative regions (*Bezirke)* of the DDR there was a defence committee (*Bezirkseinsatzleitung)* which comprised the first and second secretaries of the SED, the commander of the NVA in the region, the head of the regional office of the MfS, the regional police chief, the Chairman of the regional council (parliament) and the head of the SED's regional security department. Similar committees existed at the lower administrative unit level of *Kreis.*

THE STRUCTURE OF THE MfS

Apart from the Minister himself, hardly anyone in the MfS was expected to have a detailed knowledge of its structure. The 'need to know' principle was taken very seriously and was part and parcel of the Chekist, conspiratorial traditions of the MfS. However, many Stasi members worked in more than one department during their careers and they gradually gained some insight into the shape and size of its operations. Since the demise of the MfS it has been possible get the overall picture.

Reference has been made already to Mielke's almost impregnable position as Minister in charge of the MfS, and to the **Kollegium** of 13 generals which advised him. Four of the 13 were deputy ministers. They were Mielke's 'boys' who had been with him from the early days of the MfS. They were rivals hoping to replace Mielke in the fullness of time. The most senior, *Generaloberst* Rudi Mittag (born in 1925), was a member of the Central Committee of the SED and had been Deputy Minister since 1969. *Generalleutnant* Dr Gerhard Neiber (born in 1929) had failed to reach the Central Committee, unlike the third Deputy Minister, *Generalleutnant* Dr Wolfgang Schwanitz (born in 1930) who was elected a candidate member in 1986. It was he who took over from Mielke for a few weeks in 1989 when the Stasi colossus was already disintegrating. The fourth deputy was *Generaloberst* Werner Grossmann (born in 1929) who had reached his ministerial appointment in 1986 when he replaced General Wolf as head of the HVA. Mielke seemed to have his private empire within the MfS. This was the **Arbeitsgruppe Des Ministers (AGM)** or Minister's working party. Led by *Generalmajor* Erich Rümmler, it had 700 Stasi members attached to it. It was responsible for a wide range of activities from preparing documents for the Minister's speeches, carrying out the

Minister's orders in his various sporting activities (including both football and hunting parties), to planning measures for arrest, detention and isolation. But Mielke also had his own secretariat headed by *Generalmajor* Hans Carlsohn. This office was responsible for the personal arrangements of the Minister and often for passing on his orders to other departments and to the MfS as a whole. Within the AGM there was a special group of 50 or so officers who were responsible for planning measures in case of an emergency. This was, according to one former member, a most secret group headed by General Rümmler, and before him *Generalleutnant* Otto Geisler, who dealt directly with Mielke. They had developed **'Aktion Gipfelpunkt'**, a plan to defend the SED's DDR from internal enemies in a crisis.[19]

Generalmajor Egon Ludwig was one of many department heads who reported directly to Mielke. His responsibility was the **Büro der Leitung**, in effect the central administration of the MfS. Some 823 staff were employed there in 1989. **Der Zentralmedizinische Dienst** (The Central Medical Service, ZMD) with 1,144 staff which had its own clinics, a hospital and a prison hospital was also directly under the control of Mielke. The MfS had its own university (**Hochschule des MfS**) at Potsdam-Eiche with a staff of 761. This was a matter of increasing the prestige of the Stasi, helping it to attract brighter recruits, putting its work on the same footing as the most modern police, security and intelligence services, and dispensing a degree of patronage. Its Rector, *Generalmajor* Dr Willi Opitz, was under the direct orders of Mielke. Other training was the responsibility of **Hauptabteilung Kader Und Schulung** (Main Department Cadre and Training). With its 1,077 staff its head *Generalleutnant* Dr Günter Möller reported directly to the *Armeegeneral.*

It was a matter of prestige as well as conviction that the MfS had its own arsenal. It possessed 124,593 pistols, 76,592 light machine guns, 3,611 rifles, 766 heavy machine guns, 3,537 anti-tank weapons. The **Guard Regiment 'Feliks E. Dzierzynski'** was equipped with armoured cars, anti-aircraft artillery, grenade throwers, heavy machine guns, anti-tank weapons, water cannon and helicopters. The job of this body was protection of important party and state buildings and individuals. It could also be deployed in case of internal disorders and disasters. Finally, it was often used as an honour guard and on other ceremonial duties. In 1989 it had a strength of 10,211 and was commanded by *Generalmajor* Manfred Döhring.[20] Döhring reported directly to Mielke on all his activities. Clearly there was a great fear that the elite of the DDR could be targets of physical attack for the Main Department Protection of Individuals (**Hauptabteilung Personenschutz**) was allocated 3,772 full-time operatives.[21] Its head *Generalleutnant* Günter Wolf, as one would expect, reported directly to Mielke. Wolf was in charge of the protection of the settlement in Wandlitz where Honecker and his comrades in the Politburo lived. Wolf had 650 staff employed on these duties.

Of key importance for the whole functioning of the MfS was the **Zentrale Auswertungs und Informationsgruppe** (Central Evaluation and Information Group, ZAIG), obviously, its chief, *Generalleutnant* Dr Werner Irmler, was answerable directly to the Minister. Irmler had four deputies and a total staff of 422. Its job was to evaluate anything and everything the Minister considered of interest from the Western media to the problems of the DDR health service. Its *Arbeitsgruppe 6* (working party 6) dealt with the problems of political-ideological diversion (PID), underground political activity (PUT), church problems, youth problems, problems in the cultural sector, the reaction of the population to various developments. ZAIG prepared documents to be circulated by Mielke to his colleagues in the Politburo. It was the Stasi's representative in the mass media of the DDR. It ensured that the DDR played its full part in contributing to the databank of the 'socialist states', giving details of undesirable and subversive individuals. One unlikely activity of this body was to support Mielke's sporting interests. *Abteilung XII* (Department XII) kept the archives including all-important files on individuals of interest to the Stasi. It employed 350 operatives. *Abteilung XIII* with 447 operatives was the MfS information technology centre. Both these departments were under ZAIG control.

Not a deputy but in the *Kollegium*, *Generalleutnant* Dr Günther Kratsch was responsible for **Hauptabteilung II** (Main Department II) with 1,408 operatives at his disposal. The main function of this department was counter-espionage. He reported directly to Mielke. It was a massive operation including everything from ensuring the SED's relations with the West German Communist Party (DKP) were free from infiltrators to keeping a sharp eye on the activities of the US (Abt. 3) intelligence services. Department 9 (Abt. 9) concentrated its efforts on the British and French secret services. Even the Austrian and Swiss embassies were regarded as dangerous and were covered by Abt. 12. Postal censorship was the work of Department M within the Main Department II. Over 500 operatives were engaged on this work together with numerous IM and OibE. As in other communist states, the state security organ had its own football team. Again as in other states, it was called 'Dynamo' and had its own department in the MfS, **Büro Der Zentralen Leitung Der Sportvereinigung Dynamo**. This was run by *Generalmajor* Heinz Pommer with a staff of 1,400, 180 or so of whom were members of the MfS. Pommer was directly under Mielke's supervision. Finally, and importantly, the **Abteilung Finanzen** (Finance Department) with its 150 or so employees was directly answerable to Mielke.

One other institution that General Mielke had a direct interest in was the **Juristische Hochschule des MfS**, (**JHS**), the Ministry's own university in Potsdam Eiche. Although its origins went back to 1951, it was accorded its status as a university in 1965 and in June 1968 it received its full and final status in that it was given the right, by the Minister of Higher Education, to award doctorates. The same minister also formally appointed its academic staff.[22] After December 1985 its Rector was *Majorgeneral* Professor Dr Willi Opitz. The Rector had two deputies, both colonels in rank. It was divided into two areas, one per deputy, and four 'sections', one of these, *Sektion A*, was in fact the school of the HVA based in Gosen, Fürstenwalde. In the 1970s there was a personel of 545 at the JHS of whom about 150 were regarded as academic staff.[23] The bulk of the students were serving members of the MfS though there were a few from allied security services such as the Cuban, for instance. The normal student was expected to study for four years full-time after which he/she would graduate as a *Diplomjurist* (roughly a Bachelor of Law). It was also possible to achieve the same qualification by 'distance learning' and there were various lesser qualifications which could be gained as well as research leading to a doctorate. No final figures can be given for the total number of graduates but it can be assumed that several thousand MfS members graduated as *Diplomjurist.* The JHS was the vehicle for making the MfS a more professional service which would appeal to the better educated, and a means of patronage. High-ranking officers could have their egos massaged by doctorates based on their practical experiences and probably written up by subordinates.

The four deputy ministers of state security had their own territories. Mittag's largest department, **Verwaltung Rückwärtige Dienste (VRD)** employed 3,733 and provided the MfS with a wide range of domestic and economic services – retail stores, housing, holidays, hairdressing, dry cleaning, office equipment, printing, kindergarten, weapons and much more. The MfS attempted to ensure that its employees lived in a virtually closed community. Logically. Mittag was also involved in **KoKo.** His **Arbeitsgruppe Bereich Kommerzielle Koordinierung** employing 106 staff was responsible for protecting the commercial empire of Schalck-Golodkowski who was himself a colonel of the MfS. Mittag was also responsible for protecting state secrets. For this task his **Zentrale Arbeitsgruppe Geheimnisschutz** had a relatively modest staff of 55 members. Mittag's most politically important department was **Hauptabteilung XX** with 400 operatives. Its head was *Generalleutnant* Paul Kienberg and its mission was to prevent, discover and fight 'political-ideological diversion' (PID) and 'political underground activity' (PUT).

Neiber's empire included the **HA I** (Main Department I), one of the largest departments, in terms of those employed. This was led by *Generalleutnant*

Manfred Dietze in Berlin-Treptow. Dietze had 2,457 operatives at his disposal thus making his department the largest in Neiber's domain. Dietze's mission was to protect the armed services of the DDR from West intelligence intrusions and to gather intelligence on the Bundeswehr, the West German and Bavarian frontier forces, the Federal Customs Service and so on. Also part of Neiber's domain was **HA VI** also located in Treptow. *Generalmajor* Heinz Fiedler's 2,150 operatives were concerned with seeing to it that only the 'right' people got into the DDR, and only the 'right' people left it. Their job was to examine all the available information on those entering and leaving the DDR. They were also responsible for what they termed 'political tourism', that is to ensure that official visitors were well-protected from 'negative' individuals and experiences. Obviously they must have been seen to be failing in the second half of the 1980s and especially in 1989 as DDR citizens left for 'holidays' in Czechoslovakia and Hungary not to return. **HA VII** was run by *Generalmajor* Dr Jochen Büchner who was also directly responsible to Neiber. This 364-strong Main Department organized the work of the MfS inside the Ministry of Interior. It was to 'secure' all the elements controlled by the MdI protecting them from hostile infiltration and ensure that the two ministries marched in step. Neiber's writ also ran in **HA XXII** which with 540 staff was responsible for countering both right- and left-wing extremism and terrorism. Its chief was *Oberst* Dr Horst Franz. A sub-department of this Main Department was given the task of training cadre from the 'young national states', usually Third World states friendly to the DDR. The Central Coordination Gruppe (**Zentrale Koordinierungsgruppe** or **ZKG**) also reported directly to Neiber. *Generalmajor* Gerhard Niebling's 190 staff were mainly concerned with those who wished to emigrate from the DDR to the West. Finally, from the summer of 1989 Neiber had control of Working Party XVII (**Arbeitsgruppe XVII**). This body ran the offices of the DDR in West Berlin which handled visa applications for West Berliners wishing to visit the DDR.

In charge of **HA III** (3,000 operatives) located in Berlin-Köpenick, the Operative Technical Sector (**OTS** with 1,080 operatives) at Berlin-Hohenschönhausen and **Abteilung Nachrichten** (Department Intelligence, over 1,500 operatives) in Berlin-Lichtenberg Schwantiz was very much at the modern end of security and intelligence, controlling all electronic intelligence-gathering and counter-intelligence, and all the MfS technology. *Generalmajor* Dr Horst Männchen was directly responsible to him as head of HA III which sought to intercept all NATO, West German and West European communications as well as all those within the DDR itself.

Deputy Minister Grossmann led what could be regarded as the glamorous side of the MfS, **HVA**, which until 1986 had been the fiefdom of Markus

Wolf. The work of this Main Department's 4,126 operatives is discussed in separate chapters.

AN ARMY OF OFFICERS

It is not much of an exaggeration to call Mielke's 100,000 an army of officers. Out of 3,668 full-time MfS employees in *Bezirk* Dresden, 2,422 were officers holding the rank of lieutenant or above, and only 73 were below the rank of sergeant.[24] All, including kitchen assistants, typists, waitresses and drivers had a rank. Eberhard Ney (born 1953), worked as a photographer having joined the MfS in November 1975. He had achieved the rank of *Oberleutnant* (Ist Lieutenant in US). Sigrid Petau (born in 1941) had joined the MfS in March 1983. By 1989 she had reached the rank of *Stabsfeldwebel* or roughly sergeant, a relatively high rank for a kitchen helper and waitress. Simone Niegel (born in 1962), a typist, had advanced to *Oberfeldwebel* (roughly senior sergeant) by 1989 having been recruited in 1981. Angelika Riedel (born in 1958) had placed herself at Mielke's disposal in the same year as Niegel and had reached the rank of *Stabsfeldwebel* working as a waitress for the MfS. Veronika Rost and Eveline Rost (née Schaarschmidt), both born in 1954, recruited respectively in 1981 and 1982, both working as cleaners, had been promoted to *Oberfeldwebel* by 1989. The situation was no different in the other 14 *Bezirke*. The State Security Service of the DDR was quite consciously built up as an army of officers commanded by *Armeegeneral* Erich Mielke. His was the highest military rank in the DDR, only the Minister of Defence and Interior equalling him in this respect. For Mielke there were several advantages in all MfS employees holding military ranks. Firstly, it emphazised the seriousness of this employment. Secondly it made it easier to enforce military discipline. Thirdly, all employees were clear on their place in the hierarchy. Fourthly, everyone had a uniform which they could wear on appropriate occasions thus helping in the process of integration and the forming of a common consciousness. Finally, the ranks gave the Stasi officers higher ranks than they would have gained in the armed forces, police or in normal civilian occupations. All of this encouraged them to feel they were part of an élite.

WHO WERE THE STASI?

As we saw in an earlier chapter, the number of full-time employees of the MfS rose from 601 in 1949 to 19,803 by 1962.[25] Of these 48.1 per cent would have been too young to have served a political cause before 1945, being 30 years old or younger in 1962. Of the others, a further 19.6 per cent were between 31 and 35 years old. This means they would have been between 14 and 18 in 1945 and many could have served in the Hitlerite armed forces in the last phase of the war. Only 16.5 per cent of the 7,378 MfS personnel in the Berlin HQ were women. Surprisingly, there were more women in the older age groups than in the younger ones.[26] This could mean that the MfS had attempted to recruit more women in routine secretarial and administrative posts in the early years as they would have been less likely to have been active Nazis than the men in the same age groups. Certainly, in 1962, women were mainly deployed in the secretarial, administrative, medical and postal censorship services.[27]

Only 6.4 per cent of the 1962 MfS employees claimed membership of the KPD before 1945, 4.2 per cent the communist youth movement (KJVD) and 0.7 per cent the SPD.[28] Whichever way one looks at the limited statistics available, it appears inevitable that many of the early Stasi members were males who had served in the German armed forces in the Second World War. They had been persuaded by a variety of means, including better rations and accommodation, to enlist in the Soviet-run anti-fascist schools for prisoners-of-war, and then been asked to join the new police force in the Soviet Zone of Germany. Hans Modrow, who was a convinced supporter of the Third Reich when he was captured by the Red Army in 1945 aged 17, made this transition. He was asked to join the People's Police but was rejected because his parents had gone to live in West Germany.[29] Even former members of the SS were recruited for the People's Police. Many of those recruited into the Stasi up to this period were poached from the People's Police. On the whole, they were relatively undereducated. Of the total personnel in 1962, 84.2 per cent had finished their education in the *Volksschule*, the ordinary secondary school attended by most Germans.[30] Only 1.9 per cent were university graduates. By 1962 the Stasi was 'the sword and shield of the Party'. Over 92 per cent of its members were members of the SED. Most of those who were not, were either very young or in routine administrative, medical or similar areas.

Unfortunately, there are no comprehensive statistics on the MfS personnel in 1989. But a number of points can be made. Firstly, the percentage of women was still only 19 (in 1986).[31] Secondly, more graduates had been recruited. This had been necessary as secret police work had become more technically oriented, and because the Stasi was involved much more beyond the frontiers of the DDR. It was also a sign of the maturity of DDR society. Espionage had also become directed much more at foreign technology, both military and civilian. Specialist agents were needed who had the qualifications necessary to enable them to infiltrate Western institutions and who could sort out the wood from the trees in the scientific and technical jungle in which they operated. Werner Stiller explained[32] how he was recruited as a student of physics at Leipzig University to work as an informer in December 1970. On 1 August 1972 he took up service at the MfS headquarters on the Magdalenen Strasse in East Berlin as a full-time member of the State Security Service with the rank of lieutenant.[33] His was a typical case in the 1970s and 1980s.

MfS AND THE POLICE

Unlike the Minister for Defence and the Minister for State Security, the Minister of Interior of the DDR was not a member of the Politburo, he was only a member of the Central Committee. As mentioned above, he did enjoy the same military rank as them. *Armeegeneral* Friedrich Dickel was Minister of Interior from November 1963. Previously he had been Deputy Minister for National Defence and was an officer of the police and then of the armed services. He had joined the KPD in 1931 and was a veteran of the Spanish Civil War. His military background emphasizes the point that the SED regarded the police as a vital organ of state security to be centrally directed and organized on quasi-military lines. Publications stressed the 'military discipline' of the German People's Police (DVP). The DVP had a military command structure. At the lower levels, the ranks were traditional police titles like *Wachtmeister* and *Oberwachtmeister*, the officers had military titles like *Leutnant, Hauptmann, Major* and so on.

As head of the Ministry of Interior (MdI) Dickel was named Chief of the DVP but he was also responsible for the fire brigade, civil defence and the prison service. On the military side, the MdI had at its disposal 18,000 members belonging to the paramilitary *VP-Bereitschaften.* There were 21 battalions of these 'ever-readies', one in each of 14 DDR administrative regions, two in Leipzig, Halle, Magdeburg and Potsdam and three in East Berlin. Service in them was regarded as normal compulsory national service and members were given normal military training as well as police training. Like the Guard Regiment of the MfS, they were equipped with a variety of military weapons. From 1970 they were regarded as part of the armed forces, though remaining under MdI control, and took part in military exercises with the NVA. In addition, the Main Department of the Transport Police (*Hauptabteilung Transportpolizei*), which had the task of protecting the railways from attack, had a force of 8,500 armed with an assortment of infantry weapons including heavy machine guns and anti-tank weapons. This body was divided into units 150 strong located in key rail centres.[34] There were 15,000 policemen who were factory guards, *Betriebsschutz*. They too received military training and were responsible for training the 'voluntary' fighting groups (*Kampfgruppen*) organized in every major industrial and commercial undertaking. Their weapons were similar to those of the *Bereitschaften*.

The normal police of the DDR comprised the *Schutzpolizei*, these were the ordinary police on the beat, the traffic police, the criminal police, who investigated serious crimes when the Stasi were not formally involved, and the department responsible for identity cards, passports and registration of residents, a legal requirement and a traditional feature of German life. The strength of the ordinary police was about 73,000 men and women.[35]

Even these 'normal' police were subjected to a 'military atmosphere' in training and an American observer who interviewed policemen, reported that interviewees often indicated that their training 'had been harrowing both in the physical conditions and in the psychological pressure to conform and obey'.[36] As a matter of course the police were given ideological training which stressed the leading role of the SED, and the need to cooperate with the other defence bodies such as the MfS, NVA and the Soviet armed forces. Given the ideology, structure, training and tasks of the police most members of the force would regard it as natural that they worked closely with their colleagues from the MfS. The only hindrance would be professional rivalry.

As we saw above, it was the job of HA VII of the MfS to see to it that the police and the Stasi acted together when and where the Stasi thought it necessary. The cooperation between the MdI and the MfS took the form of the MdI extending facilities to Stasi colleagues. Members of the Stasi were equipped with IDs and uniforms of police officials on occasions when they did not wish to reveal their true identities. The departments of internal affairs of the regional or town councils, units of the MdI, were put at the disposal of the Stasi. Meetings were arranged in these departments with members of the churches, those wishing to emigrate or with other individuals of interest to the MfS, at which it was not clear to the interviewees that the interviewers were Stasi officers.[37]

The *Arbeitsgebiet I* (area of operations I) known also as KI of the Criminal Police was of particular interest to the MfS. KI had a strength of 2,300 of whom approximately 1,500 worked with informers. It was the only department which was permitted to work through informers.[38] These were known as *Inoffizielle Kriminalpolizeilichen Mitarbeiter* (IKM, unofficial collaborators with the Criminal Police). Normally they had to be at least 18 years old, have a positive attitude to the DDR, be ready to sign an undertaking to work sincerely with the police and be prepared to keep their work secret. It was not permitted to recruit full-time functionaries of the SED.[39] These 'collaborators' were often individuals with a record of crime and were known as IKMR. Taken together, there were over 15,000 informers working for KI in 1985.[40] The sub-departments of KI covered economic crimes, serious crimes, the frontier, youth, religious groups (excluding the Catholic and Evangelical churches and Jehovah's Witnesses), information and evaluation.[41] In addition, there was the highly secret 1/U unit which was concerned exclusively with clandestine observation. All its members (350–400 in 1989) worked under deep cover so that other members of the police did not know who they were. The 1/U unit worked in support of the activities of the KI. The MfS recruited officers of KI to its own ranks as 'Officers on special duty' (*Offiziere im besonderen Einsatz, OibE).* Already at the end of the 1960s all key positions in KI were in the hands of such OibE.[42] By the 1980s, however, the MfS was having difficulties with KI. Its officers were increasingly breaking the rules. Some were not reporting private contacts they had with individuals in the West. Some were exploiting IKMR for their own enrichment. Others were guilty of misusing official property and money for their own purposes. Age was also taking its toll of the officers in KI.[43]

THE MfS AND THE ARMED FORCES

'Bonapartism' was a traditional fear of communist regimes. There was always the fear that top generals would attempt to stage a coup. The execution of thousands of Soviet officers in the 1930s was partly a result of this fear. In Hungary in 1956 and Czechoslovakia in 1968, the armed forces had sided with the (legal) reform elements in their respective communist parties. Even though most officers of the DDR armed forces were SED members, many were soldiers first and party members second. They were more interested in 'the military life' than in politics. There was also the danger in the German case of nationally-inclined officers seeking to link up with their colleagues in the West German Bundeswehr. Clearly there was a great need for vigilance to ensure that the NVA remained subservient to the leaders of the SED. This was achieved by the SED organization within the NVA but also through IM and OibE at all levels of the armed forces. The MfS expected to have collaborators in every unit of any size of the army, navy and air force of the DDR. All this internal security failed to protect the armed forces from the infection from the streets towards the end of 1989. Increasingly ordinary soldiers failed to carry out the orders of their superiors. Their officers, whether MfS or not, could do nothing.

STASI DISCIPLINE

Erich Mielke prided himself on the Chekist discipline of the MfS. His service was based on hierarchy and its members had been educated to a spirit of unconditional obedience (*unbedingte Gehorsamkeit*). Those who failed in their duty could expect the worst. Given the quasi-religious, self-righteousness of the SED, deserters and traitors could expect little mercy. This was the message Mielke wanted to get across to his subordinates. Between 1950 and 1988 484 cases of Stasi desertions from East to West have been recorded. Many of them occurred before the building of the Berlin Wall in August 1961. The MfS tried hard to locate the deserters and either get them back, if necessary by kidnapping, or liquidate them. So far, 120 cases have come to light of deserters being apprehended in the West and taken back to the DDR. Up to 1995, eleven cases have come to light of MfS deserters being executed in the DDR, seven of them had been caught in the West. Among those executed were Egon Glombik, head of the MfS in Spremberg, who was accused of having contact with the West German BND. He was sentenced to death on 11 July 1975 and executed in Leipzig by shooting eight days later. Major Gert Trebeljahr, leader of an active group of the Stasi in Potsdam, was executed on 10 December 1979, after a failed attempt to flee to the West. Captain Dr Werner Teske of the HVA, had planned to escape and then called it off. Under suspicion he was arrested on 11 September 1980 and on 11 June 1981 sentenced to death.[44] The 'modern', 'humanistic', 'socialist' DDR retained the capital punishment until 1987, by which time no other state in Western Europe invoked this penalty.

Mielke's sprawling empire was weakened by rivalries, by the overlap between the departments, by its inability to cope with the ever growing 'information' from its many sources. In 1989 alone there were some 500 situation reports each of 60 pages in length about the internal situation in the DDR. At the end they were not taken seriously by the SED leaders. [45] The clash between the generations, between the old ideologues and the young security and intelligence experts also weakened it. When it was already too late, younger members of the HVA demonstrated after work in the yard of the Normannenstraße HQ, demanding an end of emphasis on ideology and more on professionalism, and an end of the struggle against the opposition in the DDR.[46]

4 The MfS as an Internal Security Organ

The leaders of the SED, first Ulbricht, then Honecker, and their colleagues, felt they needed more people employed on state security than did Heinrich Himmler to protect Hitler's Third Reich.[1] It has been estimated that proportionate to population, the density of the informer network in the DDR was seven times that of Hitler's Germany, 1933–45.[2] The number of full-time employees of the MfS was around 100,000 by the time the SED started to lose control of the DDR in 1989. Their numbers had grown steadily: 52,700 in 1973; 59,500 in 1975; 75,000 in 1980; 81,500 in 1981.[3] The actual numbers varied in the 15 administrative districts (*Bezirke)* of the DDR depending on population size, perceived security problems and geographical location. Karl-Marx-Stadt (Chemnitz) claimed the doubtful honour of having the largest number of Stasi full-timers working within its boundaries. Mielke's 3,827 officers in Karl-Marx-Stadt are explained by the fact that it bordered on West Germany and Czechoslovakia, was used as a recreation area by the SED's top brass, and was home of Wismut uranium mining company.[4] With 1,817,500 inhabitants in 1989[5] it also had the largest population. The Stasi presence worked out at about 21 per 10,000 of population or 1 full-time MfS operative per 500 of population. In Rostock, with a population of 900,000 there were 3,000 full-time MfS employees[6] or 1 per 300 inhabitants. Nationally, the 100,000 full-time employees represented 1 per 165 inhabitants in 1989. It is interesting that in the DDR, whose official slogan was 'Everything for the People', the official statistics claimed there was 1 medical practitioner per 400 in 1988.[7] The effective number of practitioners was probably considerably lower. But even if we accept the official figure, it is clear that Honecker and his comrades considered state security a far higher priority than health care. Of course, the Stasi full-timers were not alone. They were assisted by a considerable army of informers known as IM (*Inoffizielle Mitarbeiter*: see below).

The growth in the IM numbers in the 1970s and beyond was the result of the change in tactics and strategy of the SED leadership. The brutal physical repression, including torture and executions, of the 1950s, was put aside for a more selective use of force and more refined exercise of power. In this the SED was following the CPSU which under the leadership of first Khrushchev and then Brezhnev, wanted to present a more civilized face to the outside world. Given its geographical position, the difficulties of secrecy in a divided land, its fight for formal recognition, and the millions of West German visitors following its agreements with the Federal Republic, the DDR was under even greater pressure to mend its ways. Informers were seen as an excellent way of preventing trouble before it started and thus avoiding the need for unpleasantness. Many more informers would be needed, it was concluded, and their image needed polishing up.

WHO WERE THE INFORMERS?

In 1968 the MfS changed its classification of its informers ceasing to refer to them as *Geheime Informatoren* (GI or secret informants) referring to them instead as *Inoffizielle Mitarbeiter* (IM or unofficial colleages, collaborators or cooperators). The reason was that Mielke wanted to expand and upgrade this service and to do so felt it necessary to get away from any feeling that informing was 'not nice'.

Most people recoil at the thought of working as informers. They cannot conceive of doing such work themselves, nor can they contemplate members of their families or their friends being engaged in such operations. In Western democratic societies they are unlikely to be asked. However, most people would wish to support the forces of 'law and order' in their societies, and most would agree terrorism has to be countered. Most would accept that undercover operations are necessary to prevent the loss of innocent lives. The truth is, police work, including informing, becomes more acceptable, if it is regarded in the dominant culture as a respectable and responsible activity. Those brought up in the DDR were schooled in the idea that their state was a peace-loving state which would never wage aggressive war, an anti-imperialist and anti-racist state, a state in which everyone had the right to work, welfare and a place to live. There were powerful forces in the West, it was claimed, who wanted to destroy the peaceful DDR and the 'Socialist Camp' as a whole and re-introduce the exploitive capitalist system which had produced the two world wars. There were also those within the DDR who were naive enough to be led astray by Western propaganda, in the DDR, by West German radio and television. There were the charming, cunning, Western agents posing as tourists, academics, journalists, businessmen or disinterested champions of human rights. There were also the mixed-up ultra-left idealists who unwittingly did the work of the imperialists by seeking to 'reform' or 'improve' the DDR. For anyone brought up in a household in which both parents were convinced communists, members of the SED – as 2.3 million out of an adult population of approximately 12 million were – it would be difficult to resist the call to arms, if invited by the MfS to do so. Moreover, such work, either as a full-time or part-time operative, carried no risk, and brought with it considerable career advantages. In addition, for those working undercover, there is always the thrill of secret knowledge. You can feel superior to ordinary mortals who appear naive to you, because you know how the real, secret, world operates. You know who really wields the power in society. Thus the MfS could recruit idealists, the adventurous, the ambitious, the ruthless. It could also gather to itself many less willing informers. There were those who had been caught infringing the law and who accepted the 'help' of the Stasi to get them out of trouble. There were members of the opposition who were faced with the alternative of long years of imprisonment or honourable work for peace as Stasi informers.[8] Some were flattered to be asked to join the ruling class by its representatives who could be charming and kind, just as others could be brutal. One of the sad things about the democratic transformation of the DDR in 1989–90 was being forced to recognize that some of the opposition heroes were no heroes at all but instruments of the MfS. There was Ibrahim Böhme, one of the founding fathers of the Social Democratic Party in the DDR who worked for the Stasi as 'Maximillian', there was Wolfgang Schur, lawyer and defender of dissidents, and a founder of *Demokratischer Aufbruch* (Democratic Awakening), there was the dissident writer Sascha Anderson, and there were many, many others. There were also remarkable cases of those who had been recruited as IMs to infiltrate the opposition but who, against all expectations, genuinely joined the opposition. Wolfgang Templin was one of this small number. Templin had been born in Jena in 1948 in what was still the Soviet Zone of Germany. He grew up in the DDR and accepted its ideology, becoming a member of all the right organizations: the FDJ, GST, the trade union and the DSF (Society for German–Soviet Friendship). He not only took up membership, he became an activist. He applied for membership of the SED as well. He was able to study and chose philosophy, meaning Marxist-Leninist philosophy, at the Humboldt University in Berlin. By November 1972 he had been 'talent spotted' by the MfS whose representative spoke in glowing terms about him as 'an honourable, sincere and friendly person', who stood firmly behind the SED's *Weltanschauung*. Templin had been contacted first in September 1971 and had immediately declared his readiness to help. Up to May 1975 the Stasi were still able to write in very positive terms about him. By 1979, however, he had become an ultra-leftist critic of the SED and had exposed his early activity to his friends in his opposition cricle. Not surprisingly the MfS felt bitter and set to work to destroy him politically, morally and to ruin his career. By 1986 we find him surrounded by four informers claiming to be part of the opposition. His every move was monitored.[9]

Unfortunately there is no evidence which gives us a sociology of the informers throughout the DDR. It is safe to say that they came from all social and occupational groups, both sexes, and all ages. There is some evidence from Karl-Marx-Stadt from the first half of 1986. This reveals that 63 per cent of the IM were employed in the economy, above all in the industrial sector. One in three was a member of the SED and nearly half were aged between 27 and 40. Of the 395 recruited between January and June 1986 in Karl-Marx-Stadt 56 (15.2 per cent) were women. In Rostock, of those recruited in 1989 about 10 per cent were women. The Gauck-Behörde researchers believe IM activity was largely a male domain.[10]

HOW MANY INFORMERS?

It was from 1968 onwards that there was a massive expansion of the number of IM. Stasi officers had recruitment targets which they were supposed to meet. This system continued until the abolition of the MfS in 1989. Although we do not have a comprehensive picture of the build up of the IM network over time and throughout the DDR, some interesting statistics have been found. The table below for instance gives us the number of inhabitants per IM in the 15 administrative districts (*Bezirke*) of the DDR during its mature period in the years 1985 and 1986:

Below average number per IM			*Above average number per IM*		
Year	*1986*	*1985*		*1986*	*1985*
Cottbus	80	79	Dresden	128	128
Schwerin	94	96	Karl-Marx-Stadt	134	141
Rostock	100	101	Gera	125	125
Frankfurt/Oder	95	94	Erfurt	149	159
Suhl	99	95	Leipzig	141	143
Neubrandenburg	109	106	Berlin	148	146
Magdeburg	95	95	Halle	159	156
Potsdam	117	116			
DDR average	120	120			

Source: *BF informiert IM-Statistik 1985–1989 3/1993*, p.26

The figures above do not of course tell us why there were relatively more IM in Cottbus than in Magdeburg, Potsdam or Berlin. Was it due to the zealousness of the Stasi officers in that district or were there other factors involved? Cottbus was a frontier district with Poland, but so were Frankfurt/Oder and Dresden. Gera with one of the lowest IM networks relative to population was in a more sensitive Western frontier zone. The figures are for all the Stasi IM but not for those of the People's Police. It is not clear whether they include certain other Stasi operatives who worked undercover such as the so-called *Offizier im besonderen Einsatz* (OibE, officers on special duties). These were individuals in key positions in ministries, the economy, the armed forces, the education system and so on. Their remuneration and conditions were in line with those of other Stasi officers. If in their jobs they earned less than their Stasi rank, the difference was made up by the MfS.

It has proved impossible to deliver a final estimate of the number of DDR citizens involved as IM. Statistics have been found revealing the numbers in several of districts of the DDR for various periods. In Rostock, the total for 1975 was 11,508, falling to 9,436 in 1985 and 9,194 in 1989. In Frankfurt/Oder there were 7,725 in 1985 falling to 6,451 in 1989. For the whole of the DDR it is thought that from January 1985 to October 1989 about 260,000 individuals were active as IM. This figure excludes those working for the HVA, the People's Police and one or two other categories. For the whole period of the DDR it has been estimated that between one and two million citizens worked at one time or another as IM for the MfS.[11]

FOREIGNERS TARGETED

Foreigners were a favourite target for the Stasi as they were in other 'socialist' states. Western visitors to the DDR, especially West Germans, who were treated as foreigners according to DDR law, were of particular interest. They were very vulnerable. They needed a visa, they were often placed in hotels reserved for Western visitors, usually the Interhotel chain. In the more modern of them hidden television cameras were installed to observe the guests in their rooms. Receptionists, waiters, maids and other staff were required to spy on hotel guests and report to MfS officers. Groups and individuals who went either as ordinary tourists or official guests, were carefully observed and reported on by their guides. Prostitutes and other women dependent on the Stasi were introduced into the bars, night clubs and restaurants frequented by foreigners to ensnare them. In restaurants where strangers were frequently put together on one table one could never be sure whether the person opposite was an innocent diner or an agent of the MfS. Provocateurs offered tourists local currency at advantageous, black market rates of exchange. Sometimes East Germans were encouraged to ask for illegal assistance of one kind or another such as medicines, magazines and books needed for study or spare parts for scarce consumer goods. If an entirely respectable-looking woman engaged you in conversation and asked you to exchange a small amount of D-mark needed by her to buy some medicine for her sick baby, you could not know whether she was speaking the truth, or merely a Stasi agent.[12] Those who succumbed to temptation out of greed or sentiment, could then be blackmailed by the Stasi into working for them on their return to the West.

As was only to be expected, Western journalists and academics were regarded with the greatest of suspicion by the SED and the Stasi. A typical case which illustrates this suspicion is that of Peter Johnson who for many years served as the Reuters and BBC correspondent in the Soviet Union and Germany. As the Stasi knew, according to a report of December 1981, he had been expelled from the Soviet Union in February 1964, for his 'coarse vilification of the life of the Soviet people, and the home and foreign policy of the USSR'. In 1965/66 he took over as head of the West Berlin office of the BBC. He 'regularly broadcast slanders against the DDR, particularly against leading functionaries of the SED and the policies of the Party'. In connection with 'the events in the Czechoslovak Socialist Republic in August 1968' he reported in 'false and hateful form about the mood of the DDR population'. Johnson later recovered over 300 pages of Stasi reports on him stretching back to the 1960s. According to a Stasi report in December 1981, the IM 'Henry', 'Wolfgang' and 'Felicitas' were involved with 'Kent' as the MfS called Johnson. He did not know at the time of their MfS allegiance. The same report listed his contacts with the writers Rolf Schneider, Günter de Bruyn and Stefan Heym. Interestingly, Lieutenant Töpelt of HA II/13 (responsible for Western journalists) who wrote the report, admitted that it was probable that the MfS had not uncovered all 'Kent's' private contacts. On 29 March 1982, the same department initiated a programme of renewed investigation of the 'Kent' case which would be agreed with General Andrekowitsch of HA XVIII/2, General Heimann of HVA II/6 and General Reinhard of Abt. II/3 (among others). This was to be a well-planned operation!

Visiting Western academics received the same treatment as journalists from the MfS. Their hosts were expected to send detailed reports to the head of security at the university which were then passed on to the Stasi. What is more surprising is the way the Stasi sought information on British academics in the UK. In the case of David Childs reports were found, starting in 1983, of his guest lectures at the universities of Dundee, Bradford and Loughborough and his other academic activities and publications. On 20 March 1985 a report marked 'strictly secret' was circulated by HV XX about DDR researchers in Britain listing Childs, Ian Wallace and Martin McCauley as the field leaders. It was compiled by a 'leading FRG academic' (*Wissenschaftler*). Although a report of HV A III (legal residencies) on 6 December 1983 claimed to have a 'reliable source in the operational area'. The Stasi reports contained any number of factual errors. One important error was the allegation that Childs had close contact with the European Nuclear Disarmament Group, another was that he was involved with the British secret service, a third was that he associated with the East German dissidents Bärbel Bohley and Vera Wollenberger. In all three cases he had had no contact whatsoever! This nine-page gem (dated 11 April 1988) was the work of *Generalmajor* Schütt of HV A, Department IX (counter-intelligence) who in turn was relying on reports from 'METRO'. It was sent to the head of HV XX Comrade Major General Kienberg whose remit was the security of the state apparatus and the struggle against extremist forces, dissidents and ideological diversion. It even got Childs' place of employment wrong, placing him in Dundee rather than Nottingham! Childs' personal data found its way onto SOUD, the KGB's central computer in Moscow.

The evidence from Childs' file would seem to indicate that the MfS recruited agents among British academics. Independently, *Times* journalist Jamie Dettmer, believed, in 1993, 'The Stasi's most highly prized agent, code-named "Armin" was a university historian with close contacts in the Conservative government.' The British security service (MI 5) 'is also thought to be trying to discover the identity of agents codenamed "Sender", an academic who lives or worked in Leeds, and "Diana", a lecturer recruited while visiting Leipzig'. The Stasi attempted unsuccessfully to recruit Dettmer.

ESCAPES AND DEFECTIONS

West Germans offered the MfS the greatest opportunity, but also the greatest challenge. After the Federal Republic gave the DDR de facto recognition, in 1972, there was a great surge of tourists from West to East. In 1988 there were 5.5 million visits by West Germans, including West Berliners, to the DDR. The SED allowed DDR pensioners to visit relatives in the West providing their relatives would finance their stay. In 1988 3.7 million pensioners travelled West.[13] In addition, East Germans below pensionable age could make trips to the West on 'urgent family business'. This term covered visits to close relatives who were getting married, or were seriously or terminally ill. Funerals of a family member were also reasons recognized as urgent family business. Usually only one member of the family could go. A husband and wife under pensionable age would not be allowed to go, only the person directly related. The fear was if a couple went they would not return. Many categories were in any case excluded as 'holders of secrets'. Decisions were often arbitrary and permission to travel often came too late. Under pressure from both within the DDR and from the West, the number of those visiting the West rose to 1.5 million by 1988. The bulk of them returned to the DDR. Nevertheless, Mielke was worried about the increasing tendency of those going to the West to defect.[14] In the first half of 1989 4,277 citizens of the DDR did not return from private visits compared with 2,754 in the same period in 1988. In addition, 86 did not return from journeys on official business (68 in 1988), 102 tourists defected (44 in 1988) and 20 seafarers (19 in 1988) went missing. Individuals were still attempting to escape over the frontier by land, air or water. According to Mielke, 81 succeeded in the first six months of 1989 (63 in 1988) in illegal frontier crossings to the West, 203 (51 in 1988) crossed illegally into other socialist states and in a further 80 cases (51 in 1988) the way of escape was not known. These figures say nothing of course about the human drama behind them, the lengths people were prepared to go to in order to escape, the dangers they were prepared to face, including death.

In the early years of the Berlin Wall tunnels were used to escape, attempts were made to crash through the barriers with specially reinforced trucks, attempts were made using secret compartments of motor vehicles. Sometimes East Germans dressed in improvised British, French or American uniforms because members of the Allied forces in uniform did not need to identify themselves to DDR border guards but only to Soviet military personnel, who were often not available. There were even occasions when East Germans posed as Soviet officers. As Stasi methods of control got ever more sophisticated would-be escapers had to take even greater risks. Spectacular methods were employed such as successful crossings in a homemade hot air balloon and a DIY miniature submarine. Two East Germans soared over the Berlin Wall on a pulley attached to a steel cable strung from the roof of a building in East Berlin and fixed to a car hidden behind a West Berlin house.[15] To the end genuine West German passports were used by East Germans assuming the identity of West Germans. In these cases the escape was made through another Warsaw Pact state such as Czechoslovakia, Hungary or Bulgaria. Among the last spectacular escapes was that of an office cleaner who, in April 1988, got out over the Berlin Wall using a makeshift ladder. Another escapee about the same time was unsuccessful.[16] In both cases shots were fired by the DDR frontier guards. Despite the walls, barbed wire, dogs (957 of them),[17] machine guns and, not least, the informers, individuals still managed to escape. The Stasi was not as all-powerful as many believed.

FORBIDDEN CONTACTS WITH BROTHERS AND SISTERS

Mielke was also concerned in the 1980s about the rising tide of people applying to 'turn their backs on Socialism', that is, to migrate to the Federal

Republic. In the first six months of 1989 27,507 citizens of working age were allowed to leave, as compared with only 6,643 in the same period in 1988. In addition, 8,977 children left (1,744) and 2,433 (1,868) pensioners. The trouble was another 125,429 had applied to leave. The General admitted that attempts to dissuade those applying were hardly ever successful.[18] The methods of persuasion normally included denunciation at their place of work, loss of employment, loss of any privileges or social ostracism. Sometimes arrest on trumped up charges followed.

Under agreements between the two states, former DDR citizens who had fled to the West were relieved of their citizenship and permitted to visit their old home towns and relatives in the East using their West German identity documents. The challenge for the MfS with millions of West German visitors was how to secure the maximum economic advantage while at the same time achieving the minimum political disadvantage by ensuring their influence on the East Germans they contacted was limited. To be sure they were forced to exchange a minimum amount of D-mark into DDR currency for each day of their stay. Some of this money was diverted into the coffers of the Stasi. Their visits were carefully monitored. In very many cases local SED members in blocks of flats were supposed to keep their eyes open for West German (and other Western) visitors, noting car registration numbers, unknown visitors, overnight stays and so on. Many East Germans were in any case forbidden to have any contacts with Westerners, even with their own brothers and sisters, fathers and mothers, aunts and uncles. Dr Hermann Pohler, now a CDU member of the Bundestag, before 1990 an agricultural scientist, has recalled how he had to meet his brother from the West secretly at the Leipzig trade fair. It was by no means a simple matter for him to attend the trade fair. The Leipzig fair was treated to full surveillance by the Stasi as it was a channel for Western intelligence because it was an occasion for which visas were relatively easy to get even in the worst years of the Cold War. Dr Pohler has also revealed how East German participants to international conferences in the DDR were forbidden to have any kind of social contact with their colleagues from the West.[19] Heidemarie Lüth, a secondary school head, SED member and now PDS member of the Bundestag, has told how she could not even go to a café to have a chat with West German communists who were on an official visit to her school as part of a study trip to the DDR.[20] When such meetings nevertheless occurred, the Stasi was often aware of them and later found ways of exploiting them and any friendships formed. The files of the West German security organs are full of cases of attempts by the MfS to recruit individuals in this way.

POSTAL AND TELEPHONE CENSORSHIP

Once in the late 1960s a foreigner rang London from an East German provincial town. It was to be expected that she would speak in English. After a few words in English she broke into Persian. Several voices then came on the line ... confusion reigned.[21] Clearly the call was being monitored by the Stasi, and probably by other intelligence agencies as well. A fundamental of the SED's Stasi regime was, *'Vertrauen ist gut, Kontrolle ist besser'* (roughly, 'Trust is fine, but surveillence is better'). The Stasi aimed to check all calls made from the DDR to any foreign state. Mielke also wanted his operatives to be in a position to listen in on all domestic calls which could be of interest to his organization. Certainly many East Germans were aware of this. The telephone system was antiquated with long waits, as long as 20 years, for a telephone being installed. If you were unexpectedly offered installation you had to suspect you were of interest to the MfS. Department 26 was responsible for telephone and other telecommunications surveillence. Other departments presented it with its targets. Karl-Marx-Stadt was divided into four areas with a total of 430 listening units each of which had three tape recorders. There was an IM unit made up of post office employees for installing listening devices in private homes. Usually phone-tapping measures were limited to between four and six weeks.[22] In Leipzig 1,000 telephones were being tapped on a daily basis.[23] Visual surveillence of Karl-Marx-Stadt's three main hotels was organized in such a way that any room could be under observation with a video camera from the adjoining room within two hours.[24]

In Leipzig the Stasi had at its disposal 120 employees to open between 1,500 to 2,000 letters daily in its headquarters in the *Runde Ecke* (Round Corner). These letters had been removed from the normal post and dispatched to the *Runde Ecke*. Those which were cleared to be sent on to their addressees, were usually copied first by operatives wearing gloves and returned to the postal service within 12 hours. Between 3 and 5 per cent did not leave the *Runde Ecke*. These included personal pleas to Honecker for help, political letters to foreign embassies, requests to Western organizations or personalities. Among those found was a hand-painted card from a 12-year-old girl to the Swedish pop group Abba. Letters containing money often did not reach their intended recipients. The Stasi in Leipzig stole DM 180,000 annually in the 1980s.[25] In Karl-Marx-Stadt it hauled in DM 6.9 million between 1986 and 1989.[26] There, 4,000 letters were opened daily by 140 operatives. In East Berlin the MfS had an entire storey in the main railway station *(Hauptbahnof)* employing 600 operatives for their mail censorship activities. Sometimes control letters were fed into the system to ensure the reliability of operatives.[27]

In some towns every letter was opened and every second telephone conversation monitored.[28]

Department M of the MfS, with over 500 operatives, was responsible for the postal censorship. With its HQ in Berlin Lichtenberg, it operated from the central postal distribution office on Friedrichstraße. Long-serving operatives looked through the mail and cast an experienced eye over envelopes and packets, their appearance and weight, the addressees and the senders. If their curiosity was aroused, the item would be handed over to someone else for interior investigation.

THE STASI AND EDUCATION

From the discussion above, it is clear that the education system of the DDR was an important and attractive target for the Stasi. On the one hand, there was fear of revisionist ideas taking root in the universities leading to dissidence and even major opposition. On the other hand, as we have seen, the MfS wished to recruit young cadre who could be moulded into dependable IM or full-time operatives. Those recruited as under-graduates or post-graduates could then go forth into all the significant professions in all the corners of the DDR. The university lecturers and professors themselves could be recruited as specialist intelligence agents for use abroad during study trips as well as for observing their colleagues and others at home and abroad. A significant proportion of academics at every university worked for the MfS. The MfS could decisively influence who studied and who did not, who registered for research, who became a university lecturer and eventually a professor – and who was rejected whatever their academic abilities. Not surprisingly, 80 per cent or more of professors were members of the SED. Many of them would have regarded it as their duty to report for the Stasi if asked. It has been estimated that at the Humboldt University in Berlin one quarter of the academic staff worked for the Stasi. The same was true of those in the administration of higher education.[29]

One of the difficult subject areas for the MfS was theology, but even in this discipline they wormed their way in. At Leipzig University in the 1950s they were able to chalk up their first successes. Academic theologians from Leipzig were able to climb the academic ladder at various universities with Stasi help. Typical of them was Professor Kurt Meier, professor of church history at Leipzig, who was an IM from 1957.[30] The task of Meier and other 'progressive' theologians was to pass on information about their colleagues, ensure that suitable students were recruited, participate in conferences in West Germany (and other Western states) to analyse church developments there, propagate the myth of religious freedom in the DDR and to attempt to influence opinion in Christian circles in the DDR towards cooperation with the SED.

In every academy, university or school there were SED and FDJ organizations which controlled the formal governing bodies. All those responsible at such institutions were expected to cooperate fully with the Stasi if and when they were called upon to do so. Usually they did. Secondary school head, Frau Lüth, remembers several occasions when Stasi officers came to get information about the private lives and standard of work of women members of her staff. One was the daughter of an Austrian communist who had settled in the DDR. The daughter had been born there. In the second case, the teacher's son had volunteered for three years' service in the Guard Regiment Felik Dzierzynski. On another occasion, Frau Lüth was surprised to discover that one of her staff was an IM. The Stasi came to examine her file. On a fourth occasion pupils' files were scrutinized with a view to estimating likely future recruitment into the MfS or the armed forces. It was part of Frau Lüth's responsibility to encourage her pupils to volunteer for the armed forces. Frau Lüth freely admitted that, given her state of mind, given the way she had been educated and indoctrinated, she could well have become an IM had she been asked. Luckily she was not.[31]

Professor Walter Friedrich, Director of the Central Institute for Youth Research in Leipzig, 1966–90, recalls there was a 20-something young man in charge of security at the Institute, to ensure that the research results, of which there were only four copies, and other materials, remained secret. Occasionally he politely warned Friedrich that particular colleagues were going a bit too far with their lectures and were causing tongues to wag. In October 1989 Friedrich spoke critically at a meeting of FDJ functionaries and later learned that his remarks had been reported by Stasi informers and had reached the Central Committee of the SED. All universities and similar bodies had their security commissioners. Such were the conditions in education in the DDR. In a way, it is remarkable that Friedrich did not seem to find it strange.[32]

THE STASI AND THE MEDICAL PROFESSION

Between 1952 and 1962 3,948 members of the medical profession defected from the DDR to West Germany. In addition, 1,495 dentists took the same course of action.[33] Despite the Wall (from August 1961) small numbers continued to escape. Medical practitioners were regarded as amongst the most politically unreliable members of the intelligentsia in the DDR. Yet their skills were indispensable for the well-being of the population. In this situation the

MfS gave much attention to the medical institutions of the DDR. According to research completed since the fall of the DDR, the MfS had recruited doctors as informers in almost all the hospitals of the DDR.[34] Yet in all, it is estimated that under 5 per cent of the medical profession in the DDR worked for the Stasi. The MfS was interested in being warned of any political opposition among the medical staff, any likely attempts to defect, and information of the same nature about patients. Some doctors who were convinced SED members were prepared to give information about colleagues in the belief that if they were allowed to defect the health service of the DDR would be weakened. Some were of course blackmailed into informing. As far as relations with their patients were concerned it appears that the bulk of doctors kept faith with their medical oath of silence. Although some cases of the misuse of pychiatric treatment in the DDR have come to light, unlike its brother organization in the Soviet Union, the MfS was unable to use pychiatric treatment on a large scale for its political ends.

COPING WITH THE OPPOSITION

Soviet-type communism prided itself on its military and police formations. Unlike the Marxists and other socialists of old it wallowed in the glory of state power, in the paraphernalia of militarism. For the Leninist-Stalinists, deception, violence, force and fraud were the normal methods of gaining power and keeping it. To a degree, they would have welcomed armed opposition. They found it more difficult to deal with opposition which was entirely peaceful. It is far easier to crush bones and break heads if the opposition uses violent means. Of course, it must be pointed out that most of those individuals in the DDR from the 1960s onwards, who were regarded by the Stasi as oppositionists, or 'enemy-negative forces', would not have so classified themselves. In this they were different from some of the Social Democrats and others who opposed the SED before 1953.

The opposition in the DDR[35] from the 1960s onwards was pacifist in nature having been influenced by the civil rights groups in the USA, by the citizens' initiative groups in West Germany, by the Greens and the anti-nuclear protestors. Many of the DDR opposition thought they wanted 'Socialism with a human face' as attempted in Czechoslovakia during the Prague Spring. They often sought limited reforms like the right to conscientious objection to military service, the right to publish independently of the official press, the right to travel, cultural freedom, an end to discrimination against Christians and so on. Even the non-socialists among them rarely thought as far as German reunification, pluralist democracy or a market economy. They started to make reference to the DDR constitution and to the international agreements on human rights ratified by the DDR. In their campaign to strangle the opposition the SED and the MfS were limited by a number of factors. The first was the difficulty of keeping any repression secret. Because their state was part of a divided nation, it was more difficult to seal it off. There were simply too many human contacts with so many people having relatives on the other side of the border. The Berlin Wall reduced these contacts after August 1961, but after the international recognition of the DDR in the early 1970s, it became ever more hard to restrict them. As the DDR became progressively more dependent on the Federal Republic economically, West Germany could put more pressure on the DDR to behave itself and show restraint in dealing with its dissidents. Another factor was the self-image of the DDR as anti-fascism realized, as the true heir of German humanism. Its leaders did not want to appear to be following in the footsteps of Hitler and Himmler. As it was, their uniforms, parades and general military culture reminded many of the Third Reich rather than the traditional German working-class movement.

The SED regime was forced to compete with West Germany in a hearts and minds campaign for the loyalty of its inhabitants. The West German electronic media could not be denied access into the great majority of DDR homes. Viewers and listeners compared, consciously or unconsciously, on a daily basis, the two German states. They compared the abundance of consumer goods in the West to the meagre supply in the East, although to a degree many East Germans remained unclear just how great was the gap in living standards until they could visit the West themselves. They not only compared the different standards of welfare, the fashions and the pop culture, but also the style of the leaders in both states, the way in which West Germans freely voiced their criticisms and complaints and their own lack of freedom to do so. The other galling thing about the Western media for the SED was that they were usually the first with the news about dramatic happenings in the 'Socialist Camp'. Of course, for the most part, the West German electronic media were aimed at the West German population, not at the East. They were often very critical of their own society. They often provided ammunition for the SED-controlled media of the East when they exposed corruption, the drugs problem, homelessness, illegal arms exports, police brutality, pollution, racism, unemployment and mounting crime. However, this served to convince some East Germans that their own media were feeble because they dared not report on the real problems of DDR society.

Against this background, the MfS was to a degree limited in its options. It became unthinkable, for instance, to use the death penalty against dissidents and in fact it was used little after the 1960s, and then not for political opposition. It was formally abolished in 1987 just before Honecker's visit to the Federal Republic in an attempt to improve the DDR's image. Capital punishment was never part of the penal code of the Federal Republic largely because of the experience of Nazism. The proclamation of amnesties was also part of the SED's public relations campaigning. Usually these were announced on the anniversary of the founding of the DDR, as in 1951, 1956, 1960, 1964, 1972, 1979 and 1987.[36] In the 1987 amnesty 24,621 prisoners were set free. The amnesties were meant to show the generosity, humanism and progressive nature of the DDR criminal justice system and indeed of the leaders of the SED. More thoughtful East Germans concluded that thousands of those released would not have been imprisoned in any Western country. Another reason for these moves was the shortage of labour even though many of the prisoners were forced to work. The type of 'crimes' committed by many of those freed are discussed below.

A considerable number of DDR citizens would have liked to migrate to the West in search of a better life. They could not do so. Often the dissidents did not want this option but were forced to take it. By such means the Stasi was able to cut off the heads of opposition groups by expelling their leaders or potential leaders to the West. They knew the West Germans could not refuse to have them. Under the law of the Federal Republic they had an automatic right to be considered citizens of West Germany. To a degree, this particular tactic of the Stasi helps to explain the relatively limited nature of opposition in the DDR. One other aspect of this which was not widely known until near the end, was that the Federal Republic bought the freedom of thousands of prisoners, year by year, from the early 1960s onwards. Much of this money was also claimed for Mielke's MfS and was even an encouragement to the Stasi to intensify its activities! Apparently this was openly stated in a speech by a deputy Minister for State Security to his colleagues in the 1980s.[37]

POLITICAL 'CRIMES'

Although the DDR constitution of 1968 was not as liberal as that of 1949, it did proclaim the usual freedoms of speech, assembly, association and so on, in Articles 27, 28 and 29 respectively. Freedom of conscience and belief were enshrined in Article 20 and religious freedom in Article 39. The secrecy of the post and telephone was 'guaranteed' under Article 31. Compared with the 1949 constitution freedom of movement had been reduced to freedom within the DDR only. The right to strike had, however, been dropped altogether, and other freedoms could only be exercised in a socialist direction.

Moreover, unlike that of 1949, the 1968 constitution proclaimed the leading role of the 'Marxist-Leninist party', meaning the SED. In turn, the SED was, according to its constitution, subject to 'democratic centralism', which meant in practice, the dictatorship of the Politburo and its General-Secretary. Despite the fine words of the constitution, therefore, there was virtually no freedom of any kind in the DDR. Freedom of assembly was non-existent. In the 1980s massive security surrounded all public events, especially May Day, Liberation Day, Republic Day and the annual demonstration to commemorate the murder of Karl Liebknecht and Rosa Luxemburg (a fierce critic of Lenin), just two of the many historical figures hijacked by the SED. Even so, in January 1988 over 200 protestors did attempt to wrest the memory of these two German revolutionaries from SED hypocrisy by joining the official demonstration with their own banners. These quoted the words of Luxemburg against Leninism, in defence of freedom of opinion. Among the protesters were the painter Bärbel Bohley and theatre designer Werner Fischer. Others, such as Wolfgang Templin and his wife Regina, were prevented by the Stasi from leaving their home. Their planned appearances were already known to the authorities through an IM.[38] At the May Day parade in the same year, five protesters were arrested.[39] On 15 January 1989, 300 demonstrators put on their own 'Liebknecht'-Luxemburg' event at which they demanded freedom of the press and freedom of assembly. There were 80 arrests.[40] These were groups of people who were not seeking the restoration of capitalism or of German unity but rather the fulfilment of the Marxist promise. But peaceful alternative demonstrations, however mild were not tolerated by the old men of the Politburo of the SED. Even critical comments in small meetings were not tolerated.

Five cases in Karl-Marx-Stadt (Chemnitz) illustrate just how little room for manoeuvre the SED and the MfS gave the people in whose interest they claimed to exercise their power. Wolfgang Butze was sentenced to two years' imprisonment for criticizing the building of the Berlin Wall and the shooting of would-be escapers on the inter-German border. Eberhard Höfel was arrested in July 1985 by the Stasi at his place of work. He had been denounced by three SED workmates for anti-state agitation and was sentenced to one year and eight months. He was released after eleven nerve-racking months in Naumburg prison. Erwin Malinowski was sentenced to two years' imprisonment for anti-state agitation after serving seven months in a Stasi remand prison. He had written a letter of protest about the treatment of his son who, after applying to leave the DDR for West Germany, had been arrested in January 1983. The son was held in prison for five months and then expelled to the Federal Republic. He had been 'bought free' by the West Germans. All the victims in these cases reported they had been treated in a degrading manner, including beatings, by their Stasi interrogators. The fifth case was that of Josef Kniefel who in 1975 was foolish enough to attack Stalin's crimes against humanity and the part played by the SED and the block parties in this. He served ten months in prison in appalling conditions for his outburst made at a factory meeting. In March 1980 he wished to protest against the Soviet invasion of Afghanistan by blowing up the Soviet tank monument in Karl-Marx-Stadt. He was then sentenced to life imprisonment. He suffered torture and other degrading treatment in Bautzen until West German protests and money secured his release in July 1987. He was expelled to the Federal Republic.[41]

Fearing for its image, the DDR attempted, where possible, to identify and deal with potential opposition before it reached an advanced stage. This tactic is illustrated by the story of three medical friends who attempted to form an environmental group after fruitless efforts petitioning various authorities to take action against industrial air pollution. They did so after they realized that their children's illnesses were caused by the discharge of unfiltered pollutants from nearby factory chimneys. They tried to stay within the law and began to hold regular monthly meetings at a local church hall. The MfS regarded this as underground political activity but found it difficult to prosecute them. It claimed, these 'hostile-negative forces' knew how 'to remain below the threshold of prosecution and to make intervention' by the MfS more difficult, and 'By abusing the socialist restructuring in the USSR, they are trying increasingly to use the public as a cover to make themselves "immune" to measures by the security authorities … Of course, this demands a flexible counter-reaction by our agency too ….' The MfS sought to split up the friends by using different tactics in each case. One was identified as the ringleader and attempts were made to isolate him by spreading malicious rumours about him. They intervened at his place of work to get his superiors to put pressure on him for allegedly neglecting his work for his private concerns. The Stasi also sought to unnerve him by thwarting his progress. Everything he applied for was rejected. When he applied for a larger flat on the birth of his fourth child the application was simply not processed. He began to show signs of disillusionment, feeling his friends were avoiding him. The second friend had been targeted and picked up on a charge of driving under the influence of drink. He was then invited to cooperate with the MfS or face prosecution, loss of his licence and exposure. He agreed to cooperate after hours of interrogation during which the Stasi shocked him by revealing what was known about him. He was then subject to constant calls from his Stasi controller. After a few weeks he went to his friend and confided in him just what had happened. The Stasi then broke off contact. The third member of the group applied in desperation to go to West Germany. He was soon allowed to do so 'for political and operational reasons'. It was hoped that in this way the three would fall apart and the group they had organized would be smashed.[42]

HARICH, HAVEMANN AND BAHRO

As we saw in an earlier chapter, the revolt of 17 June 1953 and the denunciation of Stalin at the Twentieth Congress of the CPSU in 1956 had a major impact on the SED.The 'Harich/Janka' group in the 1950s represented elements in the SED who wanted to transform the DDR into what was later to be known as 'Socialism with a human face'. Wolfgang Harich, lecturer in philosophy at the Humboldt University in Berlin, had been greatly influenced by the Twentieth Congress of the CPSU and the subsequent hope of that it would be possible to develop genuine Socialism in the Soviet sphere. Walter Janka, a veteran of the International Brigade, was head of the famous Aufbau publishing company at the time of his arrest.[43] The MfS smashed the group making the DDR safe for Ulbricht and Stalinism and Harich was imprisoned. Remarkably, he is still politically active in the 1990s and for his own brand of democratic socialism. The Leninist-Stalinists in the SED and elsewhere feared 'revisionists' like Harich more than they feared upholders of capitalism. They thought the revisionists could more easily deceive both party members and the masses as a whole. As part of the fallout from the Harich case, there were a number of prosecutions of academics in the DDR, notably from the Humboldt University and Leipzig University. Among those arrested were Heinrich Saar and Herbert Crüger, lecturers at the Humboldt. They were sentenced to eight years for treason in December 1958 but released under an amnesty in April 1961. Saar had been an emigrant in Britain during the Nazi years and fought with the Czech Legion against the Nazis in the Second World War.[44] After Harich was neutralized, the next intellectual figure in the DDR to excite the anger of the Politburo and the Stasi was Robert Havemann.

Robert Havemann did not regard himself as an oppositionist. Havemann had joined the KPD in 1932 and was sentenced to death in 1943 for opposing the Nazis. His execution was deferred however to enable him to carry on scientific research which his captors thought important. He was saved by the arrival of the Red Army in 1945. He was in trouble again in 1950 in West Berlin because of his opposition to the development by the US of the hydrogen bomb. He was appointed to a chair of physical-chemistry at the Humboldt University in East Berlin, which he occupied until his dismissal in 1964. He was also a member of the rubber stamp parliament, the

Volkskammer. In 1959 he was awarded the National Prize of the DDR. His outspoken lectures in which he called for a dogma-free Marxism had brought him into collision with the Politburo. He openly sympathized with the Prague Spring in 1968 and published in the West (being banned in the East). His free thinking and free talking led him to be placed under house arrest by the local Fürstenwalde court on 26 November 1976. He was not even allowed to have a copy of the charge sheet. His house arrest was for an indefinite period. His tape recorder and typewriter were confiscated and up to 50 IM had the job of keeping an eye on him. The order against him was lifted in 1979 when he was fined for allegedly infringing DDR laws for allowing his work to be published in the West. He died of cancer in 1982.[45] The application for an arrest order which the MfS made to the state prosecutor of the DDR on 15 November 1976, came to light after the Stasi was abolished. He was accused of being under strong suspicion of having repeatedly collected information for institutions and individuals in the Federal Republic and West Berlin, which would assist them in their activities against the DDR. He was linked to Dr Hartmut Jäckel who was organizing this hostile activity. What also came to light was the fact that Havemann had himself worked for the Stasi in the 1950s. It appears his main activities were attempting to monitor scientific developments in West Germany and report on potential defectors among the DDR's scientific élite. No doubt the then convinced communist Havemann thought this was part of his contribution to the 'struggle for peace'. Remarkably, there is strong evidence that the lawyer who represented Havemann, Gregor Gysi, also worked for the MfS. Gysi, the son of an SED ambassador and minister, and later head of the SED successor party, the PDS, claimed the files were wrong. He represented many leading DDR dissidents, including Rudolf Bahro.[46]

Rudolf Bahro was another Marxist opponent of the SED leadership. He had been a member of the SED since 1954 and until his arrest in 1977 had held a number of jobs in the economy, party and state. He was subsequently sentenced to eight years for disclosing state secrets. However, his real crime was writing a book, *The Alternative*, which was published in West Germany by a trade union-owned publishing company. Bahro was calling for democratic communism as advocated at that time by the Italian and some other Western communist parties, the so-called Eurocommunists. He was supported by some communists in Britain and other states and by many left-wing socialists and trade unionists. An international left-wing group appealed to Honecker to free Bahro and Havemann quoting Amnesty International that there were between 4,000 and 6,000 political prisoners in the DDR.[47] He was eventually 'bought free' by the West Germans. Bahro continued his political activities in West Germany in the Green movement and subsequently attempted to influence events in the DDR during the *Wende*, 1989–90.

Bahro's case led to protests in the DDR itself. In Leipzig a group led by Heinrich Saar was formed to discuss the ideas of Bahro, Havemann, Marcuse and other Marxist thinkers. The group attempted through wall graffiti and leaflets to use Bahro's case against the SED. On the 31 August 1979 Saar and others were arrested by the Stasi. Thirteen months later a Leipzig court sentenced Saar to seven and a half years' imprisonment for agitation against the state. Others arrested with him got up to five years. In August 1982 Saar was 'bought free' by West Germany.[48]

WRITERS AND THE STASI

The DDR had always had a problem with its artists and writers. Perhaps in some cases there was disappointment at the continuing low standard of living in the DDR, but artists and writers had a material security not enjoyed by most of their colleagues in West Germany or other Western states. Much more important for most were the severe restraints under which they had to work. The SED saw the arts as a weapon in the class struggle. Writers and artists were supposed to act accordingly. Even those who regarded themselves as Marxists found it increasingly difficult to work. Some could not come to terms with what they had seen in Stalin's Russia and got out shortly after returning to the Soviet Zone from Moscow. For others the moment of truth was the rising of 17 June 1953, for others it was the Hungarian revolution. Over the four decades of the DDR any number dropped out of the communist parade and headed for the West, usually suffering severe problems of self-doubt and conscience when they did so. The veteran communist Theodor Plievier (*Stalingrad*) had been among the first to go in 1947. Uwe Johnson (1934–84, *Zwei Ansichten*) and Horst Bienek (1930–90, *Die erste Polka)* and Gerhard Zwerenz (born 1925, *Casanova*) were among those that followed but the Wall went up in 1961. The SED followed the cultural line of the CPSU, being deeply Stalinist until 1953, relaxing somewhat until 1957, increasing the pressure until the early 1960s, then pursuing a 'liberal' line from 1962 to 1965.

At the fourth session of the Central Committee of the SED in December 1971, a few months after he had replaced Ulbricht, Erich Honecker gave hope of better times for the DDR's intellectuals. He said that provided writers and artists started from a firm socialist position, there should be no taboos in the form or content of their work.[49] Some surprise and more scepticism had greeted this statement as Honecker had been at the forefront of attacks on writers and other intellectuals in the past, notably at the eleventh plenary session of the Central Committee in 1965 which had ushered in a period of greater cultural repression. The doubts were confirmed when, a few months later, it became clear that the promise amounted to very little. By 1976 the situation was as bad as ever for the writers of the DDR. Wolf Biermann, who from a committed communist family had left West Germany in 1953 to live in the DDR, was deprived of his DDR citizenship during a concert tour of the Federal Republic in November 1976. Invited by the trade union, I G Metall, Biermann was known as a pop musician who wrote his own texts. These were critical of many things in East and West. In an interview in October 1974 Biermann had explained how, when he first arrived in the DDR, he 'experienced a downright joyous, fervent unity with society. I was, as the romantic saying goes, at home in my fatherland ….' He believed he was applying a communist critique to the DDR. He opposed the 'monopolistic bureacracy, which has been dubbed Stalinism'.[50]

Once the news got out, later on the same day, of Biermann's expulsion, 12 DDR writers protested against this measure. Among the better known of them were Christa Wolf, Volker Braun, Franz Fühmann, Stephan Hemlin, Stefan Heym and Heiner Müller. During the days that followed 70 other DDR writers joined the protest. On the other hand, a smaller group declared themselves in favour of the measure including Anna Seghers (President of the Writers' Association of the DDR), Hermann Kant, Peter Hacks and the film director younger brother of Markus Wolf, Konrad Wolf. [51] The consequence of the increasing intolerance of the SED of its writers was that the exodus of those applying to go to the West increased. Once again it must be emphasized that the bulk, if not all, of the writers, painters, film directors and others in the arts regarded by the Stasi as enemies or potential enemies believed themselves to be loyal communists who were seeking to make the DDR a more civilized, and therefore more acceptable and successful place for all its citizens.

Among those DDR loyalists criticized by Honecker in 1965 was Stefan Heym. Of Jewish background Heym was born in Chemnitz in 1913. He returned to Germany as a officer of the US Army in 1945 having been forced to leave by the Nazi take-over in 1933. A communist by conviction, Heym later chose to live in the DDR when he once again took up permanent residence in Germany. He enthusiastically supported the new state and the policies of the SED but was deeply influenced by the anti-Stalin campaign in the Soviet Union after 1956. In his writing he used historical fiction to deal with modern and contemporary problems. In *Der König David Bericht* (1972) he attacked Stalinism, in *5 Tage im Juni* (1974) he examined the revolt of 1953. *Collin* (1979) although fictional, had a clear resemblance to the case of Paul Merker, the Politburo member accused of Zionism in 1952. In the book the main character is a Mielke-like minister of security. All these and other books by him were published in West Germany as they could not be published in the DDR. This led to *reprisals* against Heym (as happened to Havemann) in 1979 for breaking the rigorous DDR currency laws. Heym was fined 9,000 marks for allowing *Collin* to be published in the Federal Republic. For the remaining years of the DDR the SED played a game of cat-and-mouse with Heym. Due to Heym's international reputation as a writer, anti-Nazi past and the fact that he was Jewish, the SED and the Stasi had to handle him with care. For his part he always emphasized his loyalty to the DDR and to socialism.[52]

Erich Loest spent seven years in the notorious prison Bautzen, 1957–64. Loest, already a well-known writer, had been sentenced for treason in the last of the trials against revisionists and counter-revolutionaries. His incarceration did not break him and he continued writing. In 1978 his *Es geht seinen Gang oder Mühen in unserer Ebene* (roughly, 'It goes on as usual, or Efforts at our Levels') was published. This caused his final break with the rulers of the DDR and resulted in his move to West Germany in 1981.[53] Another prominent writer who fell foul of the Stasi in this period was Hans Joachim Schädlich. Schädlich had worked at the Academy of Sciences after completing a doctorate in linguistics in 1960. He then turned to writing giving up his Academy position in 1976. He had signed the protest in support of Biermann in that year. His *Versuchte Nähe* had been recommended to the publishers Rowohlt in Hamburg by Günter Grass and brought him acclaim in the West after publication in August 1977. By December Schädlich was in the West. His *Tallhover* (1986), is the story of a secret policeman who never dies and serves any system which needs his services including the Kaiser's regime, the Third Reich and the DDR.[54]

It is convenient to mention here the fate of Roger Loewig, a painter, writer and poet, as it illustrates the situation of DDR painters under Ulbricht and Honecker. Born in Silesia in 1930, Loewig ended up in the Soviet Zone after the Nazi capitulation. He became a school teacher but increasingly turned in his spare time to painting, sketching and writing. In the summer of 1963 he was arrested early one morning on holiday on the Baltic coast. His works were to be displayed at a private exhibition. He was charged with anti-state agitation. His art was held against him. In painting after painting he depicted Nazi crimes but also the Berlin Wall and the division of Germany. After being kept under appalling conditions for about a year, he was released. His works were, however, confiscated. He was allowed to join the VBK, membership of which was virtually compulsory for anyone wishing to be exhibited. His works were bought by galleries and museums but in 1971 he took the bold step of resigning from the VBK. He was permitted to leave the DDR in 1972. Loewig was spied upon in West Berlin. When in 1986 he wanted to travel by train through the DDR to an exhibition of his work in the National Gallery in Warsaw, he was roughly forced from the train and sent back to West Berlin.[55]

A less known, but equally disturbing example of how the Stasi attempted to destroy non-conformist writers and artists was told by the victim, Gabriele Eckart. Eckart had completed a project on the opinions of members of an agricultural cooperative. Although excerpts of the results did appear in a magazine, the book itself was dropped after a decision of the Politburo. The book later appeared in West Germany in 1984.[56] She was then physically attacked twice at night in front of her own door. A complaint to the police was rejected and the Stasi said she was suffering from a persecution complex. After consulting Rev. Rainer Eppelmann (see below) she was subjected to several house searches during which Western currency and other belongings were taken. She was also the victim of rumours spread by members of the official writers' union. She was eventually allowed to leave the DDR.

One of the saddest aspects of the break up of the old DDR literary scene were the accusations which followed the end of SED/Stasi rule. Not all the literary giants were quite what they had seemed to be. There were those who, although there is no evidence to expose them as IM, helped in the downfall of their colleagues. Anna Seghers, (1900–83 *Das siebte Kreuz*) sat by while colleagues like Janka and Biermann were persecuted. As one scholar, not unsympathetic to the ideals of the DDR put it, 'The Biermann episode demonstrated the final bankruptcy and ineffectiveness of Anna Segher's attitude ... The Janka trial serves as an illustration of the corruption of East German intellectuals who, by their inaction over decades, contributed to the final societal collapse which will ultimately reduce the GDR to a footnote in history.'[57] There were others who actually spied on their colleagues. Mention has already been made of the IM-status of Sascha Anderson, not a literary giant, but regarded as a rising star among the younger DDR writers. Much worse for admirers of DDR literature were the revelations about Heiner Müller and Christa Wolf. As we saw, both had backed Biermann in 1976. Müller was regarded by some as the most significant German dramatist since Brecht.[58] No wonder, some would say, Müller's *Quartett* was pessimistic! 'Far from denying or even regretting his contacts with the Stasi' he 'presented a list of reasons why such contacts were unavoidable and even productive'.[59] Few believed him! In the case of Christa Wolf, the best-known, and most respected, woman writer of the DDR, her known Stasi activities had been as IM 'Margarete' in the late 1950s. When she was exposed she swung 'between the poles of self-accusation ... and self-exoneration'.[60] Whether she is denounced as a hypocrite or emphasis is put on her later activities, her exposure was a body blow to the credibility of DDR literary achievements, one of the few remaining 'achievements' left in the wreckage of the DDR.

That so many writers and artists left, or were forced to leave, the DDR over its 40 years or so of existence, was a sign of its failure. In most cases they were not against the DDR or socialism. It was also a sign of the failure of the MfS, a body which had helped to alienate them and then in many cases continued to harrass then after their subsequent departure.[61]

THE CHURCHES AND OPPOSITION

On 6 March 1978 Erich Honecker held much-publicized discussions with the League of Evangelical Churches in the DDR at the conclusion of which he recognized the church as an independent organization with social relevance in the socialist society of the DDR. This was one of a number of meetings, others followed in 1985 and 1987, between church leaders and Honecker, which helped to move the main DDR Christian communities united in the BEK (*Bund der Evangelischen Kirchen in der DDR*) from conflict to limited cooperation.[62] It had been a long and tortuous road to reach this stage. During the initial Soviet occupation the churches, in this largely Protestant area of Germany, had got off relatively lightly.[63] It was in the Soviet Zone, at Eisenach in 1948, that the postwar organization of the German Protestant churches, the EKD, including the churches of all four zones had been founded. However, the churches were dismayed that the Soviets did not permit a return to denominational schooling, but theological faculties at universities were retained. In the worst Stalinist period, 1949–53, there had been clashes, particularly over attempts by the FDJ to take over all youth activities in the DDR. The churches had been upbraided for being 'reactionary'. Some relaxation followed the death of Stalin, followed by renewed attacks after 1957. The fact that the West German churches were providing chaplains for the new armed forces of the Federal Republic was regarded by the SED as proving they were siding with NATO against the Warsaw Pact. EKD Chairman, Bishop Otto Dibelius, whose seat was in Berlin, had signed the agreement. Once the Berlin Wall was in place (1961) the pressure was on to get the Protestant churches to break with their co-religionists in the West, unite with them in the EKD, and form their own organization. This they finally did, the BEK, in 1969. In 1971 the Bishop of Berlin-Brandenburg (1972–81) and Chairman of the BEK, Albrecht Schönherr, formulated his idea of the *Kirche im Sozialismus* (Church in Socialism). He wanted the churches to have their place in the socialist society of the DDR, not in a ghetto of their own making. This was an acceptance of the DDR but not necessarily of all aspects of it. Werner Krusche, Bishop of Saxony (1969–82) seemed to go further, calling for 'critical solidarity' with the DDR. On the other hand, the Bishop of Mecklenberg, Heinrich Rathke (1970–82) wanted the churches to be active for those who were either too weak or too afraid to stand up for themselves, especially prisoners of conscience, controversal writers, pacifists, environmentalists and even alcoholics. The Catholic Church in the DDR did not adopt the formula of Schönherr or anything similar. As its structure was hierarchical and it was international, it was easier to control from the top downwards. It avoided being 'suckered' by the SED but it also avoided confrontation with the SED.[64]

Under Honecker the SED gave the churches some concessions such as allowing new churches to be built, with West German money, in new towns or new large housing estates. Religious services were broadcast on the DDR television and radio (partly no doubt to make watching such broadcasts by the Western media less attractive). Some pacifists were permitted to do their compulsory military service in 'building units' of the armed forces in which they were not required to bear arms. This practice had been introduced under Ulbricht. But the SED's aims were to use the apparent freedom of the churches as propaganda that the DDR really was democratic, to entice churchmen to join the Moscow-orientated Peace Council of the DDR and the Prague Christian Peace Conference founded in 1958, to get a few selected individual church representatives to participate in Western congresses as parade horses for the regime, to encourage the churches, again with money from the West, to look after the aged and infirmed and the mentally retarded. Finally, the SED sought to enlist the churches to police their own flock and those who went to them for help and advice. 'Over and over the MfS was able through its IM to neutralize the critical potential in the churches and thus to de-politicise them.'[65]

Throughout the 1970s and the 1980s the SED and the MfS had to face opposition from Christians in the DDR. Among a new generation of churchmen who later made waves were Rainer Eppelmann, Wolfgang Thierse and Wolfgang Ullmann. Often these were individuals or groups which did not have the official backing of the churches. However, the churches were forced to address the concerns of their followers at various times. One important occasion was the introduction of compulsory military training in schools in September 1978. The BEK asked the DDR government to think again. Its response was negative. Nevertheless, it was of key importance for the credibility of the churches that they had questioned this move and promised such help as they could give to parents with difficulties. The situation in Poland in 1980 with the banning of the free trade union Solidarity caused the SED to attempt to restrict church activities as did the tension which followed the Soviet invasion of Afghanistan in the same year. The distribution of church papers by the postal system was restricted. These small papers which exercised a good deal of self-censorship were virtually the only independent medium of communication in the DDR.

In some ways the Berlin Appeal of 25 January 1982 marked a turning point. Rainer Eppelmann, Pastor at the Samaritan Church and Youth Pastor, appears to have been the chief initiator. Eppelmann had served an eight-month jail sentence for refusing to do military service. The Appeal, initially signed by Eppelmann, his wife Eva-Maria, Robert and Katja Havemann, the writer Luth Rathenow and over 30 others, was headed by the catchy slogan, 'Frieden schaffen, ohne Waffen' ('Make Peace Without Weapons').[66] The signers wanted negotiations between the two German governments on the removal of all nuclear weapons from Germany. This would be the first step towards a nuclear-free Europe. The SED and the Stasi regarded this as a deeply hostile document. By asking individuals to add their signatures the organizers were breaking new ground. The leadership of the Berlin-Brandenburg Church strongly advised its members not to collect signatures. In September 1982 the conference of church governing bodies agreed to drop the badge 'swords into ploughshares', which by then had become a popular badge especially among young people. The SED had already banned the wearing of it in schools, universities and in public even though it was a replica of the monument given to the UNO by the Soviet Union! The church leaders' decision brought them into conflict with many of their activists. Church–state relations improved in the following year in the wake of the celebrations marking the 500th anniversary of Luther's birth. Honecker chaired an official committee presiding over the celebrations, the churches constituted their own committee, but the two cooperated. For the remainder to the DDR there was growing tension between the churches and the state and, to a degree, between the church leaders and the less cautious of their followers. Peace protesters in the DDR were increasingly influenced by the example and success of the Greens in West Germany in the 1980s. The Greens succeeded, against expectations, in gaining entry to the Federal Parliament in 1983 and again in 1987. The election of Ronald Reagan to the US presidency in 1981 and of Mikhail Gorbachev as Secretary General of the CPSU in 1985 influenced opinion away from the SED as did the new round of nuclear armaments. Church leaders found themselves under pressure to speak out. In 1984 there was a wave of Western embassy occupations by East Germans demanding to be allowed to leave. Church leaders urged people to stay. At a meeting of the church synod at Görlitz in March 1984 the SED was urged to create conditions which would encourage people to remain. A similar call was heard in the same location in 1987, when the nuclear deterrent and the value of military service were also questioned. The Catholic Church also voiced criticisms of various aspects of SED practice. In July 1987, at the first meeting of DDR Catholics in Dresden, 80,000 heard Cardinal Joachim Meisner, Chairman of the Berlin Bishops' Conference, call for more career opportunities for Christians, who were still discriminated against despite earlier promises from the SED. In February (12–15) 1988 the first session of the Ecumenical Meeting of Churches and Christians took place in Dresden. This was a first also in that the Catholic Church was represented among the 150 delegates.[67] Its theme was Justice, Peace and Protection of Creation. In an open session the lack of justice, peace and environmental protection in the DDR was emphasized. Much discussion followed the Meeting and another followed in Magdeburg in October. Clearly worried and angry the SED reacted at a meeting between Werner Jarowinsky, Politburo member responsible for church affairs, and Bishop Leich on 19 February 1988. Jarowinsky accused the churches of interfering in matters which belonged to the state's jurisdiction and demanded the churches should stop using their premises as anti-state centres. The church press faced difficulties for the rest of the year. At a series of meetings over the year critical voices were heard about the situation in the DDR. However, in April at the synod of the Berlin-Brandenburg regional church, the East Berlin General Superintendent, Günter Krusche, warned of the danger that the churches could be manipulated for alien purposes which would bring them into opposition to 'the organs of the state'. The synod, as others had done, called upon Christians to remain in the DDR and Bishop Gottfried Forck called upon the Federal Government to take administrative steps designed to reduce the flow of people from the DDR. His remarks caused anger in West Germany.[68]

All these church and peace group activities over the 1980s were to culminate as a vital part of the peaceful revolution in 1989. This is discussed in a separate chapter.

After the dissolution of the MfS the churches were forced to face the painful reality that a significant number of their members at all levels had worked for the Stasi. In Saxony the church itself came to the conclusion that of 1,050 main office holders 'only' 'about two dozen' had collaborated with the Stasi.[69] Often, however, it was the quality of the IM which shocked. This is not surprising when one remembers that, for instance, at the election of the Bishop of Berlin-Brandenburg in 1981, 12 of the 110 electors were IM.[70] The leading East Berlin clergyman, Günter Krusche was known to the Stasi as IM 'Günther'. He was forced to retire in 1993. Worse still, Dr Manfred Stolpe, who had been head of the Secretariat of the BEK, was accused of being a former MfS collaborator. His defence was that Stasi contacts were inevitable in his work and he tried to help the church, and dissidents (as a lawyer), through his discussions with the representatives of the state. After he was elected SPD Minister President of Brandenburg, he convinced a Landtag committee of enquiry of his innocence in the matter. He failed to convince some former dissidents, Bärbel Bohley, Lutz Rathenow, Wolfgang Templin and Ehrhart Neubert and some others.[71] Other IM cases were Gerhard Lotz, Church Council member in Thüringia, Eberhard Natho, Anhalt Church President, and Horst Gienke, former Bishop of Greifswald.[72] An earlier Bishop of Greifswald and Chairman of the Conference of Governing Church Bodies, Friedrich-Wilhelm Krummacher (1901–74) worked both for the Soviet secret police and later for the Stasi.[73] Krummacher was a Nazi party member who collaborated with the Soviets in the National Committee for a Free Germany as a prisoner of war. Perhaps he was one of those who collaborated in the belief that they could achieve something for the churches. But any number of others did so out of cowardice, ambition or envy. The Stasi was able to use classic tactics against those who take the moral high ground. It set IM to seduce clergy at sex parties. In Berlin through one of the members of the BEK council, himself an IM, the MfS was able to infiltrate an attractive 24-year-old law student in 1973. As IM 'Micha' she organized sex-parties for churchmen, both heterosexual and homosexual. At their regular meetings her case officer gave her detailed instructions on how to behave and even what clothes to wear. She was operative until the end and only exposed two years after the collapse of the DDR.[74]

The Stasi also attempted to use its influence to help church members in personal matters to win them over. A document from the mid-1980s explains how a member of a church council was won over by helping him with his housing problem and giving assurances that his children would not be discriminated against if they wished to go on to higher education. With his help important information about church developments and the attitudes of particular clergy could be achieved.[75] No doubt influenced by the KGB's experience the Stasi was prepared to prostitute medicine to deal with clergymen who could not be bought by one means or another. Pastor Heinz Eggert who was minister in the small village of Oybin in the Zittauer mountains was one of them. As the 2,800 pages of files reveal, in 1982, about 50 IM were deployed against Eggert who was regarded as a 'reactionary'. The IM included some he regarded as close friends. After being ill with (perhaps Stasi-induced) dysentery, he was diagnosed as suffering from clinical depression and hospitalized. The head doctor was also a Stasi IM. Eggert was tranquillized and reduced to a state of apathy. He was lucky to have survived intact.[76] Richard Schröder, a member of the Protestant Church's executive council, has said that if any clergyman had dealings with the Stasi which he failed to report to his superiors, he was guilty of a clear breach of

Church regulations. Bärbel Bohley claims this frequently put the brakes on the opposition. Bishop Johannes Hempel of Saxony believes the Church realized too late how Stasi infiltrated it was. [77]

ORWELLIAN SITUATION IN THE FAMILY

The SED/Stasi system attempted to produce an Orwellian situation in which all were prepared to denounce colleagues, friends and even family members if they appeared disloyal to the Party. There was a relatively large number of cases of betrayal within families. In May 1985 an uncle and his nephew lost their jobs quite independently of each other. The uncle had warned people who wrote letters of complaint to his boss, the Minister of Justice, that they could be endangering themselves. His activities were discovered and he was sacked. The nephew was dismissed from his post of flight mechanic in the DDR air force. The uncle thought he had a close enough relationship with his nephew to confide in him his plans for escape to the West. These involved using a crop-spraying light aircraft which the nephew was invited to fly. After agreeing to his uncle's proposal the nephew made known their plans to the MfS. The uncle got two years and six months in Bautzen prison, the nephew got 1,500 marks and was reinstated in the air force. If there was a happy ending it came after German unity was restored. The nephew was convicted of depriving the uncle of his liberty.[78] Another painful case was that of Barbara Grosse who, after 15 months in Hoheneck Prison, was 'bought free' by West Germany in 1984. Her 'crime' was that she wanted to leave the DDR to settle in West Germany and had visited the Federal German Embassy in Prague and its representation in East Berlin on several occasions. After German reunification she discovered she had been spied upon by no less than 17 IM including colleagues at work, neighbours and acquaintances. Among the three identified was the writer Matthias Wedel who had reported to the Stasi on her when they both worked for Radio Leipzig. He showed little regret for his actions.[79] The worst kind of case possible was that involving Vera Wollenberger, mentioned above as a dissident who later became a Green member of the Bundestag. She had the painful experience of discovering that her husband, Knud, had denounced her and so had her lawyer, Wolfgang Schnur.[80] Unfortunately, Frau Wollenberger's experience was not an isolated case. In the DDR itself and beyond its frontiers, the Stasi attempted to exploit long-term friendships and sexual relations to gain control over its victims. One other example was the attempt to destroy the marriage of Gerd and Ulrike Poppe, two well-known dissidents, by seeking to involve an IM with Frau Poppe.[81] Out of 20-plus main members of Poppe's own group, ten had been unmasked as IM by January 1992. However, the Poppes were relieved to find that there were no informers among their close friends.[82]

Virtually all states have some sort of internal security service. Democratic states have some 'checks and balances' to ensure such forces do not become oppressive. But even in democratic states things can go wrong especially when one chief stays too long.[83] The DDR suffered from the worst possible situation. An aged tyrant who wished to die in office, no checks and balances, an ideology which produced self-righteousness and the Cold War. The MfS grew and grew until it became the largest employer in the DDR and there were plans for further expansion! All police forces in the world use informers. In democratic societies these are usually employed in small numbers and confined to the environment of common criminals. In recent years their numbers have increased to deal with terrorism such as the terrorist attacks stemming from the situation in Northern Ireland or the position in the Basque region of Spain. In the DDR the situation was quite different with the MfS seeking to know about everybody and everything in society and through this knowledge and the power it gave, manipulating an entire people. Undoubtedly, the most appalling aspect of the system of IM was the breakdown of the bonds of trust between officers and men, lawyers and clients, doctors and patients, teachers and students, pastors and their communities, friends and neighbours, family members and even lovers. It is true that the great majority of citizens of the DDR were clear that the MfS existed and that informers could be encountered on trains, planes, trams and buses, could be found at their place of work or study or even in the block of flats where they lived. Few realized how extensive the network of informers was. Fewer still expected to find them in the family or intimate sphere.

5 East German Foreign Intelligence, 1945–89

> A reason for our successes was that we always concentrated on the essential, that is on the FRG, NATO and so on.[1]
>
> Markus Wolf, former head of East German foreign intelligence, 1990

Even before the Revolution of 1989 East German intelligence had achieved international notoriety because of the operations of its foreign wing, the *Hauptverwaltung Aufklärung* (Main Department Reconnaissance) or the HVA, as it was usually referred to for short. This organization, rather than the rank and file of the MfS received the bulk of Western media coverage of the Stasi. This was ironic since the HVA had only 4,000 officers in comparison with 100,000 MfS regulars occupied on internal duties, whose number was not at that time suspected. Yet after the *Wende* a great deal was written on the Stasi as an agency of internal repression, but very little on the HVA's work outside West Germany. East German foreign intelligence has remained legendary.

The first element of the HVA myth reflects fact. Undoubtedly the organization achieved some remarkable successes. In 1974 the effectiveness of the GDR's foreign intelligence was made clear with the exposure of Günther Guillaume, the personal assistant of Willy Brandt, the West German Chancellor, as a Stasi agent. Brandt fell as a result. This case and the subsequent humiliations of the West German authorities through spy scandals created the reputation of the HVA. Yet the myth of East German espionage in the 1970s and 1980s understated the reality. The string of Stasi agents within the West German political, military and economic establishment who were uncovered after the Revolution of 1989 finally proved exactly how powerful the HVA had been.

The HVA was successful not only because it was able to penetrate the West German establishment, but also because the Western intelligence services were singularly unable to infiltrate it. Throughout the postwar period there was only one HVA defector of note. This was Werner Stiller, a regular officer from the HVA's unit dealing with the science and technology target who fled to West Germany in 1979. But Stiller does not approach the importance of the scores of West Germans working for the East Germans or the number of high-ranking KGB officers who worked for the West.[2] The West Germans' lack of knowledge about how much their establishment had been penetrated was revealed after 1989. This indicates that there were no important BND agents within the Stasi.

The second element of the HVA myth embraces both fact and fiction. The reputation of East German intelligence is linked with that of Markus Wolf, its head for over 30 years. For a quarter of a century the West was unable physically to identify the head of East German intelligence, which was a testimony to the HVA's excellent security. The West's very lack of knowledge about him generated the Wolf legend, as he became known as 'the man without a face'. Despite his anonymity, Wolf was held to have been an influence on John Le Carré when he wrote his best-selling spy novel, *The Spy Who Came in from the Cold*, in 1963.[3] In 1979 Wolf was finally identified after being photographed on a clandestine visit to Stockholm. The revelation did nothing to harm his image abroad, as excited Western journalists equated his appearance with that of the American actor, Paul Newman. Such admiration has continued to the present day. It is not difficult to see how the Wolf legend came into being. From the late 1960s to the early 1980s, observers of the Soviet Bloc consciously searched for any character who would break the greyness of the lumpish mass of Soviet Bloc leaders typified by Leonid Brezhnev himself. Wolf was such a man, so was Erich Honecker, whom the Western media often presented in the early 1970s as a dynamic force for change in East–West relations. In the case of Honecker, the liberal image created both by Western journalists and by Western politicians proved false. As will be seen in Chapter 7, Honecker was as firmly set against structural change in Eastern Europe as were his Soviet backers.

What of Markus Wolf's liberal image? In his case it is difficult to disentangle truth from fiction, particularly because, since his retirement from the secret service in 1985, Wolf has proved himself to be a formidable self-publicist. If he is to be believed, the HVA's operations were very successful, but they were harmless. By obtaining information about their adversaries, the HVA reduced the sources of distrust between East and West, creating stability in international relations.[4] The HVA's economic espionage likewise fulfilled a worthy goal, according to Wolf, since it helped East German industry to upgrade its technological base. In his writings Wolf himself appears as the virtuous head of a noble organization fighting within the system against an inadequate party leadership. He all but claims the West's gratitude for his years as head of the HVA, pointing out that by enduring that role in the face of Erich Mielke's hostility, he kept far less palatable neo-Stalinists out of the job. Then, after his retirement in 1986*, he used all the credit he had amassed in over three decades of service by furthering the cause of political and economic liberalization in East Germany. At the present time it is not possible definitively to separate fact from fiction in the Markus Wolf legend.

* The official announcement came on 6 February 1987.

The third element of the HVA myth reflects a lack of facts. Not much more is known about it after the Revolution than before. Before the fall of the SED regime in October–November 1989, the HVA had already made an effort to destroy sensitive documents *en masse*.[5] In fact, it had succeeded in destroying nearly all its archives before the mob took over its East Berlin headquarters, along with the central and regional headquarters of the MfS between December 1989 and January 1990.[6] In all the provincial capitals of the DDR, and in Berlin, Citizens' Committees were formed with the task of securing the Stasi archives.[7] Inevitably they found many HVA documents, not only because there were too many for the HVA to destroy in a short period, but also because copies were to be found in the provinces. Yet very little indeed of this information has become available, unlike material dealing solely with the domestic operations of the MfS. The caretaker regime in East Germany made an agreement with the Soviet government that the KGB should have access to the HVA's files whether in East Berlin or in the provinces and should have the right to remove any material relating to Soviet security. In effect this meant that the Soviet authorities could seize any HVA document they liked, because in a justifiable sense, East German security interests had been synonymous with those of the Soviet Bloc as a whole. Thus in 1990 KGB officers worked in the former Stasi headquarters alongside the Citizens' Committees in sorting the MfS archives.[8]

Lack of documentary material on the HVA has not been greatly improved by oral evidence since the Revolution. With the exception of Markus Wolf, HVA officers have had very little to say for themselves since the fall of the DDR, which is a last testimony to their high *esprit de corps*. Those who have spoken, like the defector Stiller, cannot speak for the HVA as whole, since it was a compartmentalized organization whose officers received information strictly on the principle of 'need to know'. So, for example, Stiller is a reliable source on the HVA's science and technology sector, but not on its operations in the Third World.

Lack of sources makes it difficult to provide definite answers even to general questions relating to the operations of East German foreign intelligence. Even the HVA's much praised success is open to dispute. Was the HVA really that superior to other foreign intelligence services? Was it so successful primarily because it was a German secret service operating in a German environment, and mainly concerned with spying on Germans? Without doubt few, if any, secret services operated in such favourable environments. With only slight exaggeration, it might be argued that the greatest successes of East German intelligence did not take place on foreign soil, but in a different state. The evidence currently available indicates that the world outside Germany was of relatively limited importance to the HVA. This evidence can be broken down into the following areas: the incidence of espionage cases involving East Germany, few of which took place outside the Federal Republic; the testimony of HVA officers, foremost among them Wolf and Stiller; the unmasking of Stasi agents abroad after the Revolution, all of whom were operating in West Germany; and the organizational breakdown of the HVA which was made public after 1989 and which shows the concentration of effort directed at the FRG. Because of its importance, HVA espionage against West Germany will be discussed separately in the next chapter. Here, East German intelligence operations in the Federal Republic will be considered only insofar as they concerned the development of the GDR's foreign intelligence service as a whole.

Lack of knowledge about the HVA's operations in the rest of Europe, the United States, and the Third World affects our understanding of its much better documented work in West Germany. One general question to which no definite answer can be given is that of the extent to which the HVA was fulfilling specifically East German needs and to which it was a weapon in the armoury of the Soviet Bloc. Of course, there could never be a firm dividing line between what benefitted the DDR and what benefited the Soviet Union. But was the overwhelming concentration on the Federal Republic the decision of the East German leadership who were following a security agenda distinct from that of the Soviet Union, or did Moscow encourage the Stasi to put all their resources into an area where they had unequalled opportunities, leaving the rest of the world to the KGB and the other satellite intelligence services?

The early development of East German foreign intelligence paralleled that of the domestic security service. Both were no more than auxiliaries of the KGB which directed their work down to the smallest details. In the case of foreign operations, continuity with the Comintern past seemed very strong, both in terms of personnel and of the kind of operations they conducted. Covert action was given a priority in the 1940s and 1950s which it was not to retain.

THE EARLY YEARS: EAST GERMAN ESPIONAGE AND SABOTAGE

When feeling between the Western Allies and the Soviet Union soured after 1946, the SED in the Soviet Zone and the KPD in the three Western Zones, already disposed of a close-knit communications centred on the '*Westkommission*' of the SED's executive in East Berlin.[9] The *Westkommission*'s organization was used to procure secret intelligence. K-5 did not operate as a foreign espionage service.[10]

At the same time that the *Westkommission* provided the KGB with an informal auxiliary intelligence agency, the SED also provided an agency for covert action abroad. In 1945 Ernst Wollweber returned from Moscow to Berlin and was made deputy director of shipping.[11] In fact, the real end of his appointment was rather destructive than constructive, for he proceeded to build up his prewar sabotage network.

Wollweber's organization was independent of the internal police and security apparatus. Little is known for certain about it. According to one of Wollweber's long-time colleagues, the organization was divided into these operations groups: sea ports; river ports; railway and transport routes; and Allied supply lines.[12] Some information was provided by one of Gehlen's agents, Walter Gramsch, codenamed 'Brutus'.

Gramsch was *Ministerialdirektor* in the state of Saxony-Anhalt. He got to know Wollweber in 1947; as a result, Wollweber had him promoted. Gramsch fled to the West in 1953.[13] He provided the West with information that the East Germans had set up schools to train saboteurs. One was the maritime school on the small Baltic peninsula of Wustrow. It was claimed that of the 180 who graduated from that institution every year, 20–30 had also received special training in sabotage. There were two other schools in the Mecklenburg towns of Goldberg and Ladebow.[14] Apparently these graduates included not only German, but also Swedish and British citizens.[15]

It is impossible to say how extensive Wollweber's organization was. Certainly the Swedish and Norwegian authorities took the threat seriously from an early date. On 6 November 1948 the Norwegian press attaché in Stockholm visited the Swedish Foreign Ministry and reported that the Norwegian authorities were 'practically certain' that Wollweber's official post was a cover for his secret work. But there was no evidence that he was involved in sabotage.[16] In 1950 the Swedish police reported that there were more than 150 eastern agents in the country.[17] The Swedes were better informed about what was going on inside their own country than the Norwegians, who had minimal experience of counter-intelligence. Nonetheless, the Norwegians later believed that Wollweber was 'in full swing building up a contact network for illegal operations in Norway'.[18]

Ørnulf Tofte, who was later to be the deputy head of Norwegian counter-intelligence was employed against Wollweber's network. Early in 1949 he was sent to watch one Asbjørn Sunde, who was suspected of making preparations for sabotage. Sunde had joined the Norwegian Communist Party in the interwar period and had fought in Spain. By his own account he had spent most of his time in a sabotage unit. He continued his work as a saboteur in the Norwegian communist resistance after the German occupation of Norway in 1940, where he had distinguished himself, later receiving a Soviet medal for his heroism. He told something of his experiences in his memoirs, *Menn i mørket* ('Men in the Dark') which included a reminiscence about how he had liquidated two wartime informers with his own knife.[19] By normal standards, Sunde seemed a strange choice as a communist agent, the majority of whom do not publish their memoirs during their active career. He made himself further suspicious by taking on a German to work at his tinsmith's works. This man had been a member of an active communist group in interwar Germany. He had come to Norway as a refugee. Despite these indications, the Norwegian authorities were never able to charge Sunde, even after he was discovered visiting the Soviet Embassy in Oslo. Finally he left for East Germany and took up residence there. He was next heard of working in eastern German harbours contacting Scandinavian seamen.[20] The Norwegian authorities never discovered exactly what Sunde had been doing in Norway. But Tofte concluded that it must have been important, since Sunde was later given a state funeral in East Germany.[21] It is hard to say whether the Sunde case reflects more the crudeness of Wollweber's methods or the inefficiency of the Norwegian police. It is fair to say, however, that the Wollweber organization also failed to leave a conclusive trail in Sweden, where the security service was very efficient.

The extent to which Wollweber had reorganized his sabotage network became particularly important after the outbreak of the Korean War. There is evidence that it was used to disrupt Allied supplies, but this is only circumstantial. It is quite possible that it was not used at all. There is some evidence that the Soviet authorities believed that the direct involvement of the KGB in sabotage was not worth the damage it would cause if discovered, though Moscow had considered aiding North Korea by covert action in the West.[22] This does of course mean that they ruled out such action by East German proxy. At any rate, there were a number of shipping accidents and acts of sabotage on British ships and in French harbours, which caused an international sensation at this time. In July 1951 HMS *Illustrious* was damaged by sabotage just as it was about to set out for Korea. Explosive devices were found on board. Then a tanker was set on fire by an explosion at Swansea. It had been intended to bring supplies to the armies in Korea. There were several explosions in British arsenals. In 1952–3 there was an unusually large number of shipping accidents. British ships were particularly affected, as were, to a lesser degree, those of the United States.[23] Sabotage was definitely the cause of fires on three big liners. There were three cases of sabotage on British warships. No ships were sunk. The total number of accidents during the Korean War which might have been caused by Wollweber's saboteurs comes to 13.[24] Not one of these accidents led to diplomatic protests from the Western powers. After the Korean War, all suspicions that the Soviet Bloc powers were active in sabotaging Western shipping disappeared and were never to surface again.

THE IWF

East Germany did not acquire a foreign intelligence service until 1951. This was the *Außenpolitischer Nachrichtendienst* or APN (Foreign Political Intelligence Service). It is much better known by its disguise, namely the *Institut für wirtschaftswissenschaftliche Forschung* or IWF (Institute for Economic Research). This was ostensibly an East–West trade organization. The IWF was separate from the Ministry for State Security as well as from Wollweber's operations.[25] It was subordinate to the Ministry of Foreign Affairs, which was then under the leadership of the SED Politburo member, Anton Ackermann. In fact, its operations were as much under the control of the KGB as were those of the MfS. The inferiority of both branches of East German intelligence to the Soviet authorities was made clear in 1954, when the KGB did not bother to inform Wollweber, then Minister for State Security, of the defection to East German of a key Western agent. This was Otto John (pronounced 'Yone'), the head of the West German counter-intelligence service, the BfV. It should further be noted that it was the KGB, not the East Germans who had been running John. Wollweber was furious at this insult.[26]

Details of the IWF's organization were revealed to the West in 1953 by the defector and former head of department (*Abteilung*), Johann Krauss. According him, the IWF was divided into four Main Departments (*Hauptabteilungen*). These were: political and military espionage; economic espionage; central evaluation of all intelligence; and general administration. Besides these there were also two independent 'operational departments' (*Operative Abteilungen*): counter-intelligence; and espionage in the field of economics and technology, as well as a personnel department. This breakdown does not reveal much about the IWF's goals, except that it indicates that even at an early date the acquisition of information about Western technology was priority for the East Germans. Less obvious is the IWF's primary concern with West Germany. Though even at this early date it was very difficult to draw the line between what concerned specifically the Federal Republic and what concerned the emerging Western Alliance. In fact, the only success of the IWF for which evidence exists at the present time was the acquisition in 1952 of the treaty document for the European Defence Community.[27]

The IWF's operations in West Germany soon ran into difficulties. Ludwig Weis, one of the IWF's officers and head of the GDR's office for inner-German trade at Frankfurt-am-Main, was soon uncovered. He was arrested on 22

August 1952 and given four years in prison. The West Germans capitalized on their success. Gerhard Schröder, the Federal Republic's Minister of Interior, told the *Bundestag* that 'He had used his position in order personally to gather secret intelligence on the economic, political and military situation in West Germany, and in order to gain further sources for his espionage work, who put themselves at his disposal either consciously or trustingly.'[28]

Worse was to come the next year. In April 1953 the West Germans arrested 38 people on suspicion of espionage, in a case which became known as the 'Vulcan Affair'. This coup was made possible by the defection of the IWF officer Johann Krauss in April 1953. Most of those arrested were released for want of evidence. Only three were sentenced to prison. Nonetheless, the IWF had been publicly humiliated and its secret intelligence had collapsed. At the end of the year the IWF ceased to exist and all foreign intelligence operations were incorporated in the Ministry for State Security as *Hauptabteilung* (Main Department) XV.

The reorganization of East German intelligence might well not have been occasioned solely by the IWF's poor performance. The merger of foreign and domestic intelligence in one organization in 1953 meant that the DDR was now following Soviet practice. There might also have been domestic political reasons for the changes, though there is no evidence for this. Certainly Walter Ulbricht now saw Anton Ackermann, the Minister in charge of foreign intelligence, as one of his enemies, along with Zaisser and Herrnstadt. Thus by removing the IWF from Ackermann's control Ulbricht might also have intended to weaken his rival by cutting the links with the KGB with which his overlordship of the IWF provided him.

MARKUS WOLF

Ulbricht took great pains to find a suitable head for East German foreign intelligence. This was Markus Wolf, who had joined the IWF in 1951. In December 1952, Ulbricht called Wolf to see him and told him that he was going to be put in charge of foreign intelligence. Significantly, two Soviet advisers were present at the interview.[29] Thus Markus Wolf became head of East German foreign intelligence at the age of 30. Ulbricht had selected him over the heads of some more senior intelligence officers, such as Gerhard Heidenreich and Richard Stahlmann who were also prominent in the IWF.

At first Wolf was directly subordinate to Ulbricht himself. But at some time early in 1953 Ulbricht changed his mind and put Wolf under the control of Wilhelm Zaisser. Strangely, though Zaisser took responsibility for foreign intelligence not in his capacity as Minister for State Security, but as member of the Politburo.[30] The next change in the organization of East German foreign intelligence was nominal. In summer 1956 its name was changed from *Hauptabteilung* (Main Department) XV to *Hauptverwaltung Aufklärung* (Main Administration Reconnaissance). This reflected its real importance. It was to retain this title until it was disbanded in 1990.

Markus Johannes Wolf was born on 19 January 1923 at a village in the Swabian mountains in southern Germany. He was the eldest son of Friedrich Wolf (1888–1953), then a country doctor of communist persuasion, by his second marriage.[31] In 1927 the family moved to Stuttgart where they lived until shortly after Hitler's seizure of power in 1933. Friedrich Wolf was not an ordinary doctor. His interests tended in the direction of natural medicine. This was reflected in the family environment. Wolf senior was obsessed with health and his family were vegetarians – a characteristic which Markus shed later in life. Friedrich Wolf governed his household according to dietary rules so strict that even a visitor from Stalin's starving Soviet Union was driven in despair into smuggling meat into his guest room. Despite this, visitors found the atmosphere in the house to be understanding and friendly. In 1928 Friedrich Wolf decided to publicize his regime for a healthy life in a book entitled *Die Natur als Arzt und Helfer* ('Nature as Doctor and Helper'). This included pictures of Friedrich doing exercises in a loincloth and his sister-in-law doing naked gymnastics. Friedrich's admiration for his own body had perhaps been indulged more fully in his student years when he had posed as a nude model for a statue commissioned by his university.

Friedrich Wolf diversified his career by becoming a writer. In the Twenties he started to write political pamphlets, social commentaries and two plays. One of these, *Cyankali*, had some success and brought the writer into prominence, for it was directed against the Prussian abortion laws. Some performances led to violent demonstrations. By 1933 Friedrich Wolf was a marked man in the eyes of the Nazis for not only was he a communist publicist who had attacked their ideas of public morality, but also he was Jewish. Friedrich Wolf took the wisest course and fled, followed by his family, to the Soviet Union. There he followed his career as a writer, and achieved distinction under the SED regime. Some of his works were required reading in East German schools. Particularly well-received was his play *Professor Mamlock*, the story of a conservative Jewish doctor who had to face up to the insecurity of his position after the Nazi seizure of power.[32] Unlike other East German writers such as Bertold Brecht and Christa Wolf (who was not a relative), Friedrich Wolf never acquired a reputation outside the DDR.

Markus and his younger brother Konrad had already started the communist career track by joining the KPD's youth movement, the Young Pioneers, in

Weimar Germany.[33] In 1934 they and their mother followed their father to Moscow. The whole family took up Soviet citizenship. Markus was educated with Russian and other German children. He acquired a fluent knowledge of Russian in the process as well as the abbreviated first name 'Misha', which is a short form of 'Mikhail'. For some reason the Russian children did not find the Romanized German 'Markus' to their taste.[34] Wolf was sometimes called by his Russian name in later life. At the age of 16 he started to train as an aircraft engineer – a prestigious calling in Stalin's Soviet Union. His technical education did not last for long, for in 1942 he was sent to a Comintern school and in the same year joined the KPD. This probably reflected the Soviet leadership's need to build up the German communist cadres for the event of victory. With the closure of the Comintern in 1943, Wolf returned to Moscow. There he started to work for the KPD's *Deutscher Volkssender*, which was one of three German-language radio programmes broadcast from Moscow at that time.

Markus Wolf was aged only ten when he first came to the Soviet Union which, as he later put it, became 'second homeland' for his family, while he was 'a half-Russian'. Wolf still felt a close affinity with Russia after returning to Germany. Throughout his adult life he visited Kamchatka almost every two years.[35] His love for Russia was also reflected in cookery, on which he prided himself. Wolf was known for his *pelmeni*, a kind of ravioli, which is a traditional Russian dish.[36]

Markus Wolf returned to Berlin at the end of May 1945. His task was to work for the KPD's German radio service as foreign commentator. He had the particularly important task of controlling the most important political broadcasts.[37] His success at his job was rewarded when he was made a reporter at the Nuremberg Trials of Nazi war criminals.

When the DDR was founded in October 1949, Wolf was transferred to the diplomatic service. He was sent to represent the DDR in Moscow with the rank of First Counsellor.[38] It was only a few months later that Wolf returned his Soviet passport.

It is difficult to describe Wolf's personality, since most that has been written about him has flowed from his own lips after 1989. He described his essential qualities as follows, at an interview in 1990: the ability to think clearly in political and strategic terms; patience; and well-balanced temperament.[39] As well as this Wolf has striven to present himself as a member of the intelligentsia rather than the Party. In his published diaries for the late 1980s he wrote more about his literary career, that of his father, and his brother Konrad who became a well-known film director. Many have found Markus

Wolf vain and his writing unrestrainedly self-indulgent.[40] No one can seriously doubt the intelligence and eloquence which spring from his pages.

One mild condemnation of Wolf and men like him came from a former German friend from the period of Moscow exile. This was Wolfgang Leonhard who fled the Soviet Zone in 1948. Leonhard had been a student at the Comintern school in Moscow with Wolf and later knew him when he was serving with the radio in the Eastern Zone. He wrote of him in his memoirs, *Die Revolution entläßt ihre Kinder* ('The Revolution Abandons her Children'):

> He was the type of very clever, calm official who stands in the background, who only regards as a game of chess everything that other comrades take seriously, that they fight for, that they are inspired by. The 'background officials' seemed to be inspired by nothing and apparently nothing could shake their cool. They confined themselves to working out the next tactical step cautiously and carefully ...[41]

It is only fair to add that Wolf claimed that Leonhard had not fairly represented him in his book, dismissing this description of him as an 'ice-cold actor' as a 'cliché'.[42]

Wolf's marital life shows him to have been anything but 'ice-cold'. He married the first of three wives in 1944. His bride was Emmi Stenzer, a German woman whom he had met at the Comintern school. The marriage broke up in the mid-1970s when Emmi found out that Wolf was having an affair. He explained that she thought more like a Russian woman. In other words, she did not forgive him but divorced him.[43] Wolf's attitude might reflect his own family life. Friedrich Wolf had fathered his first illegitimate child while fleeing from Nazi Germany and his last at the age of 65 in the year he died.

Wolf's second marriage did not last long and he was apparently unwilling to speak much about it. From these marriages he had four children. His third marriage was to a woman a good deal younger than himself, who ironically had once fallen foul of the secret police when trying to flee East Germany.

The key to Wolf's success was that the Soviet authorities liked him. From early on he had excellent relations with the most important Soviet officials. Leonhard provided a story which illustrated this. Wolf told him in 1947 that he would have to stop thinking about a 'separate German way to socialism', which was outlined in the SED's programme. Leonhard replied that he had better knowledge of the SED's political line than Wolf, since he worked in the Central Secretariat. Wolf said, smiling: 'There are higher authorities than your Central Secretariat.' Leonhard noted: 'He obviously enjoyed talking about "your" Central Secretariat.' Wolf was proved right. The Soviet authorities had informed him before the Central Secretariat that rhetoric about the 'separate German way to socialism' would come to an end.[44]

The trust in which the Russians held Wolf was the key reason for his appointment as head of East German foreign intelligence at the age of only 30. He listed three specific reasons for his advancement. First, he had no relatives in the West with whom he was in direct contact. Second, he had lived in the Soviet Union. Third, he knew Russian. He believed also that his experience as a journalist with the Eastern Zone's radio service had furthered his career in intelligence, making him seem an appropriate choice for the conduct of 'active measures'.[45]

MIELKE AND FOREIGN INTELLIGENCE

According to Wolf's evidence, relations between the domestic branch of the Stasi and foreign intelligence were very bad in the early years. Mielke received Wolf coolly when he came to see him after his appointment as head of the IWF partly because he resented the existence of an intelligence agency outside his own Ministry.[46] He had already tried unsuccessfully to avoid this situation by building up his own foreign intelligence agency.[47] According to Wolf the existence of an East German intelligence service offended Mielke's conception of state security. Wolf described this in his memoirs: 'For years he had felt the intelligence service to be superfluous and disruptive. Yes, he regarded it as a bad design, and for many of the leaders subordinate to him this service remained a foreign body within the Ministry and suspect ....'[48] 'According to Mielke, foreign intelligence ... produced only paper and created superfluous information.'[49] Thus Mielke resented Wolf's organization even after it was merged with the MfS in 1953, creating an 'unbearable atmosphere' for its officers.[50] This atmosphere had improved by the end of the 1960s thanks to the success of the HVA which, as Wolf pointed out, also improved Mielke's reputation.

> The undeniable successes of our service in the following years also improved Mielke's reputation. Finally he came to be proud of it. Foreign Intelligence played a not insignificant part in securing the détente and disarmament policies of the DDR and of the Warsaw Pact. Through its successes on the front of military, foreign policy and security policy, and the detection of hidden attacks of the other side, it won the respect of the Soviet Union and of the other socialist states. The efforts of the DDR's economy to master technical progress was given a powerful stimulus through our work. In this way Mielke's relationship with me also changed.[51]

Even Mielke's attitude towards Wolf changed: 'Undoubtedly he valued my abilities, he often made me his "token egg-head" [*Vorzeige-Intelligenzler*] in internal party affairs but with respect to power, he regarded me as unsuitable. He saw in me an abstract thinker.'[52] Wolf effected this improvement partly by his awareness of Mielke's sensitivities. He made it clear that he was neither seeking to be a party leader nor Mielke's successor.[53]

In discussing Wolf's evidence, one must never lose sight of the possible end for which it was intended. Wolf's memoirs and interviews were made at a time when he faced arrest and trial in the united Germany. Arguably an important part of his defence was to dissociate himself from Mielke and the repression of the SED regime which he personified. Central to this defence was Wolf's argument that 'Mielke did not succeed in fully integrating foreign intelligence and in reducing its relative independence.'[54] As a result, Wolf had no responsibility for internal security matters.[55] This was enough to convince a German court in June 1995 that there were no grounds for Wolf's imprisonment. Wolf was not legally held responsible for Stasi repression in East Germany. But his statements understated the close links between domestic and foreign espionage. After all, both were part of the same organization with the same main adversary, namely West Germany.

There was never a watertight distinction between internal security and foreign espionage in East Germany. After all, most of the HVA's activities took place in, or were directed against, the same people but a different state. On a practical level, relations between the HVA and the rest of the MfS had to be close. The HVA benefited from the massive phone-tapping operation conducted by the 4,500-strong Main Department III of the MfS.[56] Many foreign agents were not recruited abroad but when visiting the DDR.

THE HVA AND THE KGB

One of Wolf's great strengths in dealing with Mielke was the continued support of the Soviet authorities. This ensured that he did not go the way of Zaisser and Wollweber who had lost the goodwill of the Russians.[57] In the 1950s, the links between the IWF then the HVA and the KGB were intimate. Soviet officers worked together with their East German counterparts in all areas. Initially the KGB officers styled themselves 'advisers'. Later they became known as 'liaison officers'.[58]

The exchange of intelligence between Moscow and East Berlin was comprehensive. All the information obtained by HVA departments was sent in copy to the KGB's liaison officers attached to the HVA leadership. Three exceptions were: documents relating to relations between the DDR and the

USSR or the FRG and the USSR; English-language documents from NATO were sent to the KGB in Russian translation in order to protect the source; and HVA documents produced by the provincial administrations of the MfS only went to the KGB when they were of particular importance.[59] Information was exchanged with other intelligence services of the Warsaw Pact at regular conferences.[60] The KGB's main data base played a central role in the flow of information. It was put into operation in 1979 and was known by its known acronym, SOUD – 'System for Operational and Institutional Data'.[61] This sounds like *sud*, the Russian word for 'judge'. It was here that all the Warsaw Pact services were able to conduct central name traces. Symbolic of the close intelligence cooperation in the Warsaw Pact, the computer had been built in East Germany.[62]

The closeness of the working relationship between the HVA and the KGB extended to operations. On occasions, the MfS provided the KGB with East German citizens as regular intelligence officers. An example was Katarina Nummert. She joined the Stasi in 1972 and was trained in East Berlin and Moscow. In 1974 she married Karl Krumminsch, a Soviet citizen. The next year the couple were sent as illegals to Iran. They thereafter served in Austria, before being unmasked and arrested in Switzerland in 1981 after the authorities came into possession of decrypts of their radio communications.[63]

As with the domestic branch of the MfS, so with the HVA, intimate links with the KGB continued right till the end of the DDR and even after the deterioration in Soviet–East German relations which followed Gorbachev's accession in 1985. An example of the closeness of the bond was provided by the MfS's main headquarters in the East Berlin's *Normannenstraße* at the beginning of 1990, shortly after the East German Revolution. This was replete with decorations stressing the two agencies' common origins. Busts of Felix Dzerzhinsky predominated, followed by those of Richard Sorge. There were many examples of the bonds between the services such as photographs of football teams comprised of KGB and Stasi officers.[64]

But there were signs of trouble after 1985. According to information provided by the KGB defector, Oleg Gordievsky, Honecker resented the arrogant behaviour of Soviet diplomats and KGB officers and determined to punish them. There was an incident as early as the mid-1970s, when a KGB officer was arrested for drunken driving. In response, General Anatoli Ivanovich Lazarev, the head of the KGB in Karlshorst, complained about 'the use of Nazi methods against a fraternal power'. Honecker remained firm and Lazarev was recalled to Moscow. It is impossible to say how far KGB-HVA operations were impaired after the distinct deterioration in relations between Moscow and East Berlin after 1985. According to Gordievsky, both Mielke and Wolf complained to the KGB that Honecker was 'restricting the intimacy of Soviet–GDR intelligence collaboration'. As a result 'There were endless discussions in the Centre, some of them witnessed by Gordievsky in Grushko's [the head of the KGB's foreign intelligence] office, on how to strengthen Mielke's and Wolf's hands against Honecker ....'[65]

It is difficult to determine the extent to which East German intelligence was meeting specifically East German requirements by the 1980s. Undoubtedly the bulk of its effort was against the West German target. However, this does not imply that it was hampering the Warsaw Pact's effort elsewhere in the world. Far from it, the services of the KGB and the satellites amounted to a massive effort on a world-wide level, at least in terms of manpower. Furthermore, the HVA was present in all the major states of the world, though not in force. Such evidence as there is, indicates that the HVA operated where it was most effective according to an amicable 'socialist division of labour'. For example, in questions of nuclear weapons, the KGB dealt primarily with the USA, while the HVA dealt primarily with West Germany.[66] Finally, the HVA's activities in the FRG had a far broader relevance than Germany alone because of the concentration of NATO there.[67]

In addition to the HVA, ZAIG/5 was responsible for SOUD. Among the categories of people registered were: members of enemy intelligence services; members of centres of ideological diversion; members of subversive organizations; enemy activists; provocateurs; illegal frontier guides; expelled or undesirable individuals; enemy diplomats; enemy correspondents; members of enemy trade, economic and cultural centres; smugglers; economic criminals. The MfS provided around a quarter of all the entries in SOUD from 1979–89, which demonstrates the importance of the Stasi to the KGB.

THE STRUCTURE OF THE HVA

The HVA's concentration on West Germany is apparent from its organizational breakdown. The HVA had 15 operational departments, as well as a further department dealing with communications and supplies. Three dealt specifically with West Germany: Department I for the FRG's State Apparatus; Department II for Parties and public organizations (*gesellschafliche Organisationen*) in the FRG; and Department IV for FRG Military-strategic intelligence. Three dealt specifically with the rest of Western Europe: Department III for the HVA's residencies in the West; Department XI for North America (USA, Canada and Mexico) and Department XII for NATO and the EC. If organizational breakdown is a justifiable indicator, operations against the US appear to have been more important than those against the rest of the NATO allies since Department XI had nine sections against five in Department XII. But this does not necessarily mean that HVA officers were more active in the Western hemisphere than they were in Western Europe outside the FRG. Much of the espionage against the United States was carried out on German soil. This is also clear from the HVA's organization.

Department XI, which dealt with North America, was sub-divided into nine sections. Three dealt with the US presence in Germany: Section 2: US Embassy in Bonn and US citizens in the FRG; Section 5: US armed forces (USAREUR/EUCOM); Section 9: US military mission in Potsdam and US armed forces. According to one expert, Department XI was mainly concerned with the recruitment of US citizens travelling in the DDR.[68] Another source of recruits was US citizens working in West Germany. Discothèques and pubs were seen as good places to make contacts.[69]

Two sections dealt with US citizens on their home ground: Section 1: US/Canada/Mexico, including the infiltration of illegals; Section 4: US representation with the United Nations in New York. Section 3 dealt with US citizens in Western Europe. The other 3 sections of Department XI had a general competence: Section 6: Scientific evaluation; Section 7: Training and cadre control; Section 8: Evaluation and reporting. Of the HVA's operational departments, there was only one for the 'rest of the world'. Everything was there in it from India and Indonesia to Chile.[70]

Some of the HVA's departments with a general competence were overwhelmingly concerned with West Germany. For example sector A of Department IX which dealt with counter-espionage, was primarily concerned with the FRG. Four of its ten sections dealt with West German intelligence agencies, one with US intelligence while another was described as 'other Western intelligence services'. After Departments I (FRG State Apparatus) and II (Parties and public organizations in the FRG), Department IX was the most important in the FRG.[71] From both the offensive and defensive point of view, hostile intelligence services were a high priority for the HVA. The last basic guidelines for the HVA were 'Richtlinie Nr.2/79 für die Arbeit mit Inoffiziellen Mitarbeitern im Operationsgebiet' ('Guideline No.2/79 for Working with Unofficial Agents in the Field of Operations').[72] From this document it was clear that the three key targets were the secret services of West Germany: the BND; the BfV; and the MAD (*Militärischer Abschirmdienst*), military counter-intelligence.

THE PERSONNEL OF THE HVA

The HVA was numerically quite small, numbering only 4,000 officers in 1989.[73] This number included both intelligence officers and technical staff.[74]

However, East Germany had a higher ratio of foreign intelligence officers to population than the Soviet Union, where the KGB's First Chief Directorate numbered 12,000 in the mid-1980s.[75]

The HVA was the elite branch of the MfS, but its members were not all like Markus Wolf. In the early years, the personnel of foreign intelligence was drawn either from the KPD's *Apparat* or by the KGB from prisoner-of-war camps.[76] Many of them were narrow-minded and inflexible. Great efforts were made to improve this, and the HVA had priority in recruiting.[77] A particularly high standard of recruit was needed for two main reasons. First, HVA officers had to be of complete reliability if they were to operate abroad. Second, a vital and increasing part of the HVA's work involved espionage against science and technology. Only well-qualified officers were capable of acquiring and assessing information in this field. Not surprisingly, the HVA was particularly strict in who it employed. A prime source of recruits was the SED's youth organization, the *Freie Deutsche Jugend* (FDJ). A requirement was that recruits should have no relatives in the West with whom they were in regular contact, which was difficult to meet. Increasingly, recruits were drawn from within the *Apparat* itself and specifically from the families existing members.[78] As further guarantee of loyalty, HVA salaries were higher than those for the domestic security branch of the MfS,[79] though arguably they could be said to have earned this, since they had a particularly heavy workload, often being required to work until 9 or 10 o'clock at night.[80] Even the HVA's agents inside the DDR had to be ideologically sound, whereas the domestic branch of the MfS used students who were hostile to the regime.[81] The effectiveness of these security measures was evident from lack of HVA defectors. Even so, it was always difficult to explain why the West was able to recruit only one important HVA officer. At the time, the German character was often mentioned as the key to the HVA's impeccable discipline.

THE STILLER CASE

The experience of the HVA's main defector, Werner Stiller, is revealing about its recruiting practices. Stiller was born in 1947 in Leipzig. He studied physics and Leipzig's Karl-Marx University. It was as a student that the Stasi first approached him in April 1970. For two years he served as an *Inoffizieller Mitarbeiter*. This was effectively his probationary period, with the added advantage, from the Stasi's point of view, that he was providing information on his fellow students. He became a regular officer of the HVA in August 1972 and was allocated to Department XIII of the Science and Technology Sector of the HVA. Specifically, he was attached to section (*Referat*) 1, which dealt primarily with nuclear physics.[82] In particular, Stiller's section was concerned with obtaining information about the production and deployment of nuclear weapons.[83] In this respect Stiller was typical of the high calibre recruit which the HVA needed to fulfil the needs of modern espionage. Stiller's duties were by no means limited to the assessment of intelligence. By the time of his defection in January 1979, he had been running agents for six years and currently controlled 35 *Inoffizielle Mitarbeiter* and a number of Western agents, including the atomic physicist Rolf Dobbertin in Paris, Professor Karl Hauffe at Göttingen University, Reiner Füller at the centre for atomic research in Karlsruhe, an industrialist in Hanover and an engineer at Siemens.[84] By this time Stiller had attained the rank of *Oberleutnant* (roughly, 'First Lieutenant').

For two and a half years before his defection, Stiller had been working for the BND, whom he provided with a list of the HVA's staff.[85] After his flight to the West, 16 HVA agents were arrested in the West as a result of his information and at least 15 had to flee to the DDR. Worst of all, the BND was given a close insight into the HVA. According to one commentator, Stiller's defection was a great personal setback to Markus Wolf since it ruled out any chance he had of succeeding Mielke.[86] Even after the collapse of East Germany, Wolf had not forgiven Stiller, still referring to him as 'the traitor Stiller'.

SCIENTIFIC AND TECHNICAL INTELLIGENCE

Stiller's defection showed the West the extent to which the DDR was now engaged in espionage against the scientific and technological (S&T) target.[87] In all the Soviet Bloc countries technological espionage sections were set up in the foreign intelligence service. This was done explicitly at the request of the Soviet Union.[88] S&T intelligence was clearly important to East Germany's first regular espionage agency, the IWF. This priority was apparent from the cover which the organization took, that of an East–West trading firm, as well as from the organizational breakdown of the organization, which was described above. Thereafter S&T requirements were a powerful stimulus to the development of East German espionage. As Wolf put it, 'The efforts of the GDR's economy to master technical progress was given a powerful stimulus through our work.'[89] He did not point out, however, that the HVA was also following key Soviet requirements. Nor did he mention that from Moscow's point of view, the most crucial S&T intelligence was that with military applications, though of course in the sphere of high technology it was never easy to draw the line between what was of civilian and was of military use. This confusion is apparent from the very first paragraph of a directive on West Germany signed by Vladimir Kryuchkov, the head of the KGB in July 1977:

> Work against West Germany is assuming an increasing importance in connection with the growth of the economic potential of the FRG and the increase in its influence in the solution of important international issues.
>
> The Federal Republic of Germany is both economically and militarily the leading West European capitalist country. It is the main strategic bridgehead of NATO, where a significant concentration of the adversary's military strength can be observed ... This situation distinguishes the FRG from the other European capitalist states and makes it the most important component of the military bloc. Within the FRG military scientific-research studies in the fields of atomic energy, aviation, rocket construction, electronics, chemistry and biology are being intensively pursued.[90]

By the end of the 1970s, the HVA's operations in the field of S&T were second only to those of the KGB, with the Romanians and the Polish secret services vying for third place. The relatively easy access to the targets of West Germany made the HVA the best-placed of all the Soviet Bloc intelligence services to acquire such information. As Ion Pacepa, the head of Romanian foreign intelligence noted: 'In 1978, the largest technological espionage effort was the East German, based on its record number of illegal officers and agents documented as West Germans working everywhere in the Western hemisphere.'[91] Markus Wolf agreed that the intelligence services of the other Warsaw Pact countries were not obtaining S&T information on the same scale.[92] The HVA's organizational structure is another indicator of the priority placed on S&T intelligence. Four of the HVA's 15 operational departments belonged to its Science and Technology Sector (*Sektor Wissenschaft und Technik (SWT)*).

HVA'S CONCENTRATION ON WEST GERMANY

Markus Wolf once said that the British intelligence service was probably the best in the world, because it was the one about which he knew least.[93] If lack of knowledge about an intelligence service is a valid indicator of success, then the HVA scores very highly. Even after the Revolution of 1989, little is known about its activities outside Germany and outside the field of science and technology. In part of course, this reflects the HVA's concentration on the FRG.

Concentration on West Germany was inevitable first, because it met the requirements both of the Soviet Union and the East German leadership; and second because by the 1970s the HVA was enjoying a success there unparalleled in the work of any other satellite service. The FRG was more thoroughly penetrated than any other Western state.[94]

In the 1950s and 1960s the HVA's scope for action abroad was limited by Western foreign policy. According to the Hallstein Doctrine of 1955, the West German government announced that it would not maintain diplomatic relations with any state that recognized the DDR. None of the states of the Western Alliance did so, nor did African and Asian states which were anxious to procure West German economic aid. As a result East Berlin was left without diplomatic missions in most countries. By extension the HVA was unable to work from the cover of Residencies established under the diplomatic immunity of East German Embassies, as was the normal practice of the Soviet Bloc secret services.

The unique difficulties did not prevent the HVA working on a global level, and it undertook the passive one of building up networks abroad. The Hallstein Doctrine might have encouraged the HVA to rely more than other Soviet Bloc intelligence services on the use of 'illegals', namely intelligence officers operating abroad under the cover of a false assumed nationality. Wolf gave a slight indication that this was the case, saying that lack of diplomatic representation forced the HVA to choose this 'higher form of intelligence work'.[95] Of course, in compensation for the Hallstein Doctrine, the HVA had an advantage in its placement of illegals in the territory of its leading adversary which found few parallels in the work of other intelligence agencies. It was relatively simple for the East Germans to infiltrate agents into the FRG under false covers, posing as refugees seeking asylum. But the HVA also used foreign countries as the starting point for its illegals.[96] For example, the Stasi illegal, Siegfried Gäbler *alias* Jürgen Höfs was infiltrated into the FRG through France.

The German community abroad was large and growing. This meant that it was relatively easy for HVA illegals to avoid observation in non-German speaking countries. Furthermore, both the East Germans and the KGB saw the German presence abroad as a fertile source of agents. Kryuchkov noted in 1977:

> At the present time the FRG has roughly 400 official missions abroad. A large number of West German journalists, advisers and representatives of business circles are to be found in various countries of the world. Over 4 million Germans are living in Western Europe at the present time, while there are roughly 7 million living in the USA and Canada. German colonies

> in the countries of Latin America, Africa and Asia are expanding as a consequence of the growing penetration of West German capital into the developing countries. All this creates favourable pre-conditions for the conduct of intelligence against the FRG within the areas mentioned.[97]

Another way of circumventing the Hallstein Doctrine was to recruit agents from the foreign nationals visiting the DDR. This of course involved the close cooperation of the domestic wing of the MfS. The Stasi's campaign against tourists and visitors is described in Chapter 4. A very important source of reliable agents was students studying in East Germany. This source became particularly significant from the 1960s onwards following decolonization of Africa and the growing importance of the Middle East, both of which areas saw a struggle for influence between East and West. This struggle involved both sides attempting to infiltrate their agents into important posts in these countries. The Czech defector, Josef Frolik described how the 'Seventeenth of November University' in Prague became a gold-mine for African and Arabic agents. Analogous developments took place in East Germany and other states of the Soviet Bloc, with Moscow's 'Patrice Lumumba University' holding pride of place:

> Here were 4,500 students, predominantly coloured, from all over Africa and the Middle East, who had come to Czechoslovakia to study the normal subjects one does at university, as well as to be indoctrinated, whether they liked it or not, in communist theory and practice. Before being allowed to attend this 'university', the would-be student had to attend a one-year preparatory course in the Czech language. Here he would be checked as to his fitness for recruitment to the Intelligence Service. If he were found suitable, he would continue his studies at the University, but at the same time would be schooled for his future role as spy, ready for infiltration into his own country's infrastructure.[98]

This method of recruitment was by no means restricted to Asians and Africans. One group of Stasi students who have recently come into prominence in their home countries are the Icelanders. In this case, the recruits were already of communist persuasion when they left home. For example, Gudmundur Agustsson studied economics in East Berlin at some time around 1958–63. After his return to Iceland he became prominent as a communist journalist and reached the party's central committee. On at least one occasion he tried to recruit a sub-agent. As an Icelandic commentator noted: 'Agustsson was one of scores of promising youngsters who went to East Germany through the intermediary of the Party and were hand-picked by the chairman Einar Olgeirsson.'[99]

In the 1970s, the HVA exploited the opening up of the DDR for political and scientific visitors to recruit agents. At the same time, the development of the MfS's activities outside Germany was made possible by the increasing number of states which recognized the DDR after West Germany signed the Treaty of Moscow in 1970, which brought the implicit end to the Hallstein Doctrine. The legal representation of East Germany throughout the world also increased the East German regime's need for information about states with which it was dealing officially on the diplomatic level for the first time.

THE UNITED STATES

It was easier for the MfS to set up operations in the United States after diplomatic relations were established between East Berlin and Washington. Another advantage was the GDR's representation at the United Nations Organization in New York. Whatever the scale of the HVA's work, it was a long time before the first spy scandal occurred. This contributes to the conclusion that the MfS only gradually found its feet in the New World.[100] The espionage case started at the end of 1979 when the FBI uncovered Eberhard Lüttich, a Stasi major now working as an illegal in New York. The Americans were able to recruit him. Until 1969 Lüttich had been in the HVA's South America section (*Referat*). He had been sent out to New York in 1973 under the cover of a businessman working for a West German haulage contractor. This job had put him in contact with German diplomatic and military personnel moving between Europe and America. He had been given the task of making contacts with American universities, in order to recruit academics as agents. After Stiller, he was the West's most important East German defector.

The second espionage case involving the HVA broke in the early 1980s. Professor Alfred Zehe was a professor of physics at Dresden Technical University. In the late 1970s he was a guest lecturer at Puebla University in Mexico. At the same time he worked as an *Inoffizieller Mitarbeiter* for the MfS.

He bought weapon plans from a civilian employee of the US Marine Corps. Unfortunately for Zehe, this sub-agent disclosed what he had done and agreed to work for the FBI. In 1983 Zehe was arrested when he entered the United States. He confessed.

BRITAIN

The Stasi could fall back on a 'noble' tradition of German communist spying in Britain. One of the most successful spies was Ursula Kuczynski Beurton who as 'Sonia' worked for the Soviets in Britain from 1941 to 1950. She had been recruited by Richard Sorge (see Chapter 1) in Shanghai before the war and had gone on from there to Switzerland. She was the case officer for, among others, the German communist atom spy Klaus Fuchs. When he was exposed in 1950, she managed to evade arrest and get to East Germany, where she saw the fall of communism in 1990. She was born into a bourgeois Jewish family who were inspired by the Bolshevik take-over in Russia. Her brother Jürgen Kuczynski, who came to Britain as a refugee, worked on the evaluation of the US strategic bombing of Germany and passed all the knowledge he gained to the Soviets. After the war he pursued an academic career in the DDR. Her father René was also part of the KPD refugee group in Britain who considered it their duty to spy for the Soviets, both before and after the Hitler–Stalin Pact.

Reference was made in Chapter 4 to the Stasi surveillance of British visitors to the DDR and of attempts to recruit British journalists and academics for their cause. Writing in *The Times* (6 September 1993), Jamie Dettmer identified six high-ranking Stasi men who were based at the East German embassy in London during the 1980s. Dr Karlheinz Bauer was the chief Stasi resident in the early 1980s. He was ostensibly the commercial attaché. He returned to the DDR in 1984. Klaus Pfenning was a first secretary and the chief Stasi officer in London from December 1987 until autumn 1989. He returned to the DDR to work in the MfS monitoring the US National Security Agency and the White House National Security Council. Peter Husung, who succeeded Pfenning as first secretary was an OibE. He is said to have been responsible for guiding agents and 'moles' into service for the KGB once the SED regime collapsed. The other Stasi diplomats were Dr Oswald Schneidratus (1984–7), Dr Hans-Hendrick Kasper (1984–7) and Ulrich Kempf (1984–8). Kempf apparently watched British political developments. Commercial attachés were well placed to manipulate businessmen who tend to put business first and politics second. Given all the restrictions covering DDR trade with the outside world, all the bureaucracy and form-filling, a commercial attaché could ease the path of the British businessman, set up meetings at the Leipzig fair and elsewhere. The Stasi were particularly interested in the latest technology in all branches of the economy. No doubt they had some limited success in this sector. There has been much speculation about attempts to recruit politicians. The only politician taken to court for espionage since 1945 was Will Owen. Owen, MP for Morpeth, was accused in April of betraying defence secrets to the Warsaw Pact. He was a member of the House of Commons Defence Estimates Committee. His paymasters were the Czechs, who were very active in London circles, rather than the East Germans. He admitted receiving money but was acquitted of the charges.

(Lord) George Wigg, Paymaster-General, in the Wilson government, with responsibility for liaison with MI 5, told David Childs (1977) he thought Owen guilty. Chapman Pincher, the well-known expert on espionage, came to the same conclusion in his *Too Secret Too Long*. According to one leading Stasi officer, recruitment of Western politicians was expressly prohibited by Honecker as counter-productive. Such politicians could be drawn into friendly conversations, lunches, dinners, fact-finding visits and other hospitality through the embassy and through their counterparts in the DDR. Attempts would be made by their, often charming hosts, to nudge them a little in the direction of understanding the SED's point of view. They would give much information in conversation which was of use to the MfS and its political masters. Attempts to recruit them would only frighten them off, perhaps lead to diplomatic protests, and certainly weaken Honecker's charm offensive in the West. Journalists, on the other hand, were fair game. They had the means to provide a good deal of information and could be used to cleverly mould opinion towards a more sympathetic view of the DDR and its policies.

To some degree academics were in a similar position to journalists. They could be flattered by interest in their research, their contribution to international understanding and so on. For many years British academics interested in visiting the DDR felt it would be much easier to do so if they joined the communist-dominated British–GDR Friendship Society. They and others, especially leftists, nuclear disarmers, trade unionists, were the targets, in the first place, of East German front or mass organizations like the Peace Council of the DDR, *Liga für Völkerfreundschaft*, and similar bodies. Visits to the DDR by Western groups were carefully evaluated by their hosts and posted to the Stasi who were on the lookout for likely candidates, those who wanted to engage more actively in the fight for peace! Sometimes visitors were asked to pass on letters to friends or relatives (German prewar emigrants who had stayed). These reports could be entirely innocent, but they could also be tests. Unwitting British could be drawn into Stasi courier service in this way. Another method was for a DDR academic to ask for information about Britain, pleading he could not get such material in the DDR. Most British academics, if asked, would readily agree. This too could be the start in some cases of something more sinister. Having met British academics at conferences, exhibitions, open lectures and the like in Britain, a DDR diplomat could ask for help in the same way. 'Could you jot down a few notes on recent developments in the British economy? I'm new here, rather desperate, and know very little.' The cry for help would be answered. The East German, at a lunch for two in a good Soho restaurant, would insist on a thank-you gift. This would become a regular pattern and could become an intelligence operation.

Students were even more vulnerable than their teachers. Their lack of money and experience, their generosity, idealism and adventure lust could be exploited. In particular cases they represented a long-term investment with the possibility of eventually achieving positions of influence and authority. Over the years thousands of British students went on exchanges to the DDR. The East Germans were in a good position to carry out false flag recruitment in Britain. For this they could use genuine West Germans resident in Britain, or East Germans with false West German identities. The one spy case which reached the public domain in the 1980s involved an East German couple, Reinhardt and Sonja Schulze. They were each sentenced to ten years in prison on 10 July 1986 at the Central Criminal Court in London. They had been charged under the Official Secrets Act for preparing espionage activities calculated to prejudice state interests. They were living in London under false identities. They had been under observation for some time and were arrested within days of Hans Joachim Tiedge in West Germany. (See Chapter 6.)

The Stasi were always aware that the moves of East German diplomats and journalists were being monitored in Britain by MI 5 and other security bodies and that most of their attempts at recruitment would end in failure. However, Will Owen is said to have met his Czech controller in London parks on a weekly basis for many years.

All these methods were used in other West European countries. The chances of success were greater where there were large communist movements or traditions of neutralism as in France, Italy or Iceland, Denmark, Norway or Sweden. However, the Stasi's resources were limited and its main thrust was in Germany.

ASIA AND AFRICA

If the HVA's activities against the Soviet Bloc's leading adversary, the United States, were markedly discreet, against the second great rival, China, they seem to have been almost or entirely non-existent. Wolf has not mentioned the HVA's involvement in China, nor have other sources. It seems, therefore, that this field was the preserve of the KGB and, possibly, of the other satellite intelligence services. The HVA's activities have left equally little mark elsewhere in South-East Asia.

The same is not true, however, of Africa and the Middle East. Here East Germany provided 'fraternal assistance' to developing states by providing them with assistance in the development of their police and security services. At the same time, the DDR cooperated closely with certain 'national liberation movements', such as the Palestine Liberation Organization and the African National Congress. Some of this involvement became known at the time, though it made remarkably little public impact, far less, for example, than the CIA's alleged assistance for the Shah of Iran's notorious secret police, *Savak*, which caused an international scandal when it was exposed after the Iranian Revolution in 1979.

MfS involvement in Africa had started as early as the 1960s. After the fall of the Ghanaian president, Kwame Nkrumah in 1966, it was revealed that Stasi officers had been working as his security advisers. This led to a diplomatic crisis when the new regime arrested the Stasi major, Jürgen Rogalla. In response, East Berlin prevented Ghanaians leaving the DDR. After two and a half months Rogalla was released.

The mid-1970s was the heyday of Soviet Bloc influence in sub-Saharan Africa. A Marxist-leaning junta came to power in Ethiopia in 1974. Following the break-up of the Portuguese Empire, Marxist regimes came into existence in Angola and Mozambique. At this time the Stasi made a major contribution to the development of the police and security services of Angola, Ethiopia, Mozambique and, in the Arab world, to the People's Republic of Yemen. Besides assisting left-wing regimes, they also provided security advisers for two exceptionally brutal dictators who made little effort to legitimate their rule by any kind of ideology – President Francisco Macias Nguema of Equatorial Guinea, who fell in 1979, and President Idi Amin of Uganda. When Amin was ousted in 1980, two highest-ranking East German diplomats were killed in Kampala while trying to remove compromising documents.[101] It is not known whether they belonged to the HVA.

By 1977 it was reported that the MfS was involved in building up the security services of Angola and Mozambique. The local agents were much more brutal than the Stasi was at home in East Germany.[102] In Mozambique, for example, the local security service, the Serviçao Nacional de Segurança Popular (SNASP), sent dissenters to labour camps officially known as 'centres for mental decolonization'.[103] In Ethiopia, Colonel Mengistu's regime acquired an even more fearful reputation for brutality. A fairly large detachment of Stasi officers was stationed in Ethiopia under the command of a Stasi colonel. The East Germans trained both Ethiopia's regular and secret police. The Yemeni regime likewise had recourse to concentration camps. In this case one report stated that the MfS were even involved in running them.[104] Certainly this would account for the 300–400 Stasi officers who were reportedly present in Southern Yemen in 1978.[105]

The Soviet African adventure was turning sour by the end of the 1970s as all of its clients became involved in counter-insurgency conflicts which they had little prospect of winning. But the MfS continued to play its role as auxiliary to the KGB by training the security services of other states who entered the Soviet empire, such as the *Khad* in Afghanistan.[106] Likewise, they assisted the Sandinista regime in Nicaragua, as did the Bulgarian and Cuban intelligence services.[107]

THE STASI AND TERRORISM

The MfS's involvement with the Third World is closely linked the question of the extent to which it was involved in supporting terrorism. East Germany's support for international terrorism in the 1970s and 1980s was far greater than the Western public suspected. According to Peter-Michael Diestel, East Germany's last, non-communist, Minister of the Interior, the country became 'an Eldorado for terrorists' in this period. Revelations about East Germany's assistance to international terrorists began after the seizure of Stasi headquarters throughout the country at the end of 1989 and beginning of 1990. In just one Stasi regional headquarters, 30 briefcases were seized from *Hauptverwaltung* (Main Department) (HA) XII, which dealt with counter-terrorism as well as with hiding former terrorists in East Germany.[108] The search was helped by tips from former Stasi officers,[109] and by a former West German terrorist, Susanne Albrecht, who turned State Evidence.[110]

West German terrorists of the Red Army Faction (RAF), whose best known members were the Baader-Meinhof Gang, started receiving sanctuary in East Germany from 1977 on.[111] The Stasi gave them new identities, papers, apartments and jobs. According to one ex-terrorist, the MfS even provided the RAF with hiding places inside West Germany.[112] Whether the RAF used East Germany as a base from which to attack the Federal Republic remains unclear.

Documents proved that the Stasi not only provided shelter for RAF fugitives, but also facilitated contacts between them and the Palestine Liberation Organization (PLO). According to the West German security service (BfV), the East German authorities 'regularly closed their eyes' when RAF members went through East Berlin's Schönefeld airport on their way to Palestinian training camps in Jordan, the Lebanon, and Southern Yemen. In the 1970s, the connection between the RAF and the PLO was so close than on two occasions they collaborated in hijackings.[113]

The communist regimes of Eastern Europe made a distinction between terrorist groups and national liberation movements. Exactly how the two categories differed in their interpretation was never clear, except that they held national liberation movements to be engaged in a justified war against the military occupiers of their homeland. Thus while Soviet Bloc states condemned the RAF as terrorists, they offered logistical support to the PLO as a 'national liberation movement'. Wolf adhered to the this distinction in his public statements.[114]

Moreover, the PLO was recognized by many states. Undoubtedly the HVA had, in the words of Markus Wolf, 'very close, very intensive' links with certain Arab states such as Syria and Iraq which supported terrorism and was present there in force. Wolf equated the HVA's links with the PLO to those with these states. Wolf admitted that the East Germans trained the PLO, but not on a large scale.[115] That East Germany supported the PLO was never a secret. Yaser Arafat was received in East Germany as a state guest. During the Lebanese civil war wounded Palestinians were treated in hospitals in Prague and East Berlin.

But the extent of East German support for the PLO was far greater than Western observers suspected in the 1970s and 1980s, or than Wolf subsequently admitted. In August 1990, the East German Minister for Disarmament and Defence referred to documents which proved that the communist regime had provided military training for the PLO at the Friedrich Engels Military Academy in East Berlin.

The Stasi's support for Arab terrorists, at least on one occasion, went beyond logistical support and training for a 'national liberation movement'. Evidence now exists proving that the MfS permitted Libyan-backed terrorists to carry out the bombing of the West Berlin 'La Belle' discothèque in 1986, which led to the deaths of many US servicemen. The West German magazine, *Der Spiegel* obtained a Stasi document entitled 'State of Knowledge about the Preparation and Carrying Out of the Terrorist Attack on the West Berlin Discothèque "La Belle"'. It was drawn up by *Hauptverwaltung* II (counter-intelligence), Section 15 (Libya).[116] According to this document, the Stasi had an agent, codenamed 'Alba' inside the Libyan-Palestinian terrorist group which carried out the attack, who informed them that Libyan secret agents had smuggled weapons and explosives into East Berlin. 'Alba' stopped providing information in the days immediately preceding the bombing. Nonetheless, the MfS knew very well that the terrorist group was preparing to bomb a US military target in West Berlin, and allowed them to return to East Berlin thereafter.[117] The Stasi's complicity in the bombing was acknowledged by Diestel, the DDR's last Minister of the Interior who stated that according to information he had received from informants and seized files, Stasi agents even helped transport the explosives used in the attack to West Berlin. Furthermore, on 12 July 1990, *Die Welt* published East German intelligence files indicating that the 'highest authorities' in East Berlin had allowed the bombing to take place. Who these 'authorities' were, has remained unclear. In 1990, Wolf denied that the MfS had participated directly in acts of terrorism, such as the attack on 'La Belle' discothèque. He pointed out that though the Iraqis, Syrians and PLO were present inside the DDR, he was not involved with them.[118]

It is unclear how closely connected the Stasi were with the notorious terrorist, Ilich Ramírez Sánchez, or 'Carlos' as he is commonly known. West German investigators believed that he participated in the attack on the French cultural centre in West Berlin, the 'Maison de France', in August 1983. These suspicions were confirmed by a former high-ranking Stasi officer. Moreover, Diestel stated that well-known terrorist leaders such as Carlos, Abu Nidal and Abu Daoud, had come in and out of East Germany at will from the late 1970s until sometime in the 1980s.

One of the most important questions about the East German regime's assistance to international terrorism, is why it took such a risk. As its economy stagnated from the end of the 1970s on, East Germany became increasingly dependent on financial aid from the Federal Republic. Had the West Germans learned of even part of East Berlin's dealings with terrorists, they would certainly have cut back this aid.

The SED leadership was grateful to Iraq, which, in April 1969, was the second non-communist state to recognize the DDR. Sudan, Syria, the People's Republic of (South) Yemen, and Egypt followed in a matter of weeks. In the case of the PLO, whose leader, Yaser Arafat, first visited the DDR in 1971, the GDR was the first Warsaw Pact state to allow the PLO to set up an office on its territory. This was in 1973, more than a year before the Arab summit in Rabat (October 1974) recognized the PLO as the sole representative of the Palestinian people. One other factor in the Middle East is that the Germans were more popular than the Soviets. Perhaps this is due to the traditional ties between Germany and the Arab world. With its shaky economy the DDR was hoping to reap economic as well as political favours from its Arab friends. In these circumstances, the MfS would not shrink from giving assistance of all kinds to the PLO, Iraq, South Yemen and the other friends of the SED.

Some contacts between terrorists and the Stasi were inevitable, since the RAF found and obtained training in Arab countries, particularly Syria, Iraq and Southern Yemen, whose secret services were built up either by the MfS or the KGB. But East Germany's active support for West German and Arab terrorists may be explained by the following motives. First, there was a wish to destabilize West Germany. The East German Party leadership's eagerness to subvert the Federal Republic, given the opportunity, was revealed by captured Stasi documents, which gave details of plans to support partisan actions in the event of a possible crisis inside West Germany. Since the mid-1970s, 176 West German communists had been trained to this end in a secret camp near Frankfurt am Oder.[119] Second, support for the RAF suited the MfS's international role. The Palestine Liberation Organization was important to the Soviet Bloc in its attempts to win the goodwill of the Third World, far more of whose states recognized the PLO than did Israel. Thus, according to Peter-Jürgen Boock, an ex-RAF terrorist, the Red Army Faction gained in importance, in the Stasi's eyes, from its close connection with the PLO.[120] Third, there might have been a desire to shield East Germany from terrorist attacks by appeasing the terrorists. Fourth, the East German leader, Erich Honecker was said to have had a personal sympathy for underground 'freedom fighters'. In his youth he had been a member of the Young-Spartacus-Federation for the Fight against Exploitation and Imperialism, and according to an ex-member of the East German Politburo, revealed 'a kind of fanatical love' for the RAF.[121]

However, there were limits to the Stasi's collaboration with terrorists. The West German security service, the BfV, maintained that East German agents did not collaborate directly in terrorist attacks. This was corroborated by the evidence of captured terrorists.[122] Rather the East German leadership saw the RAF as an asset to be kept in reserve, until the time was ripe to destabilize the West in earnest.[123] Most importantly, there was no evidence that the Stasi gave orders to either the RAF, or to Arab terrorists, even though they condoned actions such as the bombing of the 'La Belle' discothèque.[124] In the case of the RAF, the Stasi remained deeply suspicious of a movement opposed to all forms of authority.[125] For their part, the RAF wished to remain politically independent, and did not regard the East German model of society as a viable alternative to capitalism. The RAF's attacks in West Germany are dealt with in the chapter which follows.

6 HVA Operations Against West Germany

On 6 May 1974 Willy Brandt, Chancellor of the Federal Republic of Germany, world-respected statesman, anti-Nazi emigrant and leading democratic socialist, announced his resignation. It sent shock waves around the world, coming as it did, less than two years after his party's best ever election result in 1972. In his letter of resignation to President Gustav Heinemann, Brandt accepted his own 'political negligence in connection with the affair of the agent Guillaume'.[1] Brandt was of course referring to the top agent of the HVA, Günter Guillaume who, together with his wife, Christel, had been arrested on 24 April. Guillaume had been working as an assistant to Brandt and, according to the Chancellor, 'arranged my contacts with the party and the trade unions, fixed my engagements and accompanied me on visits to the provinces'. Brandt had not thought it probable the DDR 'would have planted an agent disguised as a conservative Social Democrat on me when I was endeavouring to ease inter-state relations in the face of great resistance. There were certain peculiar features which encouraged my trustfulness: Guillaume was not someone who actually took part in political discussions, only a reliable aide; not a partner in serious conversation but a good, methodical worker.'[2] However, Brandt admitted that while visiting Norway with him in July 1973, Guillaume had seen 'several confidential documents'.[3] Guillaume's exposure was a considerable blow to the HVA (*Hauptverwaltung Aufklärung,* Main Administration Reconnaissance) of General Markus Wolf and of course to Erich Mielke. Wolf later regretted the fall of Brandt as apparently did Honecker.[4] The sincerity of Honecker's sorrow can be doubted. Objectively seen, the fall of Brandt would have been welcome to hardliners in the SED and the CPSU for his Social Democracy and outstretched hand were attractive to the great majority of East Germans (and East European neighbours) and this was something the SED leadership had to fear. On the other hand, the Guillaume case revealed just how successful the HVA had been in penetrating the inner circles of the West German political elite. The affair also highlighted shortcomings in the leadership of West Germany's internal security organ, the BfV. Brandt could rightly ask why nothing had been done about Guillaume before because he had been under observation for a year or more. However, he rejected the idea that the 'upper echelon' of the BfV had lured him into a trap.[5] Remarkably, the individuals most closely involved in the Guillaume case – Minister of Interior Hans Dietrich Genscher, BfV chief Günther Nollau and Chairman of the SPD parliamentary group Herbert Wehner – all came from the East. Nollau's office was later accused of slackness and negligence. Nollau, like Wehner, was, more than once, in such quarters as the *Süddeutsche Zeitung* (24 May 1974) reported, accused of being an East German agent.[6]

Another remarkable feature of the Guillaume affair was that when Bonn security officials arrived to arrest Guillaume, on the morning of 24 April 1974, he immediately confessed that he was 'a citizen of the DDR and its officer'.[7] Without this admission it would have been far more difficult, perhaps even impossible for the West German authorities to have convicted Guillaume. He claims he did it for his son who was there at the time, to give his son some orientation for the future.[8] Also surprising is Guillaume's assertion that he knew nothing of the HVA or the MfS for which he worked. Given his recruitment and training in the DDR and his long years of service, one would have expected that he knew at least the outlines of the system for which he worked. In December 1975 the Supreme *Land* Court of Düsseldorf sentenced Guillaume to 13 years' imprisonment. He served seven years and was then part of an East–West agent exchange in October 1981. His wife had been released a few months earlier. Later they were awarded the DDR's highest medal, The Karl-Marx Medal, and fêted as a heroes. However, they decided to divorce. In fact, the Guillaumes were just two of thousands of HVA agents working in West Germany. Their activities caused a political earthquake but their value to the HVA was less than that of some of their comrades. Again and again, the West German establishment was to be embarrassed from the 1950s to the 1990s by the exposure of such agents.

MARKUS WOLF AND THE IWF

The first stage of the establishment of the HVA had been in December 1951 when the Institute for Economic Research (IWF) had been set up in Pankow, East Berlin. The Institute was to be part of the foreign ministry of the DDR. Its tasks were: to gather political intelligence on West Berlin and West Germany; economic intelligence; counter-espionage; espionage outside the DDR and the surveillance of foreign missions within the DDR.[9] Those charged, by the ruling SED, with carrying on these activities were individuals who had communism in their blood, like Markus Wolf who was put in charge of counter-espionage. As we saw in Chapter 5 Wolf spent his teens in the Soviet Union. Many German communist refugees had a hard time there. Some died in Stalin's almost incomprehensible purges, others spent years in the slave labour camps. Wolf was lucky. He was sent to a secret Comintern school where the young students had codenames and were destined, after graduation, for work as full-time functionaries of the Moscow-dominated, international communist movement. Some would work openly, others undercover.[10] At the end of the war he returned to Berlin with the Red Army, working as a communist journalist before taking up his security role. He must have gone through a great deal of mental and emotional torment when one considers his childhood and teenage experiences. He could rationalize and think the Soviet Union had made 'mistakes' whereas 'Hitler fascism' was a crime from beginning to end. His friend Wolfgang Leonhard pointed out that although he was German, his nationality was of no importance. He had the same tone, the same way of lighting his cigarette as the Soviet political officers.[11] Perhaps he had felt forced to insulate himself to survive. On the other hand, the new system was already offering him a good life by the standards of Germany at that time. Leonhard, from very similar circumstances, took his chances and defected when he thought socialism had been betrayed. Wolf was of course not alone. Any number of communist-sympathizing intellectuals – Bertolt Brecht, Johannes R. Becher, Stefan Heym, Anna Seghers, Arnold Zweig, and many others – returned from exile and chose to live in the East rather than the West. It was possible to build up a picture of West Germany as a state in which Nazis were tolerated, the industrialists and civil servants who had supported or served them were restored to their property and influence, and the generals who had carried out Hitler's murderous plans were being looked after until they could once again wear uniforms. 'Mistakes', roughness, dictatorial methods in the Soviet Zone could be explained by Soviet war losses, Russian backwardness, the belief that the majority of Germans needed long re-education before they could be trusted to run a democracy.

EXPOSING NAZIS AND REVANCHISTS

From the start the Soviets stood behind the new service, they dominated it. This was inevitable. The DDR was in reality an occupied land. It was isolated diplomatically. The IWF depended on the Soviets ideologically, psychologically and for its training. Each department of the Institute had a Soviet liaison officer attached to it. By the end of 1955 the IWF was removed from the foreign ministry and taken over by the MfS. Wolf, who had taken over from Anton Ackermann as head in 1953, was made a deputy minister for state security. The Wolf organization was restricted by the attachment to the Soviets, the SED and to the narrow focus of General Erich Mielke who was appointed Minister for State Security in 1957.

Wolf's organization was used, to begin with, to dredge up dirt to bring down West German politicians and it was quite successful in doing this. In the 1950s and 1960s there were any number of ex-Nazi party members in West German politics and administration. The East Germans played on the understandable fear of many in West Germany and many more abroad, that former Nazis were regaining power and influence in the Federal Republic. A 'White Book' and then a 'Brown Book' were published to expose Nazis in West German society. The *Braunbuch* (1965), claimed that 15 ministers and junior ministers (state secretaries), 100 generals and admirals of the armed forces, 828 high judicial officials, lawyers and judges, 245 diplomats and 297 police and security officials had been far more than just nominal Nazis.[12] This was an exaggeration, but not a great one. One West German source has estimated that around 4,000 of Himmler's security officials, members of the SS or SD, found jobs in their old profession after the war.[13] As late as 1968 eight members of the 20-strong Council of the Bundesbank, 'the bank that rules Europe', had been members of the Nazi party. Taking the Council and the boards of the regional (*Land*) banks together, 18 out of 34 had been members. By then the situation was far worse in this respect than it had been in 1958 or earlier.[14] Just about the easiest target for the East Germans was Hans Globke (1898–1973). Globke was a professional civil servant and Adenauer's most important aide. He was like 'the spider in the web',[15] and had played a decisive role in building up the new ministries from 1948 onwards. He was Adenauer's constant companion and *éminence grise* of the Bonn establishment. As the hub of Adenauer's office, he worked 'with the efficiency of a computer and the discretion of a mole'.[16] The only problem was that he had, as a civil servant under Hitler, written the official commentary to the infamous 1935 Race Laws which deprived the Jews of virtually all of their rights.[17] In 1938 Minister of Interior Frick sent a glowing report about Globke to Hitler's deputy Rudolf Hess.[18] The excuse that he was such a brilliant administrator and that his commentary was lenient, seems unsatisfactory considering the fact that at least hundreds of civil servants at his level had been dismissed by the Nazis and were likely to have been available for reinstatement. Of those who had not been dismissed, it is remarkable that no one could have been found who was less compromised. The same could be asked of Dr Kurt Georg Kiesinger, Chancellor 1966–9. He had been a nominal member of the Nazi party when he worked as a journalist in the press section of the Nazi foreign ministry. He provided the DDR with an easy target. Markus Wolf could have argued that all of Globke's 'leniency' would not have saved the Wolf family from the gas chamber had they remained in Germany. Indeed, Wolf told the *International Herald Tribune* (22 November 1989) at the end of his career, that during the early Cold War years he was motivated by personal revulsion towards West Germany's intelligence service. The Jewish-American philosopher Hannah Arendt, herself a refugee from Nazism, believed Globke had become a 'symbol for the state of affairs that has done more harm to the reputation and authority of the Federal Republic than anything else'.[19] Another notorious appointment under Adenauer was Hubert Schrübbers as head of the BfV following Otto John (see below). Schrübbers, a former SA member, held this appointment from 1955 to 1972. As a lawyer in the Third Reich he had demanded extreme sentences for political anti-Nazis.[20] John Peet, a British journalist who had been Reuters correspondent in Germany, defected to East Berlin where he edited the fortnightly *Democratic German Report* between 1952 and 1975. This publication devoted much space to attacking West German politicians, diplomats, industrialists, lawyers, police officials and generals for their pasts. Peet certainly had a fairly large constituency in the English-speaking world. In retirement Peet freely admitted that he had been recruited as a Soviet spy in Spain in 1938.[21] Wolf's team often did the initial research which then went to Politburo member Albert Norden. He then made appropriate use of it. Sometimes of course the material was used to blackmail West Germans into working for the DDR. One person under attack who survived was General Reinhard Gehlen, head of the Federal Intelligence Service.

EAST GERMAN NAZIS

As a report in *Der Spiegel* (9 May 1994), based on Stasi and SED files and witnesses, was able to show, the DDR leaders were hypocritical about the use of former Nazis. A report on the SED organization in 1954 revealed that in *Bezirk* Magdeburg a quarter of SED members were former Nazi party members, in Halle and Erfurt as many as one third. In the armed forces, NVA, in 1957, three of the top 16 generals had served Hitler as generals. The Stasi itself sought former Nazis as IM. To avoid being forced to answer for their wartime activities they were prepared to make themselves useful to the MfS either in the DDR or in West Germany. One such case was Erich Gust. He was really the much sought-after SS-Obersturmbannführer Franz Erich Giese who had been the deputy commandant at Buchenwald. The Stasi kept his secret for over 20 years as he ran the Heimathof in Lower Saxony, a hotel for top people, where Willy Brandt and other SPD and CDU politicians could be seen. He died in 1992 before his accusers could catch up with him. Even in the 1960s something of this was known in the West. The organization of independent lawyers in West Berlin (*Untersuchungsauschuss Freiheitlicher Juristen*) published in 1965 details of former NSDAP members working in the DDR. It estimated that in 1963, 53 of the 500 members of the Volkskammer, the rubber stamp parliament, were former Nazi party members.

These appear to have been nominal members. Many of those listed were in the technical and medical professions. In the Central Committee of the SED five of the 121 members were former members of Hitler's party. There were those like Kurt Blecha, head of the government press office, Hans Bentzien, Minister of Culture and Professor Ernst Gießmann, Minister for Higher Education, who had been very young members of the NSDAP. In the MfS itself, General Franz Gold, a former NSDAP member, was put in charge of guarding the DDR leadership. Lieutenant General Bruno Beater advanced from the NSDAP and the Wehrmacht to become Deputy Minister for State Security. He retired in 1979. However, it could be said that, as the Stasi was so powerful in the DDR, these former Nazis were of little danger to the system.

OTTO JOHN AND THE BFV

The first major security scandal to shake the West was a Soviet rather than an MfS action. Dr Otto John, an anti-Nazi resister, was appointed as the first President of the West German *Bundesamt für Verfassungsschutz* (BfV) or Federal Office for the Protection of the Constitution. This body was established by a Law passed on 27 September 1950. This Law regulated 'the cooperation of the Federal Government and the Länder in matters concerning the protection of the constitution'. Under Article 2 the BfV was founded under the jurisdiction of the Federal Minister of Interior. Its headquarters is in Cologne. Each *Land* (region) of the Federal Republic set up its own security office which cooperates with the BfV. All the democratic parties in West Germany believed the new German state needed an internal security organ, given their experience of the rise of Nazism and given what they perceived to be the danger from the communists within Germany. Nevertheless, they did not want a strong security organ and for that reason the BfV was given no police powers and was not made part of the police.

There was obviously going to be a problem about who should lead the new BfV. Few democrats would have gained the necessary expertise in security work, most of those having such skills were not wanted as they had been implicated in criminal activities of the Third Reich. The three Western allies wanted to be sure that the person appointed was approved by them and prepared to work with them. The British, who had played an important role in setting up the BfV, succeeded in pushing the appointment of Otto John, a lawyer who, as an employee of the German airline, Lufthansa, had been implicated in the plot against Hitler in 1944. He had fled to neutral Portugal to avoid arrest and then carried on propaganda against the Nazis from London. British support, and that of Federal President Theodor Heuss, a family friend, led to his appointment as the first BfV President. His appointment was despite the hostility of Reinhard Gehlen and Federal Chancellor Konrad Adenauer.[22] John, an amateur in intelligence matters, went missing on 20 July 1954. He had been attending a ceremony commemorating the plot against Hitler in July 1944. He later appeared at a press conference in East Berlin where he supported the Soviet line on Germany and said he had decided to remain in the DDR. He voiced his fears about ex-Nazis and SS men in official positions in West Germany and his fears that re-armament in the West could dash the hopes for German unity. He made a similar attack on East German radio. In December 1955 he was driven back to West Berlin by a Danish journalist. This was of course before the Berlin Wall. On his return to the West he was arrested and put on trial in November 1956. Sentenced to four years' imprisonment he was released after 32 months, account being taken of the time he had been in custody before his trial. John always maintained that he had been drugged by a medical practitioner he knew, Wolfgang Wohlgemuth, and kidnapped on behalf of the Soviet KGB. Certainly, his criticisms of the West he had made before, but making them in East Berlin gave them added weight at the time. It now appears likely that he was indeed drugged on behalf of the KGB and held by them in the East. The affair cast doubt on the West German internal security service and on the reliability of anti-Nazi resisters as opposed to reformed Nazis for security functions.[23] It played directly into the hands of former General Reinhard Gehlen.

REINHARD GEHLEN AND THE BND

As we saw in Chapter 2, the main opponent of the MfS in the West from the 1940s to 1968 was General Reinhard Gehlen. Gehlen remains an enigma. He had made his way up the ladder of success in the Weimar Republic and under Adolf Hitler after 1933. Yet he probably never fired a shot in anger and, apart from a brief excursion during the invasion of Poland, did virtually all his fighting from behind a desk.[24] His horse-riding abilities, connections and determination had helped him in the early days of his career. Later staff work and a reputation for diplomacy took him further. In April 1942 he took over, with the rank of colonel, the army department *Fremde Heere Ost*, which was responsible for intelligence activities on the Eastern front. It must have been relatively easy to build up archives and agents at that time. Masses of Soviet prisoners, documents and equipment had fallen into German hands. Many Russians and non-Russians who knew Stalin but not Hitler were ready to collaborate with the Germans. Despite his merits he was unable to significantly change the situation and was an onlooker as his comrades were overwhelmed by the Red Army. The plot against Hitler in July 1944 passed him by[25] and he reached the rank of major general in December 1944. By then he must have known the end of the Third Reich was near and he was determined to survive it. The knack was not to be taken by the Soviets. Gehlen fell into US hands in a mountain hut in Bavaria in April 1945. Two months later he was interrogated by US intelligence chief General 'Wild Bill' Donovan. Gehlen was flown to Washington where he was able to convince his Pentagon hosts of his view of Stalin's expansive intentions and that he could help them to thwart these plans. However, shortly after his arrival Donovan's Office of Strategic Services (OSS) was closed down and it was July 1946 before Gehlen was back in Germany heading 50 of his old staff working for his new masters.[26] He had to be content to work alongside a rival German organization led by Colonel Hermann Baun. The two worked under Brigadier General Edwin L. Silbert who had in the meantime taken over all US intelligence and counter-espionage activity under General Lucius D. Clay, the US military governor. Silbert represented the Army G-2 organization. Within a short time the two German bodies were combined to form the Gehlen Organization. In December 1947 the organization moved into a renovated former SS estate at Pullach near Munich. It was to become legendary and the BND was still there in 1995. It was financed by the new CIA 'partly from its own funds, and partly by inducing the American business world to contribute large sums of money'.[27] Despite his success Gehlen had to face friction between his personnel and the Americans.[28] The Gehlen Organization was shielded behind a facade as a scientific instruments' company. It could not maintain this facade for very long. The General had sold his organization to the Americans as a body with a network of agents in the Soviet Union itself as well as in other Soviet-dominated areas. Most of its activities were, however, in the Soviet Zone of Germany, the later DDR.

In the early days (1946–8), as one Allied insider has recalled, Gehlen's operations were characterized by the widespread use of sub-agents recruited by other agents. The identities of the sub-agents were often not known to Gehlen and his staff. Often they were merely working in the hope of making some money quickly in a time of widespread unemployment. They were given a telephone number to call if they got picked up by the police or the military, and a lot of gold coin, greenback dollars, black-market goods, US cigarettes and so on, as expense money for buying information. The Americans were worried about what they believed was the lack of security in Gehlen's operations at this time. This aspect of the Gehlen Organization's work was tightened up after the CIA stepped in. Gehlen's use of sub-agents can, to some slight extent, explain his denial that there were many former SS members in the ranks of his organization. One authoritative estimate was that 30 per cent of the total personnel was drawn from the various sections of the SS including the Gestapo and the Waffen-SS.[29]

On 1 April 1956 the status of the Gehlen Organization was finally clarified when it became the official external intelligence-gathering and analysis organization of the Federal Republic – the *Bundesnachrichtendienst* (BND) or Federal Intelligence Service. Its mission is to locate any external threats to the security of the Republic and pass this information on to the government. In fact over the decade that followed Gehlen developed the BND into a body operating world-wide. He wanted the BND to stand along the US, British and French agencies as serious and respected organizations and determined opponents of the KGB and the MfS.

PROFESSOR KASTNER, HILDE HALM AND ELLI BARCZATIS

In the early postwar period it was easy for Gehlen to infiltrate East Germany just as it was easy for the Soviets/MfS to infiltrate the West. Millions of Germans had been uprooted, millions were refugees, records had been destroyed in the bombing, the chaos, the collapse, poverty and uncertainty made Germans easy targets for recruiting agents. In the East there were very many people who secretly detested the Soviets and their German communist helpers. Gehlen exploited old German armed forces networks to recruit his agents. He had many agents who regularly reported on military, economic and political developments in the other Germany. Among them was Professor Hermann Kastner, a joint chairman of the (East German) Liberal Democratic Party and deputy head of government in the DDR's first government. He and his wife fled to the West in 1956 to avoid arrest.[30] Gehlen could not get credit in public for this at the time. Another was Dr Hilde Halm, who worked as a secretary for the quartermaster's office of the Wehrmacht in the war, but soon found employment in the security section, *Kommissariat 5*, of the Soviet-German headquarters at Karlshorst. After working in the Ministry of Finance she managed to get employment in the MfS in 1954. After only 18 months there she was arrested, tried for treason and sentenced to life imprisonment.[31] A third Gehlen agent at this time was Frau Elli Barczatis who was private secretary to the DDR head of government Otto Grotewohl. Codenamed Daissy, for years she delivered copies of important government papers to the Gehlen Organization. An idealist, she was eventually detected, sentenced to death and died under the guillotine, then in use in the DDR for capital offences. These early successes of Gehlen were not easily repeated and defectors rather than sitting agents proved to be more important for the West.

Gehlen's most spectacular coup in the 1950s was achieved in cooperation with the CIA. This was a tunnel which started in the US sector of Berlin and ran for six hundred yards into East Berlin. Its purpose was to enable Western intelligence operatives to listen in on both local and long distance telephone traffic in East Berlin. The tunnel, which took nearly three months to complete, successfully operated for more than nine months. It was claimed[32] that it tapped virtually all the most important Soviet and East German diplomatic, political and military offices. On 22 April 1956 it was discovered and closed down, after which it provided the Soviets and the East Germans with a good propaganda weapon against the West.

Gehlen's activities, together with those of other Western intelligence agencies, were damaged by George Blake, a senior British intelligence officer, who was working for the Soviets for ideological reasons. Sentenced to imprisonment in London in May 1961, Blake had been working in West Berlin for some time. It was he who had betrayed the Berlin tunnel to the Soviets.[33] He later escaped to the Soviet Union where he was awarded the Order of Lenin in 1971.

Gehlen finally retired in May 1968 but not before he had warned NATO of the likelihood of the Warsaw Pact invasion of Czechoslovakia then engaged in dismantling Stalinism and attempting to build 'Socialism with a human face'. Some claim that had his warnings been heeded history could have been different. Remarkably, to the end he believed Hitler had been right to attack the Soviet Union in June 1941.[34] He did however distance himself from the methods used by Hitler in the Russian campaign. Gehlen had had things much his own way for most of his career in postwar intelligence. He had above all, the confidence of the US intelligence community and later of Dr Adenauer and Dr Globke. From late 1950 he realized that he had to go on serving Washington as well as keeping the leaders of the new Federal Republic happy. Every one or two weeks he briefed Dr Globke at the Chancellor's Office in Bonn. It was an advantage to him that Adenauer and Globke remained in office from 1949 to 1963. Once his organization was integrated into the German state structure in 1956, he had another master, the Minister of Defence. This was the right-wing Bavarian Franz Josef Strauss from 1956 to 1962. According to his memoirs, he was also sensible enough to seek an understanding with the opposition Social Democrats (SPD).[35] At this time they had their own underground organization in the DDR coordinated by the *Ostbüro* located at first in Hanover and later in Bonn. This body, which existed between 1946 and 1971, was led by Stephan Thomas until 1966 and then by Helmut Bärwald. Both of them were ready to cooperate with other Western intelligence bodies, but little is known about this cooperation.[36] For the SPD the SED was a totalitarian body which had destroyed the SPD in the Soviet Zone and had no moral or legal right to rule. Underground opposition to it was therefore justified as it had been against the Nazis. Despite his understanding with the SPD, it has been alleged that Gehlen spied on leading Social Democrats such as Erich Ollenhauer and Gustav Heinemann.[37] Some in the BND believed Heinemann, a former Christian Democrat who in 1952 founded the neutralist GVP, had got a suitcase full of money from the Soviet Embassy in Vienna.[38] Heinemann's party failed and he subsequently joined the SPD, being elected to the Presidency of the Federal Republic in 1968 – the year Gehlen retired. After the restoration of German unity files were found which did seem to indicate that Heinemann had attempted to get financial help from the SED.[39]

The BND and the BfV were to a degree in competition with each other and were in competition with the Western intelligence agencies operating within West Germany. Later they had to compete with the armed forces' own intelligence body, the *Militärabschirmdienst (MAD)* or Military Counter-intelligence Service. This was established after the setting up of the Bundeswehr in 1955. All this competition and rivalry helped Wolf's HVA.

Most of the other West German intelligence and security chiefs were not as successful as Gehlen, even in holding on to their jobs. The first five BfV presidents were forced to give up their positions:[40] John in 1954 after his 'defection' to East Berlin; Schrübbers, 1955–72, once his activities before 1945 came to light; Nollau (also a former Nazi party member), 1972–5, following the Guillaume fiasco and Dr Richard Meier in 1983. Meier was convicted by an Austrian court for manslaughter after the death of his female companion when he crashed his BMW.[41] His successor, Heribert Hellenbroich, held office until 1985, when he was moved to head the BND. He was compulsorily retired from this post after only four months in the wake of the Tiedge disaster (see below). On the whole the BND was not more successful than its rival the BfV. Although Gehlen had warned about Czechoslovakia in 1968, he had failed to predict the erection of the Berlin Wall in 1961 or the fall of Khrushchev in 1964, underestimated Brezhnev and underestimated Soviet potential in nuclear and space research. His successors failed to anticipate the fall of the Shah of Iran in 1979, the Soviet invasion of Afghanistan or the developments which led to the collapse of the DDR.[42]

HEINZ FELFE

Among the East's greatest intelligence triumphs was that of Heinz Felfe who was arrested in 1961 together with two others. Felfe, a former SS

Obersturmführer (1st Lieutenant) at Himmler's RSHA, had worked for British intelligence after the war before joining Gehlen's organization. He advanced to head of the Soviet section of Department III (counter-espionage). Felfe worked together with Hans Clemens and Erwin Tiebel, both former SS members. Both also worked for the BND. Felfe provided the Soviets at their HQ in Karlshorst, East Berlin, with copies of 'almost all the most important documents in BND files'. Urgent reports were radioed, the rest went in 'the false bottoms of suitcases, on film concealed in cans of baby food, via dead-letter drops, or through a BND courier', his comrade-in-arms Erwin Tiebel.[43] Yet all this time he was one of Gehlen's stars with a formidable reputation. The exposure of Felfe and his colleagues was the result of the defection by Günther Männel in 1961. Altogether, his defection led to the arrest of 15 East German agents. Among the others was Peter Fuhrmann, a Ministry of Defence official who had been working for the Soviets for seven years.[44] Felfe was sentenced to 14 years' imprisonment, Clemens got ten years and Tiebel three. Felfe was later exchanged to the DDR. His motivation, and that of his colleagues, apart from financial reward, was said by his defence lawyer to have been hatred of the Americans because of wartime experiences. Clemens' lawyer used the bombing of Dresden, his home town, by the Americans and British as his motive.

In a different category, but typical of the time, was Dieter Staritz, who was recruited in 1961 when he was a student at the Free University in West Berlin. He had left the DDR as a refugee sometime before. He was not exposed until after German unity was restored in 1990, having worked for the Stasi between 1961 and 1973. For four of those years he worked as an editor for the influential weekly *Der Spiegel*, using his journalistic contacts to collect political intelligence in the West and information on dissidents in the East which was then passed on to his Stasi controller. Later he emerged as a leading academic expert on DDR history at the University of Mannheim.[45] As 'Erich' Staritz, a member of the SED, he was awarded two medals by General Mielke for his loyal services. Once the Berlin Wall closed the escape route for refugees in August 1961, it became more difficult for the HVA to infiltrate its agents posing as refugees. It had therefore to be more resourceful in its recruitment methods. Equally, the Wall made it more difficult for the BND and other Western agencies to penetrate East Germany and to pull out agents in a hurry.

DEPARTMENT X

In 1966 Department X (*Abteilung X)* was established within the HVA structure. Its task was disinformation which, in the age of 'mutually assured destruction', if a superpower shoot-out took place, was seen as an increasingly important means of alternative warfare on both sides of the Iron Curtain. Wolf's colleagues in Department X stepped up their campaigns against members of the West German Establishment. By exposing leading figures, or holders of sensitive posts, in the Federal Republic as former Nazis, war criminals and the like, they hoped to cause domestic unrest and breed distrust between West Germany and its allies. One of the first recipients of the Wolf campaign was Kurt-Georg Kiesinger, who became Chancellor in 1966 at the head of the grand coalition of Christian Democrats and Social Democrats. The HVA fed documents to Western journalists attempting to show that Kiesinger had been an ardent propagandist for the Nazi regime. Usually there was some truth in the accusations, enough to make further accusations plausible. In the case of Kiesinger the fact was he had been a member of the Nazi party and the wonder was that the Christian Democrats could not find an alternative leader. The HVA also sought to show malpractice by West German government agencies such as the BND or the BfV, or that West Germany was involved in Third World neo-imperialism. It tapped the telephone conversations of Franz Josef Strauss, Helmut Kohl, Kurt Biedenkopf and others. These campaigns were successful to the extent that they got wide media coverage both in West Germany and abroad. Certainly they helped to give West Germany a tarnished image in the 1960s.

1968: THE 'YEAR OF SUICIDES'

1968 was a year of political turbulence throughout Europe. Partly growing out of the protest movement against the Vietnam war, partly because of domestic problems, partly because of the changing cultural environment of the 1960s, there was a growth of left-wing student activism throughout Western Europe. In France, campus revolts spilled over on to the streets and very nearly brought down President de Gaulle. There were riots in London and in West Berlin. In West Germany the far-right National Democratic Party (NPD) had gained entry into seven of the ten (excluding West Berlin) regional parliaments. This also excited militant student opposition. The fact that the SPD of Willy Brandt had formed a government with the CDU led by Chancellor Kurt-Georg Kiesinger, a former Nazi party member, also caused some disillusionment with 'the system'. Moreover, the 'economic miracle' appeared to be flagging. It was in this climate of opposition that the HVA was able to recruit a new generation of ideologically motivated agents in the West. It seems certain that many of these have not yet been exposed. One who was, was Rainer Rupp, who in 1977 was appointed to a senior post in NATO's economic directorate. He spied for the HVA for ideological reasons from 1970 until December 1989. He even involved his British wife, a secretary at NATO, in his activities.[46] In the year to July 1993 a record 1,425 people were prosecuted in Germany for spying. Nearly half were accused of being former Stasi agents in West Germany. The rest worked for the East either as full-time or as unofficial informers.[47]

In West Germany 1968 was known in intelligence circles as the 'year of suicides'. On 8 October 1968 Major-General Horst Wendland, deputy head of the BND, shot himself. On the same day Admiral Hermann Lüdke, deputy head of the logistics department of NATO HQ, killed himself. On 14 October Hans Heinrik Schenk, a high-ranking official of the Economic Ministry, hanged himself. Two days later Edeltraud Grapentin, who worked at the Federal Press Office, took a fatal overdose of sleeping pills. Two days after that, Lieutenant-Colonel Johannes Grimm of the Defence Ministry shot himself. The body of his colleague, Gerhard Böhm, was found by the Rhine on 21 October. About the same time four physicists, a microbiologist and two other engineers disappeared only to re-emerge in the DDR. They had originally arrived in the West as refugees and had succeeded in getting jobs in top scientific research establishments.[48] The microbiologist, Dr Ehrenfried Petras, who had headed a laboratory at the Aerobiological Institute at Grafschaft in Westphalia, was soon put to good use by the East German media claiming that West Germany was working on bacteriological and chemical weapons. John Peet ran it as his lead story in his *Democratic German Report* (11 December 1968) under the title, 'Bonn Breeds Bugs Biological Warfare Plans Exposed'. No doubt this had originated in *Abteilung X* of the HVA, the department responsible for disinformation.

Apart from Admiral Lüdke all the deaths were explained by reference to personal problems but the rumours remained.[49] Had fear of exposure prompted some of the suicides? Had disillusionment with Soviet communism prompted others? This was the year of the Prague Spring, of the attempt to introduce in Czechoslovakia 'Socialism with a Human Face'. The attempt was of course crushed by Soviet tanks and led to a further thinning of the ranks of the communist parties in Western Europe. In the case of General Wendland, a Czech defector later claimed he had been working for the KGB.[50] The formation of the Social Democratic-Free Democratic government in Bonn in the following years gave left-wing Germans an alternative to the DDR.

TERRORISM

Many of the radical students of the 1960s were placated by the government of Willy Brandt SPD and Walter Scheel's liberal FDP which took over in 1969. The communists, banned in 1956, had been legalized in the form of the DKP in 1968. Later the Greens increasingly appealed to the left radicals. However, a very small minority turned to terrorism against West Germany's democratic order which they perceived to be a sham. The terrorists drew on the example of militant Palestinian groups. A group led by Andreas Baader and Ulrike Meinhof claimed public attention by a series of terrorist attacks in the later 1960s and early 1970s. In the summer of 1970 the two attended a training course in urban guerrilla tactics at a Palestinian camp in Jordan. After this they returned to Germany to carry on their life of violence. They had decided to call their gang the Red Army Faction or RAF, a body which over the next years became notorious. In early 1972 the RAF bombed American installations in Frankfurt and Heidelberg, which resulted in the deaths of four American servicemen and the wounding of several others. Other incidents took place in Augsburg, Hamburg, Karlsruhe and Munich. In June of that year, Baader and two followers were captured in a shoot-out with the Frankfurt police. Meinhof was taken into custody two weeks later. The violence, however, continued. More arrests followed and by the end of 1974 about 90 RAF members were held awaiting their trials. A prisoner died on hunger strike; a judge was murdered. Just before the long awaited trial of Baader and Meinhof, terrorists seized the West German embassy in Stockholm demanding their release. The incident ended with two hostages and one terrorist dead, and five others captured. The terrorist trial went on from May 1975 to April 1977. Life sentences were handed down to Baader and Gudrun Ensslin and Jan-Carl Raspe.[51] Meinhof had committed suicide in prison. In revenge the RAF murdered Siegfried Buback, Chief Federal Prosecutor and his driver. On 30 July Jürgen Ponto, Chairman of the Dresdner Bank, was killed resisting a kidnap attempt. Hans-Martin Schleyer, President of the Federation of German Industry was kidnapped in September after a battle in which his driver and three bodyguards were killed. The kidnappers demanded the release of 11 convicted terrorists including Baader, Ensslin and Raspe. To reinforce their demands they joined forces with Palestinian guerrillas to hijack a Lufthansa airliner with 86 passengers and crew on board. Eventually the plane was allowed to land at Mogadishu in Somalia. A brilliant rescue operation by the special G9 unit of the Federal Frontier Force, *Bundesgrenzschutz*, was mounted. The three leaders held in Stammheim prison near Stuttgart then killed themselves in a last act of defiance. Herr Schleyer was murdered. The professionalism of the terrorists suggested outside support. Most point the finger at the PLO and the revolutionary regime in Libya.

Over the years the RAF changed the emphasis it placed on different targets: US imperialism and NATO, the military-industrial complex, the European Community and Germany unity. During the 1980s the RAF attacked the headquarters of the US Air Force in Europe at Ramstein (August 1981); attempted to blow up the NATO school at Oberammergau (December,1984); bombed the US air base at Frankfurt/Main (August, 1985); attempted to murder US soldiers at Wiesbaden (August, 1985) and attacked the US embassy in Bonn (February 1991). Numerous bankers, politicians and industrialists were the victims of assassination attempts. Among them was Alfred Herrhausen, chief executive of the Deutsche Bank, who was killed by a bomb on 30 November 1989. After German unity was restored the violence continued with the murder, on 1 April 1991, of Dr Detlev Karsten Rohwedder, who headed the *Treuhand*, the organization responsible for privatizing the DDR economy. Other terrorists groups also continued to operate in the Federal Republic. There were strong indications that in some cases they received help from revolutionary Third World dictatorships.

One of the surprising revelations which the end of the SED's rule in the DDR brought out was the fact that, to a degree, the MfS gave support to terrorists in the Federal Republic. Through its contacts with states like Chile, Cuba, Ethiopia, Iraq, Libya, Mozambique, Nicaragua, Syria and South Yemen, the MfS was well-informed about the activities and whereabouts of West German extreme-left terrorists. Apparently the *Hauptabteilung XXII*, main department XXII of the MfS, led by Deputy Minister for State Security Gerhard Neiber from the early 1980s on, had given some assistance to the RAF and other individual terrorists. The contacts were established through the PLO and the South Yemen People's Republic. Interviewed by *Der Spiegel* (2 July 1990) Markus Wolf denied any knowledge of the contacts but not that they had taken place. He thought it was likely that Mielke had got the approval of Honecker for this action. He also denied any affinity with the RAF's activities, which he thought were 'crazily damaging'. Honecker himself told *Der Spiegel* (25 June 1990) that he had known nothing of the help for the terrorists until he read about it in the press. General Gerhard Neiber also was reported in the same issue of *Der Spiegel* as saying that he found it unbelievable that Mielke would embark upon such a course without the authority of Honecker. Yet the MfS did provide RAF members with asylum, with training and with equipment. *Der Spiegel* (18 April 1994) was able to report that there were strong suspicions that the MfS provided terrorists with the timers which were used to blow up the Pan-Am air liner over Lockerbie (Scotland) on 21 December 1988. It was certain that the Stasi possessed the Swiss-made equipment. No one suggested that the Stasi knew the intended target. Among the RAF terrorists who had been given sanctuary in the DDR was Susanne Albrecht who was involved in killing her godfather, Jürgen Ponto; Sigrid Sternebeck wanted for the attempted killing of a US soldier in 1985; Henning Beer and several others wanted in connection with the bomb attack at Ramstein in 1981 and Silke Maier-Witt, wanted in connection with the Schleyer assassination of 1977. To some extent the MfS had neutralized a number of West German terrorists by giving them the chance of asylum in the DDR if they were prepared to cease their activities. In part this was a defensive action to the extent that the SED feared terrorism spilling over into the DDR. It also wanted to keep its good relations with a number of Arab states and the PLO. Full details of the MfS's activities in the Third World are dealt with elsewhere. Suffice it to say here that the HVA recruited IMs among students from these states studying in the DDR. They were used to monitor their colleagues' activities and as potential allies on their return to their own countries. HAXXII also built up an anti-terrorist capacity to ensure the DDR itself did not fall prey to terrorist attacks and to deal with them should the need arise. The Stasi connection did weaken the appeal of the RAF after 1990 but it did not result in its collapse.

No connection has been established between the MfS and the many right-wing terrorist groups operating at various times in West Germany.

THE LONELY SECRETARIES

Only about two years after the Guillaume affair, in June 1976, Bonn was shocked by another security scandal when Renate Lutze, her husband Lothar, and Jürgen Wiegel were arrested on suspicion of having passed secret documents to the MfS. Frau Lutze was the secretary to the director of the social affairs department of the Ministry of Defence. An investigation by the Defence Committee of the Bundestag came to the conclusion that the damage done by the activities of these three represented the worst case of espionage in the history of the Federal Republic.[52] Rivalries within the military establishment were identified as the cause of the affair and resulted in the premature retirement of MAD director, General Paul Albert Scherer. The matter had not been helped by the fact that both the Minister of Defence Georg Leber and the highest ranking officer, Admiral Zimmermann, were seriously ill at the time. The Defence Committee was still dealing with the Lutze case when lightning struck again. Dagmar Kahlig-Scheffler, a secretary in the Chancellor's office, was arrested for spying. Her career as an agent had lasted for only a matter of months. But her case was not uncommon. She had met a man on holiday in Bulgaria, secretly married him in East Berlin and been persuaded by him to work for the MfS. According to *Der Spiegel* (4 September 1978) the discovery of this case was due to the BfV's computer searches which exposed her controllers who were living with fictitious identities in the West.

Inge Goliath and her husband disappeared on 9 March 1979. Later they appeared before the DDR media to announce they were seeking political asylum in the Workers' and Peasants' state. Since 1966 Frau Goliath had worked as a secretary for the Christian Democratic Union (CDU), the government party in Bonn until 1969. Christel Broszey fled in the same direction the day after the Goliaths left. She was on the verge of being arrested. She had worked as 'the right hand' of four CDU general-secretaries, the last one being Professor Kurt Biedenkopf who after reunification was elected Minister-President of Saxony. One of the most damaging cases involved Ingrid Barbe, secretary to a counsellor at the West German embassy to NATO. She was jailed for four years in 1980 for sending, over a period of three years, NATO troop strength figures, details of chemical weapons, planning for the neutron bomb, crisis management plans and details of arms exports.[53] Margarete Höke was arrested on 24 August 1985. She had worked as a secretary in the Federal President's office for 21 years. Like the others, she had seen many hundreds of secret documents.[54] One report claimed she would have had access to the reports of the Federal Security Council, the Cabinet committee at which every major security, defence and foreign policy issue is discussed. Reports from all West German embassies, including NATO, would have gone across her desk, making her case potentially far more serious than that of Hans Joachim Tiedge (see below).[55] She had worked for a time for the Security Commissioner in the President's Office, with the chance of seeing the security clearances of all staff and what material they had access to. With her personal knowledge of the other secretaries, she could have passed on tips as to the vulnerability of her colleagues.[56] About the same time there was the double defection of Herta-Astrid Willner and her husband. Frau Willner had been employed in the Federal Chancellor's Office since 1973, her husband Arthur worked for the FDP, the junior coalition partner of Helmut Kohl. Frau Willner had access to sensitive documents covering Bonn's civil nuclear programme.[57] The couple had failed to return from their holiday in Spain. Another famous case was Sonja Lüneburg who worked as an agent from 1969 to 1985. From 1974 she was the secretary of Dr Martin Bangemann, who was respectively, Secretary General of the FDP, President of the Liberal group in the European Parliament (1980–4) and Minister of Economics (from 1984). These were among at least 50 cases of secretaries working for the HVA.[58] The first had been in 1958 when a secretary to Franz Josef Strauss, then Defence Minister, was exposed.[59] Many of them were the victims – if that is the right term – of a systematic attempt by the Stasi to entrap lonely women working in government or party offices in Bonn. Christel Guillaume, the wife of Günter, had spied independently of her husband when she worked as a secretary.[60] In a number of cases the East German 'Romeos' even entered into bigamous marriages to win the women for spy work. The discovery that her husband Heinz, a KGB agent, had simply married her to get her involved in spying drove Leonore Sutterlein to suicide. She had been convicted in 1967 of exploiting her position as a secretary in the Foreign Ministry to pass 3,500 classified documents to the KGB via her husband.[61]

Unlike many of the others, Sonja Lüneburg was not a lonely secretary who had been seduced into working for East Berlin. According to the *Verfassungsschutz* report for 1985 she had taken on the identity of a woman living in West Berlin who had gone in the 1960s to live in France. The 'new' Sonja had arrived in West Germany in 1967. She then found employment as a secretary with an insurance agency in Frankfurt. By 1969 she was already working for a member of the Bundestag. This case was typical of many involving HVA agents living and working under assumed identities in the Federal Republic. Even in a country in which personal identity documents were so important, and residents were required to report their arrival and departure from a particular address to the appropriate local office, it proved remarkably easy to impersonate, to assume the identity of others over a very long time.

One of the last cases involving a Bonn secretary which came to light before the collapse of the DDR was that of Elke Falk whose arrest in March 1988 after being observed for a year, caused considerable anguish in the federal seat of government. Ms Falk had been picked up by the Stasi after she had advertised for a partner in a lonely hearts' column in 1973. He was known to her as Gerhard Thieme and she was soon engaged in an intimate relationship with him. She moved from the private to the public sector, getting employment in the Chancellor's Office in 1974. There she worked until 1977. She then worked for two years in the Transport Ministry after which she moved to the Economic Aid Ministry where she worked until her exposure in 1988. Apparently she gave up her spying activities in 1985 after being warned by East Berlin that she was under suspicion. She rejected the offer of refuge in the DDR. She used classic espionage techniques such as 26 dead-letter boxes to deliver her material and collect instructions. She also received instructions by radio. She was equipped with a camera disguised as a cigarette lighter and a specially prepared hairspray container to keep the films. She is said to have received DM 20,000 (about £8,300) for her activities. Sentenced to six and half years' imprisonment in May 1989 she was on her way to the

DDR by December as part of a spy swap, the first since December 1987 when three agents on each side were exchanged.[62]

It would be inaccurate to imply that the MfS and other Soviet Bloc intelligence agencies had a free hand in attracting lonely women in Bonn and that they were unsuccessful in applying the same tactics to men. Typical was the case of a West Berliner who was given a ten-month suspended sentence in 1988 after working for the MfS since 1981. He fell for an East German woman he met at a party in 1976. As she was not willing to apply to leave the DDR, he decided to apply for residence in East Berlin. The MfS exploited his personal circumstances to enlist him in the 'fight for peace'. At about 80 *treffs* with his case officer he supplied information about West Berlin residents including those working at the Free University.[63]

MfS LEADS THE PACK

It was not all gloom on the West German intelligence scene at the end of the 1970s and the early 1980s. General Gerhard Wessel, who had taken over from General Gehlen as head of the BND, was himself replaced by civilian Klaus Kinkel (later to be the Federal Republic's Foreign Minister and FDP leader). As we saw in Chapter 5, on 19 January 1979 Lieutenant Werner Stiller of the MfS defected to the West taking with him a great deal of information about the organization and operations of his previous employers. It was a considerable blow to Mielke. In the same month there was the prospect of an even more important defector, a high-ranking officer from the DDR's navy. But the 'red admiral' as he was nicknamed, turned out to be a drunken ex-intelligence officer who had been dismissed from the NVA some years previously. He did give the BND the names of some DDR agents in the Federal Republic before his arrest. A lack of attention to detailed planning was thought to be the reason for his exposure. The result was that he was apprehended before his planned flight. Convicted of treason, he was shot in 1980. At the time the case was seen as another blow to Mielke. Nevertheless, the HVA kept up a high level of activities in the West and, as the figures (taken from the annual reports of the BfV) below reveal, remained by far the most important Warsaw Pact state involved in intelligence gathering in the Federal Republic.

The high rate of convictions in the early 1980s undoubtedly have something to do with Stiller's revelations, the increase in 1992 with information from the Stasi files after German unification.

Table 6.1 Arrests in West Germany (including West Berlin) for treason and endangering the state (paragraphs 93–101 of the criminal code)

Year	Total	SSD	Soviet	Polish	Hungarian
1983+	31	20	5	1	2
1984	29	24	4	1	–
1985	18	16	1	1	–
1986*	43				
1987*	34				

\+ 3 cases were not identified.
* As the form of reporting had changed it was difficult to give the details in these years.

Table 6.2 Convictions in West Germany (including West Berlin) for treason and endangering the external security of the state (paragraphs 93–101 of criminal code)

Year	Totals	SSD	Soviet	Polish	Hungarian	Romanian	Czech
1981	na	24	1	1	1	1	–
1982	25	22	2	–	–	–	1
1983	26	20	5	–	–	–	–
1984*	23	18	3	–	–	–	–
1985	13	12	–	–	–	–	1
1986	14						
1987	26						
1988	16						
1989	19						
1990	11						
1991	14						
1992	22						

* In this year there were two convictions of agents working for the Yugoslav intelligence service.

DDR INTELLIGENCE EFFORTS IN THE 1980s

The detailed view given below of the HVA's organizational structure indicates just how intensive its work in the Federal Republic was. From the available evidence it appears fairly certain that it had succeeded in infiltrating all the target areas and organisations though not necessarily all at the same time. Interviewed by *Der Spiegel* (2 July 1990) Markus Wolf suggested that the HVA had between 50 to 90 agents who were in close contact with leading West German politicians. *Der Spiegel*, claimed to know that the democratically elected (March 1990) Minister of Interior of the DDR, Dr Peter-Michael Diestel, had the names of two members of the Federal Government who had been working for the Stasi. In addition to the '50 to 90 agents' in touch with top people there were thousands of others at work in the Federal Republic. To protect themselves against this threat the Federal Republic in 1982 employed 3,500 full-time members of the BfV and about 13,000 part-time informants or *V-Männer*. MAD deployed 2,000 of whom half were members of the armed forces. The strength of the BND was about 6,000. It was also assisted by outside helpers who were often journalists.

The pie chart Figure 6.2 shows how the HVA distributed its espionage activities in the Federal Republic during the 1980s. It is taken from the annual report of the BfV for 1991, *Verfassungsschutzbericht 1991*. Clearly its work in the military and security fields occupied most of its efforts, but the other areas were not unimportant. The parties, churches and other organizations were important both as part of the democratic process and as opinion-formers. Clearly the media were important as opinion-formers and considerable efforts were made to plant disinformation in the right circles. The economy was of considerable interest for the new technology and for the possibility of doing favourable deals to assist the ailing DDR economy.

General Markus Wolf who, as we have seen, led the DDR's intelligence effort in West Germany from the start, retired in September 1986. This was apparently because of disagreements with Erich Mielke over his private life. He was planning his third marriage against the opposition of his minister, Erich Mielke. In retirement he turned his talent to literary pursuits and identified with Gorbachev's reforms in the Soviet Union. After the fall of Honecker in October 1989 he openly joined those calling for more democracy in the DDR and in the SED. Of his methods in intelligence work, which appeared to be so successful, in retirement Markus Wolf told the *International Herald Tribune* (22 November 1989), 'We never tried to convert people to Marxism but instead worked with their own political convictions. To get them to do what we wanted we had to mesh their personal beliefs with our own political interests.' Even when the HVA offered money its members were not expected to treat their recruits as people who had been bought but rather to reinforce a view that they were helping a moral cause. He claimed he was against blackmail with compromising material or simply seducing secretaries.

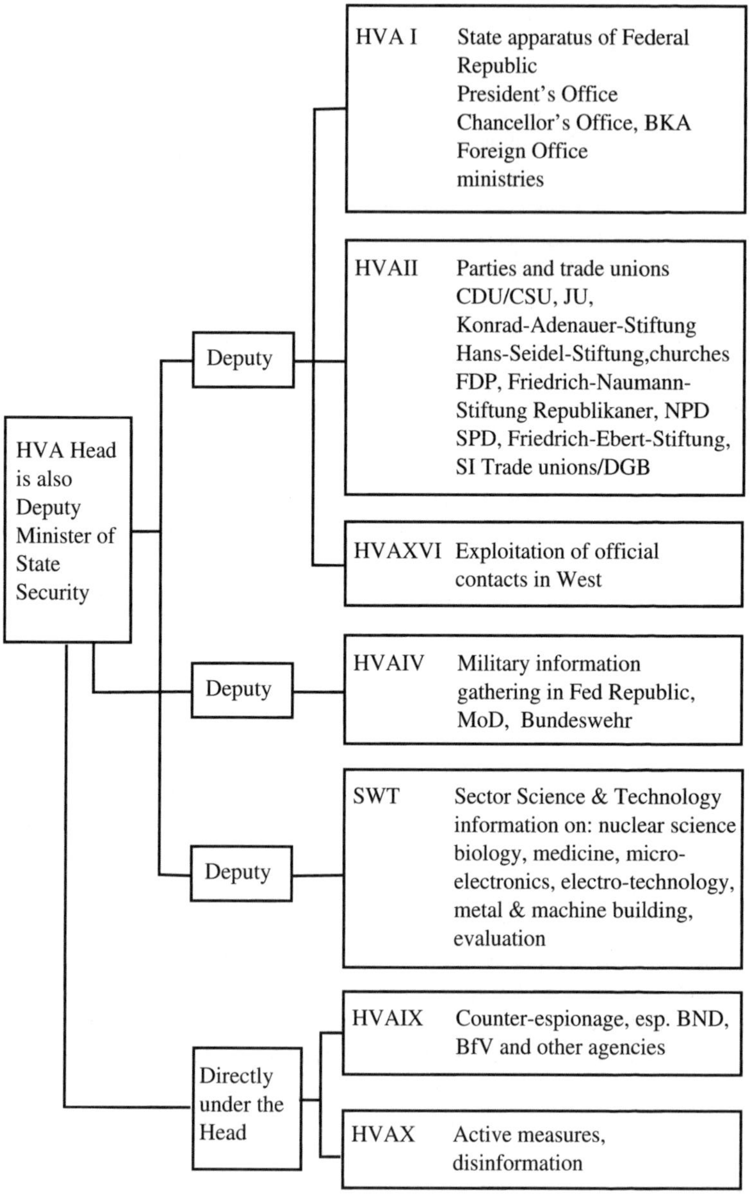

Figure 6.1 Stasi Main Departments and their West German Targets

Source: modified from *Verfassungsschutzbericht 1991*, Bonn, 1991, p.184.

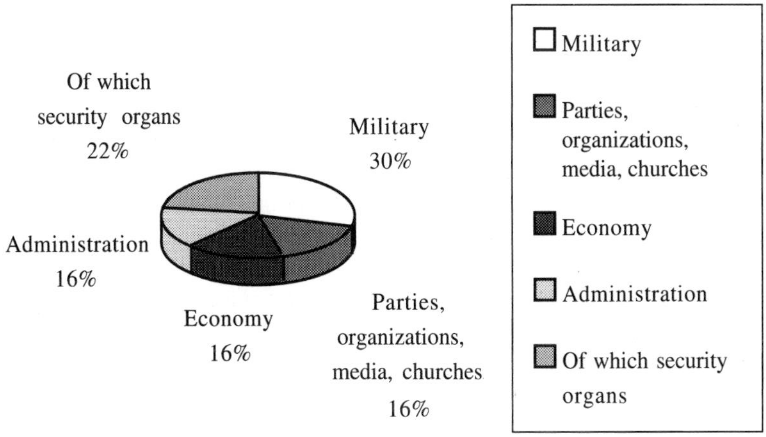

Figure 6.2 Distribution of HVA activity in West Germany

Wolf was replaced by General Werner Grossmann who then continued until the dismemberment of the MfS. He was to have continued in this capacity under the Modrow government.

GENERAL KIESSLING

Among the HVA's coups in the Federal Republic in the 1980s was the dismissal of General Günter Kiessling, a Deputy Supreme Commander of Allied Forces in Europe, on 31 December 1983. He had been accused of being homosexual by the MAD and was dismissed by Minister of Defence Manfred Wörner as a security risk. It was claimed that Kiessling had visited two homosexual bars in Cologne where he was known as 'Günter from the Bundeswehr'. Kiessling strenuously denied ever having any homosexual contacts and called for disciplinary proceedings against himself in order to bring the charges into the open. Wörner was strongly criticized for inviting, at public expense, a Swiss actor and former editor of a homosexual newspaper to travel to Bonn to discuss his claim that he had evidence proving that Kiessling was gay. Kiessling was subsequently clearly and formally reinstated. Wörner offered his resignation but this was not accepted by Chancellor Kohl. However, he was later (1988) appointed secretary-general of NATO. Many believed that behind the entire affair was the Stasi. The aim had been to derail a potentially powerful opponent, Wörner, and embitter relations between the Bonn government and its military.

MILITARY INTELLIGENCE

Like the Bundeswehr, the armed forces of the DDR, the NVA, had their own intelligence service. This service, known in its early days as *Verwaltung 19.* and then *12. Verwaltung*, was officially referred to as *Verwaltung Aufklärung* from 1966 onwards. As one would expect, its role was much more circumscribed than that of the HVA. With its HQ at the 'Mathematical-Physics Institute' of the NVA at Berlin, Köpenick, its primary targets were the NATO forces in West Germany. At one level its agents sought information on daily life in the NATO forces, daily routines, training, equipment, strengths and weaknesses and morale and discipline problems. At another level its interests were troop movements, personnel deployment, reports on manoeuvres. At the highest levels it sought access to NATO strategic planning. It sought this information through agents on the ground, military attachés of the DDR abroad, through searches of the appropriate professional literature and the media, and through its own electronic eavesdropping. As the DDR drew to a close it had a strength of seven generals and 686 officers out of a total of 1,158 staff working in 29 departments. Typical of the agents the *Verwaltung Aufklärung* ran were: Ulrich Steinmann, a building engineer in the MoD in Bonn who worked for the NVA between 1967–90 who delivered documents on armament projects and the arms trade; Heinz-Helmut Werner, a cipher officer who gave information from NATO on software and cipher technology between 1970 and 1990, and Reinhold Ginolas, a captain in the leadership staff of the air force who provided material on training and military efficiency from 1958 to 1990. Clearly, the NVA's intelligence service was a successful operation but suffered from being the poor relation to the HVA.

Lieutenant-General Jörg Schönbohm, the West German officer responsible for integrating the NVA into the Bundeswehr after reunification in 1990, found the NVA's military intelligence service had a clear picture of NATO forces. Yet the SED leadership ignored vital information provided by their military intelligence in the same way as they ignored Stasi information. Schönbohm reports in his *Two Armies And One Fatherland* that although it was known that NATO forces were almost closed down at the weekends, the political leadership of the DDR insisted that the NVA maintain 85 per cent readiness round the clock, even at weekends!

HANS JOACHIM TIEDGE

A neighbour thought he stood condemned by his overgrown and disorderly garden. His colleagues knew of his disorderly lifestyle, characterized by bad debts and alcoholism and family problems. His wife had died three years earlier leaving him to care for three daughters. He was known to suffer from depression. Yet nothing was done to bring him under control. After a warning, Hans Joachim Tiedge changed sides. He disappeared in August 1985 from Cologne and reappeared several days later on the wrong side of the Berlin Wall. The 48-year-old, who had worked for the BfV for 19 years and headed the department of counter-espionage, had crossed the lines and put himself at the disposal of the MfS. Tiedge's department had been working on the cases of Sonja Lüneburg (see page 159), Ursula Richter, who disappeared from her job with the refugee organization (*Bund der Vertriebenen)*, where she had worked from 1972, and Lorenz Betzing who had also disappeared. Betzing had been working in the information technology department of the armed forces and before that for the Labour Service of the US armed services. He was an intimate friend of Ursula Richter.[64] Tiedge was thought to have put at risk any number of East Germans working for the BND.[65] At the time, a 'terrifying catalogue' could be put together of the knowledge Tiedge took with him to East Berlin. He knew: all current West German counter-intelligence operations inside the DDR; the names of West Germans who worked for the MfS and had been turned by the BfV; the names of DDR agents who had been turned; the names of all senior counter-intelligence officers in each West German *Land* who controlled these double agents; all the techniques used by the West Germans to identify DDR agents; the top-secret evaluations prepared by the BfV which listed the strengths and weaknesses of DDR penetration; the methods and results of security vetting for senior and sensitive posts, which would have alerted the MfS to how far their moles had escaped detection; reports on his colleagues and their possible susceptibility to offers from the MfS.[66] After the collapse of the DDR Tiedge was sentenced to imprisonment. Tiedge and the other cases mentioned were just part of the Bonn spy scene in 1985. The Tiedge case was really an own goal by the BfV rather than a great victory for the MfS. Either way, it was a victory for the DDR.

Franz Arthur Roski was another MfS agent who received a good deal of media attention in 1985. Roski had worked from 1979 to 1982 at the Federal Office for the Recognition of Foreign Refugees. In that capacity he had much useful information about foreign asylum-seekers and what became of them. He went on from there to the Ministry of Interior, still dealing with refugees. His final destination before being apprehended was in the headquarters of the Federal Frontier Service. He had been recruited during a visit to his grandparents in the DDR in 1971. He claimed he had been frightened after a minor currency offence had been discovered by the DDR customs. As a student in 1971 he had received DM 250 a month from the MfS, a not unattractive sum for a student in those days. He had gone on receiving money on a regular basis ever since. He had even received special payments of DM 200 on the birth of each of his three children in 1979, 1980 and 1981. His regular monthly DM 300 appears to have been within the average range at this fairly low level of intelligence gatherer. Roski was sent to prison for his deeds.[67] In 1985 the Federal Republic was forced once again to face the fact that it was virtually powerless to protect itself from such occurrences. At this time it is thought that there were between 3,000 and 5,000 MfS spies operating in the Federal Republic.[68]

Worse was to come for the Bonn security community but, as it came after the fall of the Stasi, its impact was much less severe. Gisela Gast, who had worked for the BND since 1973, and was deputy head of the Soviet Union department, was exposed as a Stasi spy and arrested on 29 September 1990, just four days before Germany was reunited. She had been responsible for reports which went to the Defence Ministry, the Foreign Ministry and to Chancellor Kohl. She had been involved with the HVA from 1970, initially through a romantic attachment, and was regarded as so important that Markus Wolf had gone to Yugoslavia to meet and entertain her personally. Over the years they met seven times.[69] On 19 December 1991 the former Christian Democratic student who had written her doctorate on 'The political role of women in the DDR' at the Technical University in Aachen, Gabriele Gast, was sentenced to six years and nine months' imprisonment. Her East German lover received a suspended sentence. When the HVA had discovered her she had been a mere student. It was a case of excellent talent-spotting.

Gast was by no means the only agent Wolf took the trouble to meet personally, charm and motivate, nor did he simply try to captivate women. Among the others were: Alfred Spuhler, a BND captain and HVA agent from 1972 to 1989; the diplomat Klaus von Raussendorff who worked for the HVA from 1960 to 1989; Dr Hagen Blau, diplomat and HVA agent 1960 to 1990; Dr Friedrich Cremer, SPD member of the Bavarian Parliament whom Wolf went to meet in Stockholm; Johanna Olbricht, secretary to FDP politician Martin Bangemann and HVA agent from 1967 to 1985.[70] Another recruit Wolf vetted personally was Klaus Kuron.

On 6 October Klaus Kuron was taken into custody after confessing that he had been delivering information to the HVA since 1982. He had been employed by the BfV since 1962. As a result, two of his superiors were also arrested. Financial problems and a sense of injustice had led Kuron to contemplate treason, apparently supported by his wife. He claimed in court that a DM 10,000 dentist's bill had been the final straw.[71] On 7 February 1992 Kuron was sentenced to 12 years' imprisonment and fined DM 692,000, the sum he had been paid for his spying activities. Gerald Boeden, head of the

BfV, admitted to *Der Spiegel* (15 October 1990), that his organization had had not the least doubt about Kuron over the years. Unlike Tiedge, he was a typical family man, who had nothing unusual about his finances, did not drive expensive cars, nor was he attracted to drink. His job was to supervise Stasi agents who had been 'turned'. He was in the double bluff business. Through him the HVA knew which of its agents were working for the West while pretending to be still working for the East. The third of West Germany's intelligence agencies could not smile for long at the embarrassment of its colleagues. The one-time deputy head of MAD, Joachim Krause, it was discovered, had also worked for the HVA. Krause joined MAD in 1967, working for the HVA from 1973 until his death from cancer in 1988.[72] It appeared that since the Tiedge scandal there had been no improvement in securing the Federal Republic's security organs.

SCHALCK-GOLODKOWSKI AND FRANZ JOSEF STRAUSS

It was really only after the fall of the SED in the DDR that anything was known about the existence of the so-called *'Kommerzielle Koordinierung' (KoKo)* empire of Dr Alexander Schalck-Golodkowski. It later transpired that Schalck was a colonel in the Stasi, his deputy Manfred Seidel and his secretaries were OibE.[73] He worked closely together with Mielke, Honecker and Dr Günter Mittag, the Politburo member with responsibility for the economy and could, 'at any time' directly reach members of the Politburo by means of a red telephone.[74] The Schalck empire was founded in 1966 on the initiative of General Hans Fruck, deputy to Wolf at the HVA.[75] The KoKo 'empire' was basically a giant import–export organization which was free of all the normal limitations, which other DDR organizations were subject to. The DDR finance ministry was virtually banned from examining the finances of the firms which were part of the KoKo.[76] The aim of KoKo was to improve the DDR's economic position through successful exports of anything from meat products to armaments, and by importing high technology products including those on NATO's embargo list. The KoKo owned at least 160 firms[77] in the DDR and in West Berlin, West Germany, Switzerland, Austria, Italy, Liechtenstein, Luxembourg, Holland, France, Belgium, Denmark, the Grand Canaries, Panama and Caracas.[78] It is believed some of the profits were used to help to finance the DDR's espionage activities in the West.[79] Money was also used to support the activities of communist organizations in the Federal Republic and other Western countries.[80] It was controlled by the MfS through at least 200 officers[81] who worked in its different firms and who in turn acted as case officers for other IM employees. Klaus

Köhler, for instance, was responsible for MfS operatives working in the export enterprise IMES. Hanno Schütte, who was an MfS full-time operative between 1956–65, later worked for the KoKo firms Transinter, IMES and Witra. He claimed that the DDR started to export armaments to earn hard currency. It attempted to get into markets through dealers and firms in England. During the Iran/Iraq war it exported arms to both sides.[82] The DDR also exported to Africa and South America, in particular to Peru[83] and to other countries. The KoKo had its own armaments warehouse at Kavelstorf near Rostock. It was administered by an MfS officer, Major Johannes Richard Walter.[84] Schütte and another former Stasi officer reported that all directions regarding the arms deals came from Schalck directly. Some of them were approved personally by Honecker.[85] As far as arms imports were concerned, Schalck had been particularly interested in flying helmets produced in West Germany and the US and infra-red glasses for night operations.

The KoKo was in addition involved in the negotiations for the buying of political prisoners held in the DDR.[86] These are discussed in Chapter 4. It also creamed off money given by West German churches to their co-religionists in the DDR. Another task of the KoKo was offering antiques owned by DDR citizens for sale to Western collectors. Finally, it was responsible for supplying the Politburo residents of Wandlitz with Western consumer goods not available to the normal consumers in the DDR.[87]

Mielke issued an order setting up the *Arbeitsgruppe Bereich KoKo* (BKK). This body was supposed to ensure the smooth working of the KoKo in the interest of the MfS. At the same time the HVA was instructed to assist the work of the BKK by handing over all intelligence reports to it. According to Colonel Wolfram Meinel, who was in charge of the BKK, neither Markus Wolf nor his successor General Grossmann were prepared to do this.[88] There was in fact serious rivalry between the two bodies. Colonel Meinel reported that the BKK had contacts with the BND and the CIA through a person known as 'Buntsprecht'.[89]

Krenz regarded Schalck as so clever and so important that he considered appointing him head of government in October 1989.[90] Schalck is reputed to have had access to many West German politicians of all parties. Among them was Franz Josef Strauss, head of government of Bavaria, former Federal Minister for Nuclear Affairs, former Federal Minister of Defence, former Federal Finance Minister. Strauss had been at the centre of any number of alleged corruption affairs and was forced to resign in 1962 when he was Defence Minister because of his unlawful actions in having the editor and other journalists of the weekly *Der Spiegel* arrested. Strauss prided himself as an unbridled anti-communist. However, much to the surprise of many, including those in his own party, he helped the DDR to get a credit line in the West in 1983. From then until the end of his life he was a welcome visitor in the DDR. When Honecker visited West Germany in September 1987 he visited Strauss in Bavaria where he was treated to the full pomp of a state visit. Strauss was a disappointed man, feeling he should have been elected Chancellor of the Federal Republic, as the Christian Democratic choice in 1980 when he was defeated. Later he was disappointed not to be appointed to high office by Kohl in 1982. He therefore pursued his own foreign relations. Rumours abounded that he had not only made money on his deals with the DDR but that he had given Schalck valuable information. The SPD member of the Bundestag, Andreas von Büllow, went further and called Strauss, ' the most important spy the DDR had'.[91] It will be difficult to prove or disprove this. Schalck and his intimates will not be speaking publicly. Strauss is dead and cannot defend himself. The Bundestag Commission into the KoKo decided that the mass of evidence it had collected would not be available for public scrutiny until 2015. Only the Greens opposed this.[92] The jury must still be out in the case of Strauss but it seems likely, given the history of political corruption in West Germany, and the fact that the Stasi was able to recruit so many agents, that Schalck was not exaggerating when he told his boss Erich Mielke that he had a complete network of agents in the Federal Republic.[93]

One aspect of the Strauss story which came out in 1994 was that a close confidant of his had been delivering material to the MfS from 1956 to 1990. Gerhard Baumann had worked for the Gehlen Organization, was a member of Strauss' CSU and had excellent contacts with CSU leaders and the BND. He was known to the Stasi as IM Schwarz and his files in Mielke's HQ ran into 31 volumes.[94]

ELECTRONIC INTELLIGENCE GATHERING

When the East German intelligence and military machines were inspected and dismantled after 1990, there was general surprise at the extent and ease with which the Stasi had been able to monitor Western telecommunications. The Hauptabteilung III, led for 23 years by Major-General Horst Männchen, was responsible for electronic information gathering. Männchen had a staff of 4,500 to enable him to do this. From points in the DDR and Czechoslovakia the Stasi listened in to 100,000 telephones in West Germany and Austria.[95] It is estimated that 25,000 phones in West Germany were tapped 24 hours a day by the Stasi.[96] Remarkably the HAIII even had stations in Bonn and Düsseldorf and for a time in Cologne (where the headquarters of the BfV is located).[97] After investigating the HAIII's activities the West German BfV concluded that its work had been impressive.[98] This is putting it mildly. It appears that only the most carefully coded messages would not have been defenceless against the onslaught of the Stasi. One of the few limitations on HAIII's work was its inability to evaluate the mass of material pouring in, especially that in languages other than German.

Spy cases were almost routine in the Federal Republic from its establishment in 1949. This was hardly surprising given the division of Germany and the shadows of the Nazi past which haunted the corridors of power until the 1970s. The millions of East–West contacts meant that security problems were bound to be considerable. To a much lesser extent, less only because of the rigorous controls unthinkable in a free society, the MfS had the same problem. And Britain, the US and other Western states were not without security problems. Did any of it matter? For the most part, probably not. It has always been true that a great deal can be learned about the society of a potential enemy through open, legal channels – newspapers, magazines, books, radio and television programmes, and of course from personal reconnaissance. Today satellites and electronic intercepts greatly add to that knowledge. In the case of Germany there were also the military missions of the three Western Powers in the DDR, and the Soviet military mission in West Germany. The HVA's spies, it is true, would on some occasions have weakened Bonn's diplomatic room for manoeuvre by revealing its position before the start of negotiations with the DDR. In the many instances of industrial, scientific and technological espionage, the information gained by MfS agents made little difference to the relative strengths of the two societies. Certainly, the HVA was extremely successful, more successful, as Heribert Hellenbroich, one time head of both the BfV and, briefly, the BND, later admitted, than his own organization.[99] However, perhaps this success helped to reduce Cold War tensions to the extent that much of the information received ended up in the Kremlin and played a part in convincing the Soviet leadership that it had nothing to fear from NATO or the West Germans. In November 1991 the Ministry of Interior believed that there had been between 6,000 and 7,000 MfS agents at work in West Germany in 1989. Only 600 had by that time been exposed. It was thought that among those remaining were up to 400 well-trained agents, many of whom were in sensitive positions.[100] Yet the strength of the old Federal Republic was the loyalty of the overwhelming majority of its citizens despite the many Stasi agents there.This was quite a different situation from that in the DDR. In the end, the work of the HVA made no difference to the maintenance of the Warsaw Pact and the division of Germany. It was a very expensive organ of a morally and politically bankrupt state. Markus Wolf said of his old boss, Erich Mielke, after the Wall came down in 1989, 'It's hard to find a good word to say for him even before he became senile.'[101] As for General Wolf, Klaus Rösler, who served from 1952 to the end in the HVA, pointed out that he resigned but made no political gesture or statement in so doing. Rösler admitted he and many of his colleagues had increasing doubts over the years about the way things were going. In secret they discussed the situation but, 'We were too cowardly to resign ... We did not have the courage to do anything ... We were blinded by ideology ... There was a great deal of injustice in the DDR, that is so, Bautzen cannot be thought out of existence.'[102]

7 From Triumph to Catastrophe: The Stasi Under Mielke and Honecker 1971–89

> Historical experience has shown convincingly that universal models of socialism do not exist and that attempts to unify and standardize social development in various countries are doomed to failure …

Comment of V.A. Kryuchkov, Chairman of the KGB, on the East European revolutions, November 1989.[1]

> Beyond a certain level the leaders lived cut off from reality, and this was an important reason why the situation in the country could not be properly assessed. This is also why much that we informed them about was put to one side, and not taken notice of.

Anonymous officer from the Stasi's Central Evaluation and Information Group, 1991.[2]

THE ERA OF DÉTENTE

The development of the Stasi from its creation in 1950 until its collapse in 1989 took place in, from the SED's point of view, an atmosphere of unremitting ideological conflict with the West. In effect, the DDR was on a semi-war footing, with the population subject to seduction by the 'adversary'.

After Willy Brandt became Federal Chancellor, the SED's main adversary, the Federal Republic, put into full swing its *Ostpolitik* of conciliation with the Soviet Bloc. But the economic benefits which détente brought to the DDR were greatly offset by the threat which the very existence of the FRG posed to its security. The East German state incorporated only a third of the German nation. It had no other reason for being, but as an alternative to the capitalist FRG. The SED's chief ideologist, Otto Reinhold, remarked after the *Wende*: 'What justification for its existence ought a capitalist DDR next to a capitalist Federal Republic to have? None of course.'[3] Thus, in the eyes of the SED leadership, any dilution of communist ideology weakened the justification for a separate DDR. It is important to remember this in discussing the Stasi's failure to encourage the Party to reform over the course of 1989.

So even after the unleashing of Brandt's *Ostpolitik*, and its continuation into the 1980s under the direction of Hans-Dietrich Genscher, the FRG remained the SED's foe. In 1973 the DDR ratified the United Nations Treaty on Human Rights, and in 1975 signed the Helsinki Agreement on European Security and Cooperation, which expressly provided for the respect of human rights in signatory states. But the SED leadership sought to limit the effects of détente by a series of legal and security measures. For example, the category of citizens held to be party to state secrets was greatly expanded. The MfS was concerned to prevent contacts between DDR citizens and people from 'non-socialist states', including West Berlin, or at least if such contacts did occur, to ensure that they were reported. The intensity of the threat from the West, as perceived by the SED, is revealed in the statements of the Stasi's leader, Erich Mielke. In 1987, at a time when Gorbachev's rapprochement with the West was gaining momentum, he condemned the CSCE process:

> The present international situation of class war, the development of the adversary's actions and of the political-strategic situation inside the DDR fully confirm the evaluation already made that since the Helsinki Conference, Imperialism has further perfected and substantially intensified all forms of its subversive work against the socialist states.[4]

One result of this hostility to the West German state was the continuing East German espionage against the FRG throughout the 1970s and 1980s. This reflected the SED leadership's fears of the West, as much as their desire to strengthen the Soviet Bloc through the acquisition of military and technical intelligence. The East German espionage drive in the 1970s led to the fall of Willy Brandt, after the disclosure in 1974 that one of his closest advisers, Günther Guillaume, was an agent of the HVA. Despite public gloating at the effectiveness of their spies, Honecker and Mielke had never intended to bring Brandt down.[5]

Despite the bellicose attitude of the East German leadership in the 'class war', it was clear even in the Brezhnev era that the SED state did not have the powers of social control which it had even in the 1960s. Indeed, even the very restricted degree of independent political life which evolved in the 1980s, mostly revolving around the Lutheran Church, proved ultimately fatal to the Party. The MfS was, if anything, even more necessary to the maintenance of the SED's power in the 1970s and 1980s than it was in the 1950s and 1960s. The expansion of the MfS under Erich Honecker was a reflection of the leadership's feelings of insecurity.

After 1971, when Erich Honecker replaced Walter Ulbricht as SED Secretary, whom the West had perceived as even more hardline, the security apparatus was developed and activity against 'those thinking differently' (*Andersdenkende*) stepped up. Another important development of the 1970s was Erich Mielke's promotion to the Politburo which gave him greater possibilities to influence political decisions.[6] Under Honecker and Mielke the security apparatus reached a strength of 100,000 full-time employees in 1989. This was twice what it was in the 1960s. After Gorbachev's accession in the Soviet Union in 1985, Mielke called for the suppression of the growing influence of all perceived political opponents. The basis for this was his instruction No.2/85 on 'prevention, disclosure, and combating of underground political activity'.[7] After 1985 control of *Andersdenkende* amounted to 'wholesale surveillance'.[8]

In the spring of 1986, alarm grew among the SED leadership at events in the Soviet Union. Gorbachev's advocacy of the people's right to self-determination signalled that they could no longer rely on the intervention of the Red Army if serious unrest occurred in the DDR. Their remedy was to increase internal spying even more. Mielke's decree 6/86 set up a new structure alongside the MfS's existing networks of informers. Regular Stasi officers, known as officers on special assignment (*Offiziere im besonderen Einsatz*, or OibE) were infiltrated into key positions in the state and economy where important information and also property was to be protected against 'hostile' forces. For the first time, restrictions were lifted on the Stasi's spying on the Party itself.[9]

The relationship between the MfS and the SED has often been mentioned since the collapse of the communist state in East Germany. According to one interpretation, the Stasi formed a 'state within a state'. This is the argument of Egon Krenz, the former SED Secretary responsible for internal security, as he tries to exonerate himself from the excesses of the Honecker regime. This view has often appeared, without clear argument to support it, in writings on the Stasi.[10] Krenz's explanation has been refuted not only by former Stasi officers, but also by members of the Party. For example, Horst Sindermann, the last President of the Volkskammer, told *Der Spiegel* that 'in the field of State Security nothing took place without Krenz knowing'.[11]

It is much more realistic to describe the Stasi as the 'sword and shield' of the Party. This is certainly the way they viewed themselves, and they used this symbol for their coat of arms. Indeed, the close intertwining of Party and secret police apparatus was one of the main reasons why the East German regime endured for so long and with so little popular opposition. This unity between Party and security organs lay at the heart of the Stasi's work. But the Stasi and the Party were ultimately locked in a fatal symbiosis. On the one hand, intelligence conditioned the Party leadership's view of the outside world; it was always served out in the congenial clichés of Party rhetoric, which reflected the SED's 'success'. On the other hand, in its reporting, the MfS was always in a straightjacket, not just because of the restraints of a stylized language, but also because it dared not hold up a clear mirror of society to the Party.

Certainly the majority of the population of the DDR saw the Stasi as a hostile element. The Stasi's view of itself and its relationship with society must also be taken into account, if the events of the *Wende* are to be fully understood. In MfS documents, the Stasi and the Party were presented as the vanguard of society. To echo the Stasi's words, both were meant *to lead* society and *to shape* it. This sort of language clearly reflected the tenets of Marxism-Leninism, in which the Party is the vanguard of the proletariat (that is, in the context of the DDR, society as a whole). According to this argument, Party rule is no less legitimate for its lack of popular support. Rather, the Party knows better than the mass of society, and thus has the duty to lead it, because its message is 'right' in absolute terms. This outlook is important when looking at both the Stasi and the Party's view of the developing revolution.

The Stasi's 'powers of reason' were provided by ZAIG, the Central Evaluation and Information Group. ZAIG's 1,000-strong staff processed the massive amount of information provided by Stasi regulars and the IM and GMS.[12] One of their most important tasks was to draw up general reports on public morale and opinions.

The diverse tasks carried out by the Stasi reflected its role, in partnership with the Party, as the 'vanguard of society'. This attitude was clearly reflected in ZAIG's rhetoric, with its frequent references to the 'ideological offensive', with the Party leading 'social forces' (*gesellschaftliche Kräfte*) into battle. Such language, of course, was obligatory in Stasi documents. But it would be too much to say that many of the Stasi, if not the majority, did not generally believe in their task. In this respect, it is noteworthy that Stasi morale broke only after their 'betrayal' by the Party in November–December 1989.[13] Likewise, ZAIG reporting reflected a genuine hatred for 'hostile-negative' forces, as the Stasi termed its internal opponents. The Stasi regarded even people leaving the DDR for non-political reasons as traitors.[14] One of the most striking aspects of the interviews with former Stasi officers which have been published in Germany is not so much their regret at their past but that many of them simply could not understand what happened in 1989, feeling that they could have 'won', had the Party held its ground.[15]

THE STASI AND THE SED LEADERSHIP ON THE EVE OF THE REVOLUTION

Obviously, it is impossible to reduce the history of the East European revolutions to a history of intelligence. The following are fundamental reasons which led to the collapse of the East German regime, and which are independent of its decisions in the sphere of internal security. First, economic decline had set in by the end of the 1970s, leading to mounting discontent among the population about basic conditions of life. This came to a head with the stream of East German refugees leaving for the West in the late summer of 1989. Second, Gorbachev's accession to power in the Soviet Union was a disaster for the SED leadership. His reformist policies undermined the legitimacy of the East German model of socialism. Gorbachev made it clear to the East German leadership that the ultimate sanction upon which their power had always rested – Red Army intervention – no longer existed. In October 1989 Gorbachev lit the spark which finally ignited all the forces of discontent which had been accumulating within East German society. He appeared at the GDR's 40th birthday celebrations not to honour Erich Honecker, but publicly to serve him notice.

Nonetheless, to varying degrees from country to country, the intelligence element is significant in the East European revolutions. The cases of East Germany, Poland, and Romania at least, disprove de Tocqueville's maxim that the most dangerous time for a despotic regime is when it tries to introduce reforms. It was the East German leadership's inflexibility before mounting public pressure in 1989 which caused the completeness of its collapse in 1989. By October it was clear that protest could only succeed if the regime were to fall. Generally, intelligence was a factor in the East German revolution because it encouraged inflexibility on the part of the leadership by creating a sense of physical security, through the Stasi's failure to foresee the coming danger, or to urge reforms in a language that was nearly strong enough.

There were several levels to the flow of information from the grass-roots to MfS headquarters. The first tier of this relationship was the exchange of information between Stasi and Party in the provinces. The district (*Kreis*) offices of the Stasi closely cooperated with the first secretaries of the SED district executives. The information generated at this level was passed to the provincial administration (*Bezirkverwaltung*). The third tier of the information exchange was the transfer of information from the provincial administrations to MfS headquarters in the East Berlin's Normannenstraße.[16] The final level of this flow was the sending of information from headquarters to the Politburo. Here all channels were united in one man, Erich Mielke. Essentially, the MfS was conducted according to the principle of military single command. Mielke had unrestricted authority to issue instructions to all members, irrespective of their position.[17] There were two basic problems in this system. References to social discontents and the poor conditions of consumer supply were watered down at each successive level through which the information passed.[18] Most importantly, though, the dependence of the Stasi as a whole on a man like Erich Mielke in order to make itself heard at the policy-making level, proved disastrous.

Documents recovered since the Revolution show that ZAIG regularly held up to its masters an uncomplimentary picture of East German life. Over the course of 1989 they often referred to the deterioration in the supply of consumer goods, to the chronic housing shortages, to ecological disaster, to rising anger at arrogant bureaucrats and to public discontent with a lying media.[19] But this material appeared only peripherally in the Stasi's reporting. The main thrust of the ZAIG reports which reached the leadership was tactical. They were plans of action for neutralizing 'hostile-negative' forces, not for mollifying them. In the last resort, the Stasi were there to support the Party's ideological offensive, not to criticize it.

Erich Mielke, the pinnacle of the Stasi pyramid, had been Minister for State Security since 1957. In 1989 he was 81 years old, and signs of old age were clearly visible in his speech. After the Revolution he was found to be suffering from arteriosclerosis.[20] According to other reliable sources, he was also suffering from senility.[21] In January 1990, after his arrest, he spoke to a commission investigating the violent events of 7–8 October in East Berlin. The questioners said afterwards that they could not understand how such a man could have been one of the most powerful in the state.[22]

ZAIG officers compiling reports never got any positive response.[23] One of them later complained that: 'The information channel was a one-way street':

> In time my colleagues and I realised that for the most part these reports were only used as information inside the Ministry. Although they certainly ought to have left it. And of course it hurts when you know that you'd just been working for the waste-paper bin.[24]

The fact that the Party leadership did absolutely nothing to introduce reforms as the *Wende* gained momentum, confirms this statement.

After the *Wende* both Western reporters and former Stasi officers claimed that the SED leadership at its higher levels were 'cut off from reality'. Their lack of perception of the problems of society, or their lack of concern about them, are illustrated by the bizarre, but well-substantiated stories about the way in which they used the MfS not only as a source of intelligence, but also as an entertainment and shopping service. The activities of the Stasi's postal service illustrates literally how officers of the MfS served as the 'handmaidens of the Party'. Ten kilometres from Berlin a special complex was involved, among other things, with misdirecting post from inside the FRG and with purloining packages sent by West Germans to their friends and relatives in the DDR. The aim was to provide consumer goods marked down on catalogues provided by the SED leadership for their own use.[25] Other Stasi officers assisted

Honecker and Mielke on their hunting sprees. Despite the help of scores of secret policemen the two sometimes felt that the kill had not been large enough. In such cases they ordered the Stasi to obtain large numbers of frozen hares and other small animals from the deep-freezes of East Berlin meat-packing firms. These the Stasi then arrayed in neat designs on the lawns of châteaux, before which Honecker and Mielke would pose to have their photographs taken.[26]

It would be an exaggeration to dismiss the whole East German leadership as insane 'geriatrics', even though the final years of the DDR contained a certain element of farce. As argued above, their freedom of action was limited in 1989. Moreover, Egon Krenz, as member of the Politburo, dealt directly with MfS affairs. He was only in his fifties in 1989.[27]

THE REVOLUTION

Despite Gorbachev's reform policies in the Soviet Union, and despite the worsening economic situation, both the SED leadership and the MfS had no reason to expect that 1989 would be any more unsettling than other years since 1985. The Stasi's powers of repression were greater than ever, as were its means of surveillance. Manifestations of discontent had been greater in the 1980s than in the 1970s, but they did not amount to anything remotely approaching a threat to the regime. The unrest which resulted from Soviet reform policies seemed to be restricted to a narrow circle of intellectuals.[28]

The 'opposition' appeared to ZAIG to be very weak indeed. In January 1989 an unofficial demonstration in Leipzig on the 70th anniversary of the murder of Karl Liebknecht and Rosa Luxemburg drew a crowd of only 150–200. The Stasi accused the demonstrators, as usual, of permitting the Western media to launch a 'new rabble-rousing slander campaign' against the DDR. In fact, such events made very little impact on the Western media. In England for example, the *Independent* carried only a handful of short articles on East Germany before the great flight to the West started in August.[29] There was no central dissident who commanded attention like Czechoslovakia's Václav Havel. In fact, West Germany had always acted as a safety-valve because those most disaffected had somewhere to go.

The Stasi usually described demonstrators and dissidents as 'hostile-negative forces'. Quite rightly, at this stage, it never referred to them as 'the opposition', though it did refer to 'oppositionists'. Though oppositionist groups had grown in the 1980s, their numbers were very small. In June 1989, at the ZAIG's calculation, there were about 160 of them. Their total number of members – excluding sympathizers – was only 2,500. These were the people with whom Main Administration XX was chiefly concerned.[30] The Stasi felt that even this figure overrated the strength of opposition groups. They noted reassuringly that 'a "hard core" is formed by a relatively small number of fanatics, motivated by a so-called sense of mission, a personal need for admiration and a yearning for the political limelight'.[31] ZAIG mentioned only 11 people in this group of arch-enemies, locked in a duel with the Stasi's 85,000 regulars.[32] They denied emphatically that these 'deviants' had any real impact on society: 'The hostile, opposition, and other negative groups working in the DDR possess no unified political concept and no self-contained "alternative" model of society.'[33] By comparison, 800,000 citizens of the DDR expressed their 'solidarity' with Erich Honecker on May Day 1989.

ZAIG did detect some signs of trouble from the 'opposition' at the beginning 1989, though these appeared no cause for alarm. A few Lutheran clergy were increasingly active.[34] Some applicants for 'permanent departure' from the DDR were attempting to 'pressurize' the state.[35] Moreover, the number of successful emigrants from the DDR was increasing. 10,255 people had left the DDR in the first half of 1988 compared with 38,917 in the first half of 1989.[36] But those seeking to emigrate were seen as a narrow group of trouble-makers.[37] Opposition groups were becoming better organized and were attempting to form GDR-wide groupings.[38] The Stasi were also concerned about links between activists in the DDR with those in other states of the Soviet Bloc, though these did not amount to much.[39] One of the Stasi's main concerns was that the 'oppositionists' should not tarnish the GDR's image in the Western media.[40]

As late as June 1989, ZAIG ascribed the presence of oppositionists in a large part to 'political, ideological and subversive' influences emanating from Western powers. They noted that:

> One of the main objects of attack against socialism in the enemy's subversive actions against socialism, are attempts to create and legalize a so-called internal opposition, and to inspire/organize political underground activities in the socialist states, as 'potential internal pressure' for the weakening, destruction, political destabilization, and finally the elimination of socialism.[41]

Thus in the Stasi's terminology, the demands for democracy and betrayal of the DDR were one and the same thing. The remarkably hazy nature of the Stasi's depiction of the Western threat is shown by their inclusion of the Western peace movement in it.[42]

Inside the DDR, the West, along with the Lutheran Church, were rendering material support to 'hostile-negative forces':

> Since the beginning of the 1980s such people have made continuous efforts to organize and form groups and groupings, which are aimed at weakening, destroying and altering the social relations of the DDR. These are almost all included within the structure of the Lutheran Church of the DDR and are able extensively to use the material and technical potential of this Church for their activities. The accredited correspondents and officials of diplomatic missions in the DDR (amongst whom secret servicemen disguised as diplomats) of the non-socialist states, particularly the FRG, the USA and Great Britain, are of considerable importance in this process. They are inspiring hostile, opposition groups and personal associations to anti-socialist activities, are continually providing them with support, and are popularizing this kind of activity, with the aim of putting such persons and associations under the protection of international publicity ...[43]

This was not just rhetoric. The above quotations come from a secret ZAIG analysis prepared for the MfS and the SED's own consumption. The link with the Western plot emphasizes how cut off they thought opposition groups were from the rest of society. Even when discussing the increasing number of people leaving the DDR in the first half of 1989, ZAIG did not discern that the population as a whole were hostile to the Party and state. According to ZAIG, people seeking to emigrate were also inspired by 'the ideological subversion of the adversary'.[44]

But what were these groups asking for? Generally, they wanted a modicum of democracy, protection of the environment, and other limited reforms. Certainly they were not seeking to overthrow the state. ZAIG, however, would not accept that ecological and other reform groups were anything other than a camouflage for much more subversive designs.

While ZAIG saw 'opposition groups' as cut off from society, they recognized that there was discontent among the public in general. But even in October, they did not report that the population was hostile to the Party on ideological grounds.[45] The Stasi viewed the population as being essentially passive and there to be led. Thus the reforms which ZAIG proposed to mollify public dissatisfaction were not far-reaching, and were based on the premise that the SED regime could continue without structural reform. Their recommendations for preventing the spread of 'oppositionist' ideas were more far-reaching. In part they amounted to pure coercion. However, they felt that the SED and its auxiliaries should go beyond this and actively refute arguments hostile to the Party line. First and foremost, the local Party leadership ought to take the lead in countering hostile arguments. The Party was to strengthen the cohesion of its 'politico-ideological and operational collaboration' with other 'progressive' forces. The effectiveness of oppositionists should be reduced by the deployment of 'social forces' in the debate. These included rank and file members of the SED, informers, members of trade unions and members of friendly parties in the SED-dominated National Front.[46] Thus ZAIG recommended the creation of a 'positive predominance' at 'opposition' meetings, by which they meant that informers should be used 'independently' to put the Party's case. They also advised the more frequent appearance of experts with specific expertise at meetings at which 'oppositionists' attended, in order to put over a convincing representation of SED policies, as well as 'the determined use of the complex possibilities for using such people for factual and ideological influence on members of such associations, which are presented by everyday work and by social functions'.[47] These same solutions to the problem figured in all the Stasi's reporting, right up to the end.

It is interesting to note the far greater role which ZAIG ascribed to ideology, than to tactical reforms. In all totalitarian states ideology plays a crucial role in binding the state together. Even if the ideology is not believed, all strata of society and of the government must pay lip-service to it. Even though they failed adequately to respond to them, and underestimated their immediate potential, ZAIG had a strong presentiment of the potential of the handful of 'fanatics' facing them at the beginning of the year. Thus even before serious trouble started, the Stasi were concerned that the Party's presentation of its politics and ideology was stale and unconvincing.[48]

If the MfS viewed the 'hostile-negative' forces opposing it at the beginning of 1989 as a long-term threat, though their immediate strength was weak, why did it not simply dispose of them either through arrest or exile? Right up until mass demonstrations started in several East German cities in October 1989, the level of physical repression which the state deployed was very limited in comparison, for example, with the harshness of the early days of Martial Law in Poland. For a long time the Stasi had been able to prevent events organized by oppositionists from getting out of hand by a few simple measures: by warning senior Lutheran church leaders that Church–State relations were endangered; by discussing the dangers of participation with would-be demonstrators; and by putting demonstrators under short-term arrest. It is not obvious why the Stasi and the Party felt the need for such restraint. They genuinely believed until the last minute that 'oppositionists' had little influence on society; thus their arrest would not lead to protests. The imprisonment of Havel in Czechoslovakia – who was a far-better known dissident – led to only muted international repercussions. Furthermore, the Polish communists had successfully crushed Solidarity, which was a far stronger popular movement.

The SED regime may have felt that a more forceful repression would have been counter-productive. It would have led to some, albeit limited, international repercussions, as both a slap in the face to Gorbachev, and an irritation to the West Germans. But these were not the main reasons, and are certainly not mentioned in the available sources. Though the SED leadership was willing to have people crossing the Berlin Wall shot, it genuinely believed in its socialist message. This is something that is masked by all the lurid stories of Party corruption which have appeared since the Revolution. Honecker and Mielke believed that 'hostile-negative forces' should and could be defeated by the power of the Party's arguments – by the attraction of the manifest advantages of scientific socialism. It is this attitude which is clearly reflected in the Stasi's wishes to counter its opponents' arguments in words, both before and during the *Wende*.

Perestroika was the ideological threat which proved fatal to the SED. Despite the concern of the Honecker regime, which led to the expansion and ramification of the MfS after 1985, accurate reporting on it seems to have been so guarded that it might almost have been a taboo subject. A ZAIG analysis of *perestroika* dating from May 1989 was shot through with ambiguity. In it ZAIG first put the point of view of the general population, saying euphemistically, that 'the Western media's interpretation of events in the Soviet Union' has 'had its effect on the East German population'. Then, at far greater length, they described the attitude of 'progressive forces', that is, those supporting the SED leadership's line:

> opinions are now increasing in scope and intensity that the development of social democracy and the growth of an atmosphere of openness should not lead to the unrestricted expression of subjective opinions and judgements about people and processes, and the spreading of half-truths, speculation and bourgeois opinions.[49]

Members of the SED were particularly concerned about the discussion of past political errors, which they felt had reached the level of 'anarchy'.

The rejection of the need by SED and MfS leadership for even cosmetic reform of their image and political line is illustrated by the Stasi's complete failure to present a better face either to their own population or to the world. This contrasts sharply with the concerted public relations campaign which Vladimir Kryuchkov, the former head of the KGB, mounted to improve the image of the MfS's Soviet counterpart both at home and abroad.[50]

The May local elections in the DDR proved to be a major event on the road to revolution. For many people the blatant vote-rigging which the SED carried out through the agency of the MfS proved to be the last straw. ZAIG realized the value of the elections in restoring trust between the Party and the people. They reported that the people saw the elections as an 'important political high-point in the social life of the DDR, in which citizens' trust in the policies of the party and government would be strengthened once more'. They pointed out that citizens were criticizing deputies for not keeping their election promises, and for being increasingly out of touch with their constituencies.[51] But they warned that:

> Comparisons were frequently made with the elections to the Congress of People's Deputies in the USSR. Some people said that the new Soviet practices should be introduced into the DDR: for example, the use of ballot boxes; and several candidates for each seat.[52]

It is significant that in reporting this, ZAIG must have been aware that free elections would have led to at least some reverses for the Party.

Throughout the DDR Church groups tried to monitor the elections.[53] In response, Mielke gave instructions, in an order of 19 May 1989, to prevent at all costs any critical evaluation of the elections. The order supplied a list of answers to criticisms.[54] It proceeded from the assumption that 'internal enemies' intended to prove an 'alleged rigging of election results'.[55]

Despite popular disgust at the rigging of the elections, everything seemed to ZAIG basically to be in order in the middle of the year. The regime's support for the Chinese government after the Tienenman massacre caused widespread revulsion, but the Stasi were able to prevent any actions in solidarity with the Chinese protesters from gaining publicity.[56] However, Mielke saw in events in China further evidence of the Western conspiracy against 'socialism', claiming that the 'counter-revolutionary uprising in Peking' had been stimulated by the Western media. He ordered Stasi officers to show increased vigilance as the political situation in China developed. They were particularly to look out for people spreading propaganda against the Chinese authorities.[57]

The first big shock to the Stasi came in August, when thousands of East German visitors to Hungary and Czechoslovakia demanded exile in the West. This amounted to a massive failure in intelligence-gathering on the part of the MfS. Though the number of applicants for emigration in the first half of 1989 was about three and a half times larger than in the first half of 1988, the Stasi had no foreknowledge that the exodus of 1989 might occur. They had no idea that so many people were dissatisfied to such an extent with life in the DDR. Moreover, they were poorly informed about events among the would-be exiles, because their *Inoffizielle Mitarbeiter* were not present in Hungary and Czechoslovakia.[58]

The occupation of the FRG's embassies in Hungary and Czechoslovakia by East German citizens set the first alarm bells ringing among the Stasi leadership.[59] On 31 August Mielke met representatives of the Stasi provincial administrations in MfS headquarters to discuss the internal situation. In fact, by the time the conference took place, the damage had already been done in Hungary and Czechoslovakia. The Hungarian Government had informed Federal Chancellor Kohl that the borders would be opened.[60]

At the conference, the Stasi's assessment of the internal situation in the DDR can be summed up as follows. There were some districts in which the public mood caused concern. They felt that the situation in East Berlin was particularly serious, which is ironic since serious unrest was to break out first in Leipzig. Nonetheless, all the representatives agreed that generally the situation was stable, though there was widespread public sympathy with the would-be emigrants in Hungary. Some of the representatives, however, recognized that it might not remain so for long. The Leipzig Stasi reported that they had 'the situation firmly in hand', but 'a spark would be enough to set something in motion out of a situation arising by chance'. Mielke asked the Gera representative: 'Has the day before 17 June arrived?' (that is, the eve of the uprising of 1953). The answer was: 'It hasn't, and it won't arrive, that's what we're here for.'

The Stasi officers laid much of the blame for popular dissatisfaction on the Party. The SED in the provinces, like the top leadership, had failed even to speak to the people, and had done nothing to redress 'justifiable' popular grievances. Moreover, local party leaders regularly disregarded Stasi advice about how to avert popular discontent. For example, in the hospital in Karl-Marx-Stadt there was a cancer ward where there was one wash-basin for 12 patients. This situation had existed since 1980. The Stasi had repeatedly complained about this to the local Party, who had ignored them.

The MfS generals proposed the standard Stasi remedies to counter the growth of popular discontent. They recommended an improvement of consumer supply, and the unleashing by the Party of a vigorous public relations campaign. But they showed a greater flexibility towards reform than hitherto revealed in Stasi assessments by proposing a more understanding treatment of the ecology movement.

The meeting on 31 August revealed very clearly the Stasi's difficulties in disseminating intelligence through the channel of Erich Mielke. When confronted with details about the worsening situation in the provinces, Mielke reacted with angry, rambling and ungrammatical tirades. He expressed his disgust at popular demands:

> Why, so they acknowledge the advantages of socialism and all the advantages that socialism has to offer, but despite this they want out, because they take all this for granted and disregard it all, and put forward all

> possible reasons for wanting out. So what is the effect, what are the effects of our work? I don't just mean of our state security, but political influence. We will find something, search and find something, which we can recommend, something that can be improved.

The tactical need to improve the consumer situation was completely beyond his grasp:

> Socialism is so good, but they demand more and more. That's the way things are. I always think about what we lived through. I couldn't eat and buy bananas, not because there weren't any, but because we hadn't got any money to buy them with.

In what passed for a conclusion, Mielke ordered that 'good forces' should be deployed, to show that oppositionists were 'talking nonsense'. Mielke could see no further solution to the GDR's problems than making the existing system of repression function better. He ordered that informers were to work harder, while more responsibility was given to the top tier of informers, the OibE.[61]

On 11 September the Hungarian government opened its borders. This started the rapid collapse of the Workers' and Peasants' State. Even at this date, the Stasi were still looking to the Party to sort things out. ZAIG recommended that there should be closer cooperation between Party and Stasi in preparing the ideological riposte.[62] However, instead of reducing popular discontent by introducing reforms, or by arguing its case, the leadership simply closed the GDR's borders with Hungary and Czechoslovakia. Even Mielke was worried about this desperate decision. He reported to the MfS:

> A number of progressive groups advocated the measures introduced, but were surprised that such an 'unpopular' decision had been taken on the 40th anniversary of the DDR. The opinion was almost unanimous that the basic problems of the DDR would not be solved by this step, since the causes were to be found inside the DDR.[63]

The immediate effect of the exodus to the West was to bring into the open years of accumulated popular frustration. But this was not translated into political muscle until the massive demonstrations started in Leipzig in October. From the Stasi's point of view, the worst effect of the exodus was the rapid collapse in Party morale which it caused. In August, when the trouble started, the Stasi were particularly worried about the 'lousy mood inside the Party'.[64] By 11 September ZAIG were reporting that many Party members were voicing the same complaints as non-Party members – about the problems of the economy, the growth of corruption, and the SED's exploitation of the media. As a result large numbers were leaving the Party.

While the Party started to crumble, the 'hostile-negative' forces started to organize. Even ZAIG now started to talk of 'the opposition'. This was made up of various groups all of whom united in the increasingly forceful demand that the Party's monopoly on power be broken. The most important were 'New Forum' and 'Democratic Awakening', which were creations of some of the 11 'hard-core fanatics'.[65] Finally, the opposition had succeeded in creating GDR-wide organizations, whose membership included all strata of the population.[66] Mounting hostility against the SED's policies was reflected by a move of the previously passive Catholic Church towards the opposition.[67]

In ZAIG's view, the Party had abandoned the field to New Forum. They protested that

> a situation has arisen where even many citizens, in particular people from the universities, technical colleges, art and culture, as well as students, who had a positive basic outlook, are identifying with the aims and themes of the opposition movement 'New Forum', and have accepted and are spreading the political platform and demands made at the formation of this group.[68]

At the August Conference in MfS headquarters, the Stasi representatives had concluded that whenever the Stasi or the Party picked 'progressive forces' with 'the necessary backbone', and sent them to events, they always defeated opposition arguments.[69] Even now ZAIG believed that all that was needed was 'an ideological offensive' in alliance with the Party.

Gorbachev's visit to the DDR on 6–7 October set the seal on the Party's collapse. He left no doubts that he expected major reform from the SED leadership and dialogue with independent social groups. Large demonstrations broke out in several cities, which were repressed with brutality by the security forces. Yet the leadership did not understand the amount of force that was now necessary. Anticipating unrest, on 2 October Mielke stated that 'next Monday I will now once and for all deploy my special troops, and will show that our authority still has teeth'.[70] But he only intended to use truncheons and dogs on the demonstrators, whom he described as 'cowardly dogs' who would 'run like rabbits as soon as they've seen our dogs'.[71] Such methods only fuelled popular protest.

After Gorbachev's visit, a palpable note of desperation entered ZAIG's reporting. On 8 October they informed Mielke that

> According to the available information from the capital and from all the provinces of the DDR, many progressive groups, in particular members of the SED, consider that the socialist state and social order in the DDR is seriously in danger.[72]

They warned that the 'GDR already … finds itself in a situation like that shortly before the counter-revolutionary events' of 1953. They expressed dismay at the 'insecurity, helplessness and resignation among Party members'. This helplessness was so bad that the only comments on the internal situation in the DDR reaching the population, were those made in the West German media.[73] Repeatedly ZAIG made barely veiled criticism at the leadership's failure to meet the crisis with the necessary flexibility. On 16 October, ZAIG reported uncritically on disaffected Party members' claims that the SED leadership were 'to the greatest possible extent' responsible for the current situation:

> They say that because of an unreasonable attitude and a rigid adherence to an obviously not negotiable political line, the Party leadership have not reacted effectively to the worsening of political developments in the DDR since August 1989, and as a result have caused serious political damage for the SED and the DDR.[74]

Earlier in the year the SED leadership had failed to introduce even minor reforms because it had underestimated the strength of popular hostility to it. By 8 October the Party had only two options: immediately to introduce structural reforms; or to impose a Tienenman-style solution and to fire on the crowd.

Even at the very end of the SED State, the Stasi certainly had the physical force to crush the opposition, and to stop the rioting. The ease with which this could be done had already been shown by General Jaruzelski's coup against Solidarity in 1981. The Stasi had detailed information about the opposition's movements and elaborate plans to intern the ringleaders. Since 1988 the SED leadership had started to build up special forces to cope with a situation like that now existing.[75] In June 1989, a rapid deployment force was created for Berlin,[76] while after the exodus from Hungary, Mielke ordered the creation of a rapid deployment unit inside Chief Directorate VIII, which normally dealt with security of communications and special surveillance.[77] Moreover, the Stasi had plans to lock up 122 members of the opposition from the Leipzig area alone in an internment camp.[78] To the north of East Berlin, they had built a huge subterranean command bunker for the contingency of armed conflict.[79]

According to Schabowski, he, Krenz, Dickel, Mielke and others met together in the MfS in the Normannenstraße on 8 October. Mielke was still ready to use force to curb demonstrations. Just before 4 p.m. that day, provincial Stasi administrations received orders that left no doubt that a major blow was to be directed against the opposition.[80] Why force was not resorted to on Monday, 9 October in Leipzig is not entirely clear. Krenz has said that his old friend, Professor Walter Friedrich, arrived early on that Monday morning to see Krenz in the House of the Central Committee. He reported to Krenz about the situation in Leipzig and the fear there that it could come to shooting. Krenz then got in touch with all the necessary officials to ensure that firearms would not be used. Friedrich also handed Krenz a note on which was written, 'Honecker must resign'. This said Krenz further encouraged him to move against Honecker.[81] On that same day, Kurt Masur, music director of the Leipziger Gewandhaus Orchestra, and a loyal supporter of the Honecker regime, appealed with five others against the use of force. The appeal was read out in churches and broadcast on the Leipzig radio.[82] For his part, Honecker claimed that there had never been any question of using force in Leipzig except if demonstrators set fire to buildings, stormed buildings or attacked the police. Krenz, he claimed, had nothing to say in the matter.[83]

After 8 October the riot police stopped attacking the crowds, while on the 10th some of the arrested demonstrators were released. But all the security forces remained on high alert. One false move on the part of the opposition might have lead to civil war. As late as 16 October Mielke ordered that in the event of violence, the security forces were to use force if persons or buildings were attacked.[84] Undoubtedly after 8 October, the Stasi were not seeking to promote an escalation of the unrest.[85] Nonetheless their ability to repress the crowd remained considerable. The Leipzig MfS administration reported at the beginning of November that 'chemical defence measures' were still ready for use in cases where 'firearms were also justified'.[86] In the event, the crowds and the opposition groups behaved with remarkable discipline, committing no acts which the security forces might have taken for provocation.[87] Thus, the events of 8 October amounted to an abdication of political power by the SED. On 18 October the battle between the Party state and the opposition was all but over with Honecker's resignation, and his replacement by the ineffectual Egon Krenz.

After 16 October ZAIG ceased to report on the crisis. The Citizens' Committee who went through its records concluded that 'Possibly the confusion was so great after this day that a definite inability to act reigned among State Security's higher echelons.'[88] As a one former Stasi officer recalls:

> The process of disillusionment started in October was tragic. Every day it brought new, bad news, new disclosures, partly perhaps exaggerated, which now showed the top leadership to be wretched, senile men, who had been concerned above all for their own well- being, who were incapable of comprehending these numerous signals signals which had reached them, let alone to cope with them.[89]

By 15 October some of the security forces were siding with the crowd.[90] At the same time, the Stasi no longer trusted some of their informers.[91]

In the middle of November Hans Modrow's government, which had succeeded that of Krenz, replaced the Stasi with the *Amt für Nationale Sicherheit*. But little changed apart from the name. Indeed, this formed the unfortunate acronym 'NASI', which may be seen as one of the last significant failures of the SED regime to take public opinion into account.

Nonetheless, the game was not quite over as far as some of the 'Nasi' were concerned. On 10 November a Captain in the Leipzig administration wrote to his head, Lieutenant-General Hummitzsch. He argued that in the past the Stasi had neglected to make the public aware of the value of its work in defending socialist society. He noted that 'the anchoring of our organ in the working class and its high reputation among the people could have been proved not only theoretically but also demonstrated credibly and practically'. The Captain stated that he and the majority of his 'comrades' thought that the Stasi/Nasi ought no longer to be silent, leaving publicity to their 'demagogic' and 'ignorant' opponents. It was no longer enough to leave this work to informers working in narrow circles. The Stasi should put its case on the media.[92] Hummitzsch took his advice and started a media campaign. Thus the Stasi finally took over from the Party in the 'ideological offensive'.[93] The campaign, which was paralleled in other provinces of the DDR, was short-lived, since at the insistence of the opposition, now engaged in discussions with the SED, the government dissolved the Nasi on 7 December 1989.

On 13 November, a few days after the opening of the Berlin Wall, Mielke found himself in need of good public relations of his own. He appeared before the Volkskammer, the East German Parliament, attempting to justify his past, and in particular his role in the brutal attacks on the demonstrators at the beginning of October. He showed his detachment from reality by blaming all that had happened on the SED, of which he, of course, was a leading member, and by praising the now publicly execrated Stasi as 'the sons and daughters of the working class'. He concluded by telling the obviously hostile parliament that 'I love every one of you'. After this he ceased to be head of the MfS.[94] According to one Stasi general, it was this speech which caused the final collapse of the Stasi's morale throughout the DDR, when they realized who had been leading them for the past 30 years.[95]

Why then were the Stasi unable to prevent the revolution of 1989? Certain factors were outside the control of both Stasi and Party, particularly because had they so wanted, the SED leadership could not change their basic political line, by introducing structural reforms, without invalidating the justification for the existence of a separate, non-capitalist German state. It was not realistic for the Honecker regime to introduce far-reaching economic reforms, or to allow more than a modicum of freedom of expression. But this does not explain why the internal situation moved so rapidly into revolution, and why the SED leadership failed to carry out any reforms at all. Intelligence played an important part in the downfall of the DDR by its failure to perceive the deep-rootedness of discontent with the socialist state throughout society. In particular, the Stasi failed really to understand who their allies were. Though they were in one sense a massive vetting system, they did not appreciate that many members of the SED were only in the Party for career reasons, and were by no means the ideologically-committed, 'progressive forces' which they depicted.

It might be asked whether intelligence can ever prevent a revolution. In France in 1789, and in Russia in 1917, for example, revolutions have occurred through the spontaneous combustion of social discontent, usually in conditions of a sharp economic downturn. The situation in the states of Eastern Europe in 1989 was slightly different. In each case, the local regime had created an intelligence service in its own image. Like the SED, the MfS was highly centralized and ideologically motivated. Both factors served to separate it from society as a whole, within which it believed it was a leading force. Despite their vast size, the Stasi were unable accurately to assess the public mood. The tight intermeshing of secret police and Party meant that they were unable adequately to advise the Party. The distinction between an unhearing Party and a reforming Stasi should not be pressed too far. Even ZAIG wanted only cosmetic reform in the DDR. More significantly, the contradiction between the unchanged world of propaganda and reality made even the Ministry's employees to a certain degree unsure of the situation inside the country. The SED tried to use a mixture of carrot and stick as they 'led' society. They failed to see that the carrot, namely Marxist-Leninist ideology, had turned to compost. The lament of one former MfS officer is a comment on the way the Stasi appeared to society: 'Our main problem was that we tried to solve political problems by police methods, problems which we as an organization were not able to solve.'[96]

For one member of the Stasi, however, the revolution of 1989 did not spell the end. After his disastrous appearance before the Volkskammer, Erich Mielke was consigned to a prison hospital. He enraged his guards by acting as if he were still head of the MfS. In particular, he constantly demanded that they provide his cell with a telephone. Unable to bear this behaviour any longer, the prison authorities complied with his orders, and Mielke set to work giving long instructions to his subordinates. The lines were disconnected.[97]

8 The Aftermath

The East German revolution was peaceful. The restoration of German unity was achieved by peaceful diplomacy. These facts helped to set the tone of what was to come. One other factor was the experience of 'National Socialism' and the fact that the eyes of the world were on Germany. A final factor was that, as so many East Germans had been members of official organizations of one kind or another, there was a danger of placing a large number of East Germans in the status of second-class citizens or worse. This would have caused problems in the future. On the other hand, the thousands of victims wanted some visible sign that they would get justice, that those who had persecuted them would be punished. One problem was which sets of laws should be used to try those accused. Could the laws of the pre-1990 Federal Republic be applied retroactively? Most of those who worked for the DDR state felt they were obeying legitimate orders of their superiors who in turn headed an internationally recognized state. It was, therefore, decided to apply the laws of the DDR when testing individual acts carried out by state or SED officials. What were the results?

Of the 21 members of the Politburo, excluding Honecker, five had died of natural causes within five years of their fall. The rest, including Mielke, faced an uncertain fate. There were calls to prosecute at least the members of the Politburo and those who had led the organs of repression and those who had faithfully carried out unjust orders. However, some prominent individuals in West Germany criticized any prosecution of former DDR politicians or officials. They claimed reconciliation and inner unity between the inhabitants of the two parts of Germany would best be served by proclaiming an amnesty. Joachim Gauck, the East German charged with administering the files of the former MfS, believed that many West Germans were indifferent to the suffering caused by the Stasi to the East German people and that is why they could advocate closing the files and declaring an amnesty.[1] In the Bundestag, the PDS was isolated in its call for an amnesty. Dr Wolfgang Ullmann (Bündnis 90), himself a victim, thought there could be no reconciliation without the truth being established about the misdeeds of the MfS.[2] In 1991 there were indications[3] that the majority of former DDR citizens agreed with the need to find out the truth about the MfS, but equally, many felt that former Stasi members should be treated like anyone else provided they were not responsible for criminal acts.

There were those who questioned the prosecution of former DDR frontier guards who shot at would-be escapees. They were 'only obeying orders' it was claimed. The highest German court (*Bundesgerichtshof*) decided otherwise. On 3 November 1992 it gave its judgement: such acts were breaches of human rights of the worst kind. The DDR was breaking its international undertakings on human rights, it was claimed. If law is in an unbearable contraction to justice, law must give way to justice, Judge Heinrich Laufhütte, Chairman of the court, declared. He emphasized that to a degree the frontier guards were also victims. However, even indoctrinated individuals must recognize this assault on the basic prohibition on killing.[4] Two former DDR frontier guards had in fact been given suspended sentences on 5 February 1992. This judgement was regarded as forming the framework for the prosecution of the leading politicians of the DDR. No attempt was being made to prosecute former members of the MfS or other DDR bodies on the basis of membership alone.

After much embarrassment, the man who had been welcomed to Bonn with so much pomp and friendliness in 1987, Erich Honecker, was charged with a number of offences including authorizing the killing of would-be escapees on the East–West frontier and the Berlin Wall. The trial was stopped on medical advice and the ailing 81-year-old was allowed to go to Chile where he died in May 1994. His wife went there with him. She had been a hard-liner and, as a member of the DDR government, in theory also responsible for the deaths and other wrong-doings. Erich Mielke, Minister for State Security from 1957 to 1989, also had his trial interrupted on medical grounds. He was however, convicted for his part in the murder of two policemen in 1931 and sentenced to six years' imprisonment. General Heinz Kessler, former DDR Defence Minister; General Fritz Streletz, former Chief of Staff of the armed forces, and Hans Albrecht, SED First Secretary for *Bezirk* Suhl, were also charged over the shooting on the border. General Markus Wolf, head of the HVA until 1986, was sentenced on 6 December 1993 to six years' imprisonment for high treason. The sentence was suspended pending a verdict of the Constitutional Court on the constitutionality of prosecuting employees of the MfS for intelligence gathering in West Germany. Both in Germany and elsewhere some agreed with the view of Heribert Hellenbroich, former BfV head, that, 'this trial is unconstitutional … Wolf carried out intelligence by order of a then existing state'. Richard Helms, former CIA Director, believed it was 'bizarre that a fellow who was doing a job for his country as he saw it, should be prosecuted later by his enemies'.[5] The Constitutional Court suppressed Wolf's conviction in March 1996.

In May 1995 the Federal Constitutional Court in Karlsruhe reached a judgment deciding that former DDR inhabitants who pursued espionage against the Federal Republic from within the DDR should not be prosecuted for this activity. West Germans who spied for the DDR were put in a different category and could still be prosecuted with the full vigour of the law.[6] The judgment cleared Markus Wolf and his successor, Werner Großmann, from fear of prosecution for their main HVA activity.

At the lower levels most of the Stasi employees had to turn to some other means of earning their living. However, a significant number did find re-employment in police or private security work. In Saxony it was reported[7] that more than 500 ex-Stasi operatives had been taken over by the police. This included 161 former full-time MfS employees and 262 IM. In addition, 370 ex-members of the DDR criminal police were in employment in 1994.

Inevitably the hunt for IM went on. The members of the Bundestag were asked if they were prepared to be investigated for possible connections with the MfS. Only 315 of the 662 members of the 1990 parliament agreed. All members of the PDS, Bündnis 90 and FDP agreed. Almost all of the CSU declined. None of those investigated were exposed as Stasi agents. Ilja Seifert of the PDS had freely admitted he had worked as an IM from conviction.[8] The former DDR Minister of Economics and later PDS member of the German parliament, Professor Christa Luft, admitted in June 1995 that she too had worked with the MfS. The Chairman of the PDS group in the Bundestag continued to protest his innocence.[9] No doubt accusations of involvement with the MfS will continue to haunt German political, academic and cultural life for many years to come. Some of the accusations would come from former members of the Stasi who thought they had been harshly treated.

Determined to protect their interests former MfS members banded together in the Insiders group and in another organization open to all former members of the armed organs of the DDR. *Initiativgemeinschaft zum Schutz der sozialen Rechte ehemaliger Angehöriger bewaffneter Organe und der Zollverwaltung der DDR*, ISOR e.V. for short, was founded on 6 June 1991, and sees itself as a body designed to deal with all the pension and other welfare and legal issues which confront former members of the DDR's armed units. Inevitably, many of its members would be members or sympathizers of the PDS. Were the former Stasi members prepared to go beyond welfare clubs to safeguard their interests? In March 1991 there was some evidence that a group calling itself *Rote Faust* was attempting by threats and violence to frighten off would-be Stasi hunters.[10]

By 1995, at the level of the ordinary citizens, many wanted to put the whole Stasi business behind them and get on with dealing with what they considered to be the problems of today. However, between 1990 and May 1993 over 2 million individuals had made applications to see any files which had been kept by the Stasi on them. Most of the applications were from former citizens of the DDR. Information had been given by the authorities on 685,000 persons during this same period.[11] The story continues …

Appendix A
Biographical Information

Konrad Adenauer [1876–1967], Mayor of Cologne to 1933, Catholic, CDU Chancellor of Federal Republic of Germany, 1949–63.

Bruno Beater [1914–], joined MfS in 1950 rising to First Deputy Minister for State Security in 1964.

Willy Brandt [1913–92], Anti-Nazi emigrant, 1933–45, Mayor of West Berlin, 1957–66, SPD Chancellor of West Germany, 1969–74.

Fritz Dickel [1913–93], former International Brigader and Moscow emigrant, Deputy Minister of Defence then 1965 Minister of Interior of DDR and head of People's Police.

Reinhard Gehlen [1903–79], former colonel who headed German military intelligence on Eastern Front in the Second World War, he was the first head of the BND, 1956–68 after working under US direction after the war.

Werner Großmann [1929–], succeeded Wolf as head of HVA and Deputy Minister of State Security in 1986.

Otto Grotewohl [1894–1964], former Social Democrat, DDR head of government, 1949–64.

Günter Guillaume [1927–95], worked as a DDR spy in the West, 1956–74 when he was exposed working for Chancellor Brandt. The exposure cost Brandt the Chancellorship and Guillaume his freedom. In October 1981 he was exchanged and returned to a hero's welcome in the DDR.

Wolfgang Harich [1923–95], University lecturer on Marxism and SED intellectual, he was arrested in 1956 for anti-state conspiracy. He was released in 1964. After the fall of the SED he attempted to revive reform communism.

Robert Havemann [1910–82], a member of KPD anti-Nazi underground who narrowly avoided execution. Professor of physical-chemistry at Humboldt University he was removed in 1964 because of his calls for more freedom. He was later put under house arrest.

Heinz Hoffmann [1910–85], after military training in Soviet Union took part in Spanish Civil War, 1936–9. After various leading military functions, Minister of Defence of DDR, 1960–85. Member of Politburo of DDR.

Erich Honecker [1912–94], he was leader of KPD youth movement in Saar until 1933. Arrested in Berlin in 1935 he was imprisoned by Nazis to 1945. He helped to found and became First Secretary of FDJ, 1946–55. In 1958 he became Politburo member with responsibility for security. In 1971 he replaced Ulbricht as First Secretary of SED until ousted by Egon Krenz in October 1989.

Otto John [1909–97], part of July plot against Hitler, he later worked for British intelligence. He was first head of West German BfV. He disappeared in West Berlin later claiming he had been drugged and kidnapped.

Helmut Kohl [1930–], 1969–76 Minister-President of the Rhineland-Palatinate, 1982– CDU Chancellor of Federal Republic of Germany.

Egon Krenz [1937–], after various leading functions in FDJ and Young Pioneers and training in Moscow, elected First Secretary of FDJ 1974–83. Member of Politburo with responsibility for security. First Secretary of SED October–November 1989.

Erich Mielke [1907–], after elementary and grammar school [Köllnische Gymnasium, Berlin, with a scholarship] Mielke took up an apprenticeship with a road haulage firm. Both his working-class parents were communists and Mielke soon followed them into the KPD. He carried on various functions in KPD before 1933, including being active in its paramilitary wing and sports movement. He was a strict vegetarian, non-smoker and total abstainer at that time. Wanted by the police for his part in the shooting of two policemen on 9 August 1931 he escaped to the Soviet Union. There he studied at the Comintern's military school and at the Lenin School where future revolutionary functionaries were trained. As 'Fritz Leissner' he served as an officer of the communist secret police in the Spanish Civil War, 1936–9. He helped in the purge of the 'Trotskyists' but also in the evacuation of the remnants of the International Brigades to France. After working for the KPD in Brussels he crossed the frontier to France as the Nazis occupied Belgium. He was interned in St Cprien camp in southern France. By the end of the war Mielke was back in Berlin but some mystery surrounds his life between 1941–5. He later claimed to have fought on the Soviet side in the war, in other accounts he remained in France working as a building labourer. From 1945 on he played a key role in the creation of the state security system in Soviet Zone/DDR. He served as Vice-President of the Central Administration of the Interior, 1946–50; State Secretary for the MfS, 1950–3; Deputy State Secretary for State Security in the Ministry of Interior, 1953–5; State Secretary for State Security in the MfS, 1955–7; Minister for State Security, November 1957–December 1989. He was a member of the Central Committee from

1950 and Member of Politburo of SED from 1971. Mielke married Gertrud Müller, a tailor, on 18 December 1948. They had one son, Frank. Frank and his wife, both medical practitioners, worked for the Stasi with the rank of major. After his elevation to the Politburo Erich Mielke and his family lived in the top people's estate at Wandlitz. He was a mark millionaire when he was dismissed from office in December 1989.

Günter Mittag [1926–94], SED Secretary with responsibility for economy, 1962–73 and 1976–89. Member of the Politburo of SED.

Rudi Mittag [1925–94], former bricklayer and wartime soldier he became an officer of the MfS in 1950. He headed the MfS in Potsdam, 1956–64. Deputy Minister for State Security, 1969–89, member of the Central Committee of the SED from 1986.

Gerhard Neiber [1929–], he started his career as an SED functionary in Schwerin before joining the MfS. Deputy Minister of State Security, 1980–9.

Hans Modrow [1928–], after study in Moscow First Secretary of FDJ in Berlin, 1953–61, First Secretary of SED Dresden, 1973–89, head of government of DDR November 1989– March 1990 and briefly member of Politburo.

Wilhelm Pieck [1876–1960], Chairman of the KPD, 1935–46, President of DDR, 1949–60.

Helmut Schmidt [1918–], former artillery lieutenant who became Minister of Defence [1969–72], then Minister of Finance [1972–4]. He succeeded Brandt as SPD Chancellor of Federal Republic, 1974–82.

Wolfgang Schwanitz [1930–], from 1986 Deputy Minister for State Security and candidate member of the Central Committee of the SED, was briefly head of the Amt Für Nationale Sicherheit before that body was disbanded.

Horst Sindermann [1913–90], imprisoned by Nazis, 1934–45, head of government of DDR, 1973–6, President of Volkskammer, 1976–89, Member of Politburo of SED.

Willi Stoph [1914–99], Minister of Interior of DDR, 1952–5, Minister of Defence, 1956–9, head of government, 1964–73 and 76–89, head of state, 1973–6, Member of Politburo of SED.

Franz Josef Strauß [1915–88], former artillery lieutenant, Federal Minister for Special Tasks, 1953–7 and 1963–6, Minister of Defence 1956–62, Finance Minister, 1966–9. Chairman of the CSU 1961–88, Minister-President of Bavaria, 1978–88.

Fritz Streletz [1926–], wartime soldier who threw his lot in with the Soviets, he played an important role in building up the KVP and NVA. Deputy Minister of Defence of DDR, 1979–89. Member of the Central Committee of the SED.

Markus 'Mischa' Wolf [1923–], fled with his parents to Soviet Union in 1933 where he studied at a Comintern school. On returning to Germany in 1945 he worked as a journalist and then as a diplomat before embarking on his intelligence service career. Deputy Minister for State Security and head of HVA, 1958–86. In 1989 presented himself as reform communist in Gorbachev mould.

Walter Ulbricht [1893–1973], 1950–71, General/First Secretary of the SED, Chairman of Council of State, 1960–73.

Ernst Wollweber [1898–1967], leading naval mutineer 1918, KPD member of the Reichstag, Soviet saboteur in Second World War, 1955–7 Minister for State Security of DDR. Member of the Central Committee of the SED, 1954–8 after which he was purged for his opposition to Ulbricht.

Wilhelm Zaisser[1893–1958], KPD military expert, fought in Spain as 'General Gómez', 1936–9, Minister for State Security of DDR, 1950–3, purged for 'defeatism'. Member of the Politburo of the SED to 1953 and then expelled from the Party in 1954.

Appendix B
Chronology

August 1914: Outbreak of First World War.

1917: Tsar overthrown in Russia. Democratic provisional government established. October, Lenin and Bolsheviks seize power in Russia from democratic revolutionary government.

20 December 1917: Cheka established.

November 1918: Revolution in Germany followed by establishment of democratic Weimar Republic. Germans sign armistice with Allies which leads to end of war.

31 December 1918: Communist Party of Germany [KPD] set up with aim of establishing a 'Soviet Germany'.

5/12 January 1919: Communist/Spartacist attempt to seize power in Germany crushed with heavy loss of life.

October 1923: A renewed attempt by the KPD to take power in Hamburg crushed after heavy fighting.

8/9 November 1923: Hitler putsch in Munich put down with loss of life.

9 August 1931: Erich Mielke involved in killing two policemen in Berlin as part of a KPD armed group.

1933: Hitler appointed German Chancellor, communists banned.

1936–9: Spanish Civil War, KPD members Ulbricht, Zaisser, Mielke and others sent to Spain where they purge other leftists.

August 1939: Hitler–Stalin Pact, followed by outbreak of Second World War.

1 September 1939: German invasion of Poland followed by Anglo-French declaration of war on Germany on 3 September. Later Poland invaded also by Soviet Union.

22 June 1941: Nazi invasion of Soviet Union launched.

January/February 1943: Surrender of German Sixth Army at Stalingrad.

8/9 May 1945: Unconditional surrender of German armed forces to Soviets and Western allies. Walter Ulbricht, Wilhelm Pieck, Wilhelm Zaisser, Erich Mielke, Markus Wolf and other German communists return to Germany from Moscow behind advancing Soviet forces.

21 April 1946: SED formed after forced merger of SPD with the KPD.

1 August 1946: German Administration of Interior, with police functions starts work in Soviet Zone.

16 August 1947: Formation of Kommissariat 5 of the German People's Police [DVP] in the Soviet Zone of Germany by order of the Soviet Military Administration.

18 June 1948–12 May 1949: Blockade of West Sectors of Berlin by Soviets.
June 1948: Tito's Yugoslav communists expelled from Soviet-dominated Cominform.
3 July 1948: Soviets order setting up of People's Police in Barracks [KVP].
15 September 1949: Konrad Adenauer [CDU] elected Chancellor, head of government of newly established Federal Republic of Germany in West Germany.
24 August 1949: NATO becomes operative.
7 October 1949: Establishment of German Democratic Republic [DDR] in Soviet Zone of Germany with Wilhelm Pieck [SED] as President and Walter Ulbricht as key SED figure. Ministry of Interior [MdI] takes over internal security.
October 1949: People's Republic of China set up led by Mao Tse-tung.
8 February 1950: Founding of the Ministry for State Security [MfS] in DDR.
20 February 1950: Wilhelm Zaisser named as Minister for State Security with Erich Mielke as State Secretary under him.
1950–3: War in Korea after communist North invaded US-backed South.
1951: Institute for Economic Research [IWF] set up as secret service under jurisdiction of DDR foreign ministry.
16 May 1952: Frontier police put under jurisdiction of MfS.
5 January 1953: DDR Foreign Minister Dertinger arrested.
5 March 1953: Death of Soviet dictator Josef Stalin.
17 June 1953: Revolt against SED regime in East Berlin and other centres of DDR crushed by Soviet Army.
23 July 1953: Zaisser dismissed, MfS reorganized as State Secretariat for Security [SfS] under Ernst Wollweber. The SfS also takes over intelligence gathering outside the DDR by HA XV.
24 November 1955: The SfS is reorganized as MfS with Wollweber as Minister.
1956: HA XV of MfS is transformed into HVA led by Markus Wolf.
14/25 February1956: Twentieth Congress of CPSU Stalin denounced by Khrushchev.
25 October 1956: Hungarian Revolution, country invaded by Soviet armed forces.
3 March 1957: Frontier police taken over by Interior Ministry [MdI].
5 October 1957: The Soviets launch the first artificial earth satellite, Sputnik, thus inaugurating the space age.
1 November 1957 Wollweber replaced by Mielke as Minister for State Security.
13 August 1961: Building of Berlin Wall.
15 October 1963: Ludwig Erhard [CDU] replaces Adenauer as Chancellor.

October 1964: Khrushchev overthrown as CPSU leader and replaced by Brezhnev.

1966: Cultural Revolution in China.

1 December 1966: Kurt Georg Kiesinger [CDU] takes over from Erhard as Chancellor of West Germany.

20/21 August 1968: Warsaw Pact forces invade Czechoslovakia.

10 October 1969: Willy Brandt [SPD] elected Chancellor of Federal Republic.

3 May 1971: Erich Honecker becomes First Secretary of SED replacing Walter Ulbricht.

June 1971: Mielke becomes candidate member of the Politburo.

7 November 1972: Basic Treaty between DDR and Federal Republic signed. This paves the way for diplomatic recognition of the DDR by Western and neutral states. It increases opportunities for intelligence gathering. The MfS has to cope with more Western visitors.

16 May 1974: Helmut Schmidt [SPD] replaces Brandt as Chancellor after the Guillaume affair.

1976: Erich Mielke becomes full member of Politburo.

1982: Helmut Kohl [CDU] replaces Schmidt as Chancellor after coalition break up.

May 1985: Mikhail Gorbachev takes over as General Secretary of the CPSU.

6 February 1987: Neues Deutschland announces Markus Wolf resignation as head of HVA and replacement by Werner Großmann.

17 June 1987: Death penalty abolished in DDR.

7/11 September 1987: Honecker visits Federal Republic of Germany.

10/11 September 1989: Hungary opens its frontier to the West [Austria] allowing DDR citizens to pass freely. Thousands leave DDR by this route.

11 September 1989: Mass arrests during peaceful demonstration in Leipzig, beginning of large-scale demonstrations.

18 October 1989: Honecker replaced by Egon Krenz as General Secretary of the SED.

9 November 1989: Opening of Berlin Wall and other frontier points of DDR.

17 November 1989: New head of government Hans Modrow announces the abolition of the MfS and its replacement by a *Amt für nationale Sicherheit* [Office for National Security] to be led by General Wolfgang Schwanitz.

3 December 1989: Entire Politburo resigns, Honecker and 11 leading SED members expelled from party, Krenz expelled 21 January 1990.

14 December 1989: Decision of the government of the DDR to abolish the *Amt für nationale Sicherheit.*

21 December 1989: Mielke arrested on the charge of 'misuse of office'.

18 March 1990: First free elections in DDR, PDS [formerly SED] defeated.

3 October 1990: The DDR joins the Federal Republic.

Bibliography

OFFICIAL PUBLICATIONS

Bundesministerium des Innern, *Verfassungsschutzberichte* (1968, 1975, 1980–92) (These are the annual reports of the West German internal security agency).

Bundesministerium für gesamtdeutsche Fragen, *A bi Z. Ein Taschen-und Nachschlagebuch über den anderen Teil Deutschlands* (11th edn, Bonn, 1969).

Deutscher Bundestage, 12. Wahlperiode, Drucksache 12/7820, *Bericht der Enquete-Kommission 'Aufarbeitung von Geschichte und Folgen der SED-Diktatur in Deutschland'*, 31.05.94.

Statistisches Bundesamt, *DDR 90 Zahlen und Fakten* (Wiesbaden, 1990).

Publications of the Gauk-Behörde (Der Bundesbeauftragte für die Unterlagen des Staatssicherheitsdienstes der ehemaligen Deutschen Demokratischen Republik).

Abkürzungsverzeichnis Ministerium für Staatssicherheit: Häufig verwendete Abkürzungen und ausgewählte spezifische Begriffe (1993).

Ammler, Thomas and Memmler, Hans Joachim, eds, *Staatssicherheit in Rostock: Zielgruppen, Methoden, Ausflösung* (Cologne, 1991).

Auerbach, Thomas, *Vorbereitung auf den Tag X. Die geplanten Isolierungslager des MfS* (Reihe B: Nr.1/95).

Aus der Veranstaltungsreihe des Bundesbeauftragten: Bearbeiten – Zersetzen – Liquidieren (28.1.1993). *Die Inoffiziellen Mitarbeiter* (25.3.1993). *Freiheit für meine Akte!* (27.5.1993) (Reihe B: Nr.3/93).

Das Arbeitsgebiet I der Kriminalpolizei. Aufgaben, Struktur und Verhältnis zum Ministerium für Staatssicherheit (1994).

Das Wörterbuch der Staatssicherheit. Definitionen des MfS zur 'politisch-operativen Arbeit' (Reihe A: Nr. 1/93).

Die Dissertationen an der 'Juristischen Hochschule' des MfS. Eine annotierte Bibliographie (Reihe A: Nr.2/94).

Die Inoffiziellen Mitarbeiter. Richtlinien, Befehle, Direktive (Reihe A: 2 Bände).

Die Organisationsstruktur des Ministeriums für Staatssicherheit 1989. Vorläufiger Aufriß nach dem Erkenntnisstand von June 1993 (Reihe A: Nr. 2/93).

Engelmann, Roger, *BF informiert: Zu Struktur, Charakter und Bedeutung der Unterlagen des Ministeriums für Staatssicherheit* (Nr.3/1994).

Erster Tätigkeitsbericht des Bundesbeauftragten für die Unterlagen des Staatssicherheitsdiensts der ehemaligen Deutschen Demokratischen Republik (1993).

Fuchs, Jürgen, *BF informiert: Unter Nutzung der Angst. Die 'leise Form' des Terrors Zersetzungsmaßnahmen des MfS* (Nr.2/1994).

Gesetz über die Unterlagen des Staatssicherheitsdienstes der ehemaligen Deutschen Demokratischen Republik (Stasi-Unterlagen-Gesetz-StUG) Vom 20. Dezember 1991.

Gieseke, Jens, *BF informiert: Die Hauptamtlichen 1962. Zur Personalstruktur des Ministeriums für Staatssicherheit* (Nr.1/1994).

Gieseke, Jens, *BF informiert: Doktoren der Tschekistik. Die Promovenden der 'Juristischen Hochschule' des MfS* (Nr.6/1994).

Henke, Klaus-Dietmar, ed., *Hinweis: Wann bricht schon mal ein Staat zusammen! Die Debatte über die Stasi-Akten auf dem 39. Historikertag 1992* (dtv 2965).

*MfS unde Leistungssport. Ein Rechercheberich*t (Reihe A: Nr. 1/94).

Müller-Enbergs, Helmut, *Das Zusammenspiel von Staatssicherheit und SED nach der Selbstverbrennung des Pfarrers Oskar Brüsewitz aus Rippicha am 18. August 1976* (Reihe B: Nr. 2/93).

Müller-Enbergs, Helmut, *BF informiert: IM-Statistik 1985–1989* (Nr.3/1993).

Süß, Walter, *Zu Wahrnehmung und Interpretation des Rechtsextremismus in der DDR durch das MfS* (Reihe B: Nr. 1/93).

Süß, Walter, ed., *BF informiert: Erich Mielke und KGB-Vize Leonid Schebarschin über den drohenden Untergang des Sozialistischen Lagers. Mitschrift eines Streitgesprächs am 7. April 1989* (Nr.1/1993).

Süß, Walter, *BF informiert: Entmachtung und Verfall der Staatssicherheit. Ein Kapitel aus dem Spätherbst 1989* (Nr.5/1994).

Tantzscher, Monika, *'Maßnahme Donau und Einsatz Genesung'. Die Niederschlagung des Prager Frühlings 1968/69 im Spiegel der MfS-Akten* (Reihe B: Nr. 1/94).

Vollnhals, Clemens, *Das Ministerium für Staatssicherheit. Ein Instrument totalitärer Herrschaftsausübung* (1995).

Walther, Joachim and Prittwitz, Gesine von, *BF informiert: Staatssicherheit und Schriftsteller. Bericht zum Forschungsprojekt* (Nr. 2/1993).

Zastrow, Hildegard von, *BF informiert: Bibliographie zum Staatssicherheitsdienst der DDR* (Nr.4/1994).

BOOKS AND IMPORTANT ARTICLES.

Adams, Jefferson, 'Crisis and Resurgence: East German State Security', in *International Journal of Intelligence and Counterintelligence*, 1988, II, 4.

Andert, Reinhold and Herzberg, Reinhold, *Der Sturz,* Berlin and Weimar, 1991.

Andrew, Christopher, *Secret Service. The Making of the British Intelligence Community* (London: 1985).

Andrew, Christopher and Gordievsky, Oleg, *KGB. The Inside Story of its Foreign Operations from Lenin to Gorbachev* (London, 1990).

Andrew, Christopher and Gordievsky, Oleg, *More Instructions from the Centre. Top Secret Files on KGB Global Operations 1975–1985* (London, 1992).

Angress, Werner T., *Stillborn Revolution. The Communist Bid for Power in Germany, 1921–1923*, 2 vols (Port Washington, 1963).

Bahro, Rudolf, *Die Alternative* (Frankfurt-am-Main, 1977).

Bajanov, Boris, *Bajanov révèle Staline: souvenirs d'un ancien secrétaire de Staline* (Paris, 1972).

Balfour, Michael, *Withstanding Hitler* (London, 1988).

Bangerter, Lowell A., *German Writing Since 1945: A Critical Survey* (New York, 1988).

Bark, Dennis and Gress, David R., *A History Of West Germany, Vol.1, From Shadow To Substance 1945–1963* (Oxford, 1993).

Bark, Dennis and Gress, David R., *A History Of West Germany, Vol. 2 Democracy And Its Discontents 1963–1991* (Oxford, 1993).
Barron, John, *KGB Today* (London, 1984).
Behnke, Klaus, *Zersetzung der Seele: Psychologie und Psychiatrie im Dienst der Stasi* (Hamburg, 1995).
Beleites, Michael, *Untergrund: ein Konflikt mit der Stasi in der Uran-Provinz* (1992).
Berg, Hermann von, Loeser, Franz, and Seiffert, Wolfgang, *Die DDR auf dem Weg in das Jahr 2000* (Cologne, 1990).
Birke, Adolf M., *Die Deutschen Und Ihre Nation: Nation ohne Haus Deutschland 1945–1961* (Gütersloh, 1989).
Bohley, Bärbel, Fuchs, Jürgen, Havemann, Katja, *et al.*, *40 Jahre DDR ... und die Bürger melden sich zu Wort* (Frankfurt am Main, 1989).
Borowski, D., *Erich Honecker. Statthalter Moskaus oder deutscher Patriot*? (Munich, 1987).
Bortfeldt, Heinrich, *Von der SED zur PDS Wandlung zur Demokratie?* (Bonn and Berlin, 1992).
Brandt, Heinz, *Ein Traum der nicht entführbar ist* (Munich, 1967).
Brandt, Willy, *My Life In Politics* (New York, 1992).
Brant, Stefan, *The East German Rising* (London, 1955).
Brüning, Elfriede, *Und außerdem war es mein Leben. Aufzeichnungen einer Schriftstellerin* (Berlin, 1994).
Brzezinski, Zbigniew K., *The Soviet Bloc. Unity and Conflict* (Revised and enlarged edn, Cambridge, Mass., 1967).
Buber-Neumann, Margarete, *Von Potsdam nach Moskau* (Stuttgart, 1957).
Buch, Günther, *Namen und Daten wichtiger Personen der DDR* (2nd edn, Bonn and Berlin, 1982).
Bürgerkomitee Bautzner Straße e.V., *MfS – Bezirksverwaltung Dresden eine erste analyse*, (Dresden, December, 1992).
Bürgerkomitee von Leipzig, (eds), *Stasi intern: Macht und Banalität* (1991).
Carr, Edward Hallett, *A History of Soviet Russia. The Interregnum* (London,1954).
Cate, Curtis, *The Ides Of August: The Berlin Wall Crisis 1961*, (New York, 1978).
Chalet, Marcel and Wolton, Thierry, *Les Visiteurs de l'Ombre* (Paris, 1990).
Childs, David, *East Germany To The 1990s: Can It Resist Glasnost?* (London, 1987).
Childs, David, *The GDR: Moscow's German Ally* (2nd edn London, 1988).
Childs, David, *Germany in the Twentieth Century* (3rd edn London, 1991).
Constantinides, George C., *Intelligence and Espionage: An Analytical Bibliography* (Boulder, 1983).
Cookridge, E.H., *Gehlen Spy Of The Century* (London, 1972).
Cornelsen, Doris, *et al.*, *Handbuch DDR-Wirtschaft* (Reinbek, 1977).
Corson, W.R. and Crowley, R.T., *The New KGB Engine Of Soviet Power* (Brighton, 1986).
Crampton, R.J., *A Short History of Bulgaria* (Cambridge, 1987).
Crozier, Brian, *Free Agent. The Unseen War 1941–1991* (London, 1993).
Dallin, David J., *Soviet Espionage* (New Haven, 1955).
Davis, Norman, *God's Playground: A History of Poland* vol.II (Oxford, 1981).
Deakin, F.W. and Storry, G.R., *The Case of Richard Sorge* (New York, 1964).
Dean, Richard, *'C': A Biography of Sir Maurice Oldfield, Head of MI6*, London, 1985.
Degras, J., ed., *Soviet Documents on Foreign Policy* vol. 1 (London, 1951).

Dennis, Mike, *German Democratic Republic. Politics, Economics and Society* (London, 1988).
Drachkovitch, Milorad M. and Lazitch, Branko, eds, *The Comintern: Historical Highlights. Essays, Recollections, Documents* (New York, 1966).
Drews, Manfred and Stoll, Max, *Soldaten der ersten Stunde* (East Berlin, 1981).
Edinger, Lewis S., *Kurt Schumacher* (Cologne & Opladen, 1967).
Eichhorn, Alfred and Reinhardt, Andreas, eds, *Nach langem Schweigen endlich sprechen. Briefe an Walter Janke* (Berlin, 1990).
Eisert, Wolfgang, *Die Waldheimer Prozesse. Der stalinistische Terror 1950. Ein dunkles Kapital der DDR-Justiz*, (Munich, 1993).
Emmerich, Wolfgang, *Kleine Literaturgeschichte der DDR* (2nd edn, Darmstadt, 1991).
Erickson, John, 'Threat Identification and Strategic Appraisal by the Soviet Union, 1930–1941' in May, Ernest R., ed., *Knowing One's Enemies. Intelligence Assessment before the Two World Wars* (Princeton, 1986).
Erickson, John, *The Road to Stalingrad* (London, 1985).
Fejtö, François, *A History of the People's Democracies* (2nd edn, London, 1974).
Fiedler, Helene, *SED und Staatsmacht* (East Berlin, 1974).
Fischer, Ruth, *Stalin and German Communism. A Study in the Origins of the State Party* (Cambridge, Mass., 1948).
Flechtheim, Ossip K., *Die KPD in der Weimarer Republik* (Frankfurt/M, 1969).
Flocken, Jan von and Scholz, Michael F., *Ernst Wollweber. Saboteur – Minister – Unperson* (Berlin, 1994).
Foot, M.R.D., *SOE* (London, 1984).
Foot, M.R.D., 'Was SOE Any Good?' in Laqueur, Walter, ed., *The Second World War* (London, 1982).
Forster, Thomas M., *Die NVA Kernstück der Landesverteidigung der DDR* (Cologne, 1983).
Freiburg, Arnold and Mahrad, Christa, *FDJ: Der sozialistische Jugendverband der DDR* (Opladen, 1982).
Fricke, Karl Wilhelm, *Opposition und Widerstand in der DDR* (Cologne, 1984).
Fricke, Karl Wilhelm, *Die DDR-Staatssicherheit* (3rd edn Cologne, 1989).
Friedrich, Ebert Stiftung Büro Chemnitz, *Das Wirken Des Ministerium Für Staatssicherheit Insbesondere Im Bezirk Karl-Marx-Stadt* (Chemnitz, 1992).
Friedrich, Jörg, *Die kalte Amnestie NS-Täter in der Bundesrepublik* (Frankfurt-am-Main, 1984).
Frolik, Josef, *The Frolik Defection. Memoirs of an Intelligence Agent* (London, 1975).
Fuchs, Jürgen, *'... und wann kommt der Hammer?': Psychologie, Opposition und Staatssicherheit* (Berlin, 1990).
Fulbrook, Mary, *The Two Germanies, 1945–1990. Problems Of Interpretation*, (London, 1992).
Fulbrook, Mary, *Anatomy of a Dictatorship. Inside the GDR* (Oxford, 1995).
Garton Ash, T., *In Europe's Name. Germany and the Divided Continent* (London, 1993).
Gehlen, General Reinhard, *The Gehlen Memoirs* (Glasgow, 1972).
Gelb, Norman, *The Berlin Wall* (London, 1986).
Gill, David, *Das Ministerium für Staatssicherheit* (Berlin, 1991).
Glees, Anthony, *Exile Politics During the Second World War* (Oxford, 1982).

Grieder, P.E., *Tension, Conflict and Opposition in the Leadership of the Socialist Unity Party of German (SED) 1946–73* (Unpublished PhD thesis, Cambridge, 1995).
Guillaume, Günter, *Die Aussage. Wie es wirklich war* (Munich, 1990).
Hahn, Reinhardt O., ed., *Ausgedient. Ein Stasi-Major erzählt* (Halle, Verlag, 1990).
Hagen, Louis, *Der heimliche Krieg auf deutschem Boden Seit 1945* (Düsseldorf and Vienna, 1968).
Hagen, M. *DDR – Juni 1953. Die erste Volkserhebung im Stalinismus* (Stuttgart, 1992).
Halter, Hans, *Krieg der Gaukler. Das Versagen der deutschen Geheimdienste*, (Göttingen, 1993).
Hassemer, Winfried and Starzacher, Karl, (eds), *Datensch und Stasi-Unterlagen, oder Bewaltigen?* (1993).
Havemann, Robert, *Dialektik ohne Dogma?,* (Reinbek, 1964).
Heins, Cornelia, *The Wall Falls: An Oral History Of The Reunification Of The Two Germanies* (London, 1994).
Henke, Klaus-Dietmar, ed., *Wann bricht schon mal ein Staat zusammen! Die Debatte über die Stasi-Akten auf dem 39. Historikertag 1992* (Munich, 1993).
Henkel, Rüdiger, *Im Dienste der Staatspartei. Über Parteien und Organisationen der DDR* (Baden-Baden, 1994).
Herrnstadt, Rudolf, edited by Stulz-Herrnstadt, Nadja, *Das Herrnstadt-Dokument. Das Politbüro der SED und die Geschichte des 17. Juni 1953* (Hamburg, 1990).
Heydemann, Günter and Kettenacker, Lothar, eds, *Kirche in der Diktatur* (Göttingen, 1993).
Hildebrandt, Rainer, *Als die Fesseln fielen ...* (Berlin, 1966).
Hiller, Horst, *Sturz in die Freiheit Von Deutschland nach Deutschland* (Munich, 1986).
Hingley, Ronald, *The Russian Secret Police* (London, 1970).
Höhne, Heinz and Zolling, Hermann, *Network. The Truth about General Gehlen and his Spy Ring* (London, 1972).
Honecker, Erich, *From My Life* (Oxford, 1981).
Honecker, Erich, *Moabiter Notizen* (Berlin, 1994).
Hosking, Geoffrey, *The Awakening of the Soviet Union* (London, 1990).
Hurwitz, H. *Zwangsvereinigung und Widerstand der Sozialdemokraten in der Sowjetischen Besatzungszone* (Cologne, 1990).
Jäckel, Hartmut, ed., *Ein Marxist in der DDR* (Munich, 1980).
Jänicke, M., *Der dritte Weg. Die antistalinischer Opposition gegen Ulbricht seit 1953* (Cologne, 1964).
Janka, Walter, *Schwierigkeiten mit der Wahrheit* (Reinbek, 1989).
Johnson, Chalmers, *An Instance of Treason. Ozaki Hotsumi and the Sorge Spy Ring* (Expanded edn, Stanford, 1990).
Kaiser, Karl, *Deutschlands Vereinigung. Die internationalen Aspekte* (Bergisch Gladbach, 1991).
Kalugan, Oleg, with Montaigne, Fen, *SpyMaster. My 32 Years in Intelligence and Espionage against the West* (London, 1994).
Kaplan, Karel, *Report on the Murder of the General Secretary* (London, 1990).
Kluth, Hans, *Die KPD in der Bundesrepublik*, (Cologne, Opladen, 1959).
Knechtel, Rüdiger and Fiedler, Jürgen, *Stalins DDR Berichte politisch Verfolgter* (Leipzig, 1992).
Knight, Amy W., *The KGB. Police and Politics in the Soviet Union* (London, 1988).
Knight, Amy W., *Beria. Stalin's First Lieutenant* (Princeton, NJ, 1993).
Knopf, Guido, *Top Spione Verräter im Geheimen Krieg* (Munich, 1994).

Koestler, Arthur, *The Invisible Writing* (London, 1954).
Kreis, Georg, ed., *La protection politique de l'Etat en Suisse. L'évolution de 1935 à 1990* (Berne, 1993).
Krenz, Egon, *Wenn Mauern fallen. Die friedliche Revolution: Vorgeschichte-Ablauf – Auswirkungen* (Vienna, 1990).
Krisch, Henry, *German Politics under Soviet Occupation* (New York and London, 1974).
Krisch, Henry, *The German Democratic Republic. The Search for Identity* (Boulder, 1985).
Krone, Tina, *Wenn wir unsere Akten lesen. Handbuch zum Umgang mit den Stasi-Akten* (1992).
Kühnrich, Heinz, *Die KPD im kampf gegen die faschistischen Diktatur.*
Kunz, Rainer, Deckname *'Lyrik': eine Dokumentation von Rainer Kunze* (Frankfurt, 1992).
Kuusinen, Aino, *Before and After Stalin. A Personal Account of Soviet Russia from the 1920s to the 1960s* (London, 1974).
Lang, Ewald, ed., *Wendehals und Stasi-Laus. Demo-Sprüche aus der DDR* (Munich, 1990).
Lang, Jochen von, *Erich Mielke, eine deutsche Karriere* (Berlin, 1991).
Lazitch, Branko and Drachkovitch, Milorad M., *Lenin and the Comintern* Volume I (Stanford, 1972).
Lazitch, Branko and Drachkovitch, Milorad M., *Biographical Dictionary of the Comintern* (revised edn, Stanford, 1986).
Leggett, George, *The Cheka. Lenin's Political Police* (Oxford, 1986).
Leonhard, Wolfgang, *Die Revolution entlässt ihre Kinder* (Cologne, 1955).
Leonhard, Wolfgang, *Das kurze Leben der DDR. Berichte und Kommentare aus vier Jahrzehnten* (Stuttgart, 1990).
Lewis, Paul G., *Central Europe since 1945* (London, 1994).
Lintner, Eduard *et al.*, *SED-Regime und Stasi-Herrschaft: drei Jahre nach dem Fall der Mauer* (1992).
Lippmann, Heinz, *Honecker and the New Politics of Europe* (London, 1971).
Loeser, Franz, *Die unglaubwürdige Gesellschaft. Quo vadis, DDR?* (Cologne, 1984).
Loest, Erich, ed., *Die Stasi war mein Eckermann, oder, Mein Leben mit der Wanze* (Göttingen, 1991).
Loth, W., *Stalins ungeliebtes Kind. Warum Moskau die DDR nicht wollte* (Berlin, 1994).
Luxemburg, Rosa, *Die Russische Revolution*, edited by Peter Blachstein, (Hamburg, 1948).
Maaz, Hans-Joachim, *Die Entrüstung: Deutschland, Deutschland, Stasi, Schuld, und Sündenbock* (1992).
Mampel, Siegfried, *Die volksdemokratische Ordnung in Mitteldeutschland* (Frankfurt-am-Main and Berlin, 1967).
Marshall, Barbara, *Willy Brandt* (London, 1990).
McAdams, A. James, *East Germany and Détente. Building Authority after the Wall* (Cambridge, 1985).
McAdams, A. James, *Germany Divided. From The Wall To Reunification* (Princeton, N.J., 1993).
McCauley, Martin, *The German Democratic Republic since 1945* (London, 1983).

McElvoy, Anne, *The Saddled Cow. East Germany's Life and Legacy* (London: 1992).
Medvedev, Roy, *Khrushchev* (Garden City, NY: Doubleday, 1983).
Meinel, Reinhard and Wernicke, Thomas, *Mit tschekistischem Gruss: Berichte der Bezirksverwaltung für Staatssicherheit Potsdam* (Potsdam, 1989).
Mergen, Armand, *Die BKA Story* (Munich and Berlin, 1987).
Misiunas, Romuald J. and Taagepera, Rein, *The Baltic States. Years of Dependence, 1940–1980* (London, 1983).
Mitter, Armin and Wolle, Stefan, eds, *Ich liebe euch doch alle! Befehle und Lageberichte des MfS Januar–November 1989* (2nd edn Berlin, 1990).
Mitter, Armin and Wolle, Stefan, *Untergang auf Raten. Unbekannte Kapitel der DDR-Geschichte* (Munich, 1993)
Moreton, Edwina, *East Germany and the Warsaw Alliance* (Colorado, 1978).
Mosley, Leonard, *Dulles: A Biography of Eleanor, Allen, and John Foster Dulles and Their Family Network* (New York, 1978).
Müller, Michael and Andreas Kanonberg, *Die RAF-Stasi-Connection* (Berlin, 1992).
Müller-Enbergs, Helmut, *Der Fall Rudolf Herrnstadt. Tauwetterpolitik vor dem 17. Juni* (Berlin, 1991).
Müller-Enbergs, Helmut, *Das Zusammenspiel von Staatssicherheitsdienst und SED nach der Selbstverbrennung des Pfarrers Oskars Brüsewitz aus Rippicha am 18. August 1976* (Berlin, 1993).
Müller-Römer, Dietrich, ed., *Ulbrichts Grundgesetz die sozialistische Verfassung der DDR* (Cologne, 1968).
Naimark, Norman M., '"To Know Everything and to Report Everything Worth Knowing", Building the East German Police State, 1945–1949', *Cold War International History Project, Working Paper No.10* August 1994.
Nationalrat Der Nationalen Front Des Demokratischen Deutschland, *Braunbuch Kriegs-Und Naziverbrecher In Der Bundesrepublik* (Berlin, 1965).
Naumann, Gerhard, *Von Ulbricht zu Honecker*.
Nettl, J.P., *The Eastern Zone and Soviet Policy in Germany 1945–50* (London, 1951).
Nettl, J.P., *Rosa Luxemburg*, (London, 1966).
Neuberg, A., *Armed Insurrection* (London, 1970).
Nicolaevsky, Boris I., ed., *Contributions à l'histoire du Comintern: Les premières années de l'Internationale Communiste (d'après le récit du 'Camarade Thomas')* (Geneva, 1965).
Osmond, Jonathan, *German Reunification: a Reference Guide and Commentary* (London, 1992).
Pacepa, Ion M., *Red Horizons* (London, 1988).
Pechman, Roland and Vogel, Jürgen, *Abgesang der Stasi: das Jahr 1989 in Presseartikeln und Stasi-Dokumenten* (1991).
Peet, John, *The Long Engagement. Memoirs Of A Cold War Legend* (London, 1989).
Peters, Butz, *RAF: Terrorismus in Deutschland* (Munich, 1991).
Pike, David, *The Politics of Culture in Soviet-Occupied Germany 1945–1949* (Stanford, Cal., 1992).
Pincher, Chapman, *Their Trade is Treachery* (London, 1981).
Pincher, Chapman, *Too Secret Too Long* (London, 1984).
Pincher, Chapman, *The Truth About Dirty Tricks* (London, 1991).

Pittman, Avril, *From Ostpolitik to reunification. West German-Soviet political relations since 1974* (Cambridge, 1992).
Pond, Elizabeth, *Beyond the Wall: Germany's Road to Unification* (Washington, 1995).
Popplewell, Richard J., 'Themes in the Rhetoric of KGB Chairmen from Andropov to Kryuchkov' in *Intelligence and National Security*, Vol.6, July 1991, No.3.
Popplewell, Richard J., 'The Stasi and the East German Revolution of 1989', in *Contemporary European History*, I, 1 (1992), pp.37–63.
Prange, Gordon W. *et al.*, *Target Tokyo, The Story of the Sorge Spy Ring* (New York, 1985).
Przybylski, Peter, *Tatort Politbüro. Die Akte Honecker* (Berlin, 1991).
Ranelagh, John, *CIA. A History* (London, 1992).
Read, Anthony and Fisher, David, *The Deadly Embrace: Hitler, Stalin And The Nazi–Soviet Pact 1939–1941*, (London, 1988).
Reichenbach, Alexander, *Chef der Spione. Die Markus-Wolf-Story* (Stuttgart, 1992).
Reichhart, Hans J., 'Möglichkeiten und Grenzen des Widerstandes der Arbeiterbewegung' in Schmitthenner, Walter and Buchheim, Hans, eds, *Der deutsche Widerstand gegen Hitler* (Cologne, 1966).
Rein, Gerhard, ed., *Die Opposition in der DDR. Entwürfe für einen anderen Sozialismus* (Berlin, 1989).
Reuth, Ralf George, *IM 'Sekretär': Die 'Gauck Recherche' und Dokumente zum 'Fall Stolpe'* (Frankfurt, 1992).
Reuth, Ralf Georg and Bönte, Andreas, *Das Komplott. Wie es wirklich zur deutschen Einheit kam*, (Munich, 1993).
Richardson, R. Dan, *Comintern Army. The International Brigades and the Spanish Civil War* (Lexington, 1982).
Richter, Peter and Rösler, Klaus, *Wolfs West-Spione. Ein Insider-Report* (Berlin 1992).
Rieke, Dieter, ed., *Sozialdemokraten im Kampf gegen die rote Diktatur unter Stalin und Ulbricht* (Bonn, 1990).
Riecker, Ariane, ed., *Stasi intim: Gespräche mit ehemaligen MfS-Angehörigen* (Leipzig, 1990).
Rocca, Raymond, G. and Dziak, John J., *Bibliography on Soviet Intelligence and Security Services* (Boulder, 1985).
Runge, Irene and Stelbrink, *Markus Wolf, 'Ich bin kein Spion'* (Berlin, 1990).
Sass, Ulrich von, *'Feindlich-negativ'* (1990).
Schabowski, Günter, *Der Absturz* (Berlin, 1991).
Schabowski, Günter, *Das Politbüro: Ende eines Mythos* (Reinbek, 1990).
Schapiro Leonard, *The Communist Party of the Soviet Union* (London, 1970).
Schaul, Dora, ed., *Resistance Erinnerungen deutscher Antifaschisten* (Berlin, 1973).
Schell, Manfred and Kalinka, Werner, *Stasi und kein Ende* (Frankfurt, 1991).
Schlomann, Friedrich-Wilhelm, *Operationsgebiet Bundesrepublik. Spionage, Sabotage und Subversion* (Frankfurt, 1989).
Schmeidel, John, *Shield and Sword of the Party* (Unpublished PhD thesis, Cambridge, 1996).
Schmude, Klaus, *Fallbeil-Erziehung: der Stasi/SED-Mord an Manfred Smolka* (1992).
Schneider, Gernot, *Wirtschaftwunder DDR Anspruch und Realität* (Cologne, 1990).
Schoenhals, Kai P., *The Free Germany Movement. A Case Of Patriotism Or Treason?* (New York, 1989).
Scholz, Günther, *Kurt Schumacher* (Düsseldorf, 1988).

Schönbohm, Jörg, *Two Armies And One Fatherland*, translated by Peter and Elfi Johnson (Oxford: Providence, 1996).
Schops, Hans Joachim and Wild, Dieter, *Stasi-Akte 'Verrater': Bürgerrechtler Templin* (1993).
Schüddekopf, Charles, ed., *'Wir sind das Volk!'* (Reinbek, 1990).
Schwarze, Hanns Werner, *The GDR today. Life in the 'other' Germany* (London, 1973).
Seebacher-Brandt, Brigitte, *Ollenhauer Biedermann und Patriot* (Berlin, 1984).
Segert, Dieter, 'The State, the *Stasi* and the People: The Debate about the Past and the Difficulties in Reformulating Collective Identities' in *The Journal of Communist Studies*, Vol.9, No.3, September 1993, pp.202–25.
Seiffert, Wolfgang and Treutwein, Norbert, *Die Schalck-Papiere* (Vienna, 1991).
Sélitrenny, Rita, and Weichert, Thilo, *Das unheimliche Erbe, die Spionageabteilung der Stasi* (Leipzig, 1991).
Serge, Victor, *Mémoires d'un révolutionnaire* (Paris, 1951).
Siebenmorgen, Peter, *'Staatssicherheit' der DDR, der Westen im Fadenkreuz der Stasi* (Bonn, 1993).
Sinakowski, Andreas, *Das Verhör*, (Berlin, 1991).
Smith, Ken, *Berlin: Coming in from the Cold* (London: Penguin, 1991).
Sodaro, Michael, J., *Moscow, Germany and the West from Khrushchev to Gorbachev* (London, 1991)
Solberg, Richard W., *God and Caesar in East Germany* (New York, 1961).
Sorgenicht, Klaus, *et al.*, *Verfassung der Deutschen Demokratischen Republik. Dokumente, Kommentar*, 2 vols (Berlin, 1969).
Stafford, David, *Britain and European Resistance 1940–1945* (London, 1980).
Stern, Carola, *Die SED* (Cologne, 1954).
Stern, Carola, *Ulbricht* (London, 1965).
Stiller, Werner, *Im Zentrum der Spionage* (Mainz: von Hase und Kochler, 1986).
Stoltenberg, Klaus, *Stasi-Unterlagen-Gesetz: Kommentar* (1992).
Strohmeyer, Arn, *Honecker-Witze* (Frankfurt am Main, 1988).
Sudoplatov, Pavel, Sudoplatov, Anatoli and Schechter, Leona P., *Special Tasks. The Memoirs of an Unwanted Witness – a Soviet Spymaster* (London, 1994).
Suvorov, Victor, *Inside Soviet Military Intelligence* (New York, 1984).
Thomas, Hugh, *The Spanish Civil War* (3rd edn, London, 1977).
Tieding, Wilfried, *Ein Volk im Aufbruch. Die DDR im Herbst '89* (Berlin, 1990).
Tofte, Ørnulf, *Spaneren. Overvåking for rikets sikkerhet* (Oslo: Gyldendal Norsk Forlag, 1987).
Trotsky, Leon, *Revolution Betrayed* (London), 1967.
Tvigun, S.K., *et al.*, eds, *V.I. Lenin i VChK. Sbornik dokumentov* (Moscow, 1975).
Tuck, Jay, *High Tech Espionage*, London, 1986.
Turner, Henry Ashby, Jr, *Germany from Partition to Reunification* (New Haven: Yale University Press, 1992).
Untersuchungsausschuß Freiheitlicher Juristen, *Ehemalige Nationalsozialisten in Pankows Diensten* (2nd edn, 1959; 3rd edn, Berlin, 1960).
Valtin, Jan, *Out of the Night* (London, 1941).
Veen, Hans-Joachim and Weilemann, Peter R., eds, *Parteien im Aufbruch. Nichtkommunistische Parteien und politische Vereinigungen in der DDR* (Melle and St. Augustin, 1990).
Wallace. Ian *et al.*, *East Germany,* (Oxford, 1987).

Wawrzyn, Lienhard, *Der Plan: Das Spitzelsystem der DDR*, (Berlin, 1990).
Weber, Hermann, *Die Wandlung des deutschen Kommunismus*, 2 vols (Frankfurt am Main, 1969).
Weber, Hermann, *Aufbau und Fall einer Diktatur. Kritische Beiträge zur Geschichte der DDR* (Cologne, 1991).
Weber, Hermann, *'Weiße Flecken' in der Geschichte. Die KPD-Opfer der Stalinschen Säuberungen und ihre Rehabilitierung* (Frankfurt-am-Main, 1989).
Weidenfeld, Werner and Korte, Karl-Rudolf, eds, *Handwörterbuch zur deutschen Einheit* (Frankfurt-am-Main, 1992).
Wensierski, Peter and Büscher, Wolfgang, eds, *Friedensbewegung in der DDR. Texte 1978–1982* (Hattingen, 1982).
Werdin, Justus, *Under uns, die STASI* (1990).
West, Nigel, *The Illegals: The Double Lives of the Cold War's most secret agents* (London, 1993).
Wilke, Manfred, ed., *Robert Havemann, ein deutscher Kommunist. Rückblicke und Perspektiven aus der Isolation* (Reinbek, 1978).
Wilkening, Christina, *Staat im Staate. Auskünfte ehemaliger Stasi-Mitarbeiter* (Berlin, 1990).
Williams, Robert Chadwell *Klaus Fuchs, Atom Spy* (Cambridge, Mass., 1987).
Wolf, Markus, *Die Troika* (Düsseldorf, 1990).
Wolf, Markus, *In eigenem Auftrag. Bekenntnisse und Einsichten* (Munich, 1991).
Wolf, Nancy Travis, *Policing a Socialist Society. The German Democratic Republic* (New York, 1992).
Wollenberg, Erich, 'Der Apparat – Stalins Fünfte Kolonne' in *Ostprobleme*, no.19 (1951).
Wollenberger, Vera, *Virus der Heuchler: Innenansicht aus Stasi-Akten* (Berlin, 1992).
Woods, Roger, *Opposition In The GDR Under Honecker 1971–85* (London 1986).
Worst, Anne, *Das Ende eines Geheimdienstes, oder, Wie lebendig ist die Stasi?* (Berlin, 1991).
Wright, Peter, *Spy Catcher. The Candid Autobiography of a Senior Intelligence Officer* (New York, 1987).
Zeidler, Manfred, *Reichswehr und Rote Armee 1920–1933* (Munich, 1993).
Zwahr, Hartmut, *Ende einer Selbstzerstörung. Leipzig und die Revolution in der DDR* (Göttingen, 1993).
Zwerenz, G., *Walter Ulbricht* (Munich, 1966).

PERIODICALS AND JOURNALS.

Among the many publications consulted are: *Außenpolitik, Bundestag Report, Deutschland Archiv, German Comments, German Life And Letters, German Politics And Society, German Studies Review, GDR Monitor, Politics and Society in Germany, Austria and Switzerland, Das Parlament, woche im bundestag, Stern, Der Spiegel, Weimarer Beiträge, Die Zeit.*

Notes

CHAPTER 1
GERMAN COMMUNISM, THE COMINTERN AND SECRET INTELLIGENCE 1918–43

1. Irene Runge and Uwe Stelbrink, *Markus Wolf: 'Ich bin kein Spion'* (Berlin, 1990), p.11.
2. Lenin, *Collected Works*, vol.20, p.351.
3. J.P. Nettl, *Rosa Luxemburg*.
   Rosa Luxemburg, *The Russian Revolution*.
4. Branko Lazitch and Milorad M. Drachkovitch, *Lenin and the Comintern* Volume I (Stanford, 1972), p.60.
5. Aino Kuusinen, *Before and After Stalin. A Personal Account of Soviet Russia from the 1920s to the 1960s* (London, 1974), pp.35–6.
6. Lazitch and Drachkovitch, *op.cit.*, p.77.
7. Werner T. Angress, *Stillborn Revolution. The Communist Bid for Power in Germany, 1921–1923*, 2 vols (Port Washington, 1963), p.50.
8. Leon Trotsky, *The Comintern after Lenin*.
9. Lazitch and Drachkovitch, *op.cit.*, pp.154, 182.
10. *Ibid.*, p.159.
11. Boris I. Nicolaevsky, ed., *Contributions à l'histoire du Comintern: Les premières années de l'Internationale Communiste (d'après le récit du 'Camarade Thomas')* (Geneva, 1965), pp.12–13.
12. Jan von Flocken, and Michael F. Scholz, *Ernst Wollweber. Saboteur – Minister – Unperson* (Berlin, 1994), pp.28–9.
13. *Ibid.*, p.28.
14. Lazitch and Drachkovitch, *op.cit.*, pp.168–9.
15. *Ibid.*, pp.180–1.
16. *Ibid.*, p.502.
17. Angress, *op.cit.*, p.58.
18. Victor Serge, *Mémoires d'un révolutionnaire* (Paris, 1951).
19. Lazitch and Drachkovitch, *op.cit.*, pp.182–98.
20. Flocken and Scholz, *op.cit.*, p.28.
21. In the 1930s the Swedish Communist Party was able to finance itself through the proceeds of a number of working-men's cafeterias which it set up. Significantly, the Comintern disapproved of such a show of independence. At the end of the Thirties, it despatched the German communist agent, Richard Krebs, *alias* Jan Valtin, to Sweden to convey instructions to the Swedish Party that it should close the cafeterias. Jan Valtin, *Out of the Night* (London, 1941), p.318.
22. Lazitch and Drachkovitch, *op.cit.*, p.158.
23. *Ibid.*, p.166.
24. *Ibid.*, p.169.
25. *Ibid.*, p.170.

26. David J. Dallin, *Soviet Espionage* (New Haven, 1955), p.92, reference to 'D Papers' b 316.
27. *Ibid.*, p.99.
28. Lazitch and Drachkovitch, *op.cit.*, p.181.
29. R.J. Crampton, *A Short History of Bulgaria* (Cambridge, 1987), p.101.
30. Valtin, *op.cit.*, pp.180–1.
An important source for the study of the Hamburg insurrection of 1923 and the secret activities of the Comintern and Soviet intelligence in Germany thereafter is the autobiographical work entitled *Out of the Night* by the former KPD agent Richard Krebs, which he published in 1940 under the pseudonym of Jan Valtin.
It is debatable how much value to place on Valtin's account of his work for the Comintern and his subsequent experiences at the hands of the Gestapo. In his book on the failed insurrection of 1923, Werner Angress described Valtin's work as 'fascinating', but was unwilling to place any trust in it. There are four basic reasons why this work might be discounted. First, Valtin like most other authors of memoirs relating to espionage, wrote to sell his work. Inevitably the suspicion must arise that he embellished his account. Second, Valtin wrote with a purpose, which he made no attempt to conceal. He hated the leaders of Comintern and of Soviet intelligence, whom he felt had betrayed his wife. According to Valtin they had sent her on a senseless and suicidal mission into Nazi Germany in 1934, where she had inevitably been arrested by the Gestapo. Finally, *Out of the Night* contains certain factual errors. However, a strong case must be made for regarding this work as important source material. It is certainly true that the book is compelling reading, but it seems unfair to condemn the author on account of his considerable literary talent. Valtin's fundamental honesty is revealed by the lack of any attempt which he makes to conceal his bias. Most importantly of all, he does not portray himself as a hero in any sense. He appears just as confused and as incompetent as the KPD and OGPU leadership, in whose schemes he was no more than a pawn. This uncomplimentary picture of communist activities in Germany fully fits all the evidence available from other sources. Valtin does not try to be sensational over political matters. His imagination runs most freely in his graphic and frequent accounts of sex and violence. Undeniably he makes mistakes. However, none of these are of prime importance. Most of these mistakes can be ascribed to Valtin's low status in the communist hierarchy, which limited the information at his disposal, and to the Comintern's well-developed use of subterfuge.
31. It should more accurately be called in its first years, the Vecheka (the All-Russian Extraordinary Commission for Combating Counter-Revolution and Sabotage).
32. George Leggett, *The Cheka. Lenin's Political Police* (Oxford, 1986), p.299.
33. *Ibid.*, p.353.
34. Christopher Andrew and Oleg Gordievsky, *KGB. The Inside Story of its Foreign Operations from Lenin to Gorbachev* (London, 1990), p.72.
35. Dallin, *op.cit.*, p.77.
36. Andrew and Gordievsky, *op.cit.*, p.81.
37. Nicolaevsky, *op.cit.*, pp.12–13.
38. Leggett, *op.cit.*, pp.299–300.

S.K. Tsvigun *et al.*, eds, *V.I. Lenin i VChK. Sbornik dokumentov* (Moscow, 1975), pp.407, 409, 467–8, 470.

39. Dallin, *op.cit.*, statement by 'Ypsilon', D papers, XYZ, 93a.
40. Nicolaevsky, *op.cit.*, pp.17–18.
41. *Ibid.*, pp.19–20.
42. Angress, *op.cit.*, p.106.
43. J. Degras, ed., *Soviet Documents on Foreign Policy,* vol. 1 (London, 1951), pp.166–72.
44. Flocken and Scholz, *op.cit.*, p.27.
45. Erich Wollenberg, Erich, 'Der Apparat – Stalins Fünfte Kolonne' in *Ostprobleme*, no.19 (1951), p.9.
    Ruth Fischer, *Stalin and German Communism. A Study in the Origins of the State Party* (Cambridge, Mass., 1948), pp.173–4.
    'Bericht des preussischen Staatskommissars Dr Weismann', Auswärtiges Amt, Germany, microfilm, container 1405, frames D552166–D552168, National Archives, Washington, DC.
46. Fischer, *op.cit.*, p.174.
47. Wollenberg, *op.cit.*, p.11.
48. Angress, *op.cit.*, p.107.
49. *Ibid.*, p.100.
50. Branko Lazitch, 'Two Instruments of Control by the Comintern: The Emissaries of the ECCI and the Party Representatives in Moscow' in Drachkovitch, Milorad M. and Lazitch, Branko (eds), *The Comintern: Historical Insights* (New York: Praeger, 1966).
51. Lazitch and Drachkovitch, *op.cit.*, p.502.
52. Angress, *op.cit.* pp.109–10.
53. *Ibid.*, p.417.
54. *Ibid.*, p.108.
55. Angress, *op.cit.*, pp.418–19.
    Wenzel is Angress's main source. Angress notes that Wenzel 'had access to material, notably the Staatsarchiv Düsseldorf, and had the opportunity to interview Brandler, Wollenberg, and other, less well-known persons who participated in the events'.
56. *Ibid.*, p.419.
57. *Ibid.*, p.417, drawing on Wenzel, 'Die K.P.D. im Jahre 1923' (Unpublished diss., Freie Universität Berlin, 1955), pp.96–7. Angress notes that Wenzel received his information from Brandler in 1954.
58. *Ibid.*, p.325. Angress notes that Wenzel bases his information on documents which were captured by the police in August 1923.
59. Valtin, *op.cit.*, p.44.
60. Fischer, pp.319, 324.
61. For example, Dallin, *op.cit.*, p.74.
62. Angress, *op.cit.*, p.419, n.102.
63. Valtin, *op.cit.*, p.48.
64. Angress, *op.cit.*, p.418.
65. E.H. Carr, *A History of Soviet Russia. The Interregnum* (London, 1954), p.209.
    Fischer, *op.cit.*, pp.324–5.
    Flocken and Scholz, *op.cit.*, p.33.

66. Angress, *op.cit.*, p.290.
67. Angress, *op.cit.*, quoting the East German writer, Gast.
68. Valtin, *op.cit.*, p.48.
69. Boris Bajanov, *Bajanov révèle Staline: souvenirs d'un ancien secrétaire de Staline* (Paris: 1979), pp.62–4.
    A. Neuberg, *Armed Insurrection* (London, 1970), pp.9, 11.
70. Valtin, *op.cit.*, pp.48, 67.
71. *Ibid.*, p.48.
72. Kuusinen, *op.cit.*, p.62.
73. Valtin, *op.cit.*, p.50.
74. *Ibid.*, p.43.
75. *Ibid.*, p.44.
76. Angress, *op.cit.*, p.416.
77. Andrew and Gordievsky, *op.cit.*, p.21.
78. Lenin, 'Better we do less but do it better' in *Collected Works*.
79. Hermann Weber, *Die Wandlung des deutschen Kommunismus*, vol.II (Frankfurt am Main, 1969), pp.347–8.
80. Wollenberg, *op.cit.*, p.577.
81. Dallin, *op.cit.*, p.52.
82. Valtin, *op.cit.*, p.112.
83. Robert Chadwell Williams, *Klaus Fuchs, Atom Spy* (Cambridge, Mass., 1987).
84. Karl Wilhelm Fricke, *Die DDR-Staatssicherheit* (3rd edn Cologne, 1989).
85. Hans J. Reichhart, 'Möglichkeiten und Grenzen des Widerstandes der Arbeiterbewegung' in Schmitthenner, Walter and Buchheim, Hans, eds, *Der deutsche Widerstand gegen Hitler* (Cologne, 1966), p.185. The author notes: 'Das geht aus einer Reihe von Rundschreiben des Hessischen Polizeiamtes in Darmstadt im letzten Halbjahr 1932 hervor, die sich auf Mitteilungen aus Berlin stützen (Document Center Berlin)'. Cf: Dallin, *op.cit.*, who claims the German police had not significantly infiltrated the KPD Apparat.
86. *Ibid.*, p.185.
87. *Ibid.*, p.184.
88. Weber, *op.cit.*, p.182.
    Valtin, *op.cit.*, pp.337, 399.
    Andrew and Gordievsky, *op.cit.*, p.235.
89. Weber, *op.cit.*, p.182.
90. Branko Lazitch and Milorad M. Drachkovitch, *Biographical Dictionary of the Comintern* (revised edn, Stanford, 1986).
    Andrew and Gordievsky, *op.cit.*, p.237.
91. Weber, *op.cit.*, p.182.
    Lazitch and Drachkovitch, *Biographical Dictionary*, *op.cit.*
92. Norman Davies, *God's Playground: A History of Poland*, vol.II (Oxford, 1981).
    Anthony Read, and David Fisher, *The Deadly Embrace: Hitler, Stalin And The Nazi–Soviet Pact 1939–1941*, (London, 1988), p.432.
    Buber-Neumann, *op.cit.*
93. Andrew and Gordievsky, *op.cit.*, p.193.
94. For example, Fricke claims that 'After the initial shock of a defeat where no shot was fired, illegal resistance groups sprang up everywhere. Within a relatively short time the KPD succeeded in rebuilding a central leadership

with links to the provinces ... The exiled KPD sent instructors and messengers into the Reich from Paris and Moscow, as well as from bases in Prague, Berlin, Amsterdam and Stockholm. With their help, the KPD gradually succeeded in tying together a network of covert resistance groups.' Fricke, *op.cit.*, p.18.

95. Andrew and Gordievsky, *op.cit.*, pp.235, 238.
96. *Ibid.*, p.237.
    Dallin, *op.cit.*, pp.122–3.
97. Conversation with the Citizen's Committee of East Berlin and eyewitness evidence of Richard Popplewell, May 1990.
98. Chalmers Johnson, *An Instance of Treason. Ozaki Hotsumi and the Sorge Spy Ring* (Expanded edn, Stanford: Stanford University Press, 1990).
    F.W. Deakin, and G.R. Storry, *The Case of Richard Sorge* (New York: Harper & Row, 1964).
    Gordon W. Prange *et al.*, *Target Tokyo: The Story of the Sorge Spy Ring* (New York: McGraw-Hill, 1985).
99. For a discussion of Stalin's failure to interpret intelligence about the impending German invasion in 1941, see John Erickson, 'Threat Identification and Strategic Appraisal by the Soviet Union, 1930–1941' in May, Ernest R., ed., *Knowing One's Enemies. Intelligence Assessment before the Two World Wars* (Princeton: Princeton University Press, 1986).
100. Helmut Müller-Enbergs, *Der Fall Rudolf Herrnstadt. Tauwetterpolitik vor dem 17. Juni* (Berlin, 1991), p.8.
101. *Ibid.*, p.8.
102. *Ibid.*, p.14.
103. *Ibid.*, pp.22–4.
104. *Ibid.*, p.26.
105. Dallin, *op.cit.*, p.125.
106. *Ibid.*, p.125.
107. Müller-Enbergs, *op.cit.*, p.16.
108. *Ibid.*, p.31.
109. *Ibid.*, p.31.
110. *Ibid.*, p.34.
111. *Ibid.*, p.276.
112. Dallin, *op.cit.*
113. Fricke, *op.cit.*, p.205.
114. Wollenberg, *op.cit.*, p.29.
115. Fricke, *op.cit.*, p.205.
116. R. Dan Richardson, *Comintern Army* (Lexington, Ky., 1982).
117. Fricke, *op.cit.*, p.205.
118. Hugh Thomas, *The Spanish Civil War* (3rd edn, London, 1977), p.711.
     Richardson, *op.cit.*, p.68.
119. Jefferson Adams, 'Crisis and Resurgence: East German State Security', in *International Journal of Intelligence and Counterintelligence*, 1988, II, 4, pp.508–9, n.4.
120. Thomas, *op.cit.*
121. *Ibid.*, pp.780–1.
122. Flocken and Scholz, *op.cit.*, p.136.
123. Richardson, *op.cit.*, p.103.
124. *Ibid.*, p.119.

125. Wollenberg, *op.cit.*
126. Ruth Fischer, *op.cit.*, p.500n. Branko Lazitch supports Fischer's conclusion about Ulbricht in his Lazitch's *Biographical Directory of the Comintern, op.cit.*
127. Flocken, *op.cit.*, p.78.
128. *Ibid.*, p.136.
129. Valtin, *op.cit.*, p.223.
Flocken, *op.cit.*, p.14.
130. Flocken, *op.cit.*, p.15.
131. It has also been found to be untrue that Wollweber was the first to raise the red flag on the *Helgoland*. This was the act of a school friend serving alongside him. *Ibid.*, p.18.
132. Weber, *op.cit.*
133. Flocken, *op.cit.*, p.30.
134. *Ibid.*, pp.34, 37.
135. *Ibid.*, p.38.
136. Dallin, *op.cit.*
137. Flocken, *op.cit.*, p.53.
138. Valtin, *op.cit.*, p.176.
139. *Ibid.*, p.176.
140. Flocken, *op.cit.*, p.79.
141. *Ibid.*, p.54.
142. Valtin, *op.cit.*, pp.378, 609–10.
143. *Ibid.*, p.378.
144. Flocken, *op.cit.*, p.47.
145. *Ibid.*, p.48.
Fricke, *op.cit.*, Chapter 9.
146. Dallin, *op.cit.*, p.126.
147. Valtin, *op.cit.*, pp.355ff.
148. Flocken, *op.cit.*, p.48.
149. *Ibid.*, p.54.
150. *Ibid.*, p.50.
151. *Ibid.*, p.65.
152. *Ibid.*, p.67.
153. *Ibid.*, p.68.
154. *Ibid.*, p.70.
155. *Ibid.*, p.100.
156. Dallin, *op.cit.*
157. Flocken, *op.cit.*, p.103.
158. *Ibid.*, p.102.

CHAPTER 2
THE ORIGINS AND DEVELOPMENT OF EAST GERMAN STATE SECURITY: THE ULBRICHT YEARS, 1945–71

1. Details of the numerous administrative reorganizations of Soviet intelligence and brief history of the KGB can be found in Knight, Amy W., *The KGB. Police and Politics in the Soviet Union* (London, 1988).

2. Before an administrative reorganization in the Soviet Union of 1945, the two Ministries had been united in the NKVD.
   Lavrenti Beria, head of the NKVD since 1938, retained considerable control over the Soviet intelligence and its chief, V.S. Abakumov. See N.S. Khrushchev, *Khrushchev Remembers*, vol.1, p.256.
3. *Smersh* was an acronym for *smert' shpionam* or 'death to spies'.
4. Norman M. Naimark, '"To Know Everything and to Report Everything Worth Knowing", Building the East German Police State, 1945–1949', *Cold War International History Project, Working Paper No.10*, August 1994, p.12.
5. Christopher Andrew and Oleg Gordievsky, *KGB. The Inside Story of its Foreign Operations from Lenin to Gorbachev* (London, 1990), p.352.
6. Karl Wilhelm Fricke. *Die DDR-Staatssicherheit* (3rd edn Cologne, 1989), p.39, citing 'Ost-Berlin – Agitations – und Zersetzungszentral für den Angriff gegen den Bestand und die verfassungsmäßige Ordnung der Bundesrepublik Deutschland und Operationsbasis der östlichen Spionagedienste'. Author not given. (Bonn, 1960).
7. Andrew and Gordievsky, *op.cit.*, p.352.
   David J. Dallin, *Soviet Espionage* (New Haven, 1955).
8. Dallin, *op.cit.*, p.331.
   Fricke, *op.cit.*, pp.38–9.
9. Naimark, *op.cit.*, pp.4–5.
10. *Ibid.*, p.3.
11. SMAD acknowledged these problems in its order No.112 of 23 May 1946. *Ibid.*, p.6.
12. Fricke, *op.cit.*, p.20.
13. Naimark, *op.cit.*, p.7.
14. Helene Fiedler, *SED und Staatsmacht* (East Berlin, 1974).
15. Naimark, *op.cit.*, p.9.
16. *Ibid.*, p.3.
17. *Ibid.*, p.4.
18. *Ibid.*, p.19.
19. *Ibid.*, p.21.
20. Manfred Drews and Max Stoll, *Soldaten der ersten Stunde* (East Berlin, 1981).
21. J.P. Nettl, *The Eastern Zone and Soviet Policy in Germany 1945–50* (London, 1951), p.73.
22. *Ibid.*, pp.77–8. For an insight into the practice of this policy, see Wolfgang Eisert, *Die Waldheime Prozesse Der Stalinistische Terror 1950*, Munich, 1993.
23. Naimark, *op.cit.*, p.11.
24. Nettl, *op.cit.*, p.103.
25. David Childs, *The DDR: Moscow's German Ally* (2nd edn London, 1988), p.22.
26. *Ibid.*, p.21.
27. Naimark, *op.cit.*, p.11.
28. *Ibid.*, p.13.
29. *Ibid.*, p.12.
30. Dallin, *op.cit.*, p.332. Based on statement by Herr Sachse of the *Kampfgruppe gegen Unmenschlichkeit*, Berlin. D Papers, b 21.

31. Naimark, *op.cit.*, p.12.
32. Aleksandr Solzhenitsyn, *The Gulag Archipelago*, vol.3 (New York, 1978).
33. Nettl, *op.cit.*, p.73. For the Soviet Zone camps, see Jan Fiocken and Michael Klonivsky, *Stalin's Lager in Deutschland 1945–1950, Zeugen-berichte*, Berlin/Frankfurt am Main, 1991.
34. Naimark, *op.cit.*, p.13.
35. Romuald J. Misiunas and Rein Taagepera, *The Baltic States. Years of Dependence, 1940–1980* (London, 1983), Chapter III.
36. M.R.D. Foot, *SOE* (London, 1984).
    David Stafford, *Britain and European Resistance 1940–1945* (London, 1980).
37. Erickson, John, *The Road to Stalingrad*, (London, 1985), pp.78, 179, 266–7, 579, 599.
38. Gehlen, General Reinhard, *The Gehlen Memoirs* (Glasgow, 1972).
    John Ranelagh, *CIA. A History* (London, 1992), p.35.
39. Gehlen, *op.cit.*
40. Childs, *op.cit.*, pp.25–7.
41. For discussion of the role of Soviet intelligence in the 'Doctors' Plot' see Amy Knight, *Beria. Stalin's First Lieutenant* (Princeton: Princeton University Press, 1993), pp.169–75.
42. Childs, *op.cit.*, pp.25–7.
43. For events in Czechoslovakia, see Karel Kaplan, *Report on the Murder of the General Secretary* (London: I.B. Tauris, 1990).
44. Helmut Müller-Enbergs, *Der Fall Rudolf Herrnstadt. Tauwetterpolitik vor dem 17. Juni* (Berlin, 1991), pp.54–5.
45. Naimark, *op.cit.*, p.18.
46. Fricke, *op.cit.*, p.22.
47. Naimark, *op.cit.*, p.14.
48. *Ibid.*, p.14.
49. *Ibid.*
50. *Ibid.*, p.15.
51. This is the kind of argument implied in many American 'Revisionist' interpretations of the origins of the Cold War written in the late 1960s and 1970s.
52. The resolution claimed

    > that the cases of sabotage have been prepared for by increased propaganda, the rabble-rousing of RIAS [Radio in the American Sector] and the other enemy transmitters, by the distribution of illegal pamphlets, and by the overt and secret enemies of our democratic order, who live in the area of our republic and who are partly even active in state positions.

    To remedy the increase in enemy activity, the resolution proposed:

    > Through constant instruction and schooling for all *Volkspolizei*, the latter must become the first admonishers about vigilance. No measure of the enemy, no propaganda measure must go unobserved. The head of the Main Administration of the German *Volkspolizei* has jointly with the head of the Main Administration for the Protection of the National Economy to organize the system for reporting cases of sabotage, espionage, etc, in such a way that in connection with the enemy propaganda from abroad and the

activities of the agents inside the country, a general overview is constantly gained on the state of enemy activities. Operational measures must be taken accordingly.

'Beschluß über die Abwehr gegen Sabotage der Regierung der DDR vom 26. Januar 1950' in *Neues Deutschland*, 28 January 1950.

53. *Neues Deutschland*, 28 January 1950.
54. Fricke, *op.cit.*, p.25.
55. Zwischenarchiv Normannenstraße, Ordner Mielke, 879, quoted in Müller-Enbergs, *op.cit.*, p.116.
56. Knight, *op.cit.*, p.192.
57. Flocken and Scholz, *op.cit.*, p.138.
58. *Ibid.*, p.139.
59. *Ibid.*, p.161.
60. *Ibid.*, p.139.
61. *Ibid.*, p.160.
62. *Ibid.*, p.139.
63. Fricke, *op.cit.*, p.39.
64. Boris Levitsky, *From Red Terror to Socialist Legality. The Soviet Security Service.*
65. Childs, *op.cit.*, p.28.
66. Rudolf Herrnstadt, *Das Herrnstadt-Dokument. Das Politbüro der SED und die Geschichte des 17. Juni 1953,* edited by Nadja Stulz-Herrnstadt, (Hamburg, 1990), p.87.
67. François Fejtö, *A History of the People's Democracies* (2nd edn, London, 1974), p.36.
68. Herrnstadt, *op.cit.*, p.98.
69. *Ibid.*, pp.86, 89.
70. *Neues Deutschland*, 11 June 1953.
71. Herrnstadt, *op.cit.*, p.12, n.2.
72. Flocken and Scholz, *op.cit.*, p.143.
73. *Ibid.*, p.146.
74. Müller-Enbergs, *op.cit.*, p.204.
75. *Ibid.*, p.251.
76. Herrnstadt, *op.cit.*, pp.81–2.
77. Müller-Enbergs, *op.cit.*, p.172. The Federal Ministry for All-German Questions gave the figures for refugees, 1951 and 1952, as 348,046. For 1953 the figures was 331, 390, Bundesministerium für gesamtdeutsche Fragen, *ABISZ*, Bonn, 1969, p.212.
78. Flocken and Scholz, *op.cit.*, p.140.
79. Herrnstadt, *op.cit.*, p.58.
80. Herrnstadt, *op.cit.*, p.74.
81. Müller-Enbergs, *op.cit.*, pp.180–1.
82. According to Herrnstadt, the greatest danger lay not in Ulbricht himself, but in the 'little Ulbrichts' – a large number of officials. The majority of the new officials had grown up under the Nazi regime, and had learned to act and think in this environment. Herrnstadt, *op.cit.*, pp.108–9.
83. *Ibid.*, pp.67, 131.

84. See, for example, Jefferson Adams, 'Crisis and Resurgence: East German State Security', in *International Journal of Intelligence and Counterintelligence*, 1988, II, 4.
85. Müller-Enbergs, *op.cit.*, pp.253–4.
86. *Ibid.*, p.254.
87. *Ibid.*, p.280.
88. Mielke reported that Zaisser had said that the SED would not get a majority in elections in a unified Germany.
89. Müller-Enbergs, *op.cit.*, p.44.
90. *Ibid.*, p.55.
91. Zwischenarchiv Normannenstraße, Ordner Mielke, 879 quoted in Müller-Enbergs, *op.cit.*, p.116.
92. Adams, *op.cit.*
    Knight, *op.cit.*
    This view continues to find its way into general surveys such as, most recently, Paul G. Lewis, *Central Europe since 1945* (London: Longman, 1994).
93. Herrnstadt, *op.cit.*, pp.130–1.
94. The famous Russian historian, Roy Medvedev claimed that Beria flew to East Berlin shortly after the Uprising to consult with the SED leadership. If this is so, no mention was made of the visit by Herrnstadt and Zaisser themselves. See Roy Medvedev, *Khrushchev* (Garden City, NY: Doubleday, 1983), p.60. This source and Khrushchev's memoirs, seem to be the basis for Amy Knight's account of Beria's dealing with East Germany in 1953. See Amy Knight, *Beria*, pp.192–4.
95. Herrnstadt, *op.cit.*, p.59, n.9.
96. Müller-Enbergs, p.296.
97. *Der Spiegel*, p.131.
98. Herrnstadt, *op.cit.*, p.111.
99. *Ibid.*, p.139.
100. *Ibid.*, p.136.
101. As a Candidate Member of the SED Politburo, Herrnstadt was not present at this meeting.
102. Zaisser had shown a similar readiness to put the interests of the Party and the Soviet Union before all other considerations when commenting on the fate of Rudolf Slánský, the General Secretary of Czechoslovak Party, who was tried and executed on trumped up charges in December 1952. In 1953 he told Hanna Wolf: 'Well, I know Slansky, and I do not believe it all, but if Gottwald needs it, I agree with it.'
103. Herrnstadt, *op.cit.*, p.165.
104. Amy Knight, *The KGB. Police and Politics in the Soviet Union* (London, 1988).
105. Flocken and Scholz, *op.cit.*, p.144.
106. Fricke, *op.cit.*, Chapter 2.
107. *Ibid.*, p.32.
108. Flocken and Scholz, *op.cit.*, p.162.
109. *Ibid.*, p.145.
110. *Ibid.*, p.145.
111. *Ibid.*, pp.95–6.
112. *Ibid.*, p.121.
113. *Ibid.*, p.146.

114. Fricke, *op.cit.*, Chapter 2.
115. Flocken and Scholz, *op.cit.*, pp.147–8.
116. *Ibid.*, p.149.
117. Fricke, *op.cit.*, Chapter 2.
118. Flocken and Scholz, *op.cit.*, p.162.
119. Fricke, *op.cit.*, p.211.
120. Even the reports on the Securitate were exaggerated, as recent work by Dr Dennis Deletant has shown. Like the Stasi, the Romanian secret police relied much more on the threat of terror than its application. Beatings were commonly doled out to arrestees in Ceauşescu's Romania, but torture as such was not systematic. The Securitate had the distinction of maintaining the highest proportion of informers per head of population throughout the Soviet Bloc. This must have made them the most overworked secret police in Eastern Europe.
121. One former Stasi officer has recently stated about his experiences in the 1980s: 'Many people talk today about Stalinism. I don't know what this is, although I have tried hard to understand what happened. I find the term "administrative-bureaucratic system" more correct.'
    Die Informationsstrecke war eine Einbahnstraße', statement of 'Klaus, 40 years of age, *Zentrale Auswertungs- und Informationsgruppe*' in *Staat im Staate*, in Christina Wilkening, *Staat im Staate. Auskünfte ehemaliger Stasi- Mitarbeiter* (Berlin, 1990). For the death penalty see *Das Parlament*, 16/23 February 1996, p.20.
122. 'Ich war ein Teil, der zu funktionieren hatte', statement of 'Hans, 50 years of age, *Hauptabteilung XX*, in Wilkening, *ibid.*
123. Fricke, *op.cit.*, Chapter 1.
124. The situation in East German universities is well described in 'Karies, Bach und Läufer', *Der Spiegel*, 6/1990, which provides details about the Stasi's attempts to secure informers in student groups.
    I would also refer for comparison to my own experiences at the University of Olomouc in Czechoslovakia in Summer 1989. The Czechs generally held that one in five fellow-students were working for the Stasi's Czechoslovak equivalent, the Státní Bezpečnost (StB). Whether this figure was correct is unimportant from the StB, the limitations such fear imposed on all freedom of discussion were the same as if one in five students really were informers.
125. Richard Popplewell, 'The Stasi and the East German Revolution of 1989', in *Contemporary European History*, I, 1 (1992).
126. Richard Popplewell, 'Themes in the Rhetoric of KGB Chairmen from Andropov to Kryuchkov' in *Intelligence and National Security*, Vol.6, July 1991, No.3.
    Amy Knight, *The KGB*, p.64.
127. For example, in November 1953 Wollweber told 1,400 Berlin workers about the recent haul of Western agents he had thanks to Geyer.
128. Flocken and Scholz, *op.cit.*, pp.168–9.
129. *Ibid.*, p.151.
130. *Ibid.*, p.150.
131. *Ibid.*, p.151.

132. Wollweber was furious after Korotkov informed him of Otto John's defection to the DDR. Flocken, *op.cit.*, p.154.
133. Henry Ashby Turner, Jr, *Germany from Partition to Reunification* (New Haven: Yale University Press, 1992), p.84.
134. Martin McCauley, *The German Democratic Republic since 1945* (London, 1983), p.85.
135. Turner, *op.cit.*, p.85.
136. Müller-Enbergs, *op.cit.*, p.192.
137. McCauley, *op.cit.*, p.86.
Flocken and Scholz, *op.cit.*, p.186.
138. Flocken and Scholz, *op.cit.*, pp.186–7.
139. *Ibid.*, p.194.
140. *Ibid.*
141. McCauley, *op.cit.*, p.86.

CHAPTER 3
THE MfS, SED AND THE EAST GERMAN STATE

1. Dietrich Müller-Römer (ed.), *Ulbrichts Grundgesetz Die sozialistischer Verfassung der DDR,* Cologne, 1968, which gives the full text.
2. Klaus Sorgenicht, Wolfgang Weichelt, Tord Riemann, Hans-Joachim Semler, (eds) *Verfassung der Deutschen Demokratischen Republik Dokumente Kommentar*, Berlin, 1969, Vol.1, p.226.
3. David Childs interviewed Gerhard Schürer at the special party conference of the SED in Berlin, December 1989.
4. 'Wir sind keine Helden gewesen', interview with Horst Sindermann in *Der Spiegel,* 7 May 1990.
5. Interviewed by David Childs in 1994.
6. *Der Spiegel,* 2 July 1990.
7. *Der Spiegel,* 25 June 1990.
8. Bernd Heller of the Free University (Berlin), 'Stasi schützte NS-Täter doch', in *Berliner Zeitung,* 11 April 1995. In his *Im Eigenem Auftrag* Munich, 1991, p.210 Markus Wolf claims that Mielke gathered information on Honecker and all the other members of the Politburo.
9. Frank Sieren and Ludwig Koehne (eds), Günter Schabowiski, *Das Politbüro*, Reinbek bei Hamburg, 1990, pp.41–2.
10. Schabowski, *op.cit.*, p.42.
11. *Ibid.*, p.44.
12. Wolf, *op.cit.*, pp.210–11.
13. Peter Siebenmorgan, *'Staatssicherheit' Der DDR Der Westen im Fadenkreuz der Stasi*, Bonn 1993, p.14.
14. Reinhardt O. Hahn, *Ausgedient Ein Stasi-Major erzählt,* Halle and Leipzig, 1990, p.100.
15. Hahn, *op.cit.*, 109.
16. Sindermann, *op.cit.*, p.55.

17. The text is found in Thomas M. Forster, *Die NVA Kernstück der Landesverteidigung der DDR*, Cologne, 1983, pp.389–93.
18. Sindermann, *op.cit.*, pp.59–60.
19. Former Hauptmann Wilfried Mannewitz in conversation with David Childs, 4 May 1995.
20. Information on the MfS weapons is taken from *Der Spiegel*, 5 February 1995. The strength of the Guard Regiment is given in BStU, *Die Organisationsstrukur des Ministeriums für Staatssicherheit 1989, Erkenntnisstand von Juni 1993*.
21. BStU, *op.cit.*, p.86. The complete list of departments and their heads are found in this publication.
22. BStU, Günter Förster, *Die Dissertationen an der 'Juristischen Hochschule' des MfS*, Reihe A: Dokumente Nr. 2/1994, p.7.
23. BStU, Förster, *op.cit.*, p.13.
24. Bürgerkomitee Bautzener Straße e.V., *MfS Bezirk Dresden*, Dresden, December, 1992, p.76.
25. Der Bundesbeauftragte für die Unterlagen des Staatssicherheitsdienstes der ehemaligen Deutschen Demokratischen Republik, (henceforth BStU) *BF informiert Die Hauptamtlichen 1962 1/1994*, p.6.
26. BStU, 1/1994, *op.cit.*, p.15.
27. *Ibid.*, p.16.
28. *Ibid.*, p.21.
29. Interview with David Childs, 1994.
30. BStU, 1/1994, *op.cit.*, p.16.
31. *Ibid.*, p.15.
32. Werner Stiller, *Im Zentrum der Spionage,* Mainz, 1986, p.38, pp.68–9.
33. Stiller, *op.cit.*, p.18. *Ibid.*, p.30.
34. Forster, *op.cit.*, pp.168–70.
35. Hartmut Zimmermann, *DDR Handbuch, Band 1, A-L,* Cologne 1985, pp.275–6.
36. Nancy Travis Wolfe, *Policing a Socialist Society The German Democratic Republic,* New York, Westport, London, 1992, p.36.
37. Bürgerkomitee Leipzig, *Stasi intern Macht und Banalität*, Leipzig, 1991, pp.67–9.
38. BStU, *Das Arbeitsgebiet 1 der Kriminalpolizei Aufgaben, Struktur und Verhältnis zum Ministerium für Staatssicherheit*, Berlin, 1994, p.13.
39. BStU, 1994, *op.cit.*, pp.14–15.
40. *Ibid.*, p.31.
41. *Ibid.*, p.9.
42. *Ibid.*, p.41.
43. *Ibid.*, p.40.
44. These cases are taken from the research by Jens Gieseke of the BStU as reported in *Das Parlament*, 16/23 February 1996, p.20.
45. Jörg Bernhard Bilke, 'über die Arbeit der "Staatssichterheit", In Dossiers ertrunken' in *Das Parlament,* 18/25 Dezember 1992, p.21.
46. Wolfgang Büscher, 'Ein Stasi-Oberst blickt zurück', in *Das Parlament,* 23 October 1992, p.14. Also former Hauptmann Wilfried Mannewitz as above.

CHAPTER 4
THE MfS AS AN INTERNAL SECURITY ORGAN

1. Joachim Gauck, assisted by Margarethe Steinhausen and Hubertus Knabe *Die Stasi-Akten Das unheimliche Erbe der DDR*, Reinbek bei Hamburg, 1991, p.61.
2. Spiegel Spezial, *Stasi-Akte 'Verräter' Bürgerrechtler Templin: Dokumente einer Verfolgung*, Hamburg, 1993, p.166.
3. Gauck, *op.cit.*, p.61.
4. Friedrich Ebert Stiftung Büro Chemnitz, *Das Wirken Des Ministerium Für Staatssichterheit Insbesondere Im Bezirk Karl-Marx-Stadt*, Chemnitz, 1992, p.12.
5. Statistisches Bundesamt, *DDR 90 Zahlen und Fakten,* Wiesbaden, 1990, p.22.
6. Gauck, *op.cit.*, p.61.
7. *DDR 90, op.cit.*, p.25.
8. Werner Stiller, *Im Zentrum der Spionage,* Mainz, 1986, pp.68–9.
9. All these details are taken from *Spiegel Spezial, op.cit.*
10. BStU, *BF informiert IM-Statistik 1985–1989 3/1993*, p.13.
11. BStU, *3/1993*, *op.cit.*, pp.3–17.
12. This is an experience of David and Monire Childs.
13. Joachim Nawrocki, 'Die Entwicklung der innerdeutschen Beziehungen' in *DDR-Almanach '89, Daten Informationen*, Bonn, March 1989, p.79.
14. Armin Mitter and Stefan Wolle (eds), *Ich liebe euch doch alle! Befehle und Lageberichte des MfS Januar–November 1989*, Berlin, 1990, pp.88–9.
15. Norman Gelb, *The Berlin Wall,* London, 1986, p.4.
16. The *Guardian*, 23 April 1988.
17. *Der Spiegel,* 7 February 1994.
18. Mitter and Wolle, *op.cit.*, pp.82–8.
19. Interview with David Childs, 1994.
20. Interview with David Childs, 1994.
21. Experience of Monire Childs.
22. Fredrich Ebert Stiftung Chemnitz, *op.cit.*, p.19.
23. Bürgerkomitee Leipzig (ed.), *Stasi intern Macht und Banalität,* Leipzig, 1991, p.113.
24. Friedrich Ebert Stiftung Chemnitz, *op.cit.*, p.19.
25. Bürgerkomitee Leipzig, *op.cit.*, p.121.
26. Friedrich Ebert Stiftung Chemnitz, *op.cit.*, p.19.
27. Nancy Travis Wolfe, *Policing a Socialist Society. The German Democratic Republic,* New York, 1992, p.75.
28. 'Schild und Schwert der Partei' in *Der Spiegel*, 5 February 1990.
29. *Welt am Sonntag,* 10 April 1994.
30. *Der Spiegel*, 28 January, 1991, Humboldt University, see Gesellschaft für Deutschlandforschung *Rundbrief* 33, 5 Juli 1994 p.3.
31. Interview with David Childs, 1994.
32. Interview with David Childs, 1994.
33. Bundesministerium für gesamtdeutsche Fragen, *A bis Z Ein Taschen-und Nachschlagebuch über den anderen Teil Deutschlands,* Bonn, 1969 p.213.

34. Sonja Süß, '"Operative Psychologie" und das Interesse für die "medizinische Intelligenz" Psychologie und Politik in der DDR', in *Universitas,* 5/1995. Süß is a medical practitioner researching for the Gauck Agency.
35. For one of the few attempts before 1989 to document the DDR opposition in English see Roger Woods (ed.), *Opposition In The GDR Under Honecker 1971–1985*, London, 1986.
36. *Frankfurter Allgemeine Zeitung,* 15 December 1987.
37. *Der Spiegel*, 7 February 1994.
38. Spiegel Spezial, *op.cit.*, p.93.
39. *Tagesspiegel*, 3 May 1988.
40. There were 80 arrests according to the Western press at the time.
41. These cases are taken from, Rüdiger Knechtel and Jürgen Fiedler (eds), *Stalins DDR Berichte politisch Verfolgter,* Leipzig, 1992.
42. Sonja Süß, 'Persecution and the Consequences' in *German Comments*, No. 37, January 1995.
43. Walter Janka, *Schwierigkeiten mit der Wahnheit*, Reinbek bei Hamburg, 1989.
    William Abbey & Katharina Havekamp 'Our Personality: Walter Janka' in *Politics And Society In Germany, Austria And Switzerland*, Vol.4, No.3, 1992.
    Rolf Schneider, the DDR writer, 'Schwierigkeiten mit der Wahrheit' deals extensively with the case of Janka/Harich in *Der Spiegel*, 4 June 1990.
44. Karl Wilhem Fricke, *Opposition und Widerstand in der DDR,* Cologne, 1984, pp.124–5.
45. Otto Jörg Weis in the *Franfurter Rundschau*, 10 April 1992. Robert Havemann gave his views in Manfred Wilke (ed.), *Robert Havemann Ein deutscher Kommunist*, Reinbek bei Hamburg, 1978. See also Robert Havemann, *Dialektik ohne Dogma? Naturwissenschaft und Weltanschauung*, Reinbek bei Hamburg, 1964.
46. Professor Harmut Jäckel, professor of law at the Free University and SPD member knew Havemann and other dissidents. His own Stasi file was enormous. In conversation with David Childs, 1994. Havemann's Stasi activities were reported in *Stern*, 25 May 1995, pp.174–5. The case of Gregor Gysi is discussed in *Der Spiegel*, 29 May 1995.
47. Monty Johnstone in the communist *Morning Star*, 8 December 1978. Bertrand Russell Peace Foundation Ltd., *The Case Of Rudolf Bahro*, Nottingham, 1979.
48. Karl Wilhelm Fricke, *op.cit.*, p.184.
49. Wolf Emmerich, *Kleine Literaturgeschichte der DDR*, Darmstadt, 1984, p.17.
50. Wolf Biermann, *Poems and Ballads,* London, 1977, translated by Steve Gooch, pp.4–7.
51. Wolfgang Emmerich, *op.cit.*, pp.185–7.
52. David Childs interviewed Stefan Heym at his home in the 1980s. For comment on Heym and the other writers in the DDR see Wilfried Wiegand in the *Frankfurter Allgemeine Zeitung*, 11 December 1989.
53. Ian Wallace, 'Erich Loest' in *Politics And Society In Germany, Austria And Switzerland*, Vol. 1, No. 3, Spring 1989.

54. Ian Wallace, 'Hans Joachim Schädlich in *Politics And Society In Germany, Austria And Switzerland*, Vol. 4 No. 1, 1991.
55. In conversation with David Childs, 1994. Among the many publications by and on Loewig see, Roger Loewig, *Eine Hinterlassenschaft Geschichten von Käfigen und vom Zugvogeldasein*, Berlin, 1980.
56. *Die Welt*, 12 January, 1990. The book is *So sehe ick die Sache*, Cologne,1984.
57. J.K.A. Thomaneck, 'Anna Seghers And The Janka Trial: A Case Study In Intellectual Obfuscation' in *German Life and Letters*, Vol. XLVI, July 1993. See also note 51 above.
58. Emmerich, *op.cit.*, p.208.
59. Ian Wallace, 'Writers and the *Stasi*' in J.H.Reid (ed.) *Re-Assessing The GDR Papers from a Nottingham Conference*, Special issue of *German Monitor*, p.121.
60. Wallace, *op.cit.*, p.123. For a discussion of Christa Wolf see Herbert Lehnert, 'Fiktionalität und autobiographische Motive zu Christa Wolfs Erzählung "Was bleibt"' in *Weimarer Beiträge*, 3/1991. See also the assessment by Marcel Reich-Ranicki in *Der Spiegel*, 14 April 1994.
61. MfS files have revealed that Uwe Johnson was observed by the Stasi from the time he left the DDR in 1959 until at least 1974 when he went to live in England. *Der Spiegel*, 13 June 1994.
62. Robert F. Goeckel, 'Der Weg der Kirchen in der DDR' in Günther Heydemann and Lothar Kettenacker, *Kirchen in der Diktatur*, Göttingen, 1993, p.155.
63. Richard W. Solberg, *God and Caesar in East Germany. The Conflicts of Church and State in East Germany Since 1945*, New York, 1961, p.28.
64. Goeckel, *op.cit.*, p.159.
65. Deutscher Bundestag 12. Wahlperiode, Drucksache 12/7820, Bericht der Enquete-Kommission 'Aufarbeitung von Geschichte und Folgen der SED-Diktatur in Deutschland', 31 March 1994 p.163.
66. The Berlin Appeal is given in Woods, *op.cit.*, pp.195–7. The view of the church leadership is found in Peter Wensierski and Wolfgang Büscher (eds), *Friedensbewegung in der DDR Texte 1978–1982*, Hattingen, 1982, pp.283–4. Holger Wuchold, *Berliner Zeitung,* 12 March 1992, comments on Eppelmann's achievements.
67. Reinhard Henskys, 'Das Verhältnis von Staat und Kirche in der DDR' in *DDR-Almanach '89*, *op.cit.*, p.93.
68. Henskys, *op.cit.*, p.97.
69. *Die Welt,* 5 April 1994, p.2.
70. Drucksache 12/782 *op.cit.*, p.163.
71. *Der Spiegel*, 8 March 1983 and 30 August 1993. At the conclusion of its two and a half year investigation, the Brandenburg parliament (Landtag) debated the issue. For the full debate see, *Debatte zum Bericht des Parlamentarischen Untersuchungsauschusses 1/3 des Landtages* ***'Aufklärung der früheren Kontakte des Ministerpräsidenten Dr. Manfred Stolpe zu Organisationen des Staatsapparates der DDR, der SED sowie zum Staatssicherheitsdienst und der in diesem Zusammenhang erhobenen Vorwürfe'.*** *Wortprotokoll der Plenarsitzung vom 16 Juni 1994*, Schriften des Landtages Brandenburg, Heft 2 (1994).
72. Goeckel, *op.cit.*, pp.177–8.
73. *Der Spiegel*, 26 July 1993.

74. *Der Spiegel,* 21 September 1992.
75. Bürgerkomitee Leipzig, *op.cit.*, pp.162–3.
76. *Nürnberger Nachrichten,* 10 January 1991.
77. David Childs interviewed Richard Schröder in 1994. An interesting brief discussion of these views by Ludwig Harms is found in *The German Tribune*, 7 February 1992.
78. *Tagesspiegel*, 29 July 1994.
79. *Der Spiegel*, 26 September 1994.
80. David Childs interviewed Frau Wollenberger in 1994.
81. *Der Spiegel*, 13 January 1992.
82. See *The German Tribune*, 24 January 1992. David Childs interviewed Gerd Poppe in 1994.
83. Anthony Summers, *Official And Confidential. The Secret Life of J.Edgar Hoover*, London, 1993, deals with the most famous case in a democratic country, Hoover at the FBI in the United States.

CHAPTER 5
EAST GERMAN FOREIGN INTELLIGENCE, 1945–89

1. Irene Runge and Uwe Stelbrink, *Markus Wolf, 'Ich bin kein Spion'* (Berlin, 1990), p.77.
2. Gordon Brook-Shepherd, in his study of postwar Soviet defectors, believes that three KGB agents were of key importance to the West: Oleg Penkovsky; Oleg Gordievsky; and the agent codenamed 'Farewell' working for French intelligence. Gordon Brook-Shepherd, *The Storm Birds. Soviet Post-War Defectors* (London: Weidenfeld, 1988).
3. Le Carré denied that this was so and refused Wolf's requests for a meeting after the Revolution.
4. This line of argument parallels that of KGB leaders in the Gorbachev era, foremost among them Vladimir Kryuchkov, the head of that organization who was subsequently the leader of the August coup of 1991 in the Soviet Union. See Richard Popplewell, 'Themes in the Rhetoric of KGB Leaders' in *Intelligence and National Security*, Vol.6, July 1991, No.3.
5. Alexander Reichenbach, *Chef der Spione. Die Markus-Wolf-Story* (Stuttgart, 1992), p.14.
6. David Gill and Ulrich Schröter, *Das Ministerium für Staatssicherheit* (Berlin, 1991).
7. The immediate cause of the mob actions was a feeling on the part of the Round Table that the government was not providing them with sufficient information about the state security service. East Berlin ADN International Service, 16 January 1990, in FBIS-EEU-90-011, 17 January 1990.
8. The KGB also had free access to the archives of the communist foreign intelligence service of Czechoslovakia in 1990, and probably those of other states of the former Soviet Bloc.
9. After 1950 this was attached to the Central Committee of the SED.
10. Jan von Flocken and Michael F. Scholz, *Ernst Wollweber. Saboteur – Minister – Unperson* (Berlin, 1994), p.125.

11. He was promoted to full Director of Shipping in February 1947.
12. Karl Wilhelm Fricke, *Die DDR-Staatssicherheit* (3rd edn Cologne, 1989). Hermann Zolling, Hermann and Heinz Höhne, *Pullach intern* (Hamburg, 1971).
13. Flocken, *op.cit.*, p.132.
14. *Ibid.*, p.126.
15. According to one account, in 1952, 96 sailors and 18 dockers from Great Britain were trained in East Germany. Von Flocken.
16. Flocken, *op.cit.*, pp.123–4.
17. *Ibid.*, p.126.
18. Ørnulf Tofte, *Spaneren. Overvåking for rikets sikkerhet* (Oslo: Gyldendal Norsk Forlag, 1987), p.32.
19. His finest exploit had been to break into a jail dressed as a policeman and set free two Norwegian prisoners whom the Germans had arrested.
20. Tofte, *op.cit.*, pp.30–2.
21. *Ibid.*, p.32.
22. Pavel Sudoplatov, *et al.*, *Special Tasks. The Memoirs of an Unwanted Witness – a Soviet Spymaster* (London, 1994).
23. Flocken, *op.cit.*, p.130.
24. *Ibid.*, p.131.
25. *Ibid.*, p.138.
26. *Ibid.*, p.154.
27. Runge and Stelbrink, *op.cit.*, p.19.
28. Quoted in Fricke, *op.cit.*
29. Reichenbach, *op.cit.*, p.63.
30. Runge and Stelbrink, *op.cit.*, p.65.
31. Friedrich Wolf had been a strong communist sympathizer since the end of the First World War, though he only joined the KPD at the beginning of 1928.
32. Wolfgang Emmerich, *Kleine Literaturgeschichte der DDR*, (2nd edn, Darmstadt, 1991), p. 57.
33. Reichenbach, *op.cit.*, p.23.
34. Markus Wolf, *Die Troika* (Düsseldorf, 1990).
35. Runge and Stelbrink, *op.cit.*, p.57.
36. Runge and Stelbrink, *op.cit.*, p.57.
37. Wolfgang Leonhard, *Die Revolution entlässt ihre Kinder* (Cologne, 1955), p.576.
38. Reichenbach, *op.cit.*, p.61.
    Runge and Stelbrink, *op.cit.*, pp.28–9.
39. Runge and Stelbrink, *op.cit.*, p.54.
40. This is a common opinion about *Troika*.
41. Leonhard, *op.cit.*, pp.577–8.
42. Markus Wolf, *In eigenem Auftrag. Bekenntnisse und Einsichten* (Munich, 1991), p.75. Also Runge and Stelbrink, *op.cit.*, p.55.
43. Runge and Stelbrink, *op.cit.*, p.68.
44. Leonhard, *op.cit.*, p.577.
45. Runge and Stelbrink, *op.cit.*, p.15.
46. Reichenbach, *op.cit.*, p.64.
47. Runge and Stelbrink, *op.cit.*, pp.37–8.
48. Wolf, *In eigenem Auftrag, op.cit.*, p.84.
49. *Ibid.*, p.84.

50. *Ibid.*, p.83.
51. *Ibid.*, p.87.
52. *Ibid.*, p.88.
53. *Ibid.*, p.88.
54. *Ibid.*, p.26.
55. *Ibid.*, p.6.
56. Reichenbach, *op.cit.*, p.153.
57. Wolf, *In eigenem Auftrag*, *op.cit.*, p.87.
58. Runge and Stelbrink, *op.cit.*, p.15.
59. Reichenbach, *op.cit.*, p.155.
60. *Ibid.*, p.156.
61. *Ibid.*
62. Christopher Andrew and Oleg Gordievsky, *KGB. The Inside Story of its Foreign Operations from Lenin to Gorbachev* (London, 1990), p.642, n.73.
63. Fricke, *op.cit.*, pp.170–1, quoting the *Neue Zürcher Zeitung*.
64. Richard Popplewell would like to thank the members of the East Berlin Citizens' Committee for allowing him access to the MfS headquarters.
65. Andrew, *op.cit.*, pp.640–1, n.71.
66. Werner Stiller, *Im Zentrum der Spionage*, (Mainz, 1986), 'Das neue Ziel', pp.192–255.
67. Wolf, *In eigenem Auftrag*, *op.cit.*, p.342.
68. Reichenbach, *op.cit.*, p.151.
69. *Ibid.*, p.152.
70. Runge and Stelbrink, *op.cit.*, p.77.
71. Reichenbach, *op.cit.*, p.148.
72. *Ibid.*, p.71.
73. Statement of Werner Fischer, government representative for the dissolution of the MfS, cited on Hamburg DPA, 4 April 1990, in FBIS-EEU-90-066, 5 April 1990.
74. Runge and Stelbrink, *op.cit.*, p.46.
75. Andrew and Gordievsky, *op.cit.*, pp.610–11.
76. Reichenbach, *op.cit.*, p.71.
77. *Ibid.*, p.119.
78. Runge and Stelbrink, *op.cit.*, p.20.
79. *Ibid.*, p.65.
80. Stiller, *op.cit.*, 'Eine Meisterleitung', pp.165–91.
81. Reichenbach, *op.cit.*, p.119.
82. *Ibid.*, p.124.
83. *Ibid.*, p.125.
84. *Ibid.*
85. *Ibid.*, p.118.
86. *Ibid.*
87. *Ibid.*
88. Ion Pacepa, *Red Horizons* (London, 1988), p.392.
89. Wolf, *In eigenem Auftrag*, *op.cit.*, p.87.
90. Directive 2412/PR/60, dated 26 July 1977, signed 'Alyoshin', quoted in Christopher Andrew and Oleg Gordievsky, *More Instructions from the Centre. Top Secret Files on KGB Global Operations 1975–1985* (London: Frank Cass, 1992), pp.38–40.

91. Pacepa, *op.cit.*, p.393.
92. Runge and Stelbrink, *op.cit.*, p.42.
93. *Ibid.*, p.9.
94. Andrew and Gordievsky, *More Instructions from the Centre*, *op., cit.*, p.66.
95. Runge and Stelbrink, *op.cit.*, p.10.
96. *Ibid.*, p.49.
97. Directive 2412/PR/60, dated 26 July 1977, signed 'Alyoshin', quoted in Christopher Andrew and Oleg Gordievsky, *More Instructions from the Centre. Top Secret Files on KGB Global Operations 1975–1985* (London: Frank Cass, 1992), *op.cit.*
98. Josef Frolik, *The Frolik Defection. Memoirs of an Intelligence Agent* (London, 1975), pp.115–16.
99. Letter from Arni Snævarr to David Childs, dated 19 June 1995.
100. Fricke, *op.cit.*, pp.73–4.
101. Fricke, *ibid.*, citing Henning von Löwis of Menar, 'Die DDR und Afrika', in *Die Außenbeziehungen der DDR*, Jahrbuch 1980 der Gesellschaft für Deutschlandforschung (Berlin: 1980), p.224.
102. Fricke, *ibid.*, citing Henning von Löwis of Menar, '"Solidarität und Subversion", Die Rolle der DDR im südlichen Afrika' in *Deutschland Archiv*, No.6/1977, p.644.
103. Andrew and Gordievsky, *KGB. The Inside Story*, *op.cit.*, p.556, n.57 See: Thomas H. Henriksen, 'The People's Republic of Mozambique', in Bark, *Red Orchestra*, vol.II.
104. Fricke, *op.cit.*, citing Melvin Croan, *DDR-Neokolonialismus in Afrika* published by the *Deutsche Afrika Stiftung* (Bonn: 1981), p.21.
105. Fricke, *op.cit.*, p.139.
106. Stelbrink and Runge, *op.cit.*, p.81.
107. Fricke, *op.cit.*, citing Hans Lindemann, *Moskaus Traum: Nicaragua* (Stuttgart/Bonn, 1986), p.9ff.
108. 'Hier bleibt jeder für sich', *Der Spiegel*, 26/1990.
109. 'Eine perverse Kombination', *Der Spiegel*, 25/1990.
110. 'Hier bleibt jeder für sich', *Der Spiegel*, 26/1990.
111. 'Eine perverse Kombination', *Der Spiegel*, 25/1990. For the RAF see Peter Butz, *RAF*, Stuttgart, 1991.
112. *Ibid.*
113. *Ibid.*
114. Stelbrink and Runge, *op.cit.*, p.57.
115. *Ibid.*, p.78.
116. 'Bomben von Derwisch', *Der Spiegel*, 29/1990.
117. *Ibid.*
118. Stelbrink and Runge, *op.cit.*, p.79.
119. 'Oma im Altkader', *Der Spiegel*, 24/1990.
120. Interview with ex-terrorist Peter-Jürgen Boock, *Der Spiegel*, 25/1990.
121. 'Eine perverse Kombination', *Der Spiegel*, 25/1990.
122. 'Oma im Altkader', *Der Spiegel*, 24/1990.
123. 'Eine perverse Kombination', *Der Spiegel*, 25/1990.
124. Interview with ex-terrorist Peter-Jürgen Boock, *Der Spiegel*, 25/1990.
125. 'Oma im Altkader', *Der Spiegel*, 24/1990.

CHAPTER 6
HVA OPERATIONS AGAINST WEST GERMANY

1. Willy Brandt, *My Life In Politics,* New York/London, 1992, p.295. Günter Guillaume, *Die Aussage Wie Es Wirklich War*, Munich, 1990, p.38.
2. Brandt, *op.cit.*, pp.286–7.
3. *Ibid.*, p.288.
4. Markus Wolf, *Im Eigenen Auftrag: Bekenntnisse Und Ansichten,* Berlin 1991, p.269, pp.265–70 and Brandt, *op.cit.*, p.308.
5. Brandt, *op.cit.*, p.290.
6. A. Freudenhammer/K.Vater, *Herbert Wehner Ein Leben mit der Deutschen Frage,* Munich, 1978 and Günther Nollau, *Das Amt: 50 Jahre Zeuge Der Deutschen Geschichte,* Munich, 1978. These books are worth looking at but do not answer this question. The Wehner story is cover in 'Ich bin ohne Nachsicht', *Der Spiegel* (24 January 1994).
7. Guillaume, *op.cit.*, p.384.
8. *Ibid.*, p.384.
9. Peter Richter, Klaus Rösler, *Wolfs West-Spione Ein Insider Report*, Berlin, 1992, pp.20–1.
10. Wolf tells something of himself in his *Die Troika*, Berlin & Weimar, 1989 and in his *In Eigenem Auftrag: Bekenntnisse und Einsichten*, Berlin, 1991. He also appears in Wolfgang Leonhard's classic autobiographical volume, *Die Revolution Entlässt Ihre Kinder*, Cologne & Berlin, 1955. His childhood and family are discussed in Henning Müller, *Wer War Wolf? Friedrich Wolf (1888–1953) in Selbstzeugnissen, Bilddokumenten und Erinnerungen*, Cologne 1988. Also useful are Alexander Reichenbach, *Chef der Spione Die Markus-Story*, Stuttgart, 1992 and Irene Runge and Uwe Stelbrink, *Markus Wolf: 'Ich bin kein Spion'*, Berlin, 1990. Among Wolf's key interviews are: *Der Spiegel*, 20 November 1989; 2 July 1990; *International Herald Tribune*, 22 November 1989. His three marriages are covered in *Der Spiegel*, 10 May 1993. See also *Stern*, 2 February 1995.
11. Leonhard *op.cit.*, p.468.
12. Nationrat Der Nationalen Front Des Demokratischen Deutschland *Braunbuch Kriegs-und Naziverbrecher in Der Bundesrepublik*, Berlin, 1965, p.7.
13. Jörg Friedrich, *Die kalte Amnestie NS-Täter in der Bundesrepublik*, Frankfurt am Main, 1984, p.215.
14. David Marsh, *The Bundesbank: The Bank That Rules Europe,* London, 1992, p.156.
15. Hans-Peter Schwarz, *Adenauer Der Aufstieg: 1876–1952,* Stuttgart, 1986, p.658.
16. Terence Prittie, *The Velvet Chancellors: A History Of Post-War Germany*, London, 1979, p.78.
17. Schwarz, *op.cit.*, pp.658–61.
18. Friedrich, *op.cit.*, p.294.
19. Dennis L. Bark & David R. Gress, *A History of West Germany, Vol. II Democracy And Its Discontents 1963–1991,* Cambridge, Mass., 1993, p.33.
20. Hans Halter, *Krieg Der Gaukler Das Versagen der deutschen Geheimdienste*, Gottingen, 1993, p.137.

21. John Peet, *The Long Engagement. Memoirs Of A Cold War Legend*, London, pp.101–3, and pp.229–31. David Childs met Peet on several occasions. Peet claimed he carried out virtually no assignments for the Soviets.
22. E.H.Cookridge, *Gehlen: Spy Of The Century*, London, 1972, p.351.
23. *Der Spiegel*, 20 September, 1993 brought John's tale up to date. Günther Nollau, former head of the BfV, gives his views on John in *Das Amt 50 Jahre Zeuge der Geschichte,* Munich, 1978.
24. Mary Ellen Reese, *General Reinhard Gehlen: The CIA Connection,* Fairfax Virginia, 1990, claims Gehlen saw no action in Poland; Halter, *op.cit.*, p.22 believes the same, Gehlen disputes this. Reinhard Gehlen, *The Gehlen Memoirs*, London, 1972, p.38.
25. Louis Hagen, *Der heimliche Krieg auf deutschen Boden Seit 1945*, Düsseldorf/Wien, 1969, pp.36–7 discusses Gehlen's attitude to the coup.
26. Cookridge, *op.cit.*, p.185.
27. *Ibid.*, p.203.
28. Reese, *op.cit.*, pp.93–5.
29. Hermann Zolling, *Die Zeit*, 15 October, 1971. With Heinz Höhne, Zolling was responsible for, *The General Was A Spy: The Truth About General Gehlen And His Spy Ring,* New York, 1972.
30. Reinhard Gehlen, *Der Dienst. Erinnerungen, 1942–1971*, Mainz/Wiesbaden 1971, p.202.
31. Cookridge, *op.cit.*, pp.283–4.
32. *Ibid.*, p.338.
33. Leonard Mosley, *Dulles: A Biography Of Eleanor, Allen, And John Foster Dulles And Their Family*, New York, 1978, p.373.
34. Gehlen, *Der Dienst, op.cit.*, p.39.
35. *Ibid.*, p.176.
36. Wolfgang Buschfort, 'Das Ostbüro der SPD 1946–1981', in *Aus Politik und Zeitgeschichte Beilage zur Wochenzeitung Das Parlament*, 15 May 1992. There is no mention of this in Brigitte Seebacher-Brandt, *Ollenhauer Biedermann und Patriot*, Berlin, 1984. Günther Scholz, *Kurt Schumacher*, Düsseldorf/Wien/New York, 1988 contains some very limited comments on Ostbüro. For the Ostbüro see also, 'Bleibt stark, wir helfen', *Der Spiegel* 18 June 1990.
37. Zolling, *op.cit.*
38. *Ibid.*
39. *Welt am Sonntag* 3 April 1994, p.4. This is based on research by Karl-Heinz Schmidt of the Free University, West Berlin, Joachim Braun, *Der unbequeme Präsident*, Karlsruhe, 1972. A biography of Heinemann has very little to say about the GVP and nothing about its finances.
40. Halter, *op.cit.*, p.145.
41. *Ibid.*, pp.69–70.
42. *Ibid.*, p.49.
43. Christopher Andrew and Oleg Gordievsky, *KGB The Inside Story*, HarperCollins, New York, 1990, pp.448–9. Felfe's own story, no doubt cleaned up by the MfS, is found in *Im Dienst des Gegners – 10 Jahre Moskaus Mann Im BND*, Hamburg, 1986.
44. Hagen *op.cit.*, p.72, Schlomann, *op.cit.*, p.178.
45. *Der Spiegel* (19 September 1994).

46. *The Times* (5 October 1994), *Der Spiegel*, (9 August 1993).
47. *The Sunday Times* (18 July 1993).
48. Bundesministerium des Innern, *Zum Thema Hier: Verfassungsschutz 1968*, Bonn, 1969, pp.122–6.
49. Hagen, *op.cit.*, p.304.
50. Andrew and Gordievsky, *op.cit.*, p.514.
51. Stefan Aust, *Der Baader Meinhof Komplex*, Hamburg 1987, tells their story. Reference to the Stasi connection of the RAF and other terrorists is found in Peter Siebenmorden, *'Staatssicherheit' Der DDR Der Westen im Fadenkreuz der Stasi*, Bonn, 1993.
52. Deutscher Bundestag 8. Wahlperiode, Drucksache 8/2290, 15.11.78. *Beschlussemphfehlung und Bericht des Verteidigungsausschusses als 1. Untersuchungsausschuss nach Artikel 45a Abs. 2 des Grundgesetzes*, p.40.
53. The *Observer*, 1 September, 1985.
54. Schlomann, *op.cit.*, p.170.
55. The *Observer*, 1 September 1985 and 8 September 1985.
56. The *Observer*, 8 September 1985.
57. The *Guardian*, 18 September 1985.
58. Halter, *op.cit.*, p.86, Alexander Reichenbach, *op.cit.*, p.103 says there were 60 cases. According to Dr Klaus Richter, formerly in charge of the HVA's operation's against NATO and the EC, this tactic was employed against British secretaries also. Richter was interviewed by David Childs in May 1995..
59. The *Guardian*, 18 September 1985.
60. Guido Knopp, *Top Spione Verräter im Geheimen Krieg*, Bertelsmann, Munich, 1994, p.192.
61. Andrew and Gordievsky, *op.cit.*, p.514.
62. *Der Spiegel*, 28 March 1988, *Kölner Stadt-Anzeiger*, 21 December 1989.
63. *Tagesspiegel*, 27 August 1988.
64. Der Bundesminister des Innern, *Verfassungsschutzbericht 1985*, Bonn, 1985 pp.239–40.
65. The *Observer*, 1 September 1985, *Süddeutsche Zeitung*, 26 August 1985, *Tagesspiegel*, 31 August 1985, *Süddeutsche Zeitung*, 28 August 1985.
66. Ditto, agents at risk.
67. *Süddeutsche Zeitung*, 29 August 1985.
68. Halter, *op.cit.*, p.155, Markus Wolf in *Der Spiegel*, 2 July 1990 says between 3,000 and 10,000.
69. Alexander Reichenbach. *op.cit.*, p.79.
70. *Ibid.*, pp.79–80.
71. *Frankfurter Rundschau*, 11 January 1992. See also Reichenbach *op.cit.*, pp.82–5.
72. *Der Spiegel*, 29 October 1990. A former HVA colonel's evaluation of the BND is given in *Der Spiegel*, 19 December 1994.
73. *Das Parlament*, 18/25 September 1992, p.1.
74. *Ibid.*
75. *Der Spiegel*, 9 September 1991.
76. *Woche im bundestag*, (henceforth wib)30 June 1993, p.32.
77. Wib, 29 June 1994, p.53.
78. *Ibid.*, 16 December 1992, p.41.
79. *Der Spiegel*, 9 September 1991.

80. Wib, 29 June 1994, p.53.
81. *Ibid.*
82. *Ibid.*, 27 January 1993, p.33.
83. *Ibid.*, 16 December 1992, p.41.
84. *Ibid.*
85. *Ibid.*, 27 January 1993, p.33.
86. *Ibid.*, 11 June 1992, p.41.
87. *Ibid.*, 29 June 1994, p.53.
88. *Ibid.*, 16 December 1992, p.41.
89. *Ibid.*
90. *Ibid.*, 30 June 1993, p.31.
91. *Der Spiegel*, 9 September 1991.
92. Wib, 29 June 1994, p.53.
93. *Der Spiegel*, 9 September 1991.
94. *Ibid.*, 12 December 1994.
95. *Ibid.* (25 October 1993), Siebenmorgen, *op.cit.*, p.270–4.
96. *Focus*, (25 October 1993).
97. Der Bundesminister des Innern, *Verfassungsschutzbericht 1990*, Bonn, 1990, p.179.
98. *Verfassungsschutzbericht 1990, op.cit.*, p.179.
99. Insider-Komitee zur Aufarbeitung der Geschichte des MfS e.V., *Duell im Dunkeln-Spionage und Gegenspionage im geteilten Deutschland*, Berlin August 1994, p.13.
100. Wib, 13 November 1991, p.7.
101. *International Herald Tribune,* 22 November 1989.
102. Interviewed by David Childs in 1995.

CHAPTER 7
FROM TRIUMPH TO CATASTROPHE: THE STASI UNDER MIELKE AND HONECKER, 1971–89

FBIS: Foreign Broadcast Information Service.
ILEDA: Mitter, Armin and Wolle, Stefan, eds., *Ich liebe euch doch alle! Befehle und Lageberichte des MfS Januar-November 1989* (2nd edn Berlin, 1990) (A compendium of Stasi documents for the revolutionary year 1989).

1. *Pravda*, 5 November 1989.
2. 'Die Informationsstrecke war eine Einbahnstraße', statement of 'Klaus, 40 years of age, *Zentrale Auswertungs-und Informationsgruppe*' in Christina Wilkening, *Staat im Staate. Auskünfte ehemaliger Stasi-Mitarbeiter* (Berlin and Weimar, 1990).
3. Manfred Schell und Werner Kalinka, *Stasi und kein Ende* (Frankfurt, Berlin, Vienna, 1991), Chapter 8, 'Zum Äußersten bereit – SED und Stasi kämpfen gegen die Wende'.
4. Erich Mielke, *Sozialismus und Frieden – Sinn unseres Kampfes. Ausgewählte Reden und Aufsätze*, (East Berlin, 1987), p.421.
5. Irene Runge and Uwe Stelbrink, *Markus Wolf, 'Ich bin kein Spion'* (Berlin, 1990), p.50.

6. Mielke was elected as Candidate Member in 1971, and full member in 1976. *Die Staatssicherheit DDR*, *op.cit.*, Chapter 9, 'Die Chefs des MfS'.
7. Interim report on the dissolution of the former Office of National Security by Manfred Sauer, 15 January 1990, East Berlin ADN International Service, 15 January 1990, in FBIS-EEU-90-012, 18 January 1990.
8. Interim report on the state of the disbandment of the Office of National Security, presented by Manfred Sauer, Deputy Head of the GDR Secretariat of the Council of Ministers, East Berlin ADN International Service, 15 January, in FBIS-EEU-90-010, 16 January 1990.
9. *Neues Deutschland*, 9–10 June 1990, p.6.
10. For example, 'Schild und Schwert der Partei', Part I, *Der Spiegel*, 6/1990, p.50.
11. A 'former high-ranking' Stasi officer stated on West German television in April 1990:

    > Listening to Egon Krenz today, and referring to large sections of your press, I note that the term, state within the state, is used, and that the SED ranked after the State Security Ministry. That not only distorts the historic facts, it will also make it very difficult to find the historic truth regarding individual facts. The State Security Ministry was the shield and sword of the party – totally. The control of this ministry was total ... The basic orientations of the State Security Ministry's activities came from his office, from him personally, because he was the security secretary.

    Mainz ZDF Television Network, 11 April 1990, in FBIS-EEU-90-071, 12 April 1990.
12. *ILEDA*, Introduction.
13. See the plaintive letters in Bürgerkomitee zur Auflösung des MfS/AfNS (eds) *Stasi Intern: Macht und Banalität* (Leipzig, 1990).
14. For example the file of a woman from the Dresden Citizens' Committee who was engaged to a West German. 'Jeder Tag ein Alptraum', *Der Spiegel*, 17/1990.
15. Wilkening, *op.cit.*
    A. Riecker *et al.*, eds, *Stasi Intim. Gespräche mit ehemaligen MfS-Mitarbeiter.* (Leipzig, 1990).
16. East Berlin ADN International Service, 12 January 1990, in FBIS-EEU-90-010, 16 January 1990.
17. Interim report on the dissolution of the former Office of National Security by Manfred Sauer, 15 January 1990, East Berlin ADN International Service, 15 January 1990, in FBIS-EEU-90-012, 18 January 1990.
18. A former member of ZAIG recalls:

    > The bulk of reports were distributed to the former Collegium of the MfS and to the Minister [Mielke]. It is important to note here that this information really came from the grassroots. By this I mean the broadest sections of the population. I would like to stress this. Then the reports were compiled by the relevant district [*Kreis*] sections and given to the provincial [*Bezirk*] administration. Here it was condensed again, and this created the problem that we were no longer receiving the original information.

'Die Informationsstrecke war eine Einbahnstraße', statement of 'Klaus, 40 years of age, *Zentrale Auswertungs-und Informationsgruppe*' in Wilkening, *op.cit.*

19. This situation was not new to 1989. One Stasi officer claimed that 'For years shortages among the population were reported!' 'Die Informationsstrecke war eine Einbahnstraße', statement of 'Klaus, 40 years of age, *Zentrale Auswertungs- und Informationsgruppe*', *ibid.*
20. East Berlin ADN International Service, 9 March 1990, in FBIS-EEU-90-048, 12 March 1990.
21. 'Schild und Schwert der Partei (I)', *Der Spiegel*, 6/1990.
22. East Berlin ADN International Service, 26 January 1990, in FBIS-EEU-90-021, 31 January 1990.
    Günther Schabowski, a former member of the Politburo, claimed that even Honecker often complained that 'Mielke was not clever enough' and even 'clumsy'. East Berlin ADN International Service, 23 January 1990, in FBIS-EEU-90-016, 24 January 1990.
23. Armin Mitter and Stefan Wolle, introduction to *ILEDA*.
24. 'Die Informationsstrecke war Eine Einbahnstraße', statement of 'Klaus, 40 years of age, *Zentrale Auswertungs-und Informationsgruppe*' in Wilkening, *op.cit.*
25. 'Schild und Schwert der Partei (III), *Der Spiegel*, 8/1990.
    Outside this central complex, the Stasi carried out their control of the post in rooms belonging to the post office, but to which postal workers had no access. Statement of Manfred Sauer to the Round Table, 15 January 1990, East Berlin ADN International Service, 15 January 1990, in FBIS-EEU-90-010, 16 January 1990.
    Of an average of 90,000 posted every day in Erfurt, 3,000 had been opened. East Berlin, ADN International Service, 18 January 1990, in FBIS-EEU-90-013, 19 January 1990.
26. 'Doppelte Abschußquote', *Der Spiegel*, 32/1990.
27. Some Stasi officers claimed that in its last years, Krenz was responsible for the orientation of the Stasi's work, including its orders and its orientation. However, it is still hard to assess the extent of Krenz's role. The Stasi hated Krenz for the way they felt he betrayed them in 1989, and had an obvious axe to grind against him. See, for example, 'Wir waren und wurden diszipliniert', statement of 'Franz, 54 years of age, former Lieutenant-Colonel in the *Zentrale Auswertungs-und Informationsgruppe*', in Wilkening, *op.cit.*
28. Introduction to *ILEDA*, by Armin Mitter and Stefan Wolle.
29. *ILEDA*, document no. 1: Luxemburg-Liebknecht-Demonstration in Leipzig (MfS-Information 25/89, 16.1.1989), and document no. 2: Luxemburg-Liebknecht-Demonstration in Leipzig (Fernschreiben der SED-Bezirksleitung Nr.17, 16.1.1989).
30. 'Ich war ein Teil, der zu funktionieren hatte', statement of 'Hans, 50 years of age, *Hauptabteilung XX'*, in Wilkening, *op.cit.*
31. *ILEDA*, document no. 10: Oppositionelle Zusammenschlüsse (MfS-Information 150/89, 1.6.1989).
32. ZAIG noted that this 'group includes the Pastors EPPELMANN, TSCHICHE, and WONNEBERGER, as well as Gerd and Ulrike POPPE, Bärbel BOHLEY,

and Werner FISCHER; the persons RÜDDENKLAU, SCHULT, Dr. KLEIN and LEITZ'. *ILEDA* 10.

33. *ILEDA*, document no. 10, *op.cit.*
34. *ILEDA*, document no. 4: Friedensseminar Greifswald (MfS-Befehl 24/89, 10.3.1989)
35. ZAIG could not use the word 'emigrate', because these people wanted to go to the Federal Republic, which they did not regard as a legitimate state.
36. *ILEDA*, document no. 15: Ausreise in die BRD und Westberlin (MfS Analyse, Juli 1989).
37. *ILEDA*, document no. 6: Kommunalwahlen 7 Mai 1989 (MfS-Hinweise, 26.4.1989).
38. *ILEDA*, document no. 10, *op.cit.*
39. *ILEDA*, document 4, *op.cit.*
40. *ILEDA*, document no. 5: Aktion von Antragstellern auf ständige Ausreise in Leipzig (MfS-Information, 122/89, 14.3.1989).
    ILEDA, document no. 7: Kommunalwahlen 7. Mai 1989 (MfS-Information, 229/89, 8.5.1989).
41. *ILEDA*, document no. 10, *op.cit.*
42. *Ibid.*
43. *Ibid.*
44. *ILEDA*, document no. 23: Motive für Ausreiseanträge und Republikflucht (MfS-Hinweise, 9.9.1989).
45. *ILEDA*, document no. 18: Kommunalwahlen 7. Mai 1989 (MfS-Hinweise, 7.7.1989).
46. *ILEDA*, document no. 4, *op.cit.*
47. *ILEDA*, document no. 10, *op.cit.*
48. For a comparison with the role of ideology in the Soviet Union, see Geoffrey Hosking, *The Awakening of the Soviet Union* (London, 1990), Chapter 1.
49. *ILEDA*, document no. 8: Bevölkerungsreaktion auf sowjetische Medienpolitik (MfS-Hinweise, 10.5.1989).
50. Richard Popplewell, 'Themes in the Speeches of KGB Leaders from Andropov to Kryuchkov', in *Intelligence and National Security*, Vol.6, No.3, July 1991.
51. *ILEDA*, document no. 6, *op.cit.*
52. *Ibid.*
53. *ILEDA*, document no. 7, *op.cit.*
54. East Berlin ADN International Service, 17 January 1990, in FBIS-EEU-90-014, 22 January 1990.
55. *Berliner Zeitung*, 14 February 1990, in FBIS-EEU-90-040, 28 February 1990.
    ILEDA, document no. 7, *op.cit.*
    ILEDA, document no. 9: Kommunalwahlen 7 Mai 1989 (MfS-Befehl 38/89, 19.5.1989).
56. *ILEDA*, document no. 13: Ereignisse in China (MfS-Befehl 45/89, 10.6.1989) and document no. 14: Ereignisse in China (MfS-Information 321/89, 30.6.1989).
57. *Ibid.*
58. *ILEDA*, document no. 23, *op.cit.*
59. *ILEDA*, document no. 20: Oppositionsveranstaltung in Leipzig und Dresden (MfS-Information 337/89, 10.7.1989).

60. Schell and Kalinka, *op.cit.*, Chapter 8, 'Zum Äußersten bereit – SED und Stasi kämpfen gegen die Wende'.
61. *ILEDA*, document no. 21, Dienstsprechung des Ministers für Staatssicherheit (Tonbandabschrift, 31.8.1989, Auszug).
62. ZAIG recommended that: 'Under the leadership of the Central Committee, a working group should be formed from the security organs, corresponding state organs and academic institutions to study reports, tasks, arguments, as well as other bases for offensive measures.' *ILEDA*, document no. 26: Oppositionelle Zusammenschlüsse (MfS-Information 416/89, 19.9.1989).
63. *ILEDA*, document no. 35: Bevölkerungsreaktion auf Einschränkung des Reiseverkehrs (MfS-Information 438/89, 4.10.1989).
64. *ILEDA*, document no. 21, *op.cit.*
65. *ILEDA*, document no. 26: Oppositionelle Zusammenschlüsse (MfS-Information 416/89, 19.9.1989).
66. For details of the formation of New Forum and Democratic Awakening, see *ILEDA*, documents no. 29: Neues Forum (MfS-Information 429/89, 27.9.1989), no. 30: Demokratischer Aufbruch (MfS-Information 432/89, 29.9.1989), no. 31: Demokratischer Aufbruch (MfS-Information 433/89, 2.10.1989), no. 32: Neues Forum (MfS-Information 434/89, 2.10.1989), and no. 41: Oppositionelle Zusammenschlüsse (MfS-Information 451/89, 9.10.1989).
67. *ILEDA*, document no. 27: Haltung der katholischen Kirche (MfS-Information 426/89, 25.9.1989).
68. *ILEDA*, document no. 40: Innenpolitische Lage (MfS-Hinweise, 8.10.1989).
69. Mielke concluded that 'good forces, who were capable of something' could show that such people were talking nonsense, and that people were not being given correct information. *ILEDA*, document no. 21: Dienstbesprechung des Ministers für Staatssicherheit (Tonbandabschrift, 31.8.1989, Auszug).
70. Schell and Kalinka, *op.cit.*, Chapter 8, 'Zum Äußersten bereit – SED und Stasi kämpfen gegen die Wende'.
71. *Ibid.*
72. *ILEDA*, document no. 40, *op.cit.*
73. ZAIG lamented that: 'Above all, progressive groups were completely unable to comprehend the lack of offensive political discussions with hostile, opposition groups and with the anti-socialist pamphlets produced and disseminated by such groups.' *ILEDA*, document no. 40: Innenpolitische Lage (MfS-Hinweise, 8.10.1989).
74. *ILEDA*, document no. 46: Humboldt-Universität (MfS-Information 458/89, 16.10.1989).
75. *Stasi und kein Ende*, Chapter 8, 'Zum Äußersten bereit – SED und Stasi kämpfen gegen die Wende'.
76. *ILEDA*, document no. 17: 'Soforteinsatzgruppe operative Beobachtung' (MfS-Befehl 50/89, 5.7.1989).
77. Schell and Kalinka, *op.cit.*, Chapter 8, 'Zum Äußersten bereit – SED und Stasi kämpfen gegen die Wende'.
78. 'Kennwort Rosenstock', *Der Spiegel*, 30/1990.
Hamburg DPA, 1 April 1990, in FBIS-EEU-90-063, 2 April 1990.
79. Berlin ADN International Service, 2 April 1990, in FBIS- EEU-90-064, 3 April 1990.

80. For the meeting see Günter Schabowski, *Das Politbüro*, Reinbek, 1990, p.78.
For the order see *ILEDA*, document no. 39, (Fernschreiben o.Nr., 8.10.1989).
81. Krenz interviewed by David Childs, 1994 and confirmed by Friedrich.
82. Cornelia Heins, *The Wall Falls: An Oral History of the Reunification of the Two Germanies*, London, 1994, pp.228–30.
83. Reinhold Andert/Wolfgang Herzberg, *Der Sturz Erich Honecker im Kreuzverhör*, Berlin and Weimar, 1991, pp.363–71.
Walter Süß, *Entmachtung und Verfall der Staatssicherheit,* BStU, 5/1994, shows the difficulty of arriving at the final truth about the Leipzig miracle.
84. *ILEDA*, document no. 48: Montagsdemonstration in Leipzig (Fernschreiben 76/89, 16.10.89).
85. An order received by the Leipzig Stasi on 16 October read 'appeals will be made (on our side) – then if there is to be violence, no one can say he did not know about it'. DB L-BV, 16.10.90.
A general statement of intent is contained in FS Minister VVS 84/89 – 'Maßnahmen Sicherheit der Objekte', in Leipziger Bürgerkomitee zur Auflösung des MfS/AfNS (eds), *Stasi Intern – Macht und Banalität*, *op.cit.*
86. DB-L-BV, aus dem Dienstbuch des Leiters der Bezirksverwaltung, *ibid.*
87. Schell and Kalinka, *op.cit.*, Chapter 8, 'Zum Äußersten bereit – SED und Stasi kämpfen gegen die Wende'.
88. *ILEDA*, Introduction.
89. 'Wir waren und wurden diszipliniert', statement of 'Franz, 54 years of age, former Lieutenant-Colonel in the *Zentrale Auswertungs-und Informationsgruppe*' in Wilkening, *op.cit.*
90. *ILEDA*, document no. 45: Haltung der Kampfgruppen (MfS-Information 457/89, 15.10.89).
91. *ILEDA*, document no. 49: Referat des Ministers für Staatssicherheit (Protokollauszug, 21.10.1989).
92. Letter from Hauptmann 'H.U.', Abteilung II, Bezirksverwaltung für Staatssicherheit, to Generalleutnant Hummitzsch, Leiter der Bezirksverwaltung, Leipzig, 10.11.1989, in Riecker, *op.cit.*
93. Hummitzsch's arguments were based on the following lines. The attacks on the Stasi made them aware that their reputation and the people's trust in them, was not what they had assumed. Thus they were taking the initiative, making greater use of publicity. The Stasi's publicity was particularly aimed to be effective among the working class. The Stasi was given many duties which had nothing to do with the basic tasks of a socialist security service. The reasons for this should be presented honestly. Partly this was a result of Party policies. Entwurf. Leipzig, 15.11.1989. Analyse des Interviews des Leiters der BV mit dem Sender Leipzig am 14.11.1989, *ibid.*
94. Berlin Headquarters sent out the following message to the provinces:

> We have noted Comrade Erich Mielke's appearance before the Volkskammer yesterday evening with deep consternation. In agreement with the opinion of many comrades, the Secretariat of the District Management has distanced itself from these explanations of Comrade Mielke before the highest organ of the people.

Communication from H. Felber, 1. Sekretär, Sekretariat der Kreisleitung,MfS Berlin, to 1. Sekretär der Parteiorganisation der SED, alle Bezirksverwaltungen, und Parteiorganisation der Hochschule des MfS, *ibid.*

95. 'Was ist Gesetzlichkeit?' SPIEGEL-Interview mit Peter Erfurth, dem bisherigen Stasi-Chef von Greifswald, *Der Spiegel*, 7/1990, p.138.
96. 'Wir waren und wurden diszipliniert', statement of 'Franz, 54 years of age, former Lieutenant-Colonel in the *Zentrale Auswertungs-und Informationsgruppe*' in Wilkening, *op.cit.*
97. 'Schild und Schwert der Partei (I)', *op.cit.* The Berlin Citizens' Committee assured Richard Popplewell of the veracity of this *Spiegel* article.

CHAPTER 8
THE AFTERMATH

1. *Das Parlament*, 30 July 1993, p.1.
2. *Das Parlament*, 1 October 1993, p.7. Dr Ullmann was interviewed by David Childs in 1994.
3. According to a survey of the FORSA-Institut in Kiel published in March 1991. This is given in Anne Worst, *Das Ende eines Geheimdienstes Oder: Wie lebendig ist die Stasi?* Berlin, May 1991, p.274.
4. *Das Parlament*, 6 November 1992, p.1.
5. *Time*, 20 December 1993.
6. *Die Welt*, 24/25 May 1995.
7. *Frankfurter Rundschau*, 28 March 1994, p.5.
8. *Das Parlament*, 2 April 1993, p.1. The BStU felt unable to give further information according to a letter to David Childs, 19 July 1995.
9. *Das Parlament,* 9 June 1995, p.9.
10. Quoted in Worst, *op.cit.*, originally published in *Der Spiegel*, 25 March 1991.
11. BStU, *Erster Tätigkeitsbericht* 1993, p.79.

Name Index

Subject Index